MARK VOLMAN WITH JOHN CODY

HAPPY
FOREVER

JAW
BONE

HAPPY FOREVER

MY MUSICAL ADVENTURES WITH THE TURTLES, FRANK ZAPPA, T. REX, FLO & EDDIE, AND MORE

MARK VOLMAN WITH JOHN CODY

A Jawbone book
First edition 2023
Published in the UK and the USA by
Jawbone Press
Office G1
141–157 Acre Lane
London SW2 5UA
England
www.jawbonepress.com

ISBN 978-1-911036-19-7

Printed by Short Run Press, Exeter, Devon

1 2 3 4 5 27 26 25 24 23

CONTENTS

FOREWORDS
BY ALICE COOPER & CHRIS HILLMAN

The most fun I've ever had on tour was with Mark. Flo & Eddie were opening for us, and we were all at the top of our game. There were no rules, and we took advantage of that in every possible way.

Mark is one of the most indomitable yet gentle spirits I've ever met. He will always be one of my favorite artists I've ever worked with. He told me this book took him twelve years to write (I didn't know he knew that many words). I still don't know if Mark is the smartest or silliest person on this planet . . . a sign of true genius. And someday, when I grow up, I want to be just like him.

ALICE COOPER

He radiated happiness and pure love in The Turtles, dancing around onstage, waving his tambourine, and singing great duets with Howard. I loved that band. They had fun and they entertained us.

I was so fortunate to have Mark and Howard sing backup harmonies on one of my solo albums. They brought so much life to those songs.

Now, after all these years, I've come to discover that Mark and I share Ukrainian roots through our grandfathers who immigrated to America at the turn of the century. Ironically, both became tailors in Los Angeles.

Now, to see my old friend completely reinventing himself in the world of academia is such a blessing.

I love you, Mark.

CHRIS HILLMAN

CAST OF CHARACTERS

This is the story of **MARK VOLMAN**, known as **FLO**, a founding member of **THE TURTLES**. This story is told by Friends, Family, Lovers, and Losers. Whose memories are suspect at best.

All interviews conducted, edited, and compiled by John Cody.

GEORGE ATTARIAN instructor, Los Angeles Community College

PHILIP AUSTIN Firesign Theatre

ALAN BANCROFT associate pastor, Harpeth Presbyterian Church

JOHNNY BARBATA The Turtles/Crosby, Stills, Nash & Young/Jefferson Starship

KEN BARNES music writer for *USA Today/ Rolling Stone/Creem*

JEFF 'SKUNK' BAXTER Steely Dan/Doobie Brothers/session musician

ANN BECKER aunt

JIM BESSMAN journalist for *Billboard/Cashbox/ Variety*

ROLAN BOLAN Loyola Marymount classmate/ son of Marc Bolan

MARY BREDEN Professor Emerita of Music, Loyola Marymount University

HAROLD BRONSON founder of Rhino Records/ author/film producer

ANDY CAHAN Geronimo Black/Flo & Eddie/ Harry Nilsson

LINDA CAMPILLO cousin

MADELINE CAMPILLO aunt

RICK CARR president, Remote Possibilities

PEPPY CASTRO The Blues Magoos/*Hair* cast member

FELIX CAVALIERE The Rascals

MARK CHERNOFF program director, K-ROCK/ WFAN

BILLY CIOFFE musician/instructor, Mesa Community College

ALICE COOPER Alice Cooper

SUSAN COWSILL The Cowsills

DON CUSIC music historian/author

RON DANTE Archies/Cufflinks/Turtles/session vocalist

HENRY DILTZ Modern Folk Quartet/ photographer

MICKY DOLENZ The Monkees

CHIP DOUGLAS Modern Folk Quartet/The Turtles/producer of The Monkees

GEORGE DUKE Frank Zappa/Cannonball Adderley/solo

AYNSLEY DUNBAR John Mayall/Frank Zappa/ Journey/etc.

STEVE DUNCAN professor of screenwriting, Loyola Marymount University

BOB EZRIN producer, Alice Cooper/Flo & Eddie/ Lou Reed/Pink Floyd/etc.

CYRUS FARYAR Modern Folk Quartet/producer

JIMMY FINK New York radio personality

NICK FORTUNA The Buckinghams

RICHIE FURAY Buffalo Springfield/Poco/ Souther-Hillman-Furay Band

CARL GIAMMARESE The Buckinghams

RUSS GIGUERE The Association

ED GUNNEY boyhood friend and classmate

E. MICHAEL HARRINGTON professor, Berklee Online/consultant

GREG HAWKES The Cars/Flo & Eddie/Martin Mull

CATHERINE HILLMAN CLARK Loyola Marymount student/daughter of Chris Hillman

CHRIS HILLMAN The Byrds/Flying Burrito Brothers/Manassas/Desert Rose Band

GLENN HOUGHTON Nashville neighbor

URSALA HOUGHTON Nashville neighbor

DANNY HUTTON Three Dog Night/solo

TOMMY JAMES Tommy James & The Shondells

DENNY JONES aka **'EDDIE'** road manager, The Turtles/Little Feat/etc.

HOWARD KAYLAN The Crossfires/The Turtles/ Frank Zappa/Flo & Eddie

DONNIE KISSELBACH Rick Derringer/Flo & Eddie/Alice Cooper

CRAIG KRAMPF Flo & Eddie/Alice Cooper/Kim Carnes/Steve Perry/Nick Gilder

HARVEY KUBERNIK music journalist/author/ historian

CORKY LAING Mountain/West, Bruce & Laing

JOEL LARSON The Grassroots/The Gene Clark Group/The Turtles

RICHARD LEWIS comedian

MARK LINDSAY Paul Revere & The Raiders/ solo

RICK MANCZAREK Rick & The Ravens

RAY MANZAREK The Doors/Rick & The Ravens

JACKIE MARTLING comedian/New York radio personality

SPANKY MCFARLANE Spanky & Our Gang

BILL MUMY aka **BILLY MUMY** actor/musician

CHUCK NEGRON Three Dog Night

RON NEVISON engineer/producer, Led Zeppelin/The Who/Flo & Eddie/etc.

AL NICHOL The Crossfires/The Turtles

PETER NOONE Herman's Hermits

MARK PARENTEAU disc jockey, WBCN Boston

JIM PONS The Leaves/The Turtles/Flo & Eddie

DON PRESTON Frank Zappa/The Mothers Of Invention

TIM REID producer, Flo & Eddie radio show

GARY ROWLES Love/Flo & Eddie

JULIE SCHAD ex-girlfriend

ERIK SCOTT Flo & Eddie/Alice Cooper/Sonia Dada

JOHN SEITER Spanky & Our Gang/The Turtles/ Tim Buckley

TIM SEXTON producer/supervisor, No Nukes/ Live 8/etc.

HARRY SHEARER actor/director/radio host, The Simpsons/Spinal Tap

HOWARD SILVERMAN agent/co-owner, Paradise Artists

JEFF SIMMONS Frank Zappa/The Mothers Of Invention

PATRICK SIMMONS The Doobie Brothers

JOHN SNYDER boyhood friend and classmate

BILLY STEELE Flo & Eddie/Alice Cooper/Steve Perry

JOE STEFKO Meatloaf/Flo & Eddie

SHADOE STEVENS producer, *Flo & Eddie On The Air*/host of *American Top 40*

CHUCK SWENSON animator

GARRY TALLENT Bruce Springsteen & The E Street Band/producer

SKIP TAYLOR manager, Flo & Eddie/Canned Heat

MICHAEL THOMAS boyhood friend and classmate

VENNY THOMAS Rick & The Ravens

DEAN TORRENCE Jan & Dean/graphic designer

BOB TRUAX road manager, Flo & Eddie, 1974–76

JIM TUCKER The Crossfires/The Turtles

IAN UNDERWOOD Frank Zappa & The Mothers Of Invention/session musician

JACK UNDERWOOD boyhood friend and classmate

TONY VISCONTI producer, T. Rex/David Bowie/ The Moody Blues/etc.

EMILY VOLMAN second wife

PHIL VOLMAN brother

PAT VOLMAN first wife

HALLIE VOLMAN daughter

MARK VOLMAN The Crossfires/The Turtles/ Frank Zappa/Flo & Eddie

SARINA VOLMAN daughter

SUSAN VOLMAN cousin

LARRY WACHOLTZ professor of entertainment and music business, Belmont University

LESLIE WEST The Vagrants/Mountain/West, Bruce & Lang

PAUL WILLIAMS songwriter/actor/ASCAP president

HAL WILLNER producer, Lou Reed/Marianne Faithfull/various tributes

FRED WOLF animator

JIM YESTER The Association/The Four Preps

GAIL ZAPPA wife of Frank Zappa

LARRY ZINN tour manager, Flo & Eddie, 1984–95

INTRODUCTION
BY MARK VOLMAN

I don't know this room, but I'm always up for a good time. Veronica tells me to make myself comfortable. I'm going to be here a while. Her fingers feel warm as she slowly raises my sleeve to graze my arm. Veronica will take care of me. She dims the lights. Chet Baker softly sings 'My Ideal' in the background. As the drugs trickle into my body, I begin to relax and let my mind wander. What is this place? How did I get here? Who am I?

Unfortunately, this is no groovy acid trip, and Veronica is no groupie. I'm starting my second round of chemotherapy at Vanderbilt Medical Center in Nashville, Tennessee. Veronica is sweet, but if she offers me another tiny soda and package of peanut butter crackers, why, I . . .

The last time I did chemo they said I might fall asleep. I didn't. This time, my wife is with me, and she's pretty entertaining. My wife: Emily is still my wife. One month ago, we filed for divorce. Not my choice. But now that I've been diagnosed with human papillomavirus oropharyngeal squamous cell carcinoma (throat cancer, but the technical name sounded more dramatic), we have decided to postpone. Emily has also called my first wife, Pat, to come and help. Pat still lives in Los Angeles. We haven't lived together in twenty-three years. This ought to be good.

As Emily reads me an article about an actress I've never heard of, I doze off. My phone buzzes, but I let it go to voicemail.

Mark! This is Richard Lewis! I love you. And, uh, life's good. I have a new series. I play a psychiatrist. That's right, Mark. A shrink. A really cool show, man. I'm really lucky. I've been lucky since you were my butler. You and Howard. That's why I'm calling. I'm touring again. Always. And I don't know how close you are to Howard, but I'd like you to give him my phone number, if you could. I'm not sure if I have it. And whatever you do, you're alive, that's all I know. So, if you want to be my butler—you and Howard—and come on a couple of gigs . . . I'm not sure . . . you shouldn't be doing blow anymore, but if you're doing it, you can put some white powder down for me, shake powder . . . and I'll do as much as you want. You can even call me Scarface.

Mark, I will remember that night for my whole life. I mean, you two guys, just . . . just . . . took care of me. (*laughs*) Oh, God. Were we wrecked! We were so wrecked. Ha! The Mayflower! That's when they started to implode the fucking hotel. Anyway, give me a call. I'm gonna be sixty-nine, and . . . uh . . . how many phone calls do we have left, you know what I mean? I hope you're well. I want to know how you are doing. I hear this gossip . . . plus my memory is so shot about everything. In fact, I don't even know who I'm calling now. Who is this!? So call me when you can. You have my email. You really got out of it. But aren't you still gigging from time to time? I need gossip! You know, I mean, you're a genius. You were with Frank Zappa and Flo & Eddie and The Turtles. And you took me to those gigs with The Grassroots and Jerry Lewis's son.

I love you, Mark. I still ramble. I miss you. Where are you living? Somewhere in California? And where you're living, I'll try to do a gig, you know . . . in some neo-Nazi tent village . . . where you're living. Uh, just so we can hang.

I'm lying there dying, and I'm crying, I'm laughing so hard.

I'm lucky, too, Richard. For you and the many family, friends, loves, colleagues, and fans who have been part of my life. I never thought I'd have cancer. I never thought I'd be getting divorced. Actually, I never thought I'd live this long. But here I am, and my story is just beginning.

The pages you are about to read are not a biography—not according to the common use of the word. I am hoping that you will enjoy this collection of reflections, anecdotes, feelings, and memories, all nicely prepared for you, like tapas dishes to share.

The idea to do a book like this has been rolling around in my head for quite a while. I was inspired by *George, Being George*, a book that was a collection of stories from two hundred people who knew and admired George

Plimpton. I wasn't sure I could find two hundred people who tolerated—let alone admired—me. Surprisingly, over one hundred amazingly fantastic and impressive people agreed to be interviewed about me.

This book is a puzzle. The outside frame pieces are about me, but the picture wouldn't be complete without the perspectives of all the people telling you about me. Every day the list of people we wanted to talk to would grow, and every single person we talked to was just as important to the story as the next. They are actually the writers of this book. Throughout the book, I interject (hopefully without being facetious or didactic) to add insights, and sometimes self-defenses.

The logistics were insane, and this is where John Cody comes in. John was responsible for preparing the interviews, conducting the interviews, transcribing the interviews, and editing the interviews. Without John, there is no book. Imagine scanning the thousands of pages of transcribed interviews to make this collective treasure trove.

This book is dedicated to my many contributors. Without their sense of fun and observations, it would not have happened. We would have dumped it a long time ago, which we almost did. Maybe we should have. The people who wrote this gave their reflections, and we're excited to see how their memories fit in with everyone else's.

This book is also dedicated to my musical partner, Howard Kaylan, who I've worked alongside for over five decades, and who continues to be my inspirational brother. Additionally, half of my brain resides in Emily's brain, and without her we wouldn't have the ending or the beginning of this book . . . because she had to help me write them both. We wouldn't be anywhere without each other. And finally . . . I dedicate this book to my mom and dad, Bea and Joe Volman. Their love, encouragement, and laughter shaped who I am, and I will be forever grateful.

So, I hope you enjoy this book. And I hope you don't want to return it after Christmas.

BEGINNINGS
PART ONE

A true California son, Mark Volman was born at the Queen Of Angeles Hospital in Los Angeles on April 19, 1947, and grew up ten miles southwest of L.A. in the community of Westchester. It was a real nice place to raise your kids up, especially in the 1950s. The Magic Kingdom of Disneyland—which opened when Mark was eight years old—was a bicycle ride away, and there was surfing—skateboards on the streets and bigger boards in the Pacific—all year round. Classmates ran the gamut from future comedy legends to Manson Family members.

ANN BECKER He was something else; that's the only way I can describe him. Even as a child. I can remember my mother shaking her head and saying, 'That boy is so smart—he shouldn't be so silly.' And this is as a child!

I realized very early how to get attention, and I loved making my family laugh. The words 'Oh, Mark, stop' were used a lot in our house.

JACK UNDERWOOD I've known him since the fourth grade. In California at the time, they had what was called the half grades, and we were in the winter graduating class. The summer graduating classes were generally much larger. They split the year in half, and that is pertinent to a lot of the mindset that we had, because we had a very small class throughout our school years. In high school we had maybe seventy people in the class, and classes on both sides of us were three or four hundred. So, we were a pretty tight group, and we had a reputation with the teachers. We were pretty wild. We were in the same class, everything, all the way through high school.

We used to go into the boys' bathroom, having chewed a couple of Hershey bars, then we'd spit on the ceiling and have what they call 'hanger' competitions. A hanger was if you could spit on something and to see how long it would stretch before it broke. Gross little things. There would be stalactites coming down from the ceiling of dried-up spittle and Hershey bars—the Hershey gave it texture.

Jack was the king of hangers. He had the knack. It was such an innocent time. It was really full of fun.

JACK UNDERWOOD We lived about a mile apart—a bike ride apart. And from his house it was probably another mile into the little town of Westchester. We'd bump into other buddies on their bikes and go off and do things. There were a whole lot of department stores, and they had additional parking and a little café up on the roof. It was two stories plus. We'd ride up on the roof and lean over the main entrance and spit on people as they came out, then duck behind the railing so nobody would see where it came from. We didn't hit that many people, but it was fun. Kids' stuff. It didn't really hurt anybody. So that was our routine. We'd either ride into town or we'd hang out in the fields and catch lizards and snakes and slide down the grass banks on pieces of cardboard and get all beat up and have rock fights with kids from other parts of the neighborhood. All that good stuff.

In the area where we lived, there were these fields, and then what we call the canyons, but they were actually big ruts. They would go down toward Hughes Aircraft, this huge facility down below. In that era, Hughes Aircraft was experimenting with a variety of experimental aircraft, and we'd hear these weird sounds and try to figure out what the hell was going on. Of course, they had security all over the place, and we were always testing them, running onto the field and stuff. Most of the stuff would be enclosed under canvas or something to where you couldn't see what was going on, but we did see some things. For instance, they were experimenting with a helicopter that was supposed to be able to lift tanks. It had jet engines on the ends of the blades, and it was mammoth. When they fired that thing up, there was this *whoosh, whoosh, whoosh* sound that you could hear for what seemed like miles. It was kind of like the Spruce Goose, where it just lifted off for a few feet and that was it. They bounced on the runway and then they'd bring it back.

HOWARD KAYLAN My dad worked at Hughes Aircraft, which was right down the street from where we lived. He started out working at GE in Manhattan, and then went upstate for a few years in Utica before he got transferred to El Segundo. And when that job went south, he immediately got a job with Hughes Aircraft. So, I got to watch the experimental aircraft at the airfield. That was my dad, testing microwave equipment on both sides of Lincoln Boulevard back in the day. The experimental aircraft used to take off at Hughes Field and from the Cargo Terminal at what used to be LAX. That's a pretty magical upbringing. It was the X-15. It was Scott Carpenter. It was un-be-fucking-believable. Those experimental aircraft were X-15s, and we saw it. We were right there.

JACK UNDERWOOD Mark's dad was the head of our Webelos, which is like a transitional group between the Cub Scouts and Boy Scouts. And once a week we would go over to his house, and his dad would deal with us boys. You could say it was a troop. There was probably eight or ten of us at the most.

JOHN SNYDER There was never a time that you would think, *Oh my God, Mark's got problems*, or *Gee, he must have trouble at home*. Never. The guy was always clowning around, upbeat, funny, and everybody liked him. He was just fun to be around.

PHIL VOLMAN There was always music in our house; it was just a part of growing up. We would listen to everything: we'd even listen to opera. We had an LP of *Madame Butterfly* with one of the most famous sopranos of all time, Amelita Galli-Curci. It was chilling—she had such a wonderful voice. We also had some original Caruso records. We had a whole bunch of that stuff. I don't know where the opera came from, because Dad wasn't into it, and Mom certainly wasn't, but we had those records.

> **I was really affected by *Madame Butterfly*. My class went to the auditorium in downtown Los Angeles when we were about nine or ten to see a production of the opera. At the end, when she killed herself, I remember crying nearly uncontrollably until the teacher came over and calmed me down. I was really hit by the story and the music. I played that record many times after that. My mom and I talked about that.**

ANN BECKER He was not one to hold his feelings in, as a rule. He never was one to go and hide in the corner or anything like that. If something upset him, or if he wanted something, he'd let you know.

His father just loved jazz. He had quite a collection and he'd play those records over and over again. He enjoyed music so much, and I think that might have influenced Mark, too.

HOWARD KAYLAN His dad had a huge Dixieland collection, and that was the stuff I was into, because I was a clarinet player. I was playing in my own little Dixieland band in junior high.

PHIL VOLMAN Dad was a huge Dixieland fan and he had great collection, which we still have intact. Some great stuff, all 78s: Sidney Bechet, The Hot Five, Bessie Smith, King Oliver . . . lots of the old New Orleans guys. He used to take me to a place called the Beverly Caverns on Beverly Boulevard. I saw Sidney Bechet and Kid Ory there. Dad especially loved the clarinet, and so did I. I started playing when I was about seven years old, and later on I picked up the saxophone as well. We had our own little group in school. It was more bebop, and we played at a couple places around the Westchester area. I started getting into more modern jazz myself and began hanging out at the Lighthouse on Hermosa Beach. This was in the 1950s, and I was underage, but they used to get me in, and I'd sit at the bar and eat fried rice and listen to the music. I saw Cal Tjader, Howard Rumsey, The Lighthouse All-Stars. Bud Shank was there a lot. Stan Getz was there, and I watched him shoot up heroin in the bathroom. I was about sixteen, maybe fifteen.

HOWARD KAYLAN The other thing Mark's dad had lying around were records by Louis Prima and Keely Smith. In fact, both of our dads had those. They came from the same era: they were WWII vets, and everybody from that era had a passing acquaintance with that generation of lounge performer.

When I was nine and a half years old, on our trip from New York to Los Angeles, we stopped in Las Vegas and saw Louis Prima and Keely Smith. And the reason that that happened—and the reason Mark got taken as a kid to see Louis and Keely—was because they weren't a main room attraction. They played lounges. The other artists that played in Vegas—the Dean Martins, the Frank Sinatras, the Jerry Lewises—would go to see Louis and Keely after their shows. They didn't start performing until ten or eleven at night, so they took care of all the other performers. They were the entertainer's entertainers.

And Phil had this incredible doo-wop record collection. That's where a lot of our roots began. That's where we got our fondness for the song 'Teardrops,' which we later recorded, as well as having an affinity for the music that Zappa was doing. We were hearing it for the first time as Zappa was recording it when he lived out in Cucamonga or Riverside or wherever the hell he was. His first stuff was doo-wop. That was ten years before Mark and I came along, so it was an education to hear the Five Satins and that kind of stuff, the things that we couldn't really hear on the radio. Phil Volman had all those records, and they were a huge influence. So, thanks to Joe and Phil, our influences were all in place by junior high. We were ready to roll, I'll tell you.

JOHN SNYDER We were in the band together in junior high school. I played the drums, which I was terrible at, and Mark played the clarinet. He was pretty good, actually.

JACK UNDERWOOD In junior high, Mark and I both joined the school band, which was quite large. In fact, when there were over a hundred people in the band. We both played the clarinet, and we got pretty good at it. We would practice together at our homes, and at school we'd all be battling for first- or second-chair clarinet. He'd have it one period, and then I'd have it another, but he and I were right there. For us, it was like a dream to be able to play like Benny Goodman. We both would listen to music along that line. In the ninth grade, there was a Los Angeles All-City band competition, between lots of different high schools, and we wound up winning that competition. And to hear all that music in one place, it was inspiring. I think that was the birth of Mark Volman, the musician.

I was an only child, and when I was thirteen my mother died. She had a protracted illness, and my dad worked long hours, so I became what they call, here in Hawaii, *hanai*. It's when other families would take you in, knowing that there's something going on with your family. So I was what they call the neighborhood *hanai* child.

My mother had died in December, and my dad used to love to go on road trips. He loved to drive, and that following summer he was ready to get out and have some fun. He told me I could bring someone along, and my best friend at the time was Mark. Mark's folks said *sure*, so we spent this month-long road trip in a yellow and black '55 Dodge. We went along the South and then up through the Midwest and wound up in Illinois, Indiana, Missouri, and all those areas, because I had a lot of family from back in that area, and then we came back through the Dakotas.

We took our clarinets. Mark and I would be in the back, playing away with our clarinets and yelling at the herds of sheep on the side of the road, getting them to stampede some sheep herder or whatever as we went by. We would stay at roadside motels. My dad was the only one that could drive, so when he got tired, that's where we'd spend the night. Mark almost got hung one time. It was in one of the Dakotas, in a very one-horse town with maybe two or three streetlights. We were staying in the town's only motel, and Dad was sleeping. We decided to go next door to the A&W and grab a soda and just kind of hang out. There were a couple of street lights, and toward the top they had a stirrup of some sort. It was a decorative thing. And that was it for miles in any direction. I guess that was the only place the locals could cruise, and here come some cowboy types that were older teenagers, probably about eighteen or nineteen. They pulled up and started talking to Mark and I, giving us a bad time. At that time, if you were from the West Coast, the surf scene, it was all very bright, Hawaiian-oriented type clothing and streaks of bleached hair, and they didn't like that at all. One of them threw a rope, which had a noose on the end of it, up over the stirrup on the streetlight, and put it around Mark's neck, and started slowly pulling up on it. They were trying to scare us, and we were trying to be real cool and not piss them off. They had him stretched up to where he was on his toes before they cut us loose, and we went right inside the motel. *That's it, we're not gonna run around in this town anymore.*

When we were in Indiana, there was a big reunion at one of my uncles' houses. He had this huge backyard area with a bunch of tables with umbrellas set up for special occasions, and all sorts of family showed up from out of town. Mark was the only one who wasn't family there, although we considered him part of the family, but not as far as blood. Being as outgoing as he was, everybody took to him. We were at our table and he looks at me, and he's mouthing, 'I've got to fart—I can't stand it!' It was killing him. And then we started laughing, and when he started laughing, he couldn't hold it anymore and it ripped. It was huge. *Everybody* heard it. My dad was just beside himself when this went down. At first it was like they were aghast, but then there was some snickering. It was all Mark and I could do to keep from rolling on the ground laughing. So my dad sent us down into my uncle's basement to regroup. We got down there and then we really started cracking up, and then my dad came down with a stern face and proceeded to tell us that obviously we shouldn't have done that, and why did you do it? But then he started laughing about it, and we couldn't stop cracking up. Some of my relatives, in fact a lot of my relatives, remember him. Most of those folks are dead now, but they remembered him their whole life, having only met him that one time. But that does leave an image.

My father absolutely loved him, and got to know him very well when we were on that trip. He knew him before that, but when you spend a month on the road with somebody, you get to know him very well, and I knew he loved him. When my father died, Mark did the eulogy, which I'm sure— he's definitely in heaven loving Mark doing that. He did a wonderful job. It definitely brought tears to my eyes.

That trip with Jack and Rollo (Jack's dad) was my first time away from home as a young boy. I think it brought Jack and me together. My brother was nine years older, and he was not around when I was younger, so Jack was very much like a brother. Rollo, who I loved, was like a second father to me. The hanging story sounds funny but it was really scary. We didn't know what they were going to do. Jack still laughs about that, and it bugs me that my imminent death is still so funny to him.

ED GUNNEY We met when we were both nine years old. We were baby boomers, and there were a lot of kids our age everywhere. Baseball was truly the national pastime. Our dads were hardly more than ten years out of Okinawa, Iwo Jima, and Normandy. There wasn't a lot of extra money but there was time to play catch with their sons. This was going on all across postwar United States. We both lived close, and we ended up on the same team. I was a catcher and he was pitching, and he was marvelous. He was a pudgy little guy, but Phil and his dad must have played catch with him early on, because his mechanics were so smooth, and he had such great control and accuracy.

JOHN SNYDER He was always a little bit overweight. Most of us were skinny kids, but Mark was pudgy. He just had that roly-poly look. We both played Little League together. Mark was the right fielder and I was the pitcher when we were twelve years old. It was a different world. Our parents all knew each other, and were involved in our activities. His mom and dad came to every Little League game. Bea was a sweetheart—she used to volunteer at the hotdog stand—and his dad was a real character, pretty boisterous, with a great, dry sense of humor.

ED GUNNEY Both his parents were involved in helping with the Little League. Bea was chief coordinator for the women's auxiliary in 1957—that means they operated the Snack Shack—and the following year, Joe was second vice president. In 1959 he became chief umpire. So, his family was at the Little League all of the time. Our team won the league in 1956. Mark went 10 and 0. I don't think he walked anybody the whole year. The mayor, Norris Poulson, took us to lunch in the city hall when we won. We were each given a ballpoint pen with his name on it. Russ Benedetti was on the second-placed team. I remember his dad saying, 'You wouldn't have won if you didn't have that chubby kid pitching.' And he was right: Mark had such great control. He just dominated the league, and the managers and coaches from the other league must have had an eye on him, because the next year he went from this beginning division up to the major leagues, and I went to the intermediate division. Three years later, when we were twelve, there were two other kids who were as good as Mark and one of them—Roric Harrison—even made the major leagues. He was the last pitcher to hit a home run in the American League. He was a good hitter for a pitcher, and he still has the International League strikeout record. But Mark was one of the three best pitchers, and he was a heck of a good line-drive hitter. His batting average was .436, something like that. When we were thirteen, we went to Babe Ruth league. He was on a different team than I was in that league, but again, he was a very, very good stable pitcher with great, great, control.

I pitched until I was fifteen. I was pretty good till I was fourteen, and then my arm just got tired. My Babe Ruth league team (the Braves) had some good ballplayers. Tom Stephens and Don Saffer were the best on my team. Don played at UCLA and then got drafted into the majors. **My arm was gone by then. I threw a nasty curve, and a knuckleball I learned from Hoyt Wilhelm on TV. Thank God for music.**

JACK UNDERWOOD In seventh or eighth grade we started skateboarding. This was the birth pangs of the sport, when you would take your old metal skates— the old metal skates that had wheels and would clamp onto your shoe—and we would bastardize them, nail them onto the bottom of a piece of two-by-six and that became our skateboard, which was very dangerous, in hindsight.

We made this one skateboard that was probably about five feet long, and we used it like a bobsled. We packed bodies on to where the person at the back would be standing on with just his toes, because the more bodies, the faster you go. The goal was to get as heavy as we could. Whoever was in the front would be sitting on his butt, bringing his feet up almost to his crotch in order to make as small an imprint as possible. The person behind him would wrap their legs over his legs and then grab onto his back. So we could pack quite a few people onto this. There was one incline, a sidewalk that sloped down with a road on one side and various front yards on the other. At the bottom, you had to start thinking about coming to a stop before you hit a cross street, and below that was a library. There was a bunch of ivy that was maybe sixteen, eighteen inches tall in front of the library, and within this ivy was a sprinkler system, which in those days consisted of all metal elements. The sprinkler system was maybe about sixteen inches tall, hidden amongst the ivy. Mark was on the very front for this particular run. We were flying down this hill, and we lost control toward the bottom and went flying off into this ivy. We must have taken out four or five of these metal sprinkler heads with Mark's crotch, with all of our mass behind him. He's writhing on the ground, but we were just cracking up. Stupid little story, but this is the kind of stuff that we did, and it was a lot of fun.

Oh my God, skateboarding nearly killed us. Fearless—we were fearless. Jack loved it when I nearly died in crashes, and that happened most all the time.

HOWARD KAYLAN Joe was really, really into the bullfights, even though his side of the family was Russian Jewish. He was totally into the romance of it, so he and Beatrice would go down to Tijuana all the time. And they would take the kids. When they were very young, Phil and Mark went to see the bullfights.

JACK UNDERWOOD Mark's family would go down to Tijuana, to the bullfighting venues down there, and they let me go with them. The crème de la crème of the bullfighters at the time was this guy named Manolete, even though he had died years earlier. When we said that word around the Volman house, it's like everybody's head snapped around. At the Volman household, he was God. For anybody who was into bullfighting, he was like a Michael Jordan type.

HOWARD KAYLAN Joe had posters on the wall of all the famous bullfighters, and he had an album called *The Day Manolete Died*. It was very beautiful and romantic and graphic, with gorgeous flamenco guitar, lovely violin stuff and mariachis throughout, and a narration that ran all the way through, telling the story of the famous bullfight, wherein Manolete lost his life.

Manolete was the eventual foundation of the Flo & Eddie song 'Carlos And De Bull.' We took the story from *The Death Of Manolete*, by the famous writer Barnaby Conrad.

HOWARD KAYLAN Bullfighting was romanticized all over the den, and that's where Mark and I would spend most of our hangout time, because that's where the big ol' console stereo was. If we weren't sleeping in the adjoining corner units where Mark and his brother used to share the same bedroom, then we would be in the den, listening to that stuff. We would steal his parents' booze from the liquor cabinet and add water to it so they wouldn't find out, only I'm sure they did find out. We were terrible about our choice of liquors as well. We would drink the most terrible things we could find, green things and blue things, so it was just a nightmare, and we would be horribly sick. And it was really, really fun.

ANN BECKER His big thing before he got into the music was the surfing. That was the thing that he really, really enjoyed, and was really, really good at it, too. And that's so typical of Mark. If he liked something, he did it well.

PAT VOLMAN Well, you could call it surfing, I don't know if anybody else would call it that. But he thought he was a surfer. He stood up once. That's all I remember: once, he stood up. I've only seen one picture of him when he was actually standing up, and it was in the soup, it was almost at shore.

MADELINE CAMPILLO In the early 60s, the Alaska earthquake was scheduled to hit California, and it did hit up at Crescent City. I saw it afterward and it hit pretty hard up there. As I understand it, Mark and his friends went down and sat on Manhattan Beach, waiting for the tidal wave to go by. I also had a niece that stood on the other side of a latticework fence to watch the bullet fly out of a motel when there was a hold-up. I don't think brilliance runs in the family. But I really think that he was intelligent, and that he went down there out of absolute curiosity.

MICHAEL THOMAS Parts of Westchester, if you stood in certain places, you could see the beach. It was in Southern California, and sunny, and there were surfing beaches right there, that whole culture. When we got off school, we'd go surfing.

JACK UNDERWOOD We started surfing when we were around twelve or thirteen. A friend of ours lived right down in the beach at the mouth of what is now Marina Del Ray. At the time, they had not dredged yet, and it was just a couple of jetties that stuck out in the water. Everybody would keep their boards at our friend's so we wouldn't have to lug them back and forth. There could be a dozen surfboards at any given time. Mark had the goofiest board: it was pastel blue and yellow, and there were pieces of toilet paper underneath the fiberglass. Little squares of colored toilet paper underneath the resin of his board. In the winter we'd build fires in the fifty-five-gallon drums that they had for trash out by the lifeguard stands. We'd go surfing till we were purple, then we'd come out and stand around these drums and get warm. This one particular day, Mark wasn't there for some reason, and it was cold. There was no wood to burn, and we were freezing. Somebody grabbed his board and we broke it up and burned it in the fifty-five-gallon drum, and it looked like an oil fire, because fiberglass and foam produce a very dense black smoke. Nobody told Mark, and a couple of days later, he came down to go surfing, and here his board was gone. 'What happened to it?' Everybody looked at everybody else, and he figured out what happened and we wound up confessing. That was typical of the dirty little tricks we used to pull on each other.

JOHN SNYDER Mark had a club—West Bay Surfers, they were called—and I tried to get in the club but they wouldn't accept me. Mark wouldn't vote me in. It was about eight or ten guys. I wanted to get in, and I remember going to their meeting, which was held at Mark's house. I came there to say I want to join, and they made me wait outside while they voted. When I came back in, they said, 'No, you're not accepted.' Mark just didn't think I was that good. He and I never butted heads or disagreed, but my feelings were hurt, of course. They rejected me and I was upset. I went home and told my mom that Mark was a real jerk, and I hated the guy. Of course that blew over later. The thing is, I wasn't very good. In fact, I was terrible. I was a much better baseball player.

I did start a surfing club: we were the West Side Surfers. We had some good surfers from up north and I remember winning one contest against the Salt Creek Surf Club. I started my own club because I couldn't get into the West Rey Surfers. They were the best club around.

JACK UNDERWOOD We'd go down to Camp Pendleton. Now you can go, but at the time the marine base controlled the area. You would get off the highway and drive down into these very high weeds that were six to eight feet tall. You'd literally disappear with your car, and there'd be these trails that run through these weeds. We would drive in, and once you got at the high tide line, they couldn't do anything to you. So, you're out in the water, but it's getting to the high tide line—that's when they would lay for you. And literally, they would have plastic bullets. You'd hold your board up for protection as you ran along. I was never hit, but my board was. It could get serious.

I had a '57 Ford. It was my surf mobile, a station wagon with our surfboards sticking out of the back. We drove down there one time, and to give you an idea of what the marines would do, we'd gone surfing, and I parked in among the weeds. When we came back, the marines had let the air out of both of my front tires, and taken a dump next to both of them. I only have one spare, and because they flattened two of them, we had to do this twice. We had to sneak out of there with a tire that's flat, hitchhike down the road, get it fixed, and then come back just to get ourselves mobile again. It was very cunning of them to flatten both tires. Not to mention dealing with what was left next to the front tires. It was positioned in such a way so that if you had to change the tires, we'd be wading in it. We were on their land, and they were very territorial.

JOHN SNYDER Mark had a '58 Chevy, and he had installed a record player in the car. When you drove over a bump, the record would skip. Everybody wanted to ride in his car because it was so cool to have a record player. It was a big deal to hear music, besides the radio. At lunchtime we would skip out, run over to McDonald's, listen to records, and come back before the next period. We played hooky a lot in those days because he had the record player.

JACK UNDERWOOD We were blessed with a time in history and a place that was charmed. I only wish everybody could have experienced the things we did. There was a real sense of innocence. We didn't feel threatened by the things that are going on today. There were no drugs, no weapons, or anything along that line.

PAT VOLMAN In my class, Phil Hartman was the class clown. He used to sit behind me in homeroom every year. I was 'Hickey' and he was 'Hartman.' He was supposed to be in front of me, but he always ended behind me and bugging me, because we would sit in alphabetical order. He would bug me in homeroom *if* he showed up. He'd rarely show up, but when he did, he was funny. That's what he did. He was just funny.

JOHN SNYDER When we were graduating, we had a very small class, only about sixty kids. At the graduation ceremony we were all up on this scaffolding. Mark was behind my girlfriend, and he kept pushing her. She was starting to fall, and if she did, it would set it all off like dominos. It was six or seven steps tiered, and he was standing behind her, pushing her back and forth so she would feel like she was falling. If she would have fallen, she would have taken everybody in front of us down. But that was Mark. That was the clown that he was, and it was always in good nature, always in good fun, never meanspirited. I never ever saw Mark in that mode.

PAT VOLMAN In one of my school annuals, he's in every picture. He didn't belong in any of these clubs, but when he knew a picture was going to be taken, he ran and hid in behind in the back row, and when they said *smile*, he would be raised up, and he was in about eighty clubs.

All hail to thee our alma mater, fairest of them all
All hail to thee our alma mater, we will never fall
Since first we met life's noble task our hearts are still aglow
With thoughts of thee Westchester High
Loyal alma mater
Westchester hail, Westchester hail
All hail to thee

PAT VOLMAN He picked me up from school in his old '58, wearing his father's zippered zebra shirt. I said, 'Are you for real? Are you kidding me? You can't go to school wearing that.' But he did. He was a dorky, funny guy, and he was very comfortable in his dorkiness. That's why he never paid any attention at school: he was just too busy. I heard that he was sent home from kindergarten because he went into the cloak room and was making out with some little four-year-old girl. The teacher didn't know where he was. He was always doing silly stuff. I'm still laughing, and I'm not even married to him anymore.

I graduated in '66, and Squeaky Fromme graduated in '67. I never saw her. I wouldn't even know if she walked by me at that point. It's a pretty fascinating school, though. All the killers and funny people were attending—all the celebrities.

Our school had some interesting people there. Squeaky Fromme, Phil Hartman, and The Crossfires/Turtles. Squeaky (Lynette) was part of our auxiliary surfing group. Her nickname was 'Snail Butts, Inc.' Later, in 1998, Emily, my wife at the time, worked as an assistant to Phil Hartman's brother, John. When Phil died, Emily was put in charge of the memorial service. Small world, how we all came to be.

SIDE A THE SIXTIES

1

THE CROSSFIRES

Before The Turtles took off, the boys learned the ropes as The Crossfires.

ED GUNNEY We were going to Orville Wright Junior High School. I had third period PE, and in the squad next to me was a kid that had played in the Little League named Gary Whitney. All the boys were in after-school league athletics, and on Wednesdays they had a gymnastic club. Chuck Portz was also in that gymnastics club. I remember this vividly: Gary comes up to me and says, 'Hey Ed, I started a band,' and his exact words were, 'My brother Bob is going to be in it, and Pots is going to be in it'—he called Chuck Portz 'Pots.' Chuck was messing around with Gary, and they named the band The Night Riders. Dale Walton—who had gone to Cowan Avenue, the elementary school that I went to—ended up as rhythm guitarist. Bob and Gary dropped out somewhere along the line, but Dale and Chuck stayed in. When we got to high school, the group had evolved. A guy named Al Nichol was in the group, and he was an outstanding lead guitarist. The drummer was from Inglewood. I didn't know him, but you'd see the other guys on campus all the time.

AL NICHOL I started the whole thing. I was living in Ohio, and I played a few different instruments in the orchestra and the marching band. I was listening to Duane Eddy and The Ventures, all these guitarists, and I really liked that sound. Then Johnny & The Hurricanes came and played at our high school auditorium. They had had this big hit record of 'Red River Rock,' and I was mesmerized. That did it. I finally broke down and I got myself a guitar. Right about that time my father, who had been an English professor at Ohio State University, got an offer to come and take over the chairmanship and teach at USC. There was a big California craze going on, and I just said, 'Okay, that's it, I'm going to go to California and get a guitar and a surfboard and a girlfriend and a car.' And so I proceeded to do exactly that, only not quite in that order. I had picked up a guitar and was learning how to play it. I was in the a cappella choir, and I found this very talented, very musical kid named Howard in the choir.

HOWARD KAYLAN I was taking music lessons—clarinet—in a little music store in Westchester. The teacher, Mr. Ferguson, had this old, silver, beat-up used saxophone set up in the corner of my room, and I always had my eye on that thing. I kept asking, 'Aren't they very similar? If I master clarinet, can I one day move up to that thing?' And finally, he just said, 'Your parents are paying me for clarinet lessons, but what the hell, I got some extra time, the day is young. Pick the thing up and doodle around with it. You use the same fingering, it's all right.'

I honked around a bit and I really liked it, so I took a couple of lessons on that, and literally two weeks after I had started playing, just trying to get the saxophone down, I got a phone call from Chuck Portz. He was the bass player of the Nightriders, and he said, 'Hey, I hear you play sax.' Two weeks! So as, I don't know, a preservation measure, I said, 'You bet I do!' And we got together in his garage, he and Al Nichol, the lead guitar player, and Glen Wilson, this red-headed drummer guy. And that was the band, the three of us. If there was a fourth guy, it could have been Dale Walton on the bass guitar.

AL NICHOL I got together with Howard and Glen Wilson in Glen's garage. I met Chuck Portz on the beach with the surfing crowd. He had a guitar and showed me a little bit, and then I plugged in my musical knowledge and went from there. I learned the guitar very fast, and then I returned the favor and showed him how to play the bass parts. So he became a bass player right then, joined the little group with me and Howard and Glen, and that was the Night Riders. Howard was playing sax, and we did a lot of instrumentals, a lot of surfing songs. And we changed our name as well. We changed to the Crossfires. 'Crossfire' was one of the Johnny & The Hurricanes songs that I had been mesmerized by.

HOWARD KAYLAN My first contact with Mark was during tenth grade, when we were both in a cappella choir together. I was the first of the second tenors, and Mark was the last of the first tenors, so we were literally standing next to each other in Mr. Robert Wood's a cappella choir. And he would throw Mark and me out almost every day, because we were ahead of the curve: we were reading the music, we were flawless in our parts and spotless on our reading, and yet we would say things to crack each other up, and to crack the rest of the class up. And daily, we'd be out with a hall pass, prowling the corridors during third period, because he just didn't want us in that room upsetting people.

AL NICHOL We played for the surf crowd, and every time we played, this guy—this class clown—would jump up on the stage and do crazy things. Everything he did was funny. And, finally, he asked to join the group.

HOWARD KAYLAN During choir one day, Mark said he'd like to join our band. I said, 'That's great. What is it that you do?' He said, 'Nothing.' I said, 'Wow, sounds terrific. You know what? I'll ask Al after class and we'll get back to you.' So I told Al, and Al started laughing. He said, 'That's great. We could really use a guy who does nothing.' Coming from that Spike Jones Appreciation Society, as I did, and being a fan of Soupy Sales and Ernie Kovacs and that sort of nonsense comedy, I saw a shot to inject a little humor into this thing, which was at that point a humorless situation. I grew up on Louis Prima and Keely Smith, and I found myself in this band that was taking Johnny & The Hurricanes very, very seriously. And I couldn't do it. Besides, I was a fledgling sax player, remember. I was honking these notes and trying to figure out how to play solos. I was really, really subpar when I entered the Crossfires, but coming into the band I realized that everybody was just learning chords. Everybody was just figuring out how to play. We all learned together. So we wound up playing at a couple of frat parties that Al had booked, and Mark was brought along as a roadie, to schlep our equipment up and down the stairs of these enormous fraternity houses on Frat Row at UCLA.

Howard and Al were my idols. Howard was the front man and sang, and Al played guitar. I sat on the side of the stage like a groupie. I could not believe the energy coming from the stage. I have no idea what I was thinking when I asked him if I could join the band, but I did anyway. On the following Monday in the lunch yard I asked, and I was added to the band soon after. In fact, the next weekend I carried equipment at a frat party at UCLA. I was a terrible roadie.

HOWARD KAYLAN He could be clumsy from the get-go. In fact, the first or second time he was schlepping our equipment at one of these gigs, he literally dropped everything down a flight of stairs and fell down the stairs with it, and laughed the whole way down.

It wasn't too long until I was singing along with Howard onstage. He sang second tenor in choir, which was the melody. I sang the high parts, which in choir was first tenor, and Al sang baritone and Chuck sang bass. The songs we were singing were a cross of R&B and rock: 'Justine' by Don & Dewey, 'Koko Joe' by The Righteous Brothers, 'Little Latin Lupe Lu' and staples like 'Money,' 'New Orleans,' and Elvis. It made us different than the typical surf band in our area. Our stiffest competition were The Marauders and The Roosters. They fell by the wayside.

HOWARD KAYLAN From there, it was incremental. He started with simply moving gear, then he was thrown a tambourine, and then later he sang along, helping to get the crowd up on their feet and lead the choruses when we sang those R&B songs that require some kind of audience response. It wasn't so much that he began to do more and more, it's just that as things fell into his path, he would pick 'em up and smash 'em. He got very proficient, not in the playing of the tambourine, particularly, but in the spinning of the tambourine, and the tossing it over his shoulders, and even the dropping of the tambourine, which I believe even back then he was perfecting to an art form.

JOHN SNYDER I don't think Mark really had the background, other than the desire. But he was just such a likeable guy that all he had to do is say, 'Hey, I'm doing something,' and the other kids would be interested. If he said he was going to do a band, we'd all figure he'd probably do good at it, he'd make it happen.

PAT VOLMAN They used to play in the quad at lunch time. There would be a special day when The Crossfires would play. They had little wallet-size cards, with 'The Crossfires' and a picture of them all dressed up with their instruments. So he was serious.

JOHN SNYDER The Crossfires were a big deal at Westchester High. Everybody went to see them, because they were really exciting and fun to dance to. They were a little bit loud, but that was actually what we wanted as kids. They played over in Inglewood and at a bunch of little places and the kids would show up.

ED GUNNEY Somebody said, 'All the guys in The Crossfires are in the a cappella singing class at Westchester High with Mr. Wood, and they're going to start singing on some of their sock hops.' It was almost exclusively instrumental surf music, but there was a couple of numbers where Mark and Howard would sing R&B stuff. 'Justine' is the one that really stood out. That was a big bit by Don & Dewey. Their version may have been better than Mark and Howard's, but I can tell you absolutely that Mark and Howard did 'Justine' better than The Righteous Brothers. That was a hot number.

JACK UNDERWOOD I'll never forget 'Justine.' That was their signature song, and Mark was the lead singer. It used to get everybody all worked up and sweaty, and from there they could have played anything and we still would have rocked out.

AL NICHOL After a while, we decided to expand our sound a little bit and got a different drummer, Don Murray.

HOWARD KAYLAN We started making some money at these parties, and eventually Glen Wilson was replaced by Don Murray, a drummer from Inglewood High School who Al knew from one of our engagements at one of the other local teen centers. Don was really, really into it, not only as a drummer, but he fancied himself an artist, so he designed The Crossfires' logo—the business card—of an iron cross and the sunset.

JACK UNDERWOOD As somebody that wants to make everybody happy, it was the perfect vehicle for Mark. Instead of having just a couple of people around, he's got a whole audience. It played right into his hands as far as that went.

AL NICHOL This is something that Howard and I had come to realize: that this was a vital part of the group, whatever he does. He was a comedian that needed a straight man, and that right there was the birth of Flo & Eddie. And he agreed to go and get a saxophone, so we had the two-saxophone thing going. But right from the beginning, his timing was great, and he had a natural talent for communicating and entertaining audiences. That really helped the group become recognizable and popular. We became one of the most popular surf bands in Southern Cal.

PAT VOLMAN The first time I saw them, he was playing sax and tambourine. His father had come to school and said, 'You have to pay my son at least $20 to do that,' so Howard and Mark both played sax just to make money in the band. He started singing in '63 or '64.

JACK UNDERWOOD I can remember them playing sax, which was a good transition for Mark from clarinet. Howard eventually became the lead singer, but back then it was more mixed. They would trade off.

VENNY THOMAS I went to St. Bernard Parochial School, but I used to go to sock hops over there and watch them play. They were a real good band, even then. The thing about the sock hops, for me, coming from a parochial school, was that was one time where you could be with your girl. They played the right kind of tunes, too. You'd literally be dancing with your shoes off—in your socks. You'd be dancing, and all of a sudden, you'd look at each other and ask, 'You want to go play baseball?' The girl would go 'Yeah,' and then you'd go outside, where they had a couple of baseball fields, and you'd go into the dugout and make out. And then you'd come back and dance some more.

I really loved The Crossfires. You could dance to them, you could fall in love to them, and you could get laid to them. They were great.

HOWARD KAYLAN We also had a spinoff from the choir. Mark, myself, and Al brought a girl named Betty McCarty from a cappella choir in with us, to do this little talent show. The people who were headlining the talent show were a local Black act by the name of Joe & Eddie. And we were billed as The Crosswind Singers. The Crosswind Singers did a bunch of rehearsals, but we just did the one gig.

AL NICHOL This gal at school liked to sing Joan Baez, Judy Collins, and all these folk singers that were getting popular, and she needed backing, so we joined up with her. Me and Mark and Howard got up onstage with her. Of course, the whole school knew us as The Crossfires, so we billed ourselves as The Crosswinds. We changed our name once again. We did that a lot; we became other groups. That was the whole concept behind *The Battle Of The Bands*. We could be any group we wanted. Howard and Mark could go up to Hollywood and pretend they were Gerry & The Pacemakers.

CHUNKY CLUB & THE REVELAIRE

ED GUNNEY This is kind of raunchy. When I was a senior in '64, these guys, maybe six or seven guys, would kind of dance dirty with the girls in the gym and at clubs. They would have a big spoon or ladle, and they would act like they were digging it into the girl's crotch and eating it. That's the Chunky Club. I was not in the Chunky Club, but I saw this happen at dances a couple of times. They all thought they were hot stuff; they thought it was hilarious. You'd hear about it in Nutrition during school—guys were going wild and crazy.

PAT VOLMAN They were very rude. They did very nasty gestures with their hands and spoons and stuff that would be X-rated. But it was fun. I mean, those people got wild.

The Chunky Club was led by Brian Dalton. He ate caterpillars to shock people.

AL NICHOL I wrote 'Chunky' for the Chunky Club. They were part of the high-school surf crowd. They would go out and party on the weekends, and go to all these dances and everything.

HOWARD KAYLAN We were actually thrown out of the Westchester Women's Club thanks to the Chunky Club. That was their fault, not our fault. But we knew what it was like to work with a fanatical base of people, and what it took to keep them around. If it took being suggestive lyrically, we weren't the guys that were doing that moron dirty-dancing stuff, we were just the guys onstage. In fact, we were never the guys who went to dances. We were always the guys who *played* the dances. So, our social skills were nil.

VENNY THOMAS The most I saw them was in my senior year, which would have been in 1962. After 1963 I didn't go to any more sock hops. In fact, I hooked up with Jimmy and Ray Manczarek right after that. I was with that whole Doors entourage. I moved in with Rick and Jimmy and Ray. I was like the stepbrother, and we practiced in their home garage. Rick & The Ravens did surf music and sang too. We did 'Big Bucket "T",' 'Geraldine' . . . stuff like that.

RAY MANZAREK We were all fair-haired blue-eyed boys out of Chicago, and my brothers were great surfers. I couldn't surf at all. I just couldn't get my balance. I never got the hang of surfing, but my parents' house was right across from the Redondo Beach Pier. They would open the door and there was the Pacific Ocean. It was glorious. Needless to say, my family completely loved California. They never went back to Chicago. My brothers said, 'To hell with it, who cares? We're in California, man—we're Rick & The Ravens!' Rick was the center at Redondo Beach High School basketball team and had some scholarship offers, but left those behind to continue his rock'n'roll life.

MICHAEL THOMAS In Westchester, the Crossfires were the best local group. And then there was Rick & The Ravens. They were from Manhattan Beach, and they were like rivals, almost. But the Crossfires appealed to more of a cleaner-cut group of people, and they were straighter. You see Mark and Howard, and how they changed their personas, it's light years compared to what they used to be.

JACK UNDERWOOD This was the era when surf music was really coming on, where the Surfer's Stomp was happening with Dick Dale and all these other bands. In the Southern California area, it seemed like almost every weekend there was something, someplace going on where there'd be a band playing, and a lot of the times it would be Mark's band.

ED GUNNEY There was a battle of the bands at the Santa Monica Civic Auditorium. It was a big thing: you'd hear about it on KFWB or KRLA. And they won. Everybody was proud of the Crossfires and thought they were really good, but it wasn't like they were going to become a name you heard on the radio. We didn't think of possibilities in those days. We were trying to remember our locker combinations.

MICHAEL THOMAS The big battle of the bands—the surf bands—was at the Aragon Ballroom, at the end of the Santa Monica Pier. Everybody would go out there. There were surfers, and there were hodads. The hodads were the guys with the lowered cars and kind of East L.A. greaser. And surf guys were kind of bushy-bushy—like The Beach Boys, say. It was that old Fender amp and Stratocaster sound. There was definitely a competitive edge, there were individuals that maybe had an animosity toward other bands, but in general I always found it to be a cool scene.

PAT VOLMAN They won a battle of the bands, and then they worked at the Revelaire Club in Redondo Beach. It was all-ages, so a lot of kids from high school would go there and get all crazy. Everybody would look forward to going on Friday or Saturday night to the Revelaire Club.

MICHAEL THOMAS Reb Foster was a disc jockey on the radio station KFWB, and he had this club called the Revelaire on Pacific Coast Highway. It was either in Manhattan Beach, Hermosa Beach, Redondo Beach . . . almost at the border of them all. It was quite the hot spot, and as soon as you were old enough to get in, that's where everybody went.

LINDA CAMPILLO I went there one time with my aunts and uncles. I was in junior high, and I thought it was pretty cool to be in this club. It was a big space with chairs along the sides. It wasn't like people sitting at tables smoking cigarettes and drinking cocktails. It wasn't that kind of atmosphere. The focus was definitely on the band. I thought that was cool. Of course, I always thought Mark was cool anyway.

JOHNNY BARBATA I was in The Sentinels. We played R&B and rock'n'roll stuff—that's what The Sentinels were. Well, that and surf music. We played Reb Foster's Revelaire Club, but I never saw The Crossfires.

HOWARD KAYLAN We were surf boys, and we hung out with other surf boys. We worked with Eddie & The Showmen and The Challengers and all the local acts who grew up in the shadow of The Beach Boys, who had already had hit records.

AL NICHOL We played a lot at the Revelaire Club, as well as the Retail Clerks' Hall and Harmony Park Ballroom. The Crossfires, Eddie & The Showmen, The Belairs, and Dick Dale & His Del-Tones seemed to revolve around those three. But the Revelaire Club was our home base.

HOWARD KAYLAN Bill Utley was the manager of the Revelaire Club, and the only guy that we did business with on a weekly level. Reb Foster was his cousin. We didn't see Reb all that often. He was on the radio, and occasionally he would introduce a show if it was somebody he had a vested interest in, like The Righteous Brothers. But his name was attached to the club. It was *Reb Foster's Revelaire Club*, like a Dick Clark venture. It's not like Dick oversaw all of his ventures, but he had a guy who did. And that's what Bill did.

JIM TUCKER They went to Westchester. I went to Aviation High in Manhattan Beach, which was about six miles south of where they were. I was in one of the top surf bands. It was The Vibrants or The Baymen, and we were both playing at the same club. We had two bands each night, and we'd alternate sets.

AL NICHOL To this day, I can't remember what band he came from. I don't know if he was in The Baymen or The Vibrants or a combination of the two. The groups were reforming all the time under different names. Same people, just changing around as different groups. So I don't blame him—he probably doesn't remember. They were all the same, just different names.

AL NICHOL Mark, Howard, Chuck Portz, and myself we were all in the a cappella choir, and we realized we might as well change over from the instrumental stuff to include vocal performances as well. We started putting down the saxophones and singing and working on vocals, and that really pushed the group into another level of popularity.

JIM TUCKER Mark and Howard couldn't do anything. They were trying to play sax and could play on about three or four songs, and that was it. Mark was a bumbling idiot. He had no talent, and neither did Howard. But they decided they were going to start singing. Howard had a voice, and Mark did, too.

Saying we could not do anything is a bit strong. I believe we were as talented as most of the other singers in surf bands, and beyond that, eventually.

JIM TUCKER Al called me up and says, 'We're going to start singing next week, and we want you to play with us.' Well, our band was better—we had more gigs than they did—but I said, 'All right.' We learned ten or twelve singing songs in a week. And we started singing at the Revelaire. Everybody else was still doing surf music.

ED GUNNEY And then The Crossfires put a record out. Everybody thought that if you've got a record out, you're really big.

HOWARD KAYLAN The Crossfires released a couple of records. 'Dr. Jekyll And Mr. Hyde' along with 'Fiberglass Jungle,' and the second one was 'That'll Be The Day' and 'One Potato Two Potato,' which actually got some airplay, which got us on television and really, really lit a spark. It was unbelievable. We actually charted on a couple of towns. I think there were a couple of places in the Midwest where it happened, too.

AL NICHOL We fell upon this guy named Al Kavelin—he had this little label, Capco Records, in Hollywood, and he released 'Dr. Jekyll And Mr. Hyde' and 'Fiberglass Jungle.' 'Fiberglass Jungle' was a surf song that I'd written, and 'Dr. Jekyll And Mr. Hyde' was an onstage show thing featuring Howard and Mark. I played a surf beat, and Howard had a melody on his sax, and Mark would do the 'Mr. Hyde' part: he turned into Mr. Hyde, and it was theatrical performance onstage. We tried to put it on record, but of course it didn't work. It was a bomb. But it was a big highlight of our show.

Howard and I graduated in '64. Mark didn't graduate until '65. I'm a year older, but Howard skipped up and graduated early. Howard was the youngest in the group, but he always looked the oldest. When we were running around at eighteen, he was the one who would go to the liquor store and buy the beer for us. We were working two or three nights, and sometimes the whole week.

It would depend on how much they wanted to keep the club open. We were paid $150 per night. That was for the whole band. Back then, you could do a lot with twenty-five or thirty bucks in your pocket.

RAY MANZAREK I saw the Crossfires at the Revelaire Club in Redondo Beach, which was just a hop, skip, and jump down the street from where my brothers lived. They went to Redondo Beach High School, and had a surf band called Rick & The Ravens. The legendary *UR-band* of The Doors—the foundation—that's where The Doors grew out of, from Rick & The Ravens.

I was there with Rick & The Ravens auditioned at the Revelaire, and The Crossfires were rehearsing, and I must say I was very impressed, even then, with Mark and Howard's harmonies. They were good. At that time, the Revelaire was a big surf club for dancing the Surfer's Stomp. What a great dance that was. The Surfer's Stomp was, as it says, *S-T-O-M-P*. The Surfer's Stomp ultimately has more in common with the mosh pit for punk rock. I think those two styles are similar.

RICK MANCZAREK We'd play with them up at the Revelaire. We'd have one group on, the other group off. Sometimes we'd go on before them, sometimes after. The guys seemed to be very good musicians. They were so in tune with themselves, it was just amazing to see them perform, which really helped us. And they were nice guys. The whole band was so easy to get along with.

RAY MANZAREK There were not many surfing piano players. My brother Jim was the only one. And then I would sit in with Rick & The Ravens as 'Screaming Ray Daniels.' I would be the blues singer/shouter from Chicago, singing blues songs, and I would sometimes play the piano. But I never actually played surf music. Not that I couldn't—of course I understood the genre. What is there to it, after all? Well, a rather a simplistic form of music. But not without its own appeal.

HOWARD KAYLAN Mark and I had put down our saxophones, realized that we had a lot more future using our vocal talents, and were aping the hits of the day. We would do The Troggs, The Searchers, the Stones, The Beatles—all the British Invasion bands. The Crossfires became a good band, because we all started out a bad band, and we learned together. And that's the stuff that you can't replace. We'd worked for a year and a half, maybe two years, to get that good in high school. Our freshman and sophomore years were spent working in Inglewood at the teen centers on alternate weekends, and by the time The Beatles came along, we had won our battle of the bands by beating out several other groups that also came from Westchester and Redondo Beach. We had already gotten the house gig at the Revelaire Club.

AL NICHOL At the Revelaire, we backed up Sonny & Cher, Jan & Dean, The Coasters, Motown groups . . . all sorts of acts. Whoever was on their own, touring around L.A. promoting anything, they would have us as a backup band. It was just part of the gig. We were the house band, so we'd back them up. And it was a good deal both ways: they didn't have to hire a bunch of studio musicians, and we didn't have to leave the stage. We all had record collections that could probably outfit five music stores, so we knew all these songs. When it came to the instrumental arrangements, since I'd played all these different instruments, I was capable of reassigning keys and the timing and all that, and I could do it on the spot. So, we became very adept at backing up. We would do background harmonies, and Howard was good at playing the sax parts on all these old rock'n'roll things, so we did all right. We got known for that, and wound up backing all kinds of acts.

HOWARD KAYLAN The job as house band was the greatest thing, because touring acts—national touring acts—would come in and play, and we would learn their thirty-minute set every week. It taught us how to be the ultimate rock chameleons. In one week, we had to back up The Drifters—we knew all The Drifters' material, we knew where the oohs and ahhs went, we could play the sax solos—we *got* The Drifters. If it was The Righteous Brothers, we got them. If it was Dick & Dee Dee, we got them. Some soul chick, we got that. If it was Jackie DeShannon, we learned her stuff. It was a fantastic education. We were literally doing four hour-long sets a night and not repeating anything. We were varying up our show greatly, doing the instrumentals and R&B stuff and a lot of British Invasion, and that is where we honed our chops. If we owe our current and continuing success to anything, it's the fact that we're still able to work a room. And you can't work a room unless you know how to change your musical style, and you know how to work the crowd. How to make eye contact, how to talk between songs, how not to just be a talking book up there.

RAY MANZAREK Yeah! How about that, man? Jesus, The Righteous Brothers down in the South Bay, holy cow! The Crossfires sang R&B; that's where they get their soul from. It was great, they were cool. It was a good band.

HARVEY KUBERNIK They were a hard-working group, and they had something in common with The Beach Boys: they both started as surf bands and even had horn players in the group, and all of a sudden the horn players became singers. And so, Mike Love, Howard, and Mark started doing more vocals, and they both go back to the truth of rock'n'roll, that they come out of that honkin' R&B world, too. A lot of that is down to the Revelaire. Being the house band, they had to play.

MARK LINDSAY I remember The Crossfires. I didn't realize that they were R&B-based in the beginning, but that's how Paul Revere & The Raiders started as well. We were a white R&B band, and that was what made us stand out in Portland, because at that time the Brothers Four-type music was huge in that area. Everybody else was wearing slacks and sweaters, and that really set us apart. We were really the neighborhood geeks, because we were totally different than anything that they had seen in that town. And I would like to think that we helped start the pre-punk, pre-grunge revolution in the Northwest.

AL NICHOL We had a second guitarist from the beginning. After we changed The Nightriders into The Crossfires, we added Tom Stanton, who was a high school friend of ours and also a surfing buddy. And then Tom got drafted, and Jim Tucker came in as his replacement.

JIM TUCKER I replaced another guy in The Crossfires, because he couldn't cut it. It was me and Al and Don and Portz, who couldn't cut it either after the first or second album.

AL NICHOL We wanted to have six people singing and playing. Our roots were in a cappella choir, where the vocal is everything, and we wanted a big vocal sound. But there wasn't really any pressure of bringing Jim in as a vocalist. It would have been nice. We tried to get him to sing some stuff, but he just wasn't a singer.

HOWARD KAYLAN After all the dues we paid, we finally got to a position where we were getting these little groupie girls who were fifteen and sixteen years old, who came to the club every week, who hung out with us backstage, who we were actually very promiscuous with. I can't speak for Mark, but I can speak for myself and all of the other guys in the band, and there were very apparent advantages to being a musician that I had never had by being an academic Neil Sedaka. There were no academic groupies if you resemble a potato, is what I'm saying. If you look like Frankie Avalon, I don't think that was a problem for you. But if you weren't the guy who was going out with the cheerleader, if you were ogling that girl, and then you find yourself backstage and you're not in your high school persona anymore . . . you're a different guy. You're the guy they only see on Friday or Saturday night. They've got their romantic aspirations, and all of a sudden you're a Partridge Family member, as far as they're concerned, and that's a very romantic place to be. So you take that sexually to the nth degree, and find yourself in a world that you have very little knowledge of. It's the fast lane, for what it's worth, and for a high school kid, it's very, very narcotic. And once you've experienced it, it's really, really difficult to even think about not doing it—to going back to class, to continuing your life as usual. So, while I think there are a lot of people that let the rock'n'roll part of themselves go when a more practical voice in the back of their head might have whispered, 'You'll never make a living doing this. You'd better have something to fall back on,' a few of us even that far back in our lives said to ourselves, 'This is pretty sweet. If we could actually make a living doing this, this would be a wonderful life.' And not only was I personally considering it, I had considered literally nothing else. In fact, I knew from a very early age that that's what I was going to do, and I had no other plans.

I was on a full scholarship. It was all paid for, but I didn't care. When I got to UCLA, I auditioned for the radio station. I was on every single day, and I let my class stuff go to hell. It was easy, because I had been a disc jockey in my room since about the age of three years old. I had been Howard Kaylan. I don't know what made me change the letters of my name—from Kaplan to

Kaylan—when I was three years old. But I knew that when the time came, that would be my name. On the radio, I was Howie The K, in fact.

I would bring Mark on after he got done with school. He would come down to the studio and I would introduce him—these were the very early days of the British Invasion, remember, so nobody knew who anybody looked like, or sounded like—and I would introduce Mark as my cousin Van Morrison. I knew Them, and I read the liner notes, and I knew who Van Morrison was. I had the record in my hand, and I figured all we need to do is to bullshit these people for about two and a half minutes, take a couple of bogus phone calls, play 'Gloria,' and get the hell out. And that's what we did. So we created this fake reality, and he was Van Morrison, only his accent was absolutely horrible, but nobody knew. Then the next day he came on, and he was Gerry Marsden. Who just happened to be my cousin. They're all my cousins, and every day would be the same stupid accent, but it would be a different name, and I loved it. I loved it. But I was getting discouraged with college. I went to my parents and said, 'I just can't do it. But I'll make you a deal. I think that I have to pursue this record thing. And I'm positive that I can have success with it. Give me a six-month window. If I don't have a hit record in six months, I promise to go back to school.' And I quit. Had I been asked to put my career on hold until after school, that window would have closed.

2

INFLUENCES

For Mark and his peers, there were any number of influential bands, but a few stood out, from two of the biggest ever to an almost unknown local act.

THE BEATLES

FELIX CAVALIERE I actually worked with The Beatles in Europe, prior to them coming to the United States. I was with Joey Dee & The Starlighters, and I worked with them on the same bill. I could tell they were different because the audience was hysterical. I'd never seen people screaming and hollering like that in my life—people just absolutely going nuts. It was difficult to hear them, but when I did, I completely remember my reaction to their songs. I thought that they were totally unique. I'd never heard anything like that.

When they did *our*—meaning American—songs, they were okay. They just didn't get it—the feeling is entirely different. When you're doing R&B songs, and you're an Englishmen, well, I wanna wish you a lot of luck. But when they did *their* music, it was like, *What is that? Wow!* Those guys changed the entire world of music. They were like beacons, opening up new vistas and new doors for all of us. Musically, lyrically, business-wise, and then life-wise as well. That's probably where Mark first heard about the Eastern philosophies. And we tried it, too. We were all growing up on this together.

DANNY HUTTON I started at Disney Studios, literally on the ground floor. They had a record company that did the soundtracks for all their movies, and I loaded and unloaded records when the trucks came in. They had *Billboard* there, which in the early 60s was a complete trade magazine. I read it every week, and I saw a picture of this crazy, strange-looking group on the foreign section called The Beatles. They weren't featured, it was just a little two-line thing, but I was fascinated by the pictures. And then, when I heard them, I thought, *Oh, my God—that's the real deal!* So I could see a change was coming.

Right from the start, I'd buy their records on Swan and Vee-Jay, and I became a Beatles expert. I knew all about them, and I could not believe that the records kept flopping. I was living at home, up in the attic, at the time, and Kim—the notorious Kim Fowley—brought Jack Nitzsche and Jackie DeShannon over to my house for me to explain The Beatles' sound, the whole Beatles thing. Eventually, everybody got turned on, but most of them got turned on after *Ed Sullivan*. Everybody else in America thought that 'I Want To Hold Your Hand' was their first release. But I'd already been running with it for about a year.

RON DANTE I heard 'She Loves You' before it came out, and I loved it. Listen to that vocal sound—and the guitars! I was thrilled to hear guitars back on records, so I couldn't have been happier to see that happen. It did hurt some of the American artists. The British Invasion knocked a bunch of people off the charts for a couple of years, so they had to reinvent themselves. The Beach Boys and The Four Seasons had to reinvent themselves, but they got through. They managed their hits all through that. But I was never scared as a songwriter. I saw where they were going and understood exactly what Paul McCartney was doing on the guitar. He was writing songs that are comfortable for his hand positions.

E. MICHAEL HARRINGTON The Beatles ended almost every career. The only ones who were popular before and after are a few Motown acts and The Beach Boys. Elvis had seventeen #1 hits before them and only one after them. And they were accepted by everyone. It took The Rolling Stones for people to realize, *Wow, The Beatles are a nice happy bunch, especially compared to these dark guys like The Animals.* They even said it on the news reports. These bands are Britain's way of getting back at the United States for the revolution. The Beatles started a revolution.

MARK LINDSAY I heard them before they were on *Sullivan*. I was in Portland, in Lake Oswego. We had started the band and were playing on the weekends, and I was driving the hearse—that was our band car—to one of my appointments to plant some trees or something. This guy comes on the radio and says, 'Here's a new group from England with the weirdest name you ever heard.

Can you believe this? They call themselves The Beatles.' And he plays 'I Want To Hold Your Hand' or something. I remember thinking, *That sounds different than anything I've ever heard.*

The Beatles hit, and suddenly that was it. Music changed overnight. That was really the day that music changed. The day music came alive, instead of died. It was The Beatles from then on. We had this background of R&B, but suddenly here were all these beautiful melodious pop tunes, The Beatles' original songs—even though they were different and really new, at least to my ears, they were accessible, and I could hear how they built the lyrics and how the melodies fell into place. It was very much based on standards, and I knew that because I'd grown up listening to classical and standards when I was a kid. So it wasn't that hard to make a transition. And it evolved so rapidly. It was suddenly like there was a pile of music that somebody poured gasoline on it and set it on fire.

Terry Melcher had a friend in England who'd send him copies of The Kinks or The Beatles or The Animals before they got released in America. We'd listen to them and try to figure out how to top this. I remember when we got a single of 'Strawberry Fields.' We put it on, it goes, '*Let me take you down, 'cause I'm going to . . .*' then it demodulates, and Terry and I looked at each other. I said, 'What the fuck do we do now?' It was instant psychedelia from that point on.

AL NICHOL We were The Crossfires, and then The Beatles hit and every group from coast to coast wanted to be The Beatles, including us. We emulated The Beatles in a lot of ways. They were a heavy-duty influence.

CHRIS HILLMAN Everybody started plugging in. We started plugging in, we played the Troubadour Hoot Night as The Byrds, and in front of all our friends—our folk-music pals—and we got hooted off the stage. Then we came roaring back, and we showed them.

CYRUS FARYAR When the MFQ electrified, there were a bunch of snobby-nosed Baptists who said that folk could never be electrified, and they'd run out of the room if you plugged in your banjo. Get over yourself. I mean, come on.

RUSS GIGUERE I couldn't see why they were such a big thing. I thought they sounded like The Everly Brothers with an extra voice in there. Their music expanded as they got a foothold, though. They almost killed off the folk scene, but certain singers always go for it, like Gordon Lightfoot, and people like Judy Collins just go on forever. I mean, they got legs.

GREG HAWKES The Beatles were the first band I ever saw. That was in September 1964. I was eleven and I saw them in Baltimore on the first full tour. They had already done *The Ed Sullivan Show*, plus they had played in Washington DC and Miami. It definitely grabbed me, for sure. I had taken piano lessons and played clarinet in the school band, but when I heard The Beatles, that changed everything.

E. MICHAEL HARRINGTON It was *Ed Sullivan*. We always watched anyway, but that night, everything stopped. I'd just turned ten and I talked my dad into renting a guitar the next day, and I was professional two years later. Five of my friends on our street got guitars as well. We were a lower middle-class neighborhood. You couldn't afford to buy, so you rented. Everyone was watching. I went to Catholic school, and the next day, even the nuns were excited.

GARRY TALLENT In 1963, I was living in Willington, Delaware, playing guitar in a little band with accordion, guitar, and drums. These were two Greek fellows. We played at the Greek CYO or whatever they called it, the dances, and we would do 7/8 time: 'Never On Sunday' and those kinds of songs. Then The Beatles hit. Everyone else loved them, but I was still a greaser stuck in the 50s. I was saying, 'These Beatles won't last. All they're doing is rehashes of Buddy Holly and the Everly Brothers. If you want to hear something good, listen to Little Richard.' That was my thing. Then I moved to New Jersey the day after school was out in June 1964. I was all of fourteen and I didn't know anybody. Everybody in this small town grew up together and the only way I had in was through the music, because everybody wanted to be in a band. So, The Beatles were tremendously influential at that point because that was my whole social thing. I switched to bass just a little bit after that because nobody knew what a bass did. If I was in a talent show and we came in second place, the next week I joined the band that was in the first place. I figured, you wanted to play with the best people you possibly could. That's how you got better. I would play whatever instruments I could get in the band with; be it bass or guitar, or even drums, I was in that band. And that was pretty universal. Once The Beatles came along, everybody wanted to play in a band.

RAY MANZAREK The Beatles didn't change my life at all. I thought *Meet The Beatles* was profoundly juvenile, man. '*She loves you, yeah, yeah*'? I'm sorry, that did not excite me. I was listening to John Coltrane, Miles Davis, Muddy Waters, Howlin' Wolf, and Igor Stravinsky. When The Beatles finally got psychedelicized . . . I really appreciated them when they got to *Rubber Soul*. I thought, *Hey, that's a good-ass band. That's a good, tight, well-composed . . .*

Those songs are good songs, *and* they've obviously taken LSD. Look at the album cover: if you'd taken LSD, you could always see in the eyes of another person if they had ingested LSD. Their lyrics changed, too: '*I'm looking through you.*' It's like, *Uh-oh, that's acid.* And then, 'All You Need Is Love.' Ultimately, that's what was so great about dropping acid in the 60s. It turned you into a love nut. We became mystery Christians, mystics, and love nuts. And that was John Lennon saying, '*All you need is love.*' There you go man, that's it. That's what it's all about.

DANNY HUTTON I remember Mark coming by the house and saying, 'I got something special for you.' He pulled out a real good joint, we smoked it, and then he said, 'Here: *Sgt Pepper*.' He put the album on, and it was like a religious ceremony. We sat there and we're like, *Oh . . .*

MICKY DOLENZ When *Sgt Pepper* came out—and I was in some of those sessions—we were filming *The Monkees*, filming episodes, and it was the release day. We sent a runner down to Wallach's Music City to get one of the first copies and brought it back to the set, and the production stopped. They put it on a turntable and put it over the PA system. We sat and listened to the whole fucking album in the middle of the day. We stopped production.

AL NICHOL When we got the invitation to go over to Europe and we actually met them, that was big. It was mind-blowing. Something we'd always dreamed of doing, and here we were doing it. We were into their music before we ever met them, so hanging out with them, we were more taken by what it was like to *be* them: to be in the middle of their culture.

We did everything to be exactly like The Beatles. We wanted the same clothing, music, the wives, the creative freedom. In the beginning, we were already doing the same R&B songs, and we felt like we had kind of a parallel world to them.

MICKY DOLENZ There is no question that The Beatles had a phenomenal impact on all music, and socially. I've always said, and they would agree—because I talked to Paul and John and Ringo about this over the years—The Beatles were as much a product of their time as the time was a product of them. It wasn't that they came out of a vacuum and all of a sudden appeared overnight. And I don't mean just their music but their point of view, their way of life. It was postwar Britain. In Europe and the West there was a new generation, a postwar generation coming along, and that as much created The Beatles as The Beatles. It's like a biofeedback, if you will. The same thing happened in the 50s with Presley, and it happened during the war with that generation, and it has happened since then, the same sort of thing. You can't really reduce it and say that it's one or the other, because it isn't. It's a combination. What do they say, the times create the men and the men create the times? That's what happened with The Beatles, and I'm sure they would be the first to agree with that.

THE KINGSTON TRIO

RUSS GIGUERE The Trio were sort of a super-group of their own. God, they sold a zillion records. Everywhere they went people recognized them. They established their own style and really put folk music back on the map. They were not a rock'n'roll group, other than 'Greenback Dollar.'

HARRY SHEARER The Trio influenced The Turtles? [*laughs*] Well, join the club, because they've certainly influenced the Folksmen as well. They introduced many of us to folk music, because that's what you heard on the radio. I mean, my God, when I was in college, Kingston Trio music was *so* widely played on radio. You couldn't help being exposed to it, whether you reacted against it or said, 'Hey, I'd like to do that.'

It was another one of those things that you just had to mark yourself against, one or the other. They were big hitmakers—that's what they did. The

Trio were popularizers, and popularizers, especially in that era, kind of get lumped with [acts] like Pat Boone. That's what popularizers do. They take the hard edges off of a certain style of music, make it more commercially accessible. And I think for a lot of the people of that generation, hard edges were what they sought. So, the people who shaved the edges off were looked down upon.

JIM BESSMAN The Kingston Trio was a big influence on everyone at the time. They were so great, so great . . . and so important.

HARVEY KUBERNIK There's always a folk undertone, simply because groups like the Kingston Trio were playing big venues around town like the Hollywood Bowl from '58 to '63. You would hear things like 'Tom Dooley' on KFWB and KRLA. The Beatles knocked it out of the game, but there was almost a ten-year run where folk music was on L.A. radio and playing the theaters. Harry Belafonte, Odetta, Josh White, and early Peter, Paul & Mary were all coming to town. In '64, Dylan played in Long Beach at Wilson High School, not far from Westchester. A lot of that stuff kind of set the template, and on The Turtles' first album they do a version of 'It Was A Very Good Year,' which they might have gotten from The Kingston Trio.

THE MODERN FOLK QUARTET

HOWARD KAYLAN The Modern Folk Quartet were a lot like Louis Prima and Keely Smith in that they were a musician's band of musicians. Other players really, really respected them, individually and collectively. Henry Diltz was already well known, even in those days, as a photographer, and Cyrus Faryar was well known for folk influences before the band. Chip was a pop guy. They may have come from a strange place—Hawaii, and all that other background stuff—but I saw them numerous times before they went electric and did the Phil Spector stuff. I thought they were fan-fucking-tastic. I still do. They had the best variety of songs, and they had four of the greatest singers going. Any one of them at any given time could sing lead as strongly as the next. Jerry Yester was great, Chip Douglas was great. It was just a wonder to behold. They were virtuosos on their instruments.

RUSS GIGUERE I saw the first set that they did here in town. They did 'The Ox Driver's Song,' and it just kicked the audience's ass. I was there that night, and it was obvious how good they were from the first song. Everyone was amazed that of all the acts, the MFQ didn't eventually get a hit, because they were so good. They were great-looking guys, they sang their asses off, and they played a bunch of different things. I would go see them if I was in town, and when the lights came up half the musicians in town were there in the audience, because we were all fans. In fact, The Association recorded 'Come On In.' That was actually a Q song. They didn't write it, but I had been watching them do that song for years. I suggested the group do it, and we did an arrangement.

JIM YESTER When they were playing the Trip and Gazzarri's, everybody—the whole audience—was a musician. And everybody else made it and they didn't. I've had more friends that I can count ask, 'What the hell, how come they didn't make it? They were so good.'

HARRY SHEARER The MFQ? Oh God, you're talking about my favorite group. I don't think there was ever, in that era, a group that had four voices as good as that, and harmonic sense as good as that. I love that band. They were incredible, the best I'd ever heard. They were to that era what The Hi-Lo's was to the era in the fifties. I didn't get to see them in their folk persona. By the time I was going to clubs, they had picked up electric instruments. They were maybe two months late in picking up electric instruments, but in terms of the electric folk sound of Southern California, they were easily the equal of The Byrds in terms of how well they played, how well they sang, how well they rocked. All of that—they should have recorded *that*.

KEN BARNES That was another kind of survival story where they started out as a hootenanny folk band, did a couple of albums on Warners of that style, and then faced the same problem that all those folk bands did when Dylan and The Byrds added rock to the equation, and it was like either get hip or get out, pretty much. And even bands like the Serendipity Singers made a rock record. The Highwaymen made a rock record—I mean, it's just bizarre—and The Modern Folk Quartet made a few singles, plus their legendary Phil Spector record. And it's good stuff.

3

THE TURTLES

MICHAEL THOMAS When the British Invasion started, The Crossfires were playing surf music, and then they changed it—they changed their persona and their group and everything else. They sort of reincarnated themselves and became The Turtles.

HOWARD KAYLAN About two months after quitting school, the band had pretty much run its course, and I felt like a real moron. Al had a wife and a child, and he couldn't subsist on $125 split six ways, which is what we got playing at the Revelaire Club. If it was one night a week, we made $125. If we did two, we doubled our salary. It was very, very pathetic. We all knew that it couldn't continue. We had a meeting backstage at the Revelaire, and we drew up a paper of resignation that I was to take upstairs to Bill Utley, and on my way up to take the note, I was stopped by two bearded clowns in suits who had no business being at the Revelaire Club whatsoever. They had heard us perform. More specifically, they had heard us perform the newest hits of the week, which is what we were doing at that point. And two weeks previous, The Byrds had released 'Mr. Tambourine Man.' So, two weeks into The Byrds' career, we're at the Revelaire Club, Al Nichol has now purchased a twelve-string guitar. A cheap one. It wasn't a Rickenbacker, it was a Danelectro. It was cheesy sounding, but it had a twelve-string sound of its own, and it was affordable.

AL NICHOL All of us were totally into the band—there was nothing else on the side. That's where all our attention was, but unfortunately, after a while, it just wasn't making enough money. I'd gotten married and had a kid coming. Don Murray was married and had a kid on the way, too. None of us were making enough, and we didn't see any way of making more out of the band. So, we just decided to end it. All this came down at one crucial point. We were ready to call it quits, and then we were approached by Reb Foster and Bill Utley, who said, 'I got a couple of guys from Liberty Records, and they want to start a record company and sign you guys. And all you've got to do is come up with a different name.'

HOWARD KAYLAN Those two guys stopped me, and they said, 'We loved your set. We especially loved the way you did "Mr. Tambourine Man".' Now I started listening and paying attention. Because even though we had released those two other abysmal 45s in our Crossfires past, no one had ever singled out anything that we did as particularly good or commercial. When this guy said he noticed us for the twelve-string treatment on the folk-rock songs, that's when I started getting interested, because back in The Crosswind Singers, the songs that we did were songs that I wrote. Back then, I was not big into rock'n'roll yet. I was into The Kingston Trio. I had everything that the Trio ever did. I was very, very interested in them and Bud & Travis and The Limeliters and that sort of harmony and that sort of mystical, almost Appalachian folk. A folk music that later The Byrds turned into a folk-rocky kind of thing. We were able to do that, too. We were able to do that with 'The Wanderin' Kind' and 'Let The Cold Winds Blow' and all these other Dylan-esque songs I had written back in high school.

So, when the guys said, 'We want you to go into the studio and record three songs,' we took a meeting backstage, and I said, 'Look, I know we put out two records. They were both jerk-offs, this is probably going to be another jerk-off, but guys, what do we have to lose? We're breaking up *tonight*. We can either do this, or not do this. Somebody says they're going to pay for us to go into the studio and make a record. Are we really not going to do it?' So, we had a discussion about it. It was weird on many levels. It was weird because A: we're going to break up, B: we had no idea who these guys were, and C: these guys, Lee Lasseff and Ted Feigin, didn't have a name for their record company yet. They had no artists at that point, either. They just had a dream. Ted Feigin said he was the PR guy from London Records. Lee Lasseff said, 'I do the same thing for Liberty Records. And we're sick and tired of doing this crap, we wanna start our own record company, and you're the guys we're going to launch it with.'

All of a sudden now, Reb was making himself very visible. He was walking a thin line by getting involved, but he said, 'I'm your manager. Those guys found you at my club, and if you're going to continue, I think it's a good idea that I look out for your interest. I know the record business, I can handle this.'

PHIL VOLMAN Reb Foster and Bill Utley were thieves. But they got interested in them, and with Lee Lassiff and Ted Feigin, they formed White Whale, and Mark and Howard signed with White Whale. Our father had to sign everything because Mark was still underage.

HOWARD KAYLAN Mark and I were the youngest guys, and because we were so young, our parents had to sign for us, and we had to go before a judge to do it. The judge told us that we were making a gigantic mistake. He took both of our parents aside and said, 'You're doing the wrong thing. This is a contract that is going to get them in huge financial trouble. I don't know if you're reading the small print here . . .'

What it said was, in actual fact, we split among six members three percent of ninety percent of the retail price of the record, which is a losing situation by the time you paid back your recording costs and those ubiquitous if elusive recording and promotion costs, which they could pad any way they wanted to. There was no way you could make money doing this, and the judge told our parents that. But they left it up to Mark and me, and we wanted it so bad that we convinced them to sign. We figured one of two things would happen. A: this is not going to work, so it won't matter, or B: this is going to work, and we'll worry about it later. And everybody just signed it, because the odds of this working were slim and none. So Reb became our manager. And he told us, 'The first thing that's gotta go is your name.' And he came up with the new name.

JIM TUCKER We were still The Crossfires. And Reb Foster says, 'We've got to have a name for the group. We're releasing this.' We thought The Six Pack was a good one, but it was all about animal names. And then they said, 'What about The Turtles?' And we started laughing. But that's what they put it out as.

AL NICHOL We were like, '*The Turtles*? Oh, man, give me a break!' And he said, 'Well, it kinda rhymes with The Beatles, it's an animal thing, and it goes along with what's happening right now with the names of groups.' What he didn't say but implied was, 'And besides that, you guys are kinda slow and fat and goofy.' At first we thought that that was kind of degrading. Then we decided to give it a shot.

HOWARD KAYLAN In ten days we had to rehearse the songs, change our name, and sign the contract. They named their record company White Whale, they named their publishing company Ishmael Music, and we were The Turtles. And for all intents and purposes, for the first six months or so that that record was out, people though that we were British. And it saved our asses. We looked like street urchins. But those clothes were chosen to represent some sort of an image, because we were singing folk-rock music. Then Reb decided he didn't like our ratty appearance, so he took us to have our hair styled in Beverly Hills. Then he got these lime green velour shirts and little green hats made for us at a clothier that had done Jerry Lewis's clothes. Really old fashioned, old-school.

JIM TUCKER Reb and Bill brought Bones Howe down. He's there in a leather jacket and his dark glasses, and he goes, 'Can you play any Byrds music or Dylan music?' The next week we were in the studio.

Bones Howe was a drummer who became a record producer and worked with the Wrecking Crew. He produced The Turtles' first record, and then The Fifth Dimension, The Association, Tom Waits, and many others.

HOWARD KAYLAN I was trying to figure out what songs to go into the studio with. I perused all of the Bob Dylan and Kingston Trio records I had, looking for something that would distinguish us as far as putting out a Byrds-sounding record that would be recognizable as a new band.

Howard was The Turtles' main writer. His love of folk music came out when he wrote, and I think he might have felt inspiration to write from his mother, Sally. Our early albums contain Howard originals, and he and I would eventually find a style that brought us together as writers in the Flo & Eddie era.

HOWARD KAYLAN The only songs I'd written up to that point had been folk-rock songs, but I was searching for something else, and I couldn't put my finger on it until I listened to Dylan's 'It Ain't Me Babe.' And then I knew exactly what it was that the band ought to do. Unlike any of the other folk-rocky stuff that we had done, I heard it more as a Zombies record, going from very quiet minor verses to crashing 4/4 choruses. It changed the meaning of Dylan's song from a plaintive one into an angry one, by saying, 'No! No! No! It ain't me, babe!' and singing it with that sort of venom, after coming out of a very, very light, almost gay-sounding verse.

RAY MANZAREK It worked like a charm. It doesn't really matter what you do, the point is, does it work? It doesn't matter whether you cover somebody else's song, whether there's a formula there, it's just . . . does the formula work? You can be formulaic and it doesn't work. But they had the musical sense to make that song work, and it was terrific.

After struggling for years as The Crossfires, The Turtles were an overnight success, but only after countless hours spent performing in local clubs, high schools, and colleges. Over the next six years, the band would experience incredible highs and more than a few lows.

JIM TUCKER We were in Redondo Beach, and we packed up at midnight and drove to Hollywood and recorded all night. We walked out about 7:30 in the morning, and we had 'It Ain't Me Babe.' In the *Happy Together* DVD, Bones says how, in the beginning, The Byrds couldn't play. The Mamas & The Papas didn't play. None of them played their own instruments, except The Turtles. And we did. We played our own music. Two weeks later, we were on a break at the club, out on the parking lot, listening to the Top 30 survey, and the DJ says, 'This is one of the highest debuting records we've had in a long time,' and it debuted at #10 or #15 or something like that in L.A.

HOWARD KAYLAN We were in the parking lot, about to go on for our normal Friday-night set. We knew it was getting play locally, and we were waiting for it, we thought maybe that was our chance to chart. We waited and waited, and the guy kept saying, 'We've got a couple of big surprises for you on the survey,' and then he played 'Like A Rolling Stone.' We just went, 'Well, I guess not. This was a good run, anyway.' The Dylan song ended, the disc jockey came on and said, 'And if you think that's something, wait until you hear the next song that debuted even higher.' And then he played 'It Ain't Me Babe.' We were screaming and jumping around the parking lot, and we knew that night, when we went in to do the show, that we would not be back to the Revelaire Club anytime soon.

AL NICHOL All over town, they had advertisements for Alfred Hitchcock's film *The Birds*. You saw everywhere: *The Birds Is Coming, The Birds Is Coming*. We were still booked as The Crossfires, so we put a big banner up in the back of us, saying *The Turtles Is Coming*, and of course, all our regular fans said, '*The Turtles Is Coming*—what's that?' And then they played it on the radio, 'It Ain't Me Babe' by The Turtles, and the fans are getting all excited: 'The Turtles are gonna come! The Turtles are gonna come!'

They didn't know. They thought—and everybody all over the country thought—The Turtles were another band from England. And so, right in the middle of the show one night at the Revelaire Club, we took a break and put down our rock'n'roll and R&B instruments. We took off our seersucker jackets and all put on green velour hats and velour turtle necks. Reb came out and he says, 'We got a special treat for you: The Turtles!' And here come The Crossfires back out. All the people are like, *Ah—it's you guys! Oh, man!* But then we were The Turtles.

HOWARD KAYLAN We may have heard it on the radio before that night, but we had heard the Crossfires stuff on the radio, too. So, by then we were terribly jaded. We knew the music business was filled with crooks and creeps and liars. And we knew that if they said, 'Your song is #39 in San Bernardino,' that it didn't mean a lot. There was no money changing hands, there was no future, there was no album, it was just something that you did, and it had been fun. But in this case, we debuted higher than Dylan, and these DJs were saying, 'There's no stopping these guys!' We were literally on the road with the Dick Clark Caravan Of Stars, I don't think it took three weeks after that.

AL NICHOL We had a 'Dial A Hit' or 'Make It Or Break It' on KRLA, and all over L.A. they voted us #1, so we became big-time overnight. It debuted on *Billboard* nationally really high, like #12 with a bullet. That's when it really counted. We were already #1 on the local survey. About two weeks later, another rock station, KFWB, booked The Turtles and Herman's Hermits and

The Lovin' Spoonful and Cannibal & The Headhunters and all these groups together for a big show at the Rose Bowl. Herman's Hermits was the headliner, and it went over really well. They actually repeated the show. They put it on a week later in San Diego, and it was a sellout. It was mind-blowing, because we'd never played for a crowd that big. Here we are in front of a hundred thousand fans screaming and yelling; we couldn't even hear ourselves play. It was an overnight indoctrination of Beatlemania. This was something we had seen, but hadn't experienced, and then, boom! It happened.

PETER NOONE I remember it very well. We decided that we wanted to sell out the Rose Bowl, and we charged a dollar. It was a dollar because we figured that all the people who came would buy our records. It was early days for that kind of thinking. The Turtles and Lovin' Spoonful were the two opening acts. It was the first gig for The Turtles under their new name? What a lousy first gig, to play in front of seventy-eight thousand people. But they were good. They were very good right from the beginning.

LINDA CAMPILLO I got to go to that show. I was thirteen, and a huge fan of Herman's Hermits, so it was awesome. Wink Martindale was the MC, and as we were driving away from the Rose Bowl, his car pulled up next to ours, and Uncle Joe says, 'How did you like the show? What did you think of those Turtles?' And he said something like, 'They're nice kids.' And he goes, 'Yeah, I'm Mark Volman's father.' That's what Uncle Joe was like.

HOWARD KAYLAN That was the big debut, opening as we still do, all these many years later, for Peter Noone. And it wasn't just Peter Noone: it was a gigantic show. It was a twenty-act show, and we were somewhere near the bottom of the bill, because we only had one record. To go from the Revelaire to playing in front of twenty thousand people, it was unbelievable. We couldn't hear ourselves for the screaming. It was like Shea Stadium. We were living *A Hard Day's Night*. And to say that we weren't picturing ourselves as The Beatles would be a lie. Everybody was. Everybody out there making records was picturing themselves as The Beatles. And we felt an even closer affinity. Maybe because of the animal-esque name we adopted and the *-tles* ending that we got stuck with, we were mislabeled with a British tag for the first six months of our career. Even the magazines treated us that way before they realized we were L.A. guys, and that helped fuse the fantasy in our minds a little bit. It was hard to figure out where the 'British' Turtles ended and the real Turtles started for a little while. We were living the dream. Before the one-nighters and reality set in, in the form of un-air-conditioned roller rinks and other reality bringers, it was an entirely fantastic situation, and it felt very dreamlike, even in hindsight. And certainly not due to any drugs or hallucinogens. It felt very eerie, and very magical.

GARRY TALLENT When I moved to Jersey, it was just kids playing guitars. There was no chance of making a record. That was a total pipe dream for us. Anybody who was doing it, you just assumed they were either English or older cats. So they were part of the British invasion as far as we knew. Maybe they weren't The Beatles or The Rolling Stones, but they were up there, and they kind of rode that wave with that whole invasion. They were already doing it, and not a whole lot older than I was. Every three months they had a new Top 10 single out. And this lasted for years. They were a mainstay on radio that maybe I took for granted, because I didn't know how hard it was. Everybody liked them, but at least in my case, it took me growing up to realize what an impact they had. When you look back, you realize what an accomplishment that is. You realize what an impact they had.

TOMMY JAMES 'It Ain't Me Babe' was a monster record. I didn't make it myself until '66, so I actually played it in my band. We covered The Turtles.

JIM TUCKER I was barely eighteen when we hit the road. As soon as the record was out, it wasn't two weeks, and we were on the Dick Clark tour. The Shirelles, Billy Joe Royal, Peter & Gordon, Mel Carter—all these people were on it.

AL NICHOL We went on Dick Clark's Caravan Of Stars a few months later. The Caravan had some of the top Black acts at the time, with Mel Carter, The Shirelles, The Drifters, and Shirley Ellis, who had 'The Name Game.' But we weren't the only white act. Tom Jones was there, and Peter & Gordon and Bobby Goldsboro. It was an all across the board, potpourri of music in the entertainment business at that time.

PAT VOLMAN They discovered marijuana on their first Dick Clark tour.

HOWARD KAYLAN I have vivid and explicit memories. It was on the third night of a Dick Clark tour. We were in the room at the same time and the same place, and it changed both of our lives. It was Mel Carter—what a guy to turn you on. The last person on Earth you would suspect of being the guy to turn those white kids on, right? And the guys he brought with him—it wasn't just Mel. If it had just been Mel, I would have been fine with it, but it was Mel and these three incredible thugs in suits. It was the thugs in suits and the hefty bags full of product that scared the hell out of me. I hadn't yet even turned eighteen, and here were these obviously mob thugs in this hotel room, scaring the hell out of me. I knew they were packing. It was very, very bizarre. And yet Mel was calm and cool and collected, and took us through this initiation. My knees were shaking, but I remember knocking on Mel's door the next day.

JIM TUCKER Carter would say, 'I'm gonna go to my room and smoke my pipe.' His corncob pipe. Then he'd come out all smiles, and his eyes glassy. We thought he was drinking.

Mel Carter taught us how to shotgun the smoke into our mouths. It heightened the effect, but I think it placed his mouth a bit too close to our mouths.

HOWARD KAYLAN Until that night with Mel, I didn't know what marijuana was, what it smelled like, what it looked like, or how you did it. It wasn't introduced to the high school culture until two or three years later. By *Sgt Pepper*, I think everybody knew what pot was. But we're talking about Jan & Dean; this was spring '65.

AL NICHOL Everybody was smoking dope. Everybody. And we were just greenhorns when it came to actually experimenting with those things. We were just staying happy with our Jack Daniels. But it was on that tour that it actually came about. Howard, Mark . . . I wasn't part of it, so I don't know who they got it from or who they first got high with, but it was on that tour.

HOWARD KAYLAN A lot of people smoked. It was pretty accepted on the tour, but we didn't really know it. Nobody dared to light up on the bus. This was still Dick Clark, remember. This was a big national tour. Dick wasn't about to bail anybody out of jail. We were timid and paranoid and scared. We didn't know anybody, and they plunked us down next to Peter & Gordon. They had us sitting next to all of these celebrities on these eight-hour rides, and it was very, very intimidating. So, we stayed to ourselves, and we would only get high in the presence of each other.

PAT VOLMAN It didn't really faze me when The Turtles started to take off. I wasn't starstruck. I just I thought he was a silly guy: *Hey, he's popular now.* I mean, we were still kids. Nowadays I'd probably think, *Whoa!* But not back then.

LESLIE WEST When The Vagrants did our first single, we were out in the Hamptons playing, and we were listening to this radio station in Buffalo. They said they were going to play a song by this new group with a fat lead singer and we were thrilled. I said, 'It must be us.' It was the fucking Turtles. A little while later, they were playing at the Phone Booth in New York City. They were big shots. They had a hit record.

PEPPY CASTRO The Phone Booth, that's where I first saw them. I loved them. They had that good time feel and those harmonies, and Mark and Howard were these big lovable teddy bears. Where most groups were caught up trying to be cool, there was this happy, nonthreatening vibe that came across from these guys. And it was totally real. It was real playing, and the songs were real hooky; great, great songs.

AL NICHOL We were with General Artists Corporation but then we jumped to the William Morris Agency, so we were involved with the biggest entertainment industry booking agencies right from the beginning. They said, 'All this radio stuff is good, but we've got to get you on TV,' so right away we were doing things like *Shindig!* and *Joey Bishop* and all the Dick Clarks: *American Bandstand*, and *Where The Action Is* when that started up. *Shivaree, Hullaballoo, Hollywood Palace*—we did all the local stuff, and then when we went out to New York we got on the *Kraft Music Hall*. And of course, every time we were even near Philadelphia, we'd do *Mike Douglas* and *Merv Griffin*. And we got right on the early shows of the Smothers Brothers. Of course, we had to clean up the raunchy humor.

MARK LINDSAY That was exactly our experience. When we were playing for frat dances our humor was mostly blue, very sexually oriented—whatever would make the frat boys snicker and the girls blush. Toilet humor. And of course, when we got on TV, we had to totally clean up our act, because of Dick Clark and ABC. We would never have done what we did in the armories on *Where The Action Is*, that's for sure. But as we became more successful, we transitioned into the pop thing, and some of the humor that would be onstage would be between us. And probably the audience wasn't picking up on a lot of it, which I am sure that Mark and Howard did the same thing. A lot of their patter and jokes were very inside.

ALICE COOPER When The Turtles came out, I saw them on *Hullabaloo*, I saw them on *Shindig!*. I was sixteen and our band was just starting. I was one of those kids that wanted to do what those Beatles guys were doing, and The Rolling Stones guys were doing. There were all these bands from England: The Yardbirds, Manfred Mann . . . all these bands just kept coming and flooding us, and that's when we put our band together, and after we had learned all their songs—The Yardbirds and The Who and all that—I said, 'Okay, let's start being Alice.'

We used to open for everybody. I actually think—and I hope I'm not making this up—but in Phoenix we were the biggest local band. We were called The Spiders, and we always opened for everybody, from The Yardbirds to Them, to The Hollies, The Beach Boys, The Lovin' Spoonful. I'm pretty sure we opened for The Turtles, which is kind of funny—The Spiders opening for The Turtles—then later on The Turtles opening for Alice Cooper. But that's the way things work in this business.

AL NICHOL When we came out with 'It Ain't Me Babe,' we were right away labeled a protest group, folk-rockers. Mark and Howard and I had already sung folk music together in school. We all liked folk and harmonized very well as a folk trio, so we put that vocal sound to music.

HOWARD KAYLAN We spent a lot of time trying to figure out what our place was in music. We knew that we had more humor than we were getting into our folk-rock stuff, and we didn't want to be those doom-and-gloom guys that the west coast prophets—the Barry McGuire people—were turning themselves into. We figured, *What the hell are we singing protest music for, anyway? What are we protesting? We're white, middle-class, affluent kids from Los Angeles, California, with our own band and our own income.* We had everything going for us, and yet we were hypocritical enough to still call ourselves folk-rock artists. And we decided to go another route. We were looking for a way to reinvent ourselves, and it was calculated as hell. We knew exactly what we were doing. It was not like we lucked into good-time music. We knew that folk-rock was a very limited proposition.

We didn't want to be a protest band, but 'Let Me Be' was the group's way of telling the older generation—especially our parents—that we're here and we're not going away, so let us be.

HOWARD KAYLAN When we told our record company that we no longer wanted to be folk-rock, they said 'What?!' Because that's all they had seen from us. Fortunately, we were able to come up with 'You Baby'—a song from P.F. Sloan, the guy who had written 'Let Me Be,' so he was therefore a writer they respected, who they would appreciate. We stuck with Sloan for that one. We were sticking close to home, but we wanted to change our attitude, and 'You Baby' bridged the gap. It took us into good-time music, and we were no longer thought of as those folk guys. And it changed everything. After the *You Baby* album, we didn't do any more folk-rock. It turned into almost orchestral rock'n'roll for several years after that. The folk years were wonderful for us, and set us up with a rock'n'roll fan base, but if we hadn't made the move into good-time music, we would have died with Barry McGuire.

ALICE COOPER They were very commercial. They certainly weren't an underground band at all. But there was a certain comedy to them, a certain humorousness about Mark, and it just came through. You couldn't help but like him, he was a big guy with all that hair and the glasses. But when they sang, they were the best.

TOMMY JAMES In addition to singing their asses off, they had this great sense of humor. Mark was a comedian, and they pulled it off. They were multifaceted, so they were able to hit you live at a lot of different levels.

JIM TUCKER Don Murray couldn't cut it. He was on the first two albums, and then he took acid. We were on Dick Clark in Philly, and he decided to take a walk around town. We couldn't find him. We did the whole show and they never showed the drummer. He just took off. We didn't find him for two days, and so that was the end of him.

Don was having problems at home, and on our way to do the Jerry Blavat show in Philadelphia, he had a meltdown. He screamed at me: 'Volman, stop looking at me! I can feel your eyes on the back of my head!' It was a case of massive paranoia, and it scared us all until he quit at the end of the tour.

JOEL LARSON I first played with The Turtles either at the Trip or at the Whisky, when somebody didn't make the gig. I did that a couple of times; I did that with The Byrds when Michael didn't show up, and with the Buffalo Springfield and Love, but not on a consistent basis. We were all kind of interchangeable, because we all knew each other's material, I just wasn't getting as high as all the other drummers. There was no competitiveness. It was not *our band is better than yours*. Nobody was like that. I did a tour with The Turtles, and we recorded four or five songs. Bones Howe was the producer at that point.

JOHNNY BARBATA Gene Clark of The Byrds recommended me to The Turtles; he knew that they were looking for a drummer. I had never seen them. I never saw them play without me in them. I went up there and Bones Howe— who happened to be a big-time producer—after he heard me play a couple of songs, said, 'Get that drummer.' And the rest was history.

JOEL LARSON Bullshit. Bullshit. Johnny kind of has this memory problem. Actually, what happened was that I had recorded with Mark and Howard and the guys, and I got a call from Bones for another Turtles session, and I had something that was more lucrative, a Grass Roots thing, or I was going on the road and that meant big money. I wasn't going to be able to do the session, so I went down and got Johnny Barbata. Barbata was playing with Joel Scott Hill at the Action on Santa Monica Boulevard. Joel was a guitar player/singer, and his band was Lee Michaels, John Barbata, and Chris Ethridge. It was a real funky band. I said, 'John, I think you're perfect for this.' Lee Michaels had a van, and we picked up John's drums and took them over to Western Studios. We took him in, and I said to Bones, 'Man, I can't make it, but here's a drummer I think is going to do good for you.'

Both Joel and John's stories are true. Joel had the first crack at the job and actually plays drums on the song 'We'll Meet Again.' He also did a few live shows with us. John would play on 'Outside Chance' and 'Can I Get To Know You Better.' The next song was 'Happy Together.'

JOHNNY BARBATA I was a show drummer—I'd spin my sticks all the time. Mark had his tambourine, and between the two of us, you got a little more than what you would think you were going to get. I always did a drum solo, and it went over well. As a matter of fact, it would usually get the biggest applause, because people like drum solos a lot.

JIM TUCKER We got Barbata. And Barbata—you can't find a better drummer.

JOEL LARSON I just backed out. I wasn't going to make this session that I had told them I would be at, so I got Barbata. He was plopped into that, and I kick myself in the ass, because I wish I had played it. But he played it superbly. They call him a machine because he's a metronome. If you listen really closely to 'Happy Together,' it's *rup-ta-ta-rup-rup*—it's a march, a military feel, and it worked perfect. It has all those flamadiddles and turdles and all this stuff that I don't do. That was Johnny's sound. He had it down. But I took him to that session.

JIM TUCKER As time went on, the music got tougher, and after the first or second album, Portz couldn't cut it. He was strictly a three-chord, surf-band bass player.

HOWARD KAYLAN We had bass player problems. Chuck Portz left the band, and Gene Clark recommended Chip. I knew him from the Modern Folk Quartet days, but I never imagined that he would fit into our circle. And yet he did.

CHIP DOUGLAS The Gene Clark Group had just dissolved, so I needed work. Then, a week or two later, Mark came walking up the road. Joel Larson was my roommate, and Mark came up and visited our place on Wonderland Park Avenue. We'd crossed paths with those guys a couple times when I was in the MFQ, so we knew each other. He said, 'Our bass player is getting too crazy on us. We're going to let him go. Do you want to come play with us?' Things just kind of tumbled into place in those days. I think I was with them about five or six months. I can't remember the exact date we started, but I'm pretty sure it was no more than about six months.

HOWARD KAYLAN We came home long enough to record 'Can I Get To Know You Better', which White Whale believed to be the next 'You Baby,' because it was written by the same people and had the same sort of feel going for it. That was the first record that Johnny Barbata played drums on. I believe Chip and Johnny played together on that record.

CHIP DOUGLAS We went into the studio one time before 'Happy Together' and recorded some things. One of them was a novelty thing called 'Can't You Hear The Cows,' and I forget what else. It may have been some Phil Sloan song or something.

HOWARD KAYLAN There was never a time when we were making money from our records. We were making money from our shows, so the tours were booked back to back, with maybe two or three weeks in between, and in that three weeks we would go into the studio. We sometimes spent months away. We would have to be out on the road for that long a period of time.

DENNY JONES They had a DC-3. It didn't catch on fire, but it was smoking. When it came over Phoenix, there was smoke coming out of it. I don't know if they leased it or owned it, but that was their airplane. By '67, they did not have the plane. They had given it up.

We leased the DC-3. That plane was crap. It eventually feathered its engines somewhere on the side of the road in Pennsylvania. We got out and never got back in.

TOMMY JAMES The first time I laid eyes on Mark and Howard was in the spring of '67, at a show we did together in a coliseum in Alabama, and Neil Diamond and The Buckinghams were on the bill, too. We hit it right off. They were good heads, honest, very friendly to talk to. We were all doing drugs backstage; all the bands would compare their drugs.

CHIP DOUGLAS Mark was the whole show. He was the guy who was all over the stage, tossing the tambourine fifty feet in the air and catching it. He was just so much energy. He's one of the great performers.

RUSS GIGUERE Mark is the best stage tambourine player I've ever seen. He used to do this thing where he'd throw it up in the air and it would like curl—go in front of him—and make an arc, it would roll down his right hand, roll down his right arm across his shoulders and catch it in his left hand. It's one of my favorites. I've never seen a video of that. I've only seen it live. He's a fearless man.

RICK CARR I saw The Turtles at Carthage College in Kenosha, Wisconsin, '68, and they were amazing. Their vocals were just like the record and Mark was constantly throwing the tambourine up in the air. I don't think he's ever caught it in his life, but that's probably part of the show. Mark and Howard are showmen.

RAY MANZAREK He wacked that tambourine for the rest of his life, and he's probably still doing it. That man could shake and toss a tambourine in the air, and that tambourine obeyed him like a puppy. It was like a trained dog: *Is that a trained dog or a tambourine? How is he doing all those tricks?* He was—and still is—like the juggler with the tambourine. A tambourine and a voice.

DENNY JONES When I first joined, the band wanted to break me in, and they were experimenting, having me try everything. They would have me try amyl nitrate and pot and watch my reaction to these different things. At one point I felt like a chemical dumpsite. They had every new kind of drug imaginable. There was a potpourri, and it was always something new that was on the scene in some form or another. They'd smoke this incredibly potent, gummy hash that [Turtles roadie] Carlos would come up with. Oh my God, it was absolutely unbelievable. You'd get stoned and then you'd get real paranoid. Imagine it was 105 outside, you're in Salt Lake City doing an outdoor show, and you're ripped on hash. And Carlos was pretty much stoned a good percentage of the time during those years. It was all experimental, and there was no downside, because there was no AIDS or any of that kind of that stuff. Coke didn't come until a couple of years later. That came in '69.

CHIP DOUGLAS I remember getting high for the first time while driving through the desert, when we were traveling across the country. We did a couple little high schools and things, and I played the Whisky with them, but I don't have a lot of memories of being on the road. My memories are more of Mark and Howard themselves. They never took anything very seriously, and it was all just fun and games, which made it real fun. I remember us all sitting around one time in a hotel room. Mark and Howard were both hyperventilating and then holding their breath after getting ripped on pot and stuff. They'd sit there on the floor, hyperventilating, and then they'd take a big breath and bear down hard. They were trying to pass out, or just seeing how long they could go without passing out, or some darn thing like that.

DENNY JONES Sometimes after a show they would order three or four pizzas, just gorging. And there would be donut-eating contests. One night it was time to see who could eat the most doughnuts. We were at the hotel and ordered five dozen doughnuts. You had a drink of milk after each donut, and every third one had to be a bear claw. Do you know how tough it is to eat more than a couple of doughnuts? Somebody—I can't remember who—ate eleven. And the same thing happened with Bob's Big Boy. We had a Bob's Big Boy eating contest. Howard won that. He had four of them. We used to do those kinds of things when we got stoned. You'd lay around the room, bored to tears, and these are the kind of things that would happen. And Barbata hated that. He was a real fitness guy. When we stayed in New York, he'd go out and get V8 juice. He's the first guy I remember who wouldn't put it with Vodka to make a drink.

JOHNNY BARBATA Mark and Howard were kind of heavyset, so they weren't into dressing up really good. Mark had his own image, of course, and so did

Howard, but they all tried to dress better because of me. Even when I was in the Sentinels, I was into choreography. I'd show them all what steps to do and all that.

Obviously, the band were not fashion trendsetters. Size 36 and higher was our fashion, and Barbata hated that. If he could have dressed us, that would have pleased him. That was a battle always waiting to start, because we were in the front and he was in the back. That really bugged him.

HARVEY KUBERNIK It's good to address survival aspects of rock bands, especially as things became more telegenic, so I don't consider Johnny Barbata making those overt suggestions anything negative. No matter how you slice it, as Mick Jagger said, rock'n'roll, half of it's always been about haircuts, and the rest is about clothing. Things like hair and clothes and, unfortunately, body type—that's usually associated with women or girl groups—but that concern exists in male dominated rock'n'roll. Witness people like Gene Simmons who have an almost military approach to music and business too. You've got to look good and look sharp. For bands, hair and wardrobe and being perfectly immaculately kept was always very important.

HAPPY TOGETHER

We met Alan Gordon and Gary Bonner in Long Island. They were the opening act for The Turtles, and they asked us if we were looking for songs to record. We said, 'Send them along to us.' The Vogues, The Happenings, and The Tokens had all turned the song down before we heard it.

JIM TUCKER Howard used to carry this little portable 45 player around. Little teeny thing, you could put it in your suitcase. We had Bonner and Gordon's acetate of 'Happy Together.' Nobody else wanted it. There wasn't much to it.

HOWARD KAYLAN We went through all of these masters, and we found one that everyone else had passed on, including The Vogues, and when The Vogues pass on something, it can't be good. We tried to make it more palatable than that horrible demo record that we had heard from Bonner and Gordon, who hadn't had any success at that point. But we had seen them performing live as The Magicians at the Night Owl Café in Greenwich Village. And The Magicians had written all their own tunes. We were very aware, when we got these songs, from whence they had come.

PHIL VOLMAN Bonner and Gordon had taken that song to other acts, and nobody wanted it, and Mark and Howard made it, and of course it became their theme song. It went all the way to #1.

HOWARD KAYLAN We really, really worked on the song while we were out on the road. And when I say we, I mean largely Chip Douglas. Chip was responsible not only for the bass part on that song, but for a lot of the vocal arranging, and a lot of the horns, and all the strings. Everything but the mix on that record. The only thing that Joe Wissert did in his function as Turtles producer was to let everybody have enough space to do what we needed to do.

CHIP DOUGLAS I had these ideas for a bassoon and oboe part and some double flutes and trumpets, which I wrote out for them. I had never really done that kind of work, but I thought, *This can't be that hard*. I had written out a lot of four-part harmony vocals for The Modern Folk Quartet, but I had no understanding of how to write the rhythm into music. I could get the notes down on paper, but the actual way they came out—the phrasing—was a whole lot different than what I intended, so I just went over and sang it to them, and they adjusted their notes for me.

It turned out to be quite a memorable record, and it was because we had time to let the thing age and work out the stuff we were going to work out. We all had our parts down pat before we went in the studio, so it just took a matter of half an hour to cut the track once everything was set up. A couple of takes and that was it. It was all figured out beforehand, and that made it easy. Mark wasn't playing guitar at that point, but he would kind of slap his knees and be singing a harmony part, and just kind of putting juice in there one way or the other. He was mainly the harmony singer at that point.

HOWARD KAYLAN Everybody looked at each other before the horns went on, before anything was mixed, and we just said, 'Holy shit, this is it. This is our #1 record.' We knew it before it came out. It was the weirdest thing in the world. It was the only time in my entire career that I ever knew, leaving a recording studio that we were part of a #1 record. I never felt that with 'Hungry Heart,' I never felt that with 'Bang A Gong.' I never felt that with any song we were ever a part of, with the exception of 'Happy Together.'

CHIP DOUGLAS I knew it was a good record, but I was too busy thinking about the final mix—how come I couldn't hear my bassoon part a little louder, and things like that. When it was done I was just hoping for the best. I'd been doing so many records and trying so many things, and I kind of didn't expect it was going to be as successful as it was.

RICHIE FURAY Mark came home with the acetate. Both of us probably got a little self-indulgent in things that maybe we shouldn't have gotten self-indulgent in, and because he was pretty happy about it, he put that acetate on. So there we were, man, literally, we were happy together as we listened to it. I mean, it was like, *This is awesome, man!* We *knew.* I knew it right away, listening to it: *This is a hit record.* And we enjoyed it to no end, and of course it turned out to be a #1 record.

RAY MANZAREK 'Happy Together' was a perfect song. The band was a good time rock'n'roll band, and you'd have to smile when you were watching them. 'Happy Together' has a little bit of an old-fashioned, oompah beat. They're like a two-man barbershop quartet, with a happy oompah band playing. And the song was just such a natural, it just exploded. As a matter of fact, 'People Are Strange' was our version of 'Happy Together.' After Jim came in with the lyrics and we worked out the chord changes, we were trying to find out how we play this song. What's the backing going to be? What is the music behind it? And I said, or Robbie said or John said—who knows, man—*somebody* said, 'Happy Together.' And we all went, 'Yeah!' Like a minor, dark 'Happy Together.' And that was it. Like an actor always has to find some little thing that will help him get into the character, we couldn't get into the song until somebody said, 'Happy Together.' And that's what it was, man. That's an exclusive—nobody knows this. I've never told anyone before. 'Happy Together' for The Doors became 'People Are Strange,' and 'Happy Together' is the thing that kicked it off for us, that locks it in. Yeah! That's how to do it. Except, we're dark and minor, and The Doors.

DON CUSIC 'Happy Together' came out during the Summer Of Love, and that was 'San Francisco (Be Sure To Wear Some Flowers In Your Hair),' 'All You Need Is Love,' and all of that. It just sort of fit in there. The interesting thing is that here is a pretty tradition love song in the era of free love.

KEN BARNES I'm sure they knew it was a hit, but I'm not sure they realized what a millstone around their necks it would be in a sense. It's such an interesting song when you analyze it. It's almost like 'Born In The USA,' for a song that's misunderstood, too, because it's remembered as the most blithe, happy pop tune of the 60s, just about—pure sunshine played at weddings and all that kind of stuff. And it's actually kind of a wistful: *Wouldn't it be great*. A fantasy. It's almost more like 'Wouldn't It Be Nice,' but it's not even *that* hopeful.

That record just sounded special. It had everything a record needed to be a hit. It was a bit of a surprise that it could happen on such a small record label, but it did, and it changed our lives forever.

SHADOE STEVENS 'Happy Together' is generally considered, cross-generationally, as one of the happiest, most enjoyable, catchy, songs of all time. It's in commercials, it's in television shows and movies. It's the go-to feel good song for all kinds of things.

TOMMY JAMES I'll never forget, it was a real epiphany. I've got the radio turned up and I hear 'Happy Together' for the very first time, and you just knew immediately it was going to be a smash. And the next record was 'Strawberry Fields' by The Beatles. Both came out the same moment, and I remember thinking to myself that the industry had just divided in two. On one side, you have Top 40 pop with The Turtles, and on the other you have this sort of underground, not quite discernible record of 'Strawberry Fields' that's going down a very different path. And that turned out to be a very insightful moment, because the industry divided into two camps. AM radio was playing Top 40 music, and FM radio was playing what was called underground music, or album rock. You had this division between singles and albums, and 'Happy Together' and 'Strawberry Fields' represented that to me, more than anything else.

JOHNNY BARBATA Nobody ever told me what to play in The Turtles. Everything I ever did was my idea. I always came up with my parts. 'Happy Together'— that stylized me. That was the forefront runner.

HOWARD KAYLAN Everything changed with that song. The fact we'd already had a couple of Top 10 hits two years earlier wasn't really common knowledge. Until you got into the #1 situation, I don't think anybody really paid attention. As soon as the record became a hit, Chip got an offer to work with The Monkees, and he was gone.

CHIP DOUGLAS I really hated to quit playing with them. When I got the offer to go do The Monkees, I was having a really, really good time, but I wasn't making much money, so it was a matter of having to pay the bills, and the offer sounded pretty good. Mike Nesmith said, 'You'll be making six figures in six weeks.' I didn't quite believe it at first, but after a while I realized it was the real thing. I had met Nesmith before, he was kind of a fan of mine in The Modern Folk Quartet and the group in general, and he singled me out. So, I started working with those guys, and that was a whole different thing, because they weren't as tight a band as The Turtles were. The Turtles had a pretty solid drummer and everything, and Micky was just learning the drums.

Mark was the one least happy about me leaving the group. I think there was a little bit of resentment on his part, and the relationship was never quite the same for a number of years. We're all older and past all of that now, but I always wanted to tell him that I really didn't want to leave. It was a matter of survival. I had to make some money. And I wanted to continue making records with them, so we worked on *Battle Of The Bands* later, and that was good. We all had fun during that period of time.

HOWARD KAYLAN Chip jumped off. He was gone, replaced by Jim Pons, who played on everything else. We knew Jim from way back in the days of The Leaves.

JIM PONS & ED SULLIVAN

JIM PONS I was the social director of my fraternity at Cal State Northridge and in charge of hiring bands to play at our parties. When I first saw The Beatles, I decided to start my own group and formed The Leaves. I didn't know anyone who could play guitar, but I picked out five of the best-looking guys in the fraternity, thinking if we didn't sound good at least we could look good. We were very amateurish but so were the songs in those days, so we learned fast. We got big largely because local rock bands were so few and far between. We had a hit with 'Hey Joe.' I can't recall ever seeing money from the single, but we didn't really care, because we were getting gigs and going on the road all of a sudden.

The Leaves were hanging together by a thread after recording our second album. The hits had stopped coming, and jobs had become fewer and farther between. In the middle of all this, one night Mark Volman and Johnny Barbata asked if I'd be interested in joining The Turtles, and I decided to accept the offer. 'Happy Together' had just been released, and it was a culture shock. From the humble beginnings of a homemade garage band, all of a sudden I had stepped into a showbusiness career.

For well over two decades, an appearance on *The Ed Sullivan Show* brought instant credibility. Sunday nights at eight, Sullivan presented a wide variety of acts, including 'something for the youngsters'— rockers from Elvis to The Beatles and beyond.

DENNY JONES I've been in the music business forty years as a tour manager, and I started with The Turtles. Pons and I went to high school together, and then we were in the same fraternity at San Fernando Valley State College. Pons joined The Turtles, and that was my shot later on.

Jim was married on November 11, 1967, and I was his best man. It was in a little town in Oregon, and Mark and Al Nichol flew up for it. A week later, they were on *The Ed Sullivan Show*. That was a big deal—unbelievable. That's when I came aboard, and the first tour I did with them was at the end of November '67, and they were huge, man. We played Arizona State University, and we flew into Phoenix, and my God, it was like Beatlemania. There were hundreds of girls waiting to meet us. That band had so many hits between 1965 and 1969, just one after the other.

JIM PONS My dad thought I was being led down the primrose path, that I'd just waste my life. He warned me about it all the time, and then all of a sudden he liked it. When I got him tickets for *The Ed Sullivan Show*, and we sang 'Happy Together,' he was all for that. Everything was fine by then.

E. MICHAEL HARRINGTON You're on *Ed Sullivan*? Now you're big. Before that, you should have gone to med school and done something useful.

LINDA CAMPILLO When our grandmother saw The Turtles on *Ed Sullivan*, she said that then she knew they had made it. She was so proud. They were on *Ed Sullivan*, so they had really made it. That was a big thing. It was just Grandma and me at that point, but she was having little strokes and dementia was setting in, so at the end of that summer we moved in with Aunt Madeline and Uncle Bob. That's where she passed away. She had a stroke later that year, when we were living with them. But she was healthy when she saw them on *Ed Sullivan*.

JOHN SNYDER In those days, parents thought you had to go to college or get a job. Mark's dad wasn't real thrilled that Mark was going into the music industry, and there were some negative feelings. He wasn't real happy about it. And then they played on *Ed Sullivan*. That's what turned everything around. The whole world knew they were for real.

AL NICHOL We got a lot of media coverage early on in our career, so by the time 'Happy Together' came out we were nationally known and met the qualifications of *The Ed Sullivan Show*. That was wonderful. We did *Ed Sullivan*, and the response was so good we did it three more times.

SUSAN COWSILL Whoo! *Ed Sullivan*! I remember thinking how in the heck is this even real, because I was sitting on the couch that night in '64 like everyone else. In 1964 we were watching The Beatles, and in 1967 we're on the same stage as The Beatles. How does that happen? And I'm five-six-seven while all this is brewing, so once we get where we're going, it was insane. At first, I was too young to even be in the band, but I managed to get in two months before we were on Sullivan. Have you looked at the clip? When you see me, I'm just like, *Tah-dah! I managed!*

NICK FORTUNA All national TV was important, but *Ed Sullivan* was the premier show to be on, and the hardest of them all to get booked on. You had to have something special in order to get on that show. The best of the best were on *Sullivan*, so that was a great honor for us and it definitely helped our career, because now every other TV show wanted you. Once you did *Sullivan* it was easy to get on every other show.

RAY MANZAREK *Ed Sullivan* was national—you had made the upper rung. You were now one of the gods. If you were rock'n'roll—because they would bring on other genres—and you made it onto *The Ed Sullivan Show*, you had become one of the immortals, and you entered Valhalla and were now residing on the top of Mount Olympus. From there it was national tours, more records, more idolatry. And if you were good and could continue making good songs, you just went on and on and on. Your life was made. Your career was now secure.

We were very excited about playing on the show. The Beatles had played *The Ed Sullivan Show*, The Rolling Stones were on *The Ed Sullivan Show*, and Elvis Presley, Jerry Lee Lewis, and the 50s rockers, and then the 60s, and the British Invasion. So, to be on *The Ed Sullivan Show* meant that you had entered the pantheon. And you were now absolutely famous. It was a *Good Housekeeping* Seal Of Approval from Ed—he put his imprimatur on you. Like the Pope would do the same thing, so you had your imprimatur from Ed Sullivan.

RUSS GIGUERE Everyone knew who Ed Sullivan was. We were on that show many times, and it's hard to explain today how important it was. There's nothing like it. There are no variety shows today. Variety died.

HOWARD KAYLAN My folks just didn't know what to make of it when I quit school. One minute I was the bum for giving up the already paid for UCLA education, and then I end up on *Ed Sullivan*. I bought them this gigantic GE color TV, and I got my brother a car, and I sent them all on a trip to Hawaii. And I never again heard a bad word about choosing music as a career.

JOHN SNYDER We were all so happy when The Turtles took off. Everyone from Westchester High was bragging that we used to go to their dances when they were The Crossfires. Obviously, once the band got going, our friendships just kind of moved to the back burner. He was traveling, they had a #1 record, and there was a lot going on. They were rock stars in those days; I mean, come on, it's a big deal. Everybody wants you. But that was okay. We were happy for Mark. He was big-time and making lots of money. And it wasn't like he was above it all and he was so superstar that didn't have time for us. We never felt that. When we talked to him, he always wanted to know how we were doing, what's going on. He never shunned anybody that I was aware of.

MARK PARENTEAU I grew up in Massachusetts, and California was the Promised Land. It was palm trees, movie stars, and everything we dreamed about in the cold, white north, this magical place with all the TV shows and especially the music. Seeing The Turtles on *Shindig!* and *Hullabaloo* and *American Bandstand* and *Where The Action Is*, and of course *The Ed Sullivan Show*, you couldn't watch and not be affected by Mark's *je ne sais quoi*. He just had that look in his eye. He was a character, a little odd-looking with that fuzzy hair and glasses and that tummy. And it tied in to that free spirit that California represented—that loose shirt, Bermuda shorts kind of thing. While we had to go to school in shirts and ties and jackets, California was loose and carefree, sunshine and surfing and palm trees. And Mark fit right into that. He was to me the essence of what California was all about.

RICK CARR The Turtles were on television all the time, and as a kid growing up in Southern Wisconsin, where it's zero degrees and you've got two feet of snow on the ground, when you turn on the TV and see them on the beach or someplace with palm trees, to me, that was the California dream. I grew up with the white snow and pine trees, and Mark and Howard were white sand and palm trees.

AL NICHOL We had transitioned from an instrumental band to a vocal band. We were getting a lot of bookings on the college circuit with vocal groups like Spanky & Our Gang and The Association. And we still did a lot of shows with The Beach Boys and other groups that were hitting things hard vocally.

SPANKY MCFARLANE We probably met Mark in 1967. We met on the road several times, and if they were playing, we'd come and see them, and they would come and see us if we were playing. I remember one incident in a club on the north side of Chicago. The Turtles were playing and we—Spanky & Our Gang—had played somewhere, and then we went to see them and we sang with them and somehow wound up in a pile up on the floor. It was hilarious. I don't know what we were doing. We had our clothes on of course, but it got real crazy. It usually did with a late-night set at a night club.

In 1967, a trip to perform in the UK brought out many of The Turtles' heroes, including The Beatles. Years later, Howard would write and release a film inspired by this trip, *My Dinner With Jimi.*

JIM TUCKER We went to England and played this club called the Speakeasy. The Beatles came in. Hendrix came in dressed in his flower thing. Graham Nash came in with Brian Jones from the Stones. Our first set, all these guys are sitting there, and nobody clapped or anything. Everybody was quiet, and we thought, *Oh boy, we're screwed.* Well, they came in every night. Paul and John and Ringo were all there. The only one that never came in was Harrison. And by the end of the night, Lennon was under the table.

Howard did this thing about having dinner with Hendrix. I saw the film, and that never happened, that I know of. The whole time I was there, I never saw it. I said, 'Shit, where were we? Why are you going to dinner and we didn't?' I never saw that. I don't think it ever happened.

JIM PONS Jim was upset with the drudgery of the road, and somehow meeting The Beatles was a major disillusionment.

JIM TUCKER I left right after that. Me and Howard got really sick, and we had to cancel three or four dates. We couldn't get out of bed. And after about three or four days, I walked over to the window, and I just went, 'You know what? I think I'm done.' We were leaving England the same day, and they had two weeks back east before we were due back in L.A. Reb Foster and Bill Utley were over there, and I got on a plane with Bill and flew back to L.A.. They kept saying, 'C'mon, we got two more weeks back east.' And I said, 'You know what? Screw it.' So that was it. Packed the bag, flew out to see my parents.

They used this story about how I was obsessed with The Beatles. They said I left because of The Beatles. That was all bullshit. When they first came out, I didn't even like them. I didn't even care about them. It was just *Beatles! Beatles!* So what? To be honest, I think it was Howard. He was the one that was so obsessed. But I didn't even really like 'em. But when you watch the DVD [*Happy Together*], Mark tries to give his explanation why I left. It's just like when you read magazines; it's all bullshit. But they put it on the DVD. That was their excuse for me leaving.

HOWARD KAYLAN Jim's quitting had nothing to do with The Beatles. It's not like he was a dynamic personality or anything, but I think even he realized a good thing when he saw it. He didn't really have to do much to remain a member of The Turtles. He played rhythm guitar—all he had to do was strum. We didn't ask him to sing, we didn't ask him to look British, he did that by himself, but I think he let himself down. I think he wanted himself to be a Beatle. It wasn't so much that *we* didn't become The Beatles, I think it was that he didn't. I think that he found his role in the band a subservient one, but he was never going to bust out and be the John Lennon rhythm player, because he wasn't a writer. So, knowing that, it was like he was butting his head against a wall. He couldn't take it any farther. He didn't have the chops to turn it in to a lead player, he couldn't write and he couldn't sing well enough to be a singer of his own material. He was sort of resting on our coattails.

Now, if I were given that situation today, I would be thrilled to ride along on somebody else's talent and reap the benefits, but I think after a few years, Jim's guilt started getting the better of him. If you weren't triggered by something like that Lennon incident, then what would make you leave a group like that? It's not like—as Don Murray thought—we were all paranoid and 'after him.' Tucker knew that we weren't out to get him, we just wanted him to shut up and do his gig. And he couldn't do it. He excluded himself from our social circle, and The Turtles band was always a social club first and a band second. Still is. If you can't get along with us right now then you can't play in our band, period. We would rather have players we can get along with than the best virtuoso players who ride some kind of a high horse.

LINDA CAMPILLO Jim had what they used to call a nervous breakdown. He was very quiet and not really outgoing onstage. I'm sure he was a good guitar player, but he was not like a major part of the show.

PAT VOLMAN Jim Tucker had some problems because he was so hurt. His feelings were hurt. And it's kind of sad. That's a long time ago. Get over it, right? You've got to grow up sometime. But I don't know the real story. Maybe, because he's so bitter, maybe that was one of the reasons why they didn't want him around. I don't know what happened. Sometimes you just don't want to know. Like, I can tell it's band stuff.

JIM TUCKER I don't regret quitting, not really, because they ended up getting rid of Barbata. I mean, come on, he's one of the best drummers there is. I don't know what happened there. I think it all goes back to Mark, and maybe Howard for a while. Seiter couldn't hold a candle to Barbata. The stuff I was getting was that he fit more into the group. But you talk about a drummer? Shit, he wasn't half what Barbata was. I moved to Grass Valley and played in the band in a couple of bars up here. And because of who I was, shit, the place was packed every goddamned night. They were lined up around the corner, and the cops said, 'You gotta get in or leave,' and nobody would leave.

AL NICHOL It didn't change a whole lot when Jim left. In the studio it didn't change at all, because I would simply overdub all the parts. Tucker was able to cover the rhythm guitar parts live, so I had to be a little more versatile onstage, but we couldn't see bringing somebody else into the group replacing him. We decided to just go with what we had. We got down to just using guitar, bass, and drums, and I think we probably had a better, tighter, rhythm section with just the three of us. Then we focused on our vocal power, arranging songs with a lot of background parts for all the guys. Having a tight rhythm section backing an expanded vocal section made our live performances really domineering. So I think it probably helped. We thought we'd miss that extra support, but it actually made us concentrate on what we had.

JIM TUCKER Those guys were lucky to even stay in the group. Because it was surf music and they couldn't do anything. And now he thinks he owns everything—the whole ball of wax.

AL NICHOL Jim kind of got his head twisted around there for a while. About the point when he left the group over in England, he was swirling in the dark.

I think that ever since, deep under, he's probably been very unhappy with his decision to leave the group. He missed a lot of years with the band. And he feels that he was cheated out of all those years. He's bitter about it, but he also knows that nobody cheated him out of those years except himself.

PETER NOONE You know, all I've got to say about the guitarist is, when you hear a Turtles record, do you see the guitar player in your visual? If you play The Beatles, you might see Ringo or Paul or George or John. But there isn't a person on the planet—except that guitar player's mum—who thinks about him when she hears 'Happy Together.' Not one single person. And I saw them in that lineup! That's the lineup I know. I've got that video with them then, but he's not the guy I see. I see—it's amazing—I see Flo and Eddie. I just don't see anybody else.

DENNY JONES 'She'd Rather Be With Me' was June of '67, and that was a huge, huge hit. That was Bobby Kennedy's kid's favorite song. The Turtles played the World's Fair in Montreal, and all of Bobby's kids wanted to get their autographs.

HARVEY KUBERNIK I can't believe all the crazy yelping on 'The Story Of Rock And Roll'—the wild, unabashed background vocals Mark is tossing in—it's such a great counterbalance to the precision vocals, and it captures the essence of Flo & Eddie, where you have Howard like Picasso, with his precise, pinpoint vocal narratives taking you through the geographical history of rock'n'roll, and then you have Mark doing class-clown shtick on the same song, and then they all come together in harmony. It made me realize that in a weird way, a lot of the Turtles songs are like audiobooks, because they're storytelling.

KEN BARNES 'Happy Together' forced them into a very above-ground pop mold that didn't necessarily suit them. There was far too much talent and innovative ability in the band to be contained by the pigeonholing that they suffered. And if you look at the singles before, you see at least three different bands. You see a folk-rock protest group on 'It Ain't Me Babe' and 'Let Me Be,' and then the first glimmerings of a real pop/happy sort of sensibility with 'You Baby.' And then they turn it around and do 'Grim Reaper,' which is about the dirgiest sitar-oriented modal garage rock ever. The whole thing is like, *Wow! What an image change, and what a great, great, record.*

They did the Warren Zevon song next: 'Outside Chance,' which is again, a kind of a garage-rock classic. And then, all of a sudden, this switch into 'Happy Together.' 'She'd Rather Be With Me' is a wild little song, and then they got really strange after that. 'She's My Girl' and 'You Know What I Mean' are very adventurous. If they were done by somebody else—a group with more of the underground credibility of The Byrds, for instance—they would be looked at a whole different way. Then you get to 'Elenore,' another where most people were oblivious to the sarcasm and the satire. And then a gorgeous record like 'You Showed Me.' Where did that come from? That was pretty interesting too. They dug up an old, primitive, early Byrds song and turned it into a masterpiece.

I've thought about it a lot over the years, and it's really interesting, the whole career of that band, from visiting the White House with Tricia Nixon to hanging out with Hendrix. *Rolling Stone* never really appreciated them, but at the same time, what other band of the 60s could have pulled off *Battle Of The Bands?*

HENRY DILTZ I photographed The Turtles a number of times, including going on the road with them. I took some pictures of them for *Battle Of The Bands.* Not the whole album, but I did Chief Kamanawanalea, the Hawaiian group. The *Turtle Soup* day was terrific, out at the beach. There's a ton of pictures from that—of them all standing with the water up to their waist. There were a lot of funny shots that happened out there that day.

DEAN TORRENCE *The Turtles' Golden Hits* was my first album cover. I was a fan of the band, but I knew the guys that owned the record company as well. They were looking for somebody to do some of their graphics, and they weren't sure how to go about doing that. So, I filled that void for them. And two years later, I did *More Golden Hits* for them as well.

I set up the [*Surfer Dan*] photo sessions, since that was part of my domain. I probably hired the photographer, and I was there to oversee what was being done. In that particular one, I ended up in the picture. I was to bring the props. I was the only one that had the surf boards, so those are my surf boards.

Released in late 1968, *The Turtles Present The Battle Of The Bands* marked the first time an entire album project was to be the focus, rather than the earlier, more rudimentary notion of a collection of singles. Chip Douglas was back as producer, and the concept of a dozen different bands showcased the group's wide-ranging talent.

HAL WILLNER That's one of the great obscure records. Anyone who has ever heard it will go, *Oh!* like one's in a secret club. That record was so far ahead of its time. A band playing twelve different groups battling, and all those songs are amazing. 'Elenore' is on that record, and 'You Showed Me' of course has its own history, when it was done later. The De La Soul story.

CHIP DOUGLAS It was a fun album to make. It was their tunes, and we were all part of it. I would chime in, but they had an idea of what they wanted to hear and how they wanted it to go, and I said, 'Great, let's do that.' I had learned with The Monkees to just kind of let everyone contribute, and have some creative process going on. By this point, Mark was singing lead on some songs, and he had a lot of ideas as far as chords, structure, word ideas, pretty much everything. They were good songwriters. I mean, *The Battle Of the Bands* is really a classic little album. I had a few ideas in 'Elenore,' on how to tighten it up and get the arrangement going, and, being a bass player, I got pretty specific with Jim Pons on the bass part. But other than that, it was just drum fills and those kinds of things. The general arrangement of it.

'You Showed Me' was a co-write by Jim McGuinn and Gene Clark. We heard the song at Chip Douglas's house. He had a harmonium that played by pumping the pedals with your feet, and one of the bellows had a hole in it so he could only play it so fast. He said it should be faster, like The Beatles. We loved the slowed-down version he could only play due to the hole. We recorded it slow. It was a big hit.

RUSS GIGUERE I was driving up Beachwood Canyon the first time I heard it. The record came on the radio as I was driving to my friend's house, so when I got there I asked them if they had heard the new Turtles record. They said, 'No, what's it like?' I had only heard it once, but I sang part of it, and Gene Clark was there. He wrote it, but I didn't know that, and I was singing it to him. He asked me if I really like the song. I said, 'Yeah, I think it's the best thing they've ever done.' He said, 'Well, I wrote it.' It reminds me of a sort of Jewish folk song. I always thought it was really sweet.

CHIP DOUGLAS I used to hear 'You Showed Me' at the Troubadour bar all the time when The Byrds were just getting started. McGuinn and Crosby and Gene Clark would sit around on Monday nights doing Beatles songs, things like 'I Should Have Known Better,' and other Beatles-sounding things. So I knew how it went from hearing it live so many times, and when I played it for Mark and Howard, they loved it. On that one, they both sang the lead until the bridge. I guess I suggested that. It was more of a haunting sound that way, and then Howard sang lead on just the bridge.

Around that time, 'Ode To Billie Joe' had been a hit, and I loved the strings on there, so I wrote some string parts for it. I was going for the 'Ode To Billie Joe' feel, that's how it wound up sounding like it did. And I brought Paul Beaver in. I'd used him with The Monkees, because Micky was experimenting with synthesizers, and Paul was the only guy who played synthesizers at that point. He had a keyboard and all of the plug-ins; the synthesizers in those days were a big deal. They were in three different wooden cabinets, and you'd set them up and start patching things into one another. It was enormous.

MICKY DOLENZ Paul Beaver had come over to the set one day, and I messed around on his and ordered one. We used it on two songs. I'm pretty sure that I was the first to use it on any kind of popular record. As far as I know, Walter Carlos, who did a thing called *Switched On Bach*, was the only one before that.

CHIP DOUGLAS The Monkees were the first to use a synthesizer on a pop record, and The Turtles would have been the second. Unfortunately, *Battle Of The Bands* wasn't a big hit, but the album that came into Gold Star Studios right after us—they were booked, and we had to finish up and get out of there—was Iron Butterfly doing *In-A-Gadda-Da-Vida*. That album followed us in Gold Star Studios, and I think it sold eight million copies or something. It was a big one.

4

THE SCENE

SUNSET STRIP

Every place was hopping, and all the clubs had house bands. The Mothers were at Bito Lito's, The Doors and The Turtles at the Whisky, The Daily Flash, The Chocolate Watch Band . . . it was busy.

DEAN TORRENCE California was a unique place that a whole lot of people worldwide wanted to know something about, unbeknown to us. In the beginning we didn't get that part. We didn't really realize that it was so unique that people were extremely interested in it.

HOWARD KAYLAN We'd gone to see The Byrds. We wanted to be those big boys, too. We saw them just as 'Mr. Tambourine Man' was coming out. Literally two weeks before, Al, Mark and I had gone to see them at Ciro's on Sunset Boulevard. This was one of their first shows, and they were so new to their electric instruments, and we were just taken aback by how wonderful the twelve-string electric guitar sounded on traditional songs. Only Roger had a twelve-string. David had a six. And then Gene also was playing an acoustic/electric. So we witnessed this for the first time.

DANNY HUTTON The Byrds were different. They were almost a revolution, because they had all of these artists—Vito the sculptor and all of those people—coming to see them. So, when you went to see them, it was more like a Grateful Dead kind of a vibe. They brought their own party. I saw them at Ciro's, and it was amazing, with Roger and Gene up front, David with all the attitude, and then Michael on drums trying not to lose the beat. He would be struggling. And Chris, real sweet, more like a mandolin player playing bass, kind of faking it a little bit. So you had the shaky kind of a thing, but it was wonderful watching them. I loved The Byrds.

CHRIS HILLMAN I met them in '66, right around when The Byrds started at the Whisky A Go-Go, after we had success. Prior to that—to our first #1 single— we had been working at Ciro's. I know they were greatly influenced by The Byrds. We sort of set the town on fire for a brief period of time. They were following that old formula in the record and movie business, where they find a thing that works and then the powers that be duplicate it for profit. But that's fine. Yeah, a Dylan song, 'It Ain't Me Babe.' I remember that.

HARVEY KUBERNIK In L.A., 'It Ain't Me Babe' had just as profound an influence on disc jockeys, rock bands, and listeners as the opening strands of 'Mr. Tambourine Man,' because these were local kids. The Byrds seemed so much older than us. They wore capes and granny glasses and had perfect hair and looked like pop stars. The Turtles looked like schmendricks. They would do goofy things like photo sessions at the beach, stuff that The Byrds would never do, because they weren't caught up in image. They seemed like guys you'd see at fast food restaurants in Culver City. There was no mystique to them. They weren't English, they were Americans, and they were fucking fat Americans too.

PHIL VOLMAN 'It Ain't Me, Babe' became a huge hit, and it just went from there. It was the right time—everything was happening on the Sunset Strip. The Byrds and all the big bands were playing there, and they fit right in with what was going on. They connected so quickly, because they were very good.

CHRIS HILLMAN Mark and Howard were a couple years younger than me, and I was the youngest in The Byrds, but they had the [Crossfires experience] going for them. In the case of The Byrds, we didn't know what the hell we were doing. We had no blueprint. What struck me was that they were very outgoing onstage—the opposite of The Byrds. We were so aloof when we played, and The Turtles were having fun. We were taking ourselves a bit seriously. There wasn't really a competitive nature at all between The Turtles and The Byrds, they were just a bunch of guys having a great time. They weren't doing anything that I felt was stretching the boundaries that much, but it didn't really matter. They were great onstage. They were competent musicians, and they were having a wonderful time. They were more of a pop band, more of an entertaining band. But me, I was the guy in the back line of The Byrds. See, Mark was the gregarious out-front guy with Howard, and I'm in the back of The Byrds, barely able to look at the audience, scared to death, but absorbing it all. So, it's now turned where you can't shut me up anymore.

DANNY HUTTON On every block there was another club, with incredible bands every night. There was that innocence, that energy, all that that newness going on. Acid had started happening and it was just magical.

CHUCK NEGRON It was a great place. You could go into the Whisky and see just about anybody: Cream, The Doors ... you could go up the street to what was the Galaxy and Iron Butterfly was the house band, and at the Trip you could see The Temptations. There was something everywhere.

RAY MANZAREK It was amazing, absolutely amazing. We were the house band of the Whisky A Go-Go for the summer of 1966, and the summer of '66 was the Sunset Strip's Summer Of Love. All the freaks—the people who let their hair grow long—came to the Sunset Strip. The longhairs were everywhere on the Sunset Strip—unbelievable—and people started dressing like gypsies, like pirates. They were putting on costumes and putting on new personalities. The whole surf movement left the South Bay and migrated up to the Sunset Strip. The surfers came up to the Strip and became psychedelicized. They dropped acid and many of them had Nietzschean visions of Zarathustra and the Übermensch. As they rode the waves, they felt on top of the world. The Übermensch is the Überman in Nietzsche's philosophy, that you will rise above the constraints of your society and become ultimately a free man on the planet, beholden unto no one except for the basic decency and goodness and power of your own mind, your own heart. And the surfers took to that instantly. Of course, the music was entirely different. It was no longer surf music but it was still rock'n'roll—the beat is on two and four. And the blues is the basis of all rock'n'roll. So, they just morphed into something a little more trippy, a little more psychedelic, a little more far out. And people were dancing furiously, madly on the strip. It was an amazing time.

DANNY HUTTON The thing that bothers me—that no one has really written about, or they've always gotten it wrong—was that whole Summer Of Love crap in San Francisco. That actually all started a year before, in L.A. I did *The Dick Clark Show* with The Lovin' Spoonful, and later, Zally invited me to a session at RCA Studios right off the Sunset Strip, and the Jefferson Airplane were in the other room, recording *Surrealistic Pillow*. All of this stuff that supposedly happened in San Francisco was happening here first. That whole Summer Of Love was Sunset Strip. People were walking up and down the Strip and hitchhiking in the Canyon. At the Whisky, somebody would shout, 'Hey! Party up in Laurel Canyon!' and everybody would leave the club, doing what Andy Kauffman did later with meeting up after a show with cookies. There was that kind of vibe, where everybody would meet up at some house.

MARK AND PAT

PAT VOLMAN I'm a year younger than Mark. I was raised in Inglewood, which is a couple of miles from Westchester. We met in '62—I can't remember exactly how. I think he was playing someplace, and I must have gone and seen him, and then I saw him again when I started high school—he was already at Westchester High, and then I started going in '63—and he kept bugging me. He wouldn't leave me alone. We used to go over to his place after school. He was supposed to do chores when he got home, and I was the one who was doing the dishes and cleaning up the house before his parents came home. See how that worked? He was good at manipulating.

Mark and Richie Furay shared a place before we got married, and then Richie and his new wife moved in with us, so the four of us were living in this teeny weenie little Canyon house. That didn't last long, though, because it was driving everybody crazy. Newlyweds, living like that? No.

DANNY HUTTON I was best man at Mark and Pat's wedding. It was at the Little Brown Church. Ronald Reagan got married there, too. It's literally a little brown church in the Valley, near Ventura Boulevard on Coldwater Canyon Boulevard. I remember I wore my sandals. We were all hippies.

LINDA CAMPILLO The whole band was at Mark's wedding. There was a reception at my aunt and uncle's house and all of The Turtles were there. In fact, the whole band came over a few times, and they would get Uncle Joe to play stuff for them. Everybody loved having them there.

SARINA VOLMAN When I was born, my mom was by herself with my dad's aunt and his mother. My grandma and aunt were with her, but Dad was on the road.

FELIX CAVALIERE We were backstage together in a dressing room when his daughter was born, and he was so ecstatic about the birth that his voice went up a couple of octaves: 'I've got a little girl and she's okay!' I remember him vividly, like it was yesterday. That stuck in my mind because it showed me the guy's personality. That he was very family-oriented, very loving. Of course, most people would be excited, but I'll never forget that one.

SARINA VOLMAN He's a great father. He just wasn't around a lot for our childhood. That's just how it was from day one. We always knew he was going away; he's going to go tour. And he loves his job, so why take that away? This is what he has to do. He was the breadwinner and Mom would take care of us. And when he came home, we definitely went out and did things together as a family. We knew it was limited time, so we'd all be involved.

TIM SEXTON Mark and Pat were really good parents, really grounded. Part of it was Mark's South Bay middle-class upbringing, and part of it was *Sarge*. That was what Mark used to call Pat, because she kept everybody on the straight and narrow. They were comfortable, as Mark remains, with who he is. A lot of other people were trying to be something else because there was a ridiculous amount of money floating around. We were all young men with unlimited capital, in our twenties and filled with the arrogance of youth. Lots of people frittered away fortunes, but Mark was always level-headed, always responsible, and that was part of how we connected. We knew that about one another, so we could have fun, but . . . everything in moderation, including moderation. We could wink and laugh about it, but we made sure it didn't get too out of control. And Pat was an incredible moderating influence in Mark's life, because of the girls. Hence the name Sarge: Sergeant Pat wasn't going to let anything interfere with raising those girls right. Pat is a great gal, and I will always love Pat and Sarina and Hallie. They were great kids.

LAUREL CANYON

Laurel Canyon, as Van Dyke Parks sang, was the seat of the beat. Where many of the L.A.'s creative elite chose to live. Of that group, Mark was one of the first to arrive, and last to leave.

RICHIE FURAY In '67, the Buffalo Springfield played a show with The Turtles somewhere around Redondo Beach. I was about ready to lose my apartment. I didn't have a place to stay, and I didn't even know Mark. I knew The Turtles and all, but I don't think we really knew too much about each other. Mark got wind of the fact that I needed a place to stay, and man, he is just one big friendly guy, and he says, 'Why don't you come and stay here with me up on Lookout Mountain?' So, I took the invite and bunkered down there with him for, golly, it was several months. That's how that all got started. He was about ready to get married, and it wasn't long that I was also planning to get married, but in the meantime we shared his house up there on Kirkwood. They got married while we were living there, and then Nancy and I got married shortly after. After I moved out, Mark and I remained friends, throughout the whole course, right up to today.

The house I rented was at 8530 Lookout Mountain, and when Richie moved in, I was paying $195 a month. It was a three-bedroom across from the school and it was next door to Jim Pons. Isn't that just crazy? By 1967 I had bought a home up the hill at 8760 Lookout. It had a great half-acre lot in the middle of the Canyon, and when the fences went up it was a great place for the kids to play without getting hurt. The house cost $40,000. I didn't have enough money for a down payment, so the realtor Wally Mann loaned me $5,000, which was half of the $10,000 down payment. I lived there until 1994. Okay, Pat lived there until 1994. I moved out in 1993. It was part of our divorce: we split the sale and left the Canyon.

PHILIP AUSTIN In the early days, there was a Laurel Canyon sensibility that had a sort of camaraderie to it. I lived in Laurel Canyon early on, and the downstairs apartment in my house was rented by hundreds of girls who worked with Zappa. Many musicians and music people were around.

HENRY DILTZ We were neighbors in Laurel Canyon. I moved there in '67. Mark and Pat were there a little earlier. My wife Elizabeth and I lived across the street, and we would go over to play different board games with them. We loved playing a card game, Mille Bornes.

To get a hug from Mark was always amazing. It was like hugging a huge teddy bear, and that's kind of what I thought of him: he was like a huge teddy bear. He was always friendly and upbeat and positive. When he'd come to my house he had the really long frizzy hair, almost like a big Afro, and he was already a big guy, so he would completely fill the doorway. When you opened the door, there would be no light coming in. It was impressive.

PHILIP AUSTIN I first met Mark at a party at Henry and Elizabeth Diltz's house in the Canyon. We were part of the same general crowd of people. After I moved to the Farm, I became good friends with Henry and Cyrus Faryar of The Modern Folk Quartet, and they were connected to Mark and Howard through folk music and their partner Chip Douglas, who lived across the street from Henry and Elizabeth in the Canyon. But the relationships between musicians and the kind of Firesign Theatre world I was in were not much connected, except that we all made records, and we've all been allied with the guys at Rhino Records for thousands of years.

CYRUS FARYAR The Farm was a forty-acre parcel of property just off Barham Boulevard. There were two homes, and mine was the house where all the musicians hung out, so it was a lively environment. In between the houses was a place called Chicken Flats, which had a big teepee, and John Sebastian spent some time there and got himself into tie-dyeing. So did Mark and Howard. They were all wearing tie-dye for a while. We were all doing what we did, playing and singing, and we didn't conceive of anything otherwise.

It was a 60s experience, and it was wonderful and charming and delightful in just about every way. This was before anything weighty really had happened. There was a flow of people in and out. Crosby, Stills & Nash stopped by one day and sat down at my piano and sang me one side of their album, right in my living room. It was unforgettable. Oddly enough, one of the people that I met was Squeaky Fromme, who went to Westchester High with Mark and Pat. She was there one day as someone's accompaniment. I don't know the exact connection, but I know that I met a person who later became famous for terrible reasons.

PAT VOLMAN We used to go to Alice Cooper's house all the time and go swimming. Cyrus Faryar's place—the Farm—was pretty unique. But all those people just seemed normal to me. They were my friends. We used to go to The Monkees' house, and The Lovin' Spoonful . . . Danny Hutton would come over all the time. They were all our neighbors. Living in Laurel Canyon wasn't a big deal to us, because we were just part of the neighborhood. But it was an amazing time. And I didn't find out that Jim Morrison lived up the street, because Mark never told me. I wish I would have known that, because when he went out of town, I would have gone to visit him. Darn!

DANNY HUTTON I remember the young Mark, barefoot. He was doing the whole hippie thing. I didn't know he was from Westchester and all that, more of a straight kind of a background, but he was feeling his oats. He was the Nature Boy. He moved up the street with Pat, and he just loved tacos and stuff, so I remember going there having little taco dinners. I was going through kind of a rough period then, and in Mark's backyard he had probably eight, nine feet high and fifteen feet long of soda pop bottles, returnable soda pop bottles. I was smoking cigarettes at the time, and many a day he saved the day when I went down there with a bunch of bottles and returned them.

MICKY DOLENZ I don't remember first meeting Mark. I just remember him always being around, mainly because we lived very close to each other. Back in those days, it was a very, very communal thing. Up the street was Danny Hutton, down the street was Graham Nash and Joni Mitchell, next door was Alice Cooper, across the street was Henry Diltz, and then Mark was up in his house, and literally, you'd just wander around and hang out. It was just one long Summer Of Love.

HENRY DILTZ We were all good friends living up in Laurel Canyon, and when my wife passed away, we had a little tribute and remembrance. Elizabeth taught nursery school, so we all gathered out in the backyard of the school, and talked about her. A few people got up and said how wonderful she was with our kids, and Mark talked for a while. I really appreciated that, but I can't really summon up the image of it. That was kind of a hard day. It's on a video tape somewhere that I've never looked at, but someday, I'll look at it.

PAUL WILLIAMS We were neighbors in Laurel Canyon, a couple of houses apart. Any time we saw each other, we'd wave. We were big wavers, but we didn't hang together a lot, because it seemed like Mark was always on the road. But there was always a lot of affection there.

Chip lived across from Henry, and when Chip left, Paul Williams moved in, and then Cheryl Bentyne from Manhattan Transfer. In a matter of five houses you had, at different times, myself, Chip, Paul, Cheryl, Mentor Williams (Paul's brother and songwriter), Jeff Gonzer (DJ at KMET), Joe Schermie from Three Dog Night, Ken Forssi (the bass player from the group Love), Paul Rothchild, who produced The Doors and Love, plus James Spader and some other Hollywood hipsters.

HARVEY KUBERNIK Mark left in 1994. He was the last to leave of the originals. He put in thirty years, and he was a big part of the community.

5

THE BUSINESS

The music business, especially when it came to rock'n'roll, was hardly an industry when The Turtles first had their hits. Still, there was money to be made. Just rarely by its creators.

DEAN TORRENCE If I had bet the farm on whether or not it would last much in the 60s? Not a chance. In essence, that's why we didn't really pay a whole lot of attention to contracts and all that stuff. We paid enough attention, but you let some of the details fly, because you figured you're going to have a run at this for three or four years at most, and then it's on to the next thing. And that would overlap things like writing songs. You may not even fight for credit on a song, because you figured, at worst, the damn thing is probably only on the radio for three months anyway. Big deal. Or it doesn't make it anyhow, so why get in a fight over it? That's the nature of the business. The suits don't particularly care about art. They just want product; they've got to keep the pipeline full of the product. If they burn you out? Big deal. It doesn't matter. We've got to get as much as we can out of these folks, and then the guys that are right behind them on the treadmill, we'll take that stock when we burn the guys in front of them out.

DANNY HUTTON I was young and naïve. I gave away writing and I gave away publishing—I didn't know about that stuff. I tell my kids I really, *really* know what I'm doing, because I was so stupid through my whole life. I've gotten screwed so many ways, that I look at a contract now and I can tell you, 'Don't—that's bad.' Not because I'm a genius, not because I'm smart, because I *was* so stupid. Because I had signed all of those things.

WHITE WHALE

GARRY TALLENT Mark and Howard knew what a long shot it was, and that's the offer they had to take. I get that. Everybody was saying, *Don't do it, you'll get ripped off,* but nothing ventured, nothing gained, in a sense. And, yes, they were ripped off. But look what their legacy is. So, it all worked out fine, and that's the bottom line. And a lot of it has to do with their perseverance: they fought for it; they didn't just grow embittered. They kept playing, they did other things, and at the same time they did what had to be done to make sure that that legacy belonged to them. They took care of it and they got the music back.

DEAN TORRENCE Jan & Dean were on Liberty, and Liberty could kind of handle a single. They were not very good in LPs, unfortunately. It would have been nice to be on a bigger label, but we weren't. In those days, indie labels were doing well. A hit record could come from anywhere. Of course, the larger labels had all the different promotional offices, the public relations office and huge mail rooms where they could respond to stuff pretty quickly, but the down side to that was they could also afford to have tons of artists, and what you gained in one area, you lost in another. So, six of one, a half-dozen of another.

RON DANTE Some record companies wouldn't pay, like Roulette Records. Morris Levy once told my group, 'All your records came back,' and we knew we'd sold about nine hundred thousand singles. He said, 'If you want to see the books, I'll show you, but we keep two sets anyway.' Levy was unbelievably straightforward about how he was being a crook. We walked out of there saying, 'Thank you, Mr. Levy.' We didn't want to mess with him. Morris got involved in some heavy-duty hurting. But I was lucky—me and Tommy James—nobody was twisting our arm or breaking legs. We were just not getting paid. And we couldn't complain, because Morris had connections. It was old-time music business. Where there's big cash money, you're going to find the underworld, and they were there.

TOMMY JAMES We got an education at Roulette that we couldn't have had anywhere else. We weren't getting paid, but we were running our own careers creatively, right on into the marketing and the album covers and everything else. And, just like The Turtles, we got to play on our records, too. I'm surprised the way White Whale treated them, because they really were a pretty good label, aesthetically: from a selling-records point of view. The Clique were on White Whale, and they did one of my songs, 'Sugar On Sunday,' from the *Crimson And Clover* album. I'm really shocked at the way The Turtles were treated, and it was very unfair.

KEN BARNES It was a small label up against giants. The Turtles were their meal ticket and they probably tried it as best as they could, but I don't think White Whale particularly understood how music was evolving in the 60s, going from singles to an album-oriented mentality. But there was obviously some sort of intelligent A&R sensibility going on at the label, to have people like Warren Zevon hanging around and Danny Whitten from Crazy Horse with The Rockets, even Nino Temple and April Stevens, and Judee Sill late in the game. There were some really interesting one-shot records on that label too.

DEAN TORRENCE Ted Fagen and Lee Laseff were old pros. They both went through Liberty Records at one time or another, so they had done their networking. They knew the right people. I think they had The Turtles' best interests at heart, and they were trying to keep their company going, too. It was like any business: you write off so much pilferage. That's just part of the biz. And you had to make sure your contracts were written properly and that you could audit and keep everybody straight. But you always knew there was going to be some slippage in there, and don't get hung up over it.

PAUL WILLIAMS The first deal I ever got as a songwriter was a contract at White Whale Records. I wanted to be there so badly that when they offered me a contract, I didn't even look at it. I just signed it, because The Turtles were there. So that was huge for me. And about five weeks into the contract, Ted Feigin and Lee Lasseff called me in and said, 'We don't think you have a future in the music business.' I walked out of there going, *Oh fuck, what am I going to do? I thought I was a songwriter.* And then about a month later I wound up signing with A&M Records. I found my career, my life . . . but thank God for White Whale kicking my ass out. One of the first things I did when I made a little money was buy a flashy automobile. I bought this Type 35 Bugatti. It was a one-off with no doors, you just stepped into it. A beautiful red with big straps on the hood. And when I'd run up to the bank at the end of Sunset, I'd go right by White Whale, and every now and then I'd see Lee or Ted outside. I would honk and wave as I would go by, and they would be putting their faces in their hands and going, 'What have we done? What have we done?'

NICK FORTUNA In 1967 we had three hits in the Top 10 at one time, and we were named the most listened to American act. We did 312 one-nighters that year, and we didn't see any of the money. Your manager and the booking agent and your lawyers and accountants all realize that you are stupid, business-wise, which we were, and our parents had no idea of what the music business was about, and after everything is said and done, we *owed* money. But we signed the contracts. We were over eighteen. You think that the money is an automatic, and it's not. It's an automatic if the people working for you are honest and are worried about your future. Bottom line is, they are manipulating their asses off trying to figure out how to steal every penny you've got. And they do a great job.

CARL GIAMMARESE When you've hit #1, your manager or agency wants to keep you out on the road playing and taking advantage of the fact that you had a hit record. And we played three hundred dates that year. That's all we ever did; we would take a break only to come in to New York to cut another record. And then we'd go right back out again. It was crazy, and I'm sure The Turtles had a lot of crazy stuff, too, because we all got ripped off by managers and record labels, and it's the classic 60s story. I was in my late teens, and all you want to do is go out there and play your music and have fun and meet girls and get crazy. You're not really thinking about the business. You think it's going to go on forever and I'm sure they felt the same way at that point. I don't think when you're twenty years old you're supposed to think about the future. Somebody else is supposed to be looking out for you, and, unfortunately, many times that doesn't happen.

SUSAN COWSILL We own our catalogue, but up until a few years ago Universal Music Group owned everything. We got no money all through the years. None—zero, zip, zilch—because we were part of the 60s brigade that lined up with all the nice New York mafia guys to sign our lives away. My dad sure as hell had no education and didn't know what was going on, so he said, 'Yes, sign here kids,' and we did. Our 'Rain, The Park & Other Things' is in the film *Dumb And Dumber*, which I didn't know beforehand, so I'm sitting in a theatre going, *Wait . . . what?!* and wondering who got that money. We found out it was $40,000 just to get the rights to license it. That would have sent my kids to college, instead of me being in debt for them to go. That's the tip of the iceberg of what monies were generated, but not for us.

We finally found a guy who was willing to go pro bono and hunt it down and find all of our signatures, my little second-grade signature on a contract, agreeing that they can have all of our money. A contract that states in word that Bill and Bob Cowsill are of age to be making these commitments, and then at the bottom of the contract where their names and date of births are, it showed that they were *not* of age. Oh, it was hysterical! Like, *Hello?* So, they had to give us our money back. And they had everything. So, the stuff that's out there now, all the stuff that they put together, they had to cut us in.

RON DANTE I don't own any of my hit catalogue. There's a big dispute about who owns it. Don Kirshner sold it off to five different people, so every time, you never know who's going to claim ownership of those records. But if they play it on any kind of medium—TV, movies, or commercials—I have to be paid, because I'm a member of the union, and the union says whoever the singer is gets paid. So I do make money that way. My album *Ron Dante Brings You Up* is available on Amazon, but who gets the money for that? I don't know. I know it's not me, and, like Mark and Howard, you get tired of spending money on lawyers. You spend $100,000 to get $10,000 back. That's not gonna work. And today with the streaming and everything else, I'm not worried about it.

PEPPY CASTRO We didn't sign directly to a label, we signed to our producers and managers, so we got caught up in the same stuff. The Blues Magoos didn't own their name. Our managers and producers had everything, and at seventeen years old, you don't understand the business, yet because of the statute of limitations, I couldn't go back after the fact and contest anything. We never really had any of our publishing. You see your performance rights, but all our publishing was taken, which was pretty standard, especially back then. And now we want to contest that, because none of us has seen any royalty statements from the publisher in fifty years. This stuff is still being repackaged and put out, so at some point we're going to collectively get an attorney to put a hold on everything. We don't want to see royalties going to somebody else after all this time, so we're going to contest it. We're going to come up with something.

DEAN TORRENCE We stayed in school. Jan was premed, and we didn't run into too many premed students. And I had a master's in design. There were not many college graduates, and certainly not from major universities. That's exactly why we stayed in school, because we didn't trust the business. We didn't trust that we would be able to make it last that long anyway, because we didn't really see anybody else that was. Very few people were able to make it last much longer than a couple of years, so going to school was all by design, and I think it worked out great.

There was music business taking place all around us. There was a record company, publishing, touring: all the things you consider today to sell music. But we didn't get into the business with any idea of how it would feel to have a #1 record. We were excited every time a new record came out, and by the time 'Happy Together' happened, we were more seasoned, I guess . . . a bit more jaded. By then, it was tour, tour, tour, and more touring. We were international. Our music was being played around the world.

JIM PONS Howard did write 'Elenore,' with some help from the rest of us. But you don't have hit records, you don't have gigs, and you wind up opening for people that used to open for you. You had to be on the road all the time to make any money. It got tough. We should have been more willing to acquiesce when Bill Utley and Reb Foster wanted us to do other songs, but we thought we were The Beatles, and that was our downfall. Because of our insistence on doing our own songs, which weren't that good, things began to deteriorate. We weren't gifted that way. We were good entertainers, good presenters of material, but we weren't good songwriters, and it was our downfall. We didn't have any more hit records. So, they formed Three Dog Night and made them stars instead.

CHUCK NEGRON Three Dog Night were just starting, and The Turtles were opening up for us. That's when they were back with Bill Utley. I never will understand that. If I was in a group that had several hits, and it was a band that was just working on their first or second album, I would never let my band open up for them. I felt bad for Mark and Howard, but they were back with Bill, and they listened to what he said. They had left Bill earlier for this young kid, Bill's assistant. He was the road manager, and then he became the manager, because The Turtles were unhappy with Bill, and this guy got in their ear, and of course they left. But this kid wasn't a manager, so they ended up having to go back. With the hits they had, compared to a new band, they shouldn't have done it. They deserved a better chance, and it was wrong. Management was really putting it to them.

DANNY HUTTON When we ended up with Reb Foster Associates, they had Steppenwolf, who were huge. So it wasn't really like the payout from The Turtles [to get out of the management deal with Foster] was paying for us to get started. Probably from Mark's perspective it was, but we came in late in the game. Utley was already in Beverly Hills with the big offices and all these groups, so we were just another one-off until we started having some consistency.

FELIX CAVALIERE I hate to be naive, but I've never really understood that lack of paying the people who sing and play. I guess there's just not enough money for these people to spread around. In their eyes, they have to keep every dime. It was like that on Atlantic with The Rascals. It's like that everywhere. I don't get that, but that's what's there. And most of us are right brain/left brain heavy, and we're not really good at those things. So, we have to hire people, and then you're at the mercy of how trustworthy they are. But the more you take an interest in learning your craft—which obviously Mark did—the more you understand exactly what these guys are doing, and you have a voice in it. A lot of musicians say, 'Don't bother me. I just want to play my music, man.' And then they get ripped off. I mean, it's your fault. So, I don't blame anybody. That's the way it is.

RICK CARR I've seen that so many times throughout the years. It's just business, and if you are going to be in the rock'n'roll business, you expect it. When I started out at seventeen years old, I had no clue of how nasty things would get, but as I worked my way up, I saw people getting screwed over constantly. I got screwed over a few times, and I'd go, 'Gee, why'd they do that?' And I realized it's a part of the business. For all the years of doing this professionally, I know exactly what Mark is saying. It's just business.

TOPPING THE CHARTS

FELIX CAVALIERE We didn't know 'Groovin'' was going to be a #1 record, but people in the room did. Murray The K was in the room, and he knew. He went to the record company, who did not like the idea of us not having a drum on that record. We have a conga on the record, so we were messing with the formula.

RUSS GIGUERE 'Windy'? Oh yeah, I knew it would reach the top. As we were recording the song, it occurred to me that Chicago is the windy city, and I said out loud, 'This is going to kick butt in Chicago.' We recorded it right up to the end. We left the studio and got on a plane and went around the world, literally. Over the next few shows, they released the record, and it became a giant success and we had to learn the fucking song, because we had not had a chance to add anything to the set. So we had to add it right then, and the next show during the soundcheck we put it all together and did it that night. Pretty weird, huh?

RAY MANZAREK We knew 'Light My Fire' was going to be a #1 hit. Absolutely. We had played the song over and over on the Strip. The Doors opened for The Turtles at the Whisky. They were on their way up at that point, because the Whisky was the club where all the visiting English bands would play, and bands almost ready for the top rung would play. The first week we played it—we were the house band in early summer—we knew.

CARL GIAMMARESE When the guy who wrote 'Kind Of A Drag' gave it to us, it was just him strumming an electric guitar that wasn't even plugged in. He just sang it real quick. I thought it was catchy, it had something to it, but after we recorded the basic track I realized that the hook is there in the first line of song—it's right there. We knew we had something and then our producer had the brains to add horns to it. That really made it sizzle. It changed everything in such a way that the track came alive. But it was a great song.

TOMMY JAMES Certain records, you just had this sense of predestination about them. With 'Crimson And Clover,' we made a strategic decision that we were going to produce our own records and write our own songs. It was a departure from how we had done business before. We basically got rid of our producers at that point, and began doing everything ourselves. And we knew we had to, because that was the only way we were going to be taken seriously as artists. The whole single came together in about five and a half hours, and we just knew. Everyone who heard it just loved it. We really felt we were working on something unique. It was important for us on so many different levels. It turned out to be our biggest single, but it also allowed us to have another half of our career.

RON DANTE We worked on 'Sugar, Sugar' longer than any other Archies record. Usually it was twenty minutes, this one took a couple of hours. Jeff Barry, the producer and writer, worked on the rhythm track a lot longer than he usually worked. He kept rewriting the bass part, and the acoustic guitar wasn't sounding right, so they replaced that, and I worked on the vocal a little harder in terms of time taken and approach. So, we knew we had something, but you could have knocked me over with a feather when it became #1 around the world. I thought it was maybe going to be a hit in America, but it transcended the language and became #1 in almost every country. It was amazing. People didn't care that they couldn't understand the words, they just liked the sound.

ALICE COOPER When I heard 'School's Out' at the playback, I knew it was #1. And that's only happened once to me, and that was on that song. I think that maybe you get one of those in your life. The Beatles had 400.

DANNY HUTTON Three Dog Night had three. 'Mama Told Me Not To Come,' I thought that would go to #1. Now, we're talking about Randy Newman—a Randy Newman demo—okay? But when we got into rehearsal, it started. We flipped it and did things to it. Then in the studio, we were doing the choruses— doubling the choruses—and I knew. I knew that one was happening.

'Joy To The World'? No way! Are you kidding? That was like, *What!?* We were working in the studio, and Hoyt Axton comes in. He's this big, huge guy, all sweaty and says, 'I want to play you a song. Check this out.' Hoyt had this big baritone voice, plus, he's not like a real virtuoso guitar player, so he kind of bangs on the guitar and sings, in his rough baritone voice, 'Jeremiah was a bullfrog.' We ended up doing it. Our guitar player and bass player came up with some really hooky things. We put the album out, and they released one or two singles first. We just thought it would be an album track. All of a sudden, DJs from across the country started telling us they were getting requests for the song, so, okay, let's put it out. And eleven million records later ... what the hell is going on? Who knew? You just never know.

I knew 'Black And White' was destined for the top. I was in Holland and I heard it on the radio and went, 'Oh my god, what a great, hooky chorus.' I found out who it was, went home and waited about four months, and nothing. That's the time when records would fall through the cracks, so I went, 'Let's do it, man. This song is great.' So that one, when we did the basic track, we all looked at each other and went, 'Ooh yes—that's *real* interesting.' It was one of the early reggae records.

MICKY DOLENZ They knew in the studio that it would go to #1? I find that hard to believe. You can *hope* it's going to go to #1, you can plan for it and you can do your best, but to say that you *know* you're going to have a hit record, or a hit movie or a hit TV show or a hit book? If it was that easy—if there was that kind of formula—you'd never have a flop.

AM/FM

The rules were changing fast, and this year's shiny new thing was not always relevant twelve months later, so the jump from AM to FM was what we really wanted to do. Everybody was hoping to bridge over from being a singles act to an FM artist. AM radio was a two-minute-and-thirty-second lifespan, and FM radio was full of albums, and you wanted to be respected by your peers by making that transition. We wanted to be accepted in FM radio.

MARK LINDSAY Once FM came along, bands like us no longer mattered. It became embarrassing to be commercial. If it wasn't being played on FM, it was, like, old-school. We were still having chart records, but our peers . . . there were spears from our peers. You wanted big long album cuts that were obscure and multilayered and slightly hard to fathom. There had to have a lot of hidden meaning in the groove, so the audience didn't just listen and say, 'I got it.' You'd listen to it and say, 'Oh, I really see what they are doing here, wow, yeah.'

PEPPY CASTRO We toured with The Who and Herman's Hermits in '67, and it was clear the Hermits were at the end. By the time you put The Blues Magoos out there with their electric suits, and then The Who comes on and destroys the gear, the audience was just dumbfounded. So 'I'm Henry VIII, I Am' was a real letdown. What was funny was the audience was split. Half were these whacked-out hippies who were there to see The Who and the Magoos, and the other half were parents bringing their kids to see Peter Noone. The parents were shocked, but it sold tickets. I don't think Peter understood. I don't think anybody in that position thinks that it's ever going to end, but FM was coming on strong, without a doubt.

Later, I did the lead in *Hair* on Broadway. I had come off the hit record, so they hired me very quickly. Mark and Howard were offered parts in *Hair* in L.A.? Oh, they would have been perfect. Mark would have been a perfect Berger and Howard would have been a perfect Claude.

TOMMY JAMES In August of '68 we went out on the road with Hubert Humphrey, who was running for president. When we left to go on the campaign, the hot acts on Top 40 radio were The Rascals, The Turtles, Gary Puckett, The Buckinghams, The Grass Roots . . . when we came back, ninety days later, it was all albums. It was Joe Cocker, Crosby, Stills & Nash, Led Zeppelin, and Neil Young. The industry turned inside out in those ninety days. It was that fast. Almost overnight, there was this mass extinction of so many of my friends. As a culture, we went musically from Lesley Gore to Led Zeppelin in three years.

MARK PARENTEAU They were in that period between being Top 40 and FM radio: did you want to have a Top 40 single, or did you want to sell albums and be a touring group that people would go see? I mean, 'Elenore' was a wonderfully crafted song, but just a little too Top 40, so The Turtles definitely were pigeonholed. Even though they were hippies and had long hair, they weren't like other bands that were able to make that transition, like Eric Burdon with The Animals. He went from Top 40 well into the FM thing, and there were bands that went opposite, that started as Fillmore-type bands, like Alice Cooper, and went to Top 40. But they never were able to bridge that gap as The Turtles, and it's too bad, because musically they always had a lot to offer.

HARRY SHEARER   I don't think The Turtles were seen by the FM cognoscenti—the B. Mitchel Reeds of the world—as still relevant. There was a kind of unspoken but very strict hipness code. And as guys who had first come to public prominence as Top 40 hitmakers, they violated rule #1 of the hipness code. Your approved way of getting ahead was do some artsy albums, and then, hopefully, you get some underground airplay. And they had violated that code by becoming Top 40 hitmakers. It was typical of what was going on in the youth culture in general at that point. It seems goofy, and yet when you look back on it from this vantage point, the idea of some skepticism for the 'machine' seems almost charmingly quaint.

FELIX CAVALIERE   I think that we all—everybody—attempted to adapt to the marketplace that was burgeoning in terms of FM radio. The record companies really promoted that. They wanted you to become a so-called album act, because obviously they make more money off an album than they do off a single. It's interesting that the marketplace has kind of rejected that whole album concept. Primarily because they're sick and tired of buying ten songs when they only like one. There's a tremendous backlash.

DANNY HUTTON   There was a time when you'd get hounded for that. If you did a cover, you were not considered hip.

PAUL WILLIAMS   Basically, I have a lifetime of writing codependent anthems. All these guys that are in this book are at the hardcore center of the rock'n'roll world and all. I was living in Laurel Canyon and writing for The Carpenters, God bless them, and a lot of middle-of-the-road, codependent anthems.

You know, *Ouch! Mommy* songs: 'I'm nothing without you ... Pick me up and love me!'

RAY MANZAREK Times change. I can imagine they wanted to be dark and heavy and psychedelic, too. But they just weren't. That's not who they are. They're great singers and they're fun to watch onstage. I always thought of them—and I'm sure they'll be offended—as the Tweedle Dum and Tweedle Dee of rock'n'roll.

JIMMY FINK They had hit singles and they were famous, but their albums were not the sort of deep, meaningful things some people were putting out. They were not part of album-oriented-rock, although I personally believe that they have some pretty deep and meaningful songs, aside from the 'Elenore's and the 'Happy Together's.

JIM PONS Everybody was trying to be like The Beatles, and they were writing their own material. What it meant to be a rock band was changing. You were supposed to be doing what you believed. And what you believed, you wrote. Big mistake.

DON CUSIC Just like The Byrds, The Turtles covered a Dylan song. It was okay to cover Dylan. But it wasn't okay to be a pop act. It wasn't cool to be commercial. And The Turtles were commercial. There was a very serious undertow that an act couldn't be an entertainer: they had to be an artist. The Beatles and Dylan merged the idea that if an artist did not write, they were not authentic. So, therefore, The Turtles were not authentic. Even though they ended up writing their own material, they weren't the big impact songs. They kind of fell in the crack between not quite bubblegum and not the underground stuff. They were hipper than the vocal groups like The Association, but they had great harmonies. So, it's quite a mess to sort out.

It was hard to peg The Turtles during that period. In terms of historical perspective, I think the *songs* were more influential than The Turtles as a group, because there were The Beatles and the Stones—the elite groups—and then there's everybody else. They kind of got lost in the shuffle with all those other groups, like The Hollies and The Bee Gees. That's why the songs were bigger than the group. Everybody knows the songs, but they don't always know who did them.

JOHNNY BARBATA I didn't see it going anywhere when they started to write their own stuff. It didn't sound that good, and, other than 'Elenore,' they never wrote a hit. Even that was a joke, but it turned out to be a big smash-hit single. I love it. Next to 'Happy Together,' it's their second-best song. It's recorded really well, and it was another shuffle. And that was my idea, because 'Happy Together' was a shuffle.

JIM PONS Johnny got to be a little irritable. He started to think of himself as the star of the show, demanding more airtime, more publicity, longer solos ... he thought he was pretty special. He wanted us to dress differently and eat better, and all the things that were funny in the beginning became tedious. Then John Seiter comes along. We had become friends with John during shows with Spanky & Our Gang, and when we decided we couldn't take it anymore from Barbata, Seiter was the obvious choice to replace him. He was just like us—easygoing and funny and relaxed—and we said, 'Let's get John in here instead.' Not thinking how different it was going to be.

DENNY JONES Johnny definitely made an impression, because he would flick his sticks, and he was flamboyant. He also had an ego that wouldn't quit. But if you've seen footage of The Turtles, you definitely know that Mark was the real front guy. There was no question about that. You never really focused on the drummer because Mark was all over the stage, always running around, throwing his tambourine way up in the air, and sometimes he'd have to jump off the stage and run into the audience to catch it. He was doing those kinds of things all the time, but it never took away from how great their harmonies were. Howard and Mark used to come together, and Al was the perfect fit on guitar: understated. But the drummer never got off the drum throne. So, although Johnny would be more of an attention-getter because he was flashier, I never thought of it being a drop in quality with Seiter. Seiter wasn't the greatest, but he was solid. He just didn't have the flair.

JIM PONS The record company didn't want us to fire Barbata, because he was a great drummer. He was the driving force on all those hit records. But we didn't care about what they thought. We didn't listen to anybody. We wanted to do everything our way.

JOHN SEITER I was born in St Louis. Right out of high school I went to Los Angeles and played with a little blues trio until I got an offer to go on the road with a folk band. I was an R&B guy. I didn't know what folk music was. I'd never heard it. I'm eighteen. I go to this rehearsal in Laurel Canyon, and it's Judy Henske. She'd had some folk hits and was coming off her second album. I had never heard of her, obviously, but I got the gig, and the next day we drove to Cleveland. After that we played in Chicago, and that's where I met Spanky, because she was a fan of Judy's. And that's where I met Odetta.

When we got back to L.A. I played with Tim Buckley. Herb Cohen was managing, and he was managing the Mothers at the same time. The Mothers were playing in New York, and we got the opening slot, so the four of us drove from Los Angeles. We get there, and Tim is opening for Frank. Jac Holzman [Elektra Records head] came backstage and announced to us that we are about to play our last gig, because they were going to make Tim like Bob Dylan. They were going to make him a solo artist. As it turned out, he went on to have another band, a jazz kind of band. But that was our last gig.

Now, I'm in New York and out of a gig. I'm living downtown with the Mothers in the Van Rensselaer Hotel, and I see a sign for Odetta at the Village Gate. She was looking for somebody to go on the road, and I was lucky enough to get that gig. She knew I was a folk guy. I was playing a lot of brushes and sometimes just tambourine. I couldn't be too loud, but in those days it was wide open. You could do anything. We came out to the coast and did an album, and after that we played at the Apollo in Harlem. I'm the only Caucasian in the building. It's summer of '67, with Wilson Pickett and Sonny Terry & Brownie McGee, and there I am with my Beatles haircut, and the crowd was nasty—they called her out about having a white drummer: 'Whose side you on, baby?' They were a rough crowd, and you never knew what was going to happen.

Odetta's manager knew Spanky. She told her that she was downtown at the Bitter End and would like her to come by. I went along, and their act just killed me. I went backstage and said, 'Your act is great, but your drummer sucks.' Spanky said, 'That's good, because he can't travel with us. So, you want the gig, you got it.' I accepted that night. I just knew that I had to be part of it. I joined the circus, basically. We took off right away. We did all the television shows and we opened for everybody: The Turtles, The Rascals, The Association, anybody who was out there, really.

SPANKY MCFARLANE Was Mark partially responsible for breaking up Spanky & Our Gang? Well, in a way that was true. They courted my drummer, John Seiter, and probably offered him more money, but he became interested in one of the band member's wives. So that kind of lured him away from us. So I guess Mark could take some credit, on a deceitful level, of sneaking around, trying to court John. But John, of course, was his own man and could make up his own mind, and he did. He did leave, and he did pursue one of The Turtles' wives. I just say, 'No, no, Nanette.' He'll hate me for saying that.

JOHN SEITER That had nothing to do with why I joined The Turtles. I'd never even met her when I joined the band. That came after. We had a relationship, yes. I had a relationship with her for sure. We did get together and lived together, but that wasn't my reason for joining the band. When I joined I didn't know her.

JOHNNY BARBATA I had played with the Joel Scott Hill Trio before. I loved playing R&B and blues, so I left The Turtles and went back to Joel and we made an album called *L.A. Getaway*. We had Booker T. and Leon Russell and Dr. John and Chris Ethridge. I mean, I'm playing with much better musicians. It was my decision to leave, and they never liked that. There was a little animosity. Mark and Howard were in the Troubadour and made a remark—and I love the guys, but this is kind of funny—'What's he going to do next? He's finished now.' And I got with Crosby, Stills, Nash & Young, the biggest group in the world. But that was cool. And later, when I was with the Jefferson Starship and The Turtles opened for us, I sat in with them.

JIM PONS Funny how everyone remembers things the way they want to. Unfortunately, the way I remember it—very vividly—we told Johnny we wanted to replace him. We were in Howard's living room in the Hollywood

Hills, and I'm pretty sure he was there with us to discuss it. Our paths were beginning to go in very different directions, and he may very well have been intending to join Joel and Chris. We had had our feelers out for John Seiter for quite some time, and we notified him that he was in that very same day.

JOHN SEITER The phone rang one night, and it was Mark. He said, 'Johnny is leaving, and we've always been four fingers and a thumb, and we want to be a whole hand. Are you interested?' That's exactly what he said. And they *were* kind of four fingers and a thumb. Johnny had his own publicist and was doing his own thing. They'd go to the gig in the same limo, and Johnny would have his own limo. I was already a friend, I knew them all, and we always had a good time hanging out, so I said yes. But I don't know why they called me, because I thought I was absolutely the wrong call, musically, for this gig. I didn't play like Johnny at all and I wasn't a rock'n'roll guy. I didn't listen to rock'n'roll.

JIM PONS The difference between Johnny and John was pretty obvious from the first studio session. I hate to say it, but it was.

JOHN SEITER I didn't have the chops that Johnny had. I was totally trying to mimic, to play like the record sounded. That's all. I was playing the book, at least initially. They asked me if I wanted to play a solo during the gig, because Johnny always played a solo, and they got to leave the stage for fifteen minutes and take a break. I said, 'Absolutely not!'

Johnny was like Gene Krupa: Johnny had his own little show. I said, 'No, man, no! Come on, dudes . . . no way.' I'd gone from a six-piece band to a power trio. It was just Al and Jim and me, and I'm playing so loud and so hard. It's just balls to the wall, every tune.

AL NICHOL We spent hours sitting around working out vocals, and when Seiter joined, that added a whole new dimension. John Seiter was very conscious of group harmonies, because he had come from Spanky & Our Gang. We could arrange a four-part background behind Howard's lead voice.

JIM PONS Our first gig with John was the White House. It was huge. The

Secret Service met us at the airport with the limousines. We had tours of parts of the White House that nobody was ever allowed to go into. We were pretty much on our best behavior. There was no alcohol, but we managed to sneak coke in. Somehow, we did that. And while sitting on a table in one of the rooms they left us alone in, we snorted cocaine off the bust of Lincoln. I do remember that.

DENNY JONES The *New York Times* had a headline and a big front-page picture of The Turtles with Tricia Nixon. She said they were her favorite band. We played the East Room and The Temptations played the other end of the hall, and I mixed both bands. In a funky tuxedo I rented in Reseda, which seemed to add a little more luster to it. Imagine Mark and Howard walking around in their tuxedos mingling with these people.

HOWARD KAYLAN After the White House, The Turtles somehow elevated ourselves to a position where it was okay to hire us for big social occasions, because, after all, we were Tricia Nixon's favorite group. If we had played the White House, we could play anywhere. However, things in the band were not so great. Drugs were very much still a part of our lives, at least in my case, and I really didn't like the direction that the band was going in. Al and Jim were taking the group into sort of a country direction, and then White Whale started coming up with material that I didn't like very much. When we started going away from pop music and turning country, I was distraught.

DENNY JONES Howard was furious, because where they were playing totally went against the grain from where they were at that time. They played this big elaborate place with all these people showing up in limousines, and The Turtles are playing for their daughter; this graduation party for the daughter of U.S. Steel. I remember that like it was yesterday. It was around the pool, a pool party.

HOWARD KAYLAN I had done LSD two or three nights before, but I hadn't slept, and I hadn't really come down. And while the performance itself was acceptable, I couldn't understand the audience reaction. We had just come off three or four giant hit records in a row. We had just played the White House.

We were at the top of our form, and yet we would finish our songs, and there wouldn't be any applause at all. You'd just hear the clicking of plates and the chattering of little teenage girls. And their parents over in the corner, belching and making stock deals and stuff. Normally, this wouldn't bother me. It's a normal day in suburbia. But at that particular time, it was the straw that broke the camel's back. And I was not afraid to go right into the microphone and call these people out by name and just go, 'You lousy hypocrites!'

The band just stopped in their tracks, obviously. I mean, if I heard that coming out of the PA system, *I'd* stop in my tracks, too. And I didn't stop there. I went on, and I gave quite a tirade: 'You son-of-a-bitches have no idea what you're doing, You capitalist pigs! You Republican bastards! What's happening to America?' I mean, I went nuts. I threw the microphone into the pool along with a bunch of lawn chairs. And I kicked and I stormed my way out, and I quit. I just went home and I quit.

I sat there in my house, not really knowing what the hell was going on, stewing in my own juices. Angry for what I had done, but angrier about what everything had turned into. I really didn't like where anything was headed. I hated the direction of the band and the music. I didn't like working for 'the man,' and our Nixon association had been highly publicized. We were becoming like the Lester Lanin of rock, and I was bitter about it. I didn't regret what I had done, but I was well out of the band. And the problem was I had cut myself off from my only income stream. So, things were not looking too rosy.

It was maybe six weeks later when I finally decided to see what was going on. I had no intention of re-joining or anything, I just wanted to see what they were doing. I popped over to Al's house, and everybody was busy at work on their own songs. Songs that would later become *Turtle Soup*. And it was amazing to me. Not because I thought I was particularly great, but that everybody was doing their own thing. That all of a sudden Al had his songs he was working on. Mark had his songs he was working on. And so, fine, that's the way it should be. There isn't a focal point to the band and you guys might as well do your own thing. It'll probably work. Good luck, congratulations. I think you found something there. More power.

I got ready to leave, and I think Jim was the guy that said, 'Hey, you want back?' 'What?' 'You want back in? I mean, you wouldn't have to do very much now, 'cause we're all just gonna do our own stuff, but if you wanna be a part of this new record, we're kind of more a democracy now. So, if you wanna write a couple of songs, and be a part of the new project . . .' 'What the hell, why not?'

So, I came back to the band, with those mitigating circumstances, knowing that it wasn't gonna be the same as it was before. That I put myself in a position of supplication, for lack of a better word.

KEN BARNES Democracy is rarely a good idea. Just look at how Creedence broke up: they did one democratic album, and it was far below their usual standards. Without Howard? That would have been quite an un-commercial album.

CHIP DOUGLAS They were getting into their real sort of hippie phase, with the moustaches and the long hair and all of that stuff. We had done *Battle Of The Bands* and were going to talk about doing some more things. I said, 'The way I see it, fellas, you've got to feature Howard more as the lead singer on all the tunes on the album. You know, a little more of Howard, and Mark with that high harmony.' That was the sound that I was most stoked about, that's the way I liked to hear music. One guy sings lead, and he's the signature sound of the band, and then another guy will sing harmony.

Howard was clearly the voice of The Turtles. He did all the hits, and so I was suggesting we maybe make the album a little more like that, get Howard singing on a few more songs. And I'll never forget, they all almost unanimously looked at me and said, 'No, Chip, that's not the way we see it. We're a family here. We all must have an equal part in everything, and we divide everything five ways. So no, we don't agree. Everybody gets to sing a song.'

I look back on *Battle Of The Bands* and I wouldn't want to see it any other way. And to have made a subsequent album—which I wanted to do at that point—would have been great. You can start looking for some really good tunes that would be potential hits, and stuff like that. But that was the end of my working with them.

JIM PONS Chip knew what would work. He also knew what wouldn't. He knew we were stepping outside of our natural abilities. We decided we were going to mix it up. We demanded that freedom.

DANNY HUTTON Yeah, that sounds like the Vanilla Fudge scenario. You get to the third or fourth album, where either you turn it into democracy, where you let some schlub in the group put in two songs that suck, or you stick with what works.

HENRY DILTZ Before that, there were the songwriters and there were the singers. But that joined together somewhere in the middle of the 60s. So that added a whole other thing, and it doesn't work. You lose your focus. And that's the problem: everybody wants to write their own songs. Some people did really well, and others didn't. Just because you're a writer . . . look at Frank Sinatra. Elvis didn't write any songs. And Linda Ronstadt didn't write any of her songs.

JOHN SEITER They had been a surf band, and they had been a showband, and they were successful and able to work, but they really wanted to write their own songs. They wanted to be Buffalo Springfield, and they weren't.

Here's how that all went down: Al had a garage that was empty, and we set up and started writing. This guy would have a verse, and this guy would have a bridge, and this guy would have some sort of melody thing, and a lot of those songs were Frankenstein kind of tunes. That's why they're so weird. All of a sudden, the bridge goes somewhere totally out there. That's because it was Al's bridge and it was Mark's verse. Well, sometimes that works, and sometimes that doesn't work. But we were experimenting, and we did the best we could.

What did it sound like? We sucked. We were terrible, man. The record company would say, 'What is this shit? What happened to this hit machine? What happened to The Turtles?' Well, what the company didn't understand, is, that *was* The Turtles. Those five guys—me included—that's what we came up with. That's what we sounded like, and they didn't like that. They *really* didn't like that.

HOWARD KAYLAN It was the stupidest thing we ever did. The only thing we had going for us was that so-called 'Turtles' sound. The Turtles sound was soft into loud, it was my airy voice into the screaming chorus, it was the jangling guitars and the big orchestra. There was a formula, and it had worked since the first record through 'Happy Together,' through 'Elenore.' It was the same formula. We knew what we sounded like and to screw with it was absolutely stupid. It was taking another shot at stardom and throwing it away. The Turtles were really good at that. We tossed success at every turn. Just when we had a production company that was delivering nothing but Top 5 records, we'd dump 'em. That's just the way we were.

AL NICHOL We scattered ourselves over so many different styles that it was a detriment in the end, because it made us more or less style-less. We had a lot of records, but each was different from the one before. All that jumping around probably kept us from being catapulted up into the realm of Led Zeppelin or whoever. We were too scattered; we could sound like anything we wanted to at that point, and we very often did. It was a positive as far as our own artistic development, of course, but it diminished the 'star' image. We didn't get in the Rock and Roll Hall of Fame or get our star on Hollywood Boulevard, or any of those. But we did have a lot of #1 records. People bought the records.

JIM PONS The live shows could be interesting. I'm pretty sure we dressed in lounge-act-like costumes with matching blazers and greased-back hair for the Miami Pop Festival. When we played at the Fillmore East, Creedence opened for us, and we had a bunch of topless dancers come out onstage for an encore on that show. I have a picture of that, so I know that's true. I don't remember where we got them, or why we thought we needed them or why we used them, but I remember them coming out on the last number.

DONNIE KISSELBACH I saw The Turtles in '69. I took my high school girlfriend— we were juniors. I saw them with Three Dog Night and Hoyt Axton in Allentown, and they were just great. They didn't even have a keyboard player, they played all the hits, and there were no holes in it. That took a lot of balls. They just went out there and made it work. Everybody was singing and there was just one guitar, bass, and drums. It was unbelievable. I'll never forget it.

JOHN SEITER There was a lot of sleight of hand when we played live, because it was just a trio: a rhythm section and one guitar. But we pulled it off. Al made every tune sound different. He got everything out of that one axe. Al was the short guitar player who sang background, Pons looked good and played okay, but he was just kind of there, and I did my thing. Howard had the voice, but he didn't make a lot of moves, either. He walked up to the microphone and sang the hits, sang it just like the record.

Mark was the show, there's no doubt about it. His stage persona was very, very, important. He was funny and did weird shit, did his thing with his tambourine and was all over the place. He had his look, his tie-dyed shirts, and was just full-on Mark at every moment. You couldn't ask for a better diversion, if you will. There was always something going on.

END OF THE ROAD

The final album released during the band's lifetime, *Turtle Soup*, was a major change in direction. This time, lead vocals were shared between members and Chip Douglas was out as producer, replaced by Ray Davies of The Kinks.

CHIP DOUGLAS You gotta have those hit singles in there to sell an album.

HOWARD KAYLAN Evidently, my hardcore stance on the establishment and the Republican pigs was the wrong way to go. 'Sorry, I won't be political anymore. I'll just shut up and do what I'm told.' So, The Turtles that recorded *Turtle Soup* was that group. It was me shutting up and not having any real say in the band or the politics of the band. The only thing we could agree on at that point was that we wanted Ray Davies, and that was enough of a focal point to make that album work.

JIM PONS Ray didn't give us a whole lot of time. He came for ten days and then another ten days. He wasn't able to stay longer than that, but when he was here, he spent all of his time working with us. I'm embarrassed now to think of what we gave him to work with. These were songs that we had written, and he's one of the great songwriters. But I got to be real good friends with him.

JOHN SEITER They idealized Ray, but he didn't have any real input. Other than having his name attached, I can't see what his contribution was. They thought he'd be great for the whole process, and that it would actually make a difference. They put out a whole album, and none of them were hits. Nothing made it on the chart—nothing. I joined the band when 'You Showed Me' was

#1 in the nation, and we never had another hit. I tell people that I joined the band and it went down the tubes. But the real reason it stopped was because we didn't do the formula. We did Al's garage, and the stuff that came out of Al's garage was not hits and nobody cared, because the material wasn't there.

JIM PONS Seiter thought he'd been strung along. He'd been taken out of Spanky & Our Gang, into a group that was dying and involved in lawsuits. He really resented Mark and Howard because we never had any hit records after he joined. We wanted to, and we thought he was capable enough. He wasn't as good as Barbata, but he was more like us than Johnny was, and that's why we liked him. We all liked John a lot but let's just say, playing with Barbata was wonderful.

JOHN SEITER The phone would ring, and Mark says, 'Be ready in a half hour, we're going to pick you up.' 'Okay, what's up?' 'We're going to fire our agent today.' And the van would show up and I'd get in the van, and sure enough, we went somewhere and we fired somebody. And one day it was the manager. We fired the manager, and we fired the agent, and these are people that had been with them for a long time. I don't know if they all talked it over and then the word went down. Nobody ever said anything to me. I was the new guy; I was not involved in any of that. I would just be told to be ready for the van to come by.

HOWARD KAYLAN After the Ray Davies album, we went back into the studio to do our final work with Jerry Yester on an album, but they locked us out of the studio and we weren't allowed to complete the record. It came out eventually, but unfinished, after we left the label. That was headed back into the right direction. It was starting to improve.

JOHN SEITER I'm not sure that we were very in touch with the sliding scale of reality at the time, about how things were perceived and what was really going down. I'm not saying we were in denial. We may have been to a certain extent, but there was a cash cow, and we wanted that to all keep going, and the gigs were getting weird. They weren't good-time concerts, necessarily. It was a different thing, and it really changed everything.

DENNY JONES Then Seiter started sleeping with Jim's wife. I remember them being together in Reno. I was shocked to see that he was already traveling openly with her. She was out there on the road with us. Jim accepted it. I mean, he went along with it. My brother was there to help me with gear, and he was shocked. It was wide open in those years. You name it and it was available. Anything, from sex, drugs, rock'n'roll . . .

JOHN SEITER Carlos slept with both Al and Jim's wives. So, Carlos was very busy. Oh, man, it was the era. But it's an old story; those things don't change. I'm sure Woody Herman had those stories. Being on the road with a band is being on the road with a band.

DENNY JONES Carlos was chasing Al Nichol's wife. And she was from a little tiny town in Oregon. Imagine her parents—she was probably nineteen—letting her go with a rock'n'roll guy, just take off in a car and drive to California. She and Jim's wife got into all kinds of trouble with drugs and stuff. But Carlos was chasing her.

JIM PONS It was enormous fun to be on the road in a popular rock band during the sexual revolution. It's just that too much of anything has its consequences. For me, the one-night stands and the newness and variety of sexual encounters created an appetite for more of the same that lasted after the days of celebrity vanished. Not the best training for forming lasting relationships.

DENNY JONES The last show they did was March '70, up in Billings, Montana. I remember that distinctly. Even Pons didn't have the interest any more. I think Al did more than anybody. Al was more entrenched, because the other guys had options. Mark and Howard were more visible—people knew about them—but Al didn't have as much recognition. Not as many doors would open for him. The very month that they called quits was the very month The Beatles disbanded. It was April of '70, same month as The Beatles.

JIM PONS We broke up because we ran out of hits.

JOHN SEITER It was over. Changing everything took such a toll, and there was no success. Mark and Howard were moving on, and they were going to stick together. Because of the lawsuits, they couldn't use their real names, so they changed to Flo & Eddie, and Flo & Eddie—the Phlorescent Leech & Eddie— were our roadies, Carlos and Denny.

DENNY JONES Carlos was the Phlorescent Leech and I was Eddie. They called me Eddie because I looked like an all-American guy, and Carlos used to wear all these big flamboyant shirts and he had hair out to here—a big Afro—and he just looked like . . . a Phlorescent Leech. It was perfect. And I was Eddie. Just Eddie. Who the hell else could it be? We were the Phlorescent Leech and Eddie, and it stuck. And after The Turtles broke up, Mark and Howard started using the names.

HAROLD BRONSON In '91, Rhino put out a documentary on The Turtles, and what's interesting is that Howard and Mark are the whole show and everybody else, well, nobody is really that interesting. When you have that many people it corroborates their story, but it's almost like it would have been as good or maybe better without all those people.

The other thing I realized was that, generally speaking, they had consumed a lot of drugs in their lives, but what was remarkable was how good their memories were, how much they remembered. Even people who didn't do drugs at all had memories that weren't as good as theirs. For the most part, whatever Howard and Mark's recollection was, it was confirmed by what the others said. That would have been twenty or twenty-five years ago for a lot of that stuff, and for everybody's memories to be in the same place, that was really cool. You don't expect that.

AL NICHOL I saw [the breakup] coming, I just wasn't really ready. I didn't want it to happen, but it was clear that that this was the end. After that, it was a big party of legal eagles throwing contracts and lawsuits back and forth.

PHIL VOLMAN I wasn't surprised. They were very young. They were not too sophisticated yet, and the guys that they were in business with were crooks. It happened to a lot of people.

AL NICHOL When we broke up, the rest of us said we're gonna do this, that and the other, but Howard and Mark decided music was the only thing they knew how to do. So they were going to try to get the masters cleared free from White Whale. They stayed involved with the lawsuit, as well as releasing their own product with Flo & Eddie. So they took on a bunch of problems as well as responsibilities. It took about ten or twenty years for that to iron out to any kind of a substantial gain for them.

PHIL VOLMAN In retrospect, it's the best thing that ever happened to them, because as part of the court case, they got the masters. They controlled their own stuff from that point on. They got the masters, and they were able to sell all their stuff to Rhino. They didn't have to do anything. And it went to many other labels after that. They licensed it out for use. They owned it, and they own it to this day.

AL NICHOL We had a corporation where we sold each other all our shares; we sold our share for $5,000. Mark and Howard took the money that was left over from all of us paying and made a settlement with White Whale's lawyers in the bankruptcy lawsuit, so they were able to keep the masters. And so, really, everybody wound up with a fair deal at that point. Mark and Howard treated us fairly, but you get lawyers fighting with each other, and pretty soon whatever you want or stand for is out of the picture. And Howard and Mark were caught in the middle of that. They were actually caught in it more than I was or Jim Tucker or Jim Pons were, because they opted to carry licensing for the name and still wanted to use it.

JIM PONS I remember having my deposition taken, which was pretty grueling. I can't remember much after that. It went on well after I had parted ways with Mark and Howard. I had already decided to move on and sold my rights to The Turtles catalogue voluntarily. I have never looked back in regret.

JIM TUCKER I was bought out, but I still get royalties from before, whatever it is. TV commercials and all the other stuff, just what's due me. This guy approached us, and he gets half. We signed a contract and he gets 50 percent. In the last couple, three years, he's probably gotten about thirty or forty grand for me. He says, 'There's money out there for you.' He's doing it for Al and Portz. But Portz wasn't in on 'Happy Together,' and that's when the real money started. And Murray—the original drummer—died. I don't know about Pons—I've never asked him. And I don't know about Barbata—I've never asked him.

MADELINE CAMPILLO I hear 'Happy Together' every now and then, and I can see money falling from the sky.

With the band finished, players scattered in varying directions. Al was hit the hardest.

PAT VOLMAN Al was very intelligent. He was really a brainiac, like Howard.

HAROLD BRONSON When we put out the documentary, we couldn't find Al. Nobody could find him. I even put an ad in *Billboard*: 'If you know where he is . . .' And then, much later, he said he would have participated, but he didn't know about it. He kinda blamed it on his wife, or his ex-wife, at the time.

AL NICHOL After the band folded, I moved up to Humboldt County. I more or less semi-retired for a couple of years. I performed locally, but no big contractual things or recordings really, and then I got remarried and moved to Montana and put another band together. Our sound became Cajun country-rock, and we did lots of tours, mostly clubs. We had a pretty good name, but we didn't release any records. After I traveled for a while, my wife and I and our kids moved to Washington State, and I went out in the woods. I became a logger. After a while, I decided I was too old for that stuff, so I quit the logging business. And about that time, my wife and I were having problems. Not really serious, but we decided to call it quits and got a divorce.

Eventually, I bowed out of the music business and went to work in retail. And then I met another woman and got married again. I got involved with Sherman-Williams, and moved with the company over to Nevada, and worked thirteen years there. And then I took early retirement. I was gonna try to put together some music there, but it was chaos. Just wasn't working. So, I came over to California. I got my social security and retirement going, and about three years ago I got involved with Goodwill Industries. I'm just a clerk and a stock position. But I open and close the store. I'm back to working there, forty hours a week. I play whenever I can, with whoever I can, and I'm still doing a lot of writing.

HOWARD KAYLAN It was obvious from a very early age he was headed in that direction. When he was sixteen I knew what he was going to look like, and how he was going to act later on in life, because his father was a drunk. His mother was a drunk, and I don't say that in the most disparaging way. I say that knowing that my ex—my last wife—was a drunk. There are just people that I feel very, very sad for and the Nichols—John Nichol—I felt that way about him. I felt that way about Al growing up, and Al needed a crutch. Al always needed a crutch, whether it was a woman or whether it was a drink. He couldn't do it on his own. He would try to enlist our help. For instance, I co-wrote a lot of songs with Al. Songs that he could not have possibly finished on his own. I didn't do it out of the kindness of my heart or anything; he had some good ideas, it's just that he really, really couldn't think outside the box very much, and I think he was very inhibited by his upbringing. By what was acceptable in the Nichol household and what wasn't. He was already so outside of the box. His parents were both college professors, and Al blew away all of that stuff.

CHUCK NEGRON He was totally fucked up. I tried to get him into rehab but he wasn't ready to go. He's probably going to be one of the casualties.

AL NICHOL My father was chairman of the English Department at USC, and had been in the education system his whole life, so it was hard for him to relate to something else. Everybody said, 'How could you go off be a stupid rock'n'roll star when your father is a professor?' But eventually they got into it. My mother kept scrapbooks and was always supportive of what we were doing, and my father was always amazed as to just where I got musical talent when he had absolutely none. He and my mom both would come to our performances. When we performed at the Whisky with The Doors, they'd have a table right in the front.

JIM TUCKER I worry about him. He just don't know what he's doing. He just needs … I don't know. If something was to come together, something concrete, I think he'd straighten up.

JOHNNY BARBATA I'm one of the fastest drummers you'll ever see. I was on twenty hit singles and over a hundred albums. That's a lot of airplay. And I was actually in the groups, I wasn't just a studio musician. I did Linda Ronstadt, The Everly Brothers, and a lot of stuff you never heard; all kinds of stuff. Fortunately, for me, I still look great, and I can still play my butt off. I got all my hair. I'm a health freak, like Mark is, but I'm probably healthier than him, because I was doing it from back in the day. I was taking Nutrilite, which was Amway back then.

JOHN SEITER After The Turtles, I played on Tom Waits' first album, I was on Aztec Two Step's first album … but when it was over for me, it was really over. I did construction and all kinds of other things to make money. I could no longer say I'm this guy from the past.

JIM TUCKER I still play. I can still play, and there are people out there that want the originals to come back. Everywhere I go, people wanna see The Turtles do one last thing. I've talked to Barbata. I've talked to Al. Al's having a tough time with alcohol and stuff now, but he would straighten out. He's just trying to make music happen. And I know Pons would. Everybody would. But Mark won't let it happen. He says, 'I own everything. I'll sue. Nobody does anything without me. I'll sue.'

JIM PONS Al's called me a couple of times over the years when he's been drunk, and he wants to reform The Turtles, and he goes on and on, and I finally have to hang up on him. Poor guy. Al, Johnny Barbata, and Jim Tucker have spoken to me a few times about forcing ourselves back into the group, but it's been more about trying to cash in than getting back at Mark and Howard for some wrongdoing. I'm pretty sure everyone knows they were bought out fairly and squarely.

JIM TUCKER Howard and I always got along. It's just Mark. I'm sorry, but he's just selfish. It's all him and his band, and they were lucky to get in the band.

I don't know what his deal is. Nobody does. He screwed everybody, and he only calls when he wants something. When I talk to him, it's like, 'Yeah well, my band, my band.'

AL NICHOL Over the years, several other people have been trying to sell Turtles things to people, and Jim Tucker thinks that Howard and Mark were part of that. He thought Howard and Mark were somehow involved in getting money that we—the other members—weren't seeing. And that's not true.

JOHNNY BARBATA Mark had a great harmony voice and was a great entertainer. Just the way he moved, the big Afro, and he always had a smile on his face. He played the clown, and Howard was the circus announcer. And then you had a really showy drummer. So, when you saw The Turtles, you got a little more for your money than most groups. Not like The Mamas & The Papas, who stood there. We were entertainers, and we tried to be professional.

SIDE B THE SEVENTIES

6

FRANK ZAPPA

Concurrent with The Turtles' rise to fame, another L.A.-based act, Frank Zappa and his band The Mothers Of Invention, were blazing a singular path with a unique blend of high-grade musicianship, scathing sociological commentary, and a large dose of humor. Their debut, *Freak Out!*, was released in June '66, a year after 'It Ain't Me, Babe.' By the time Mark and Howard came on board four years later, Zappa had already released ten LPs. During their tenure, three albums were issued. Well over a dozen have appeared in the years since, with a steady release schedule continuing unabated.

We didn't plan on joining the Mothers, but it could not have been planned any better. Our relationship with Frank goes back to 1965 when the Mothers were in Bido Lito's. And we were at the live recordings for the *Freak Out!* album.

JIMMY FINK The Mothers Of Invention went off into topics and scenarios where your average band didn't go. I wouldn't even call them a band. They were something more. And especially the Flo & Eddie version. There was no other Mothers like that, no question about it.

ALICE COOPER It didn't surprise me when they ended up with Frank, because when they were out with us on the road, we'd spend all of our time doing movie trivia and TV trivia. But the amazing thing was, when you were with Frank Zappa, you had to have a memory like an elephant. You had to know how to read music, how to interpret his music, when to come in, because he did all these insane directions. He only picked the best of the best, so, to be a Mother, you had to be the best bass player, best keyboard player, the best horn player, the best drummer and the two best singers. Frank recognized greatness.

SHADOE STEVENS They really crossed over when they joined with Frank, because nobody was more out there or more respected as a brilliant musician than

Frank Zappa. When they joined The Mothers Of Invention and did 'Happy Together,' it was one of the great moments in music. I remember it vividly.

HARVEY KUBERNIK It didn't surprise me when they joined, because I saw the Mothers at the Shrine Exposition Hall in late '68, when Frank had the GTOs, Alice Cooper, and Wild Man Fischer onstage, and that kind of congregation was almost an open house party for Mark and Howard to join. It was kind of a logical extension of that. And *Battle Of The Bands* was kind of like a Zappa concept.

HOWARD KAYLAN Mark and I had been on the *Freak Out!* sessions. We were just two of the street bums that were hanging around and wound up at RCA Studios one night between midnight and six in the morning. I was drunk, and I have very little memory of being there, but I do know that the most oft-quoted line from that album is, '*I'd like to clean you boys up a bit. I'll make you as big as The Turtles.* A noted L.A. Disc Jockey.' And, of course, that was Reb. So, Zappa always knew who we were. You've got to remember that Frank was managed by Herb Cohen, and Herb Cohen was my cousin. So there's always been that link to the Zappa thing, even before I really knew it or took advantage of it.

I don't know if he was a fan of The Turtles going that far back, but you can look at the quote from Reb on *Freak Out!* In those days, The Turtles represented everything he was not trying to be. And Clive Davis said, 'No commercial potential.' Well, they were both right. Frank had no commercial potential, and if he'd only let them clean him up, he might have been as big as The Turtles. But I don't think Frank ever wanted to be that big. He didn't chase success—or, if he did, he wanted it on his terms, and the terms he eventually got it on were his.

DON PRESTON He always wanted better sales. The funny thing about Frank was, he would take some really strange song and tweak it and tweak it and tweak it until it was even stranger, and then put it out on a single, thinking that it was a hit. And it never happened, of course. And partially that was because of the way he promoted the band in the first place, us being these old, ugly guys playing rock music. I was the oldest one, and I was only in my late thirties.

AL NICHOL I wasn't surprised. All during The Turtles, we would get together with Frank for various little things, like at the Garrick Theatre in New York. And Gail and Frank lived right down the street: they had the big old log cabin up there in Laurel Canyon, and we'd go there all the time. We knew Frank and all the guys in the band, and we were all friends.

GAIL ZAPPA I already knew Jim Pons, but I didn't know Mark and Howard before I met Frank.

JIM PONS I used to go out with Gail, Frank's wife, before they got married. We used to date. We went out to dinner a couple of times, and I brought her to Santa Barbara to hear us—The Leaves—when we had the #1 record in California with 'Hey Joe.' I really liked her a lot. I mean, I loved her. I didn't know her that well, but I thought that she was a wonderful person.

GAIL ZAPPA We hung out together would be more accurate. He took me out to Santa Barbara for a concert and all that stuff. But we were just hanging out.

DANNY HUTTON I knew Frank right from '66. We were both young guys, and both just signed to MGM. We got along great. He was a very, very clever guy. But that persona . . . Frank was such a straight guy, but he had the ability to make himself seem very exotic. And he was really a straight-on, hard businessman. It's funny, but I never saw Frank as musical. I think he was like a mathematics genius, but he was no idiot savant. There are guys that will sit down on guitar and blow you away. You'll say, 'Wow, where does that come from?' 'I don't know, man, it's transmitted from the heavens or the spirit—it entered me.'

I don't think that ever, ever hit Frank. Ever. I could be completely wrong, but I always felt everything was so controlled, so written, so mathematical, and very smart. But, really, not musical. It wasn't Otis Redding, you know. Sometimes it was very successful. It was very, very clever, but not musical in that sense, although technically, of course, it's very musical. He could write all the notes, play all the instruments. He could do all that. But that little intangible thing . . . and that's why it's very hard to write a hit. That little funnel from wherever it comes from, I don't think he had that.

DON PRESTON In the first band, you had Jimmy Carl Black and Roy Estrada, and they couldn't read music. They didn't know anything about that, but somehow they managed to play songs like 'Little House,' where you had one part of the band playing 12/8 and part of the band playing in 11/8. And that was Zappa's magic, if you will—being able to pick people, maybe by luck. Even though they didn't know that much about music, they were capable of doing it. On the other hand, you had Art Tripp and Bunk Gardner and Ian Underwood. Art and Bunk had both played in orchestras before they got in the Mothers, and Ian was a concert pianist who also played alto sax. It was a strange combination of people, and I was kind of in the middle of all that. Before I joined, I had been in a group for about five years, playing in 19/8 and all kinds of time signatures.

JOHN SEITER When I was playing with Odetta at the Apollo, I was living with the Mothers at the Van Rensselaer Hotel. Billy Mundi and I shared a room, and I would come downtown and play with them after I finished up at the Apollo. Jimmy Carl Black wanted to be a trumpet player, and he would stand up in front with Bunk Gardner and play. But there had to be two drummers. Frank wouldn't allow him to get up unless there were two drummers. So, I would come down and play the last set. I hung around the Mothers all the time, for two, three years.

IAN UNDERWOOD I first saw the Mothers while they were at the Garrick Theatre. I didn't know anything about the band or Frank. I was just coming along in the evenings as an audience member. I had grown up playing classical music, and when I was around twelve I started playing Dixieland and jazz, so I had a background in both, but rock'n'roll was something I knew absolutely nothing about. I heard the Mothers, and it was all the kinds of music that I was interested in, done with humor and in a very, very interesting way, and it just seemed like something I wanted to do. It wasn't that I wanted to be in a rock'n'roll band. I really wasn't interested in being in any band at all, ever, and I wasn't even heading in that direction. Then I joined the Mothers.

When he finished *Ruben & The Jets*, he played it for Howard and me when we were in New York. We saw many, many shows at the Garrick. Frank would pull people out of the audience and they would play with puppets and all kinds of goofy stuff.

DON PRESTON We never had a set list. We never knew what we were going to play. Zappa would jump up in the air, and when he landed we were supposed to start playing with him, not knowing what song it was. And we usually wound up being right. Sometimes we would only do three songs during a three-hour concert, and the rest would all be improvised. That didn't happen with the second band.

HOWARD KAYLAN We must have gone twenty times. Those shows were fantastic. Of course, the great part is you never knew what you were going to get. One night you would walk in there and Frank would literally do nothing but make barfing noises for forty-five minutes. Depending on the way he felt, some nights he wouldn't even do music. He would just conduct the band in a freeform fuck-fest, for lack of a better word, and they would all just . . . attack a section of something, and Frank would look out and see if the audience appreciated it. 'Er . . . yeah, screw it.' And then just leave. You either got it or you didn't. Some nights were two-hour brilliant musical interludes that you've never seen or heard the like of before, and other nights were total throwaway theater pieces. And it didn't really matter what you got to see—they were all sides of Frank. And that impacted us. Of course it did.

IAN UNDERWOOD Just after I joined the Mothers, Frank booked his first European tour, and the first show we played was the Royal Albert Hall. So we went directly from the Garrick Theatre to the Royal Albert Hall, and Frank really started to get a feeling of responsibility to the audience. There were more people coming to see the band and it was clear that the kind of things that worked at the Garrick Theatre—which were very funny and oddball and quirky and worked really well with a very small space and a very small audience—that kind of humor doesn't have the same impact at all in the larger spaces. So, Frank wanted to organize things better. We still had the humor in the show, but it was not just something that might happen that might work. It was something that could not, to a certain extent, be repeated.

JEFF SIMMONS I was installed in the Mothers after my group broke up. Frank brought us down to L.A. from Seattle, and we played one gig at the Shrine and then we folded up. I was hovering, and Herb Cohen gave me a biker soundtrack [*Naked Angels*] to do while I sat there on retainer. I went to Frank's house to borrow a hundred bucks, and he said, 'Gail, make Jeff some spaghetti.' He listened to my solo album, which was bogged down, and helped me finish it. He actually played on a couple cuts and co-wrote some stuff with me, which now I look back on and think, *Man, no one wrote stuff with him.* I was operating on a lot of chutzpah and energy and probably not very sophisticated. I was pretty green.

Lowell George had left and taken Roy Estrada with him to start Little Feat, and after helping finish my album, Frank asked me to join The Mothers Of Invention. It was the old crew: Motorhead Sherwood, Ian Underwood, Billy Mundi, Ray Collins, Don Preston... the original guys, and we toured Fillmore East, Fillmore West. I was just getting my feet wet, and I was thinking, *Wow, this is kind of weird, to be in a kind of a sort of Fugs-like group.* I was all of twenty years old, so I didn't really know what I was doing or talking about. The old guys, especially Artie, resented the fact that all of a sudden here's this broccoli-haired folk-head sitting there. Jimmy Carl Black was brusque. But I can understand where they were coming from, in hindsight. They'd worked all these years with Roy, and Roy just booked.

GEORGE DUKE My first gig with Frank was at the Pauley Pavilion, doing *200 Motels* with Zubin Mehta. That particular show was more orchestral, so I was reading everything, and I enjoyed that because I was into the new classical music. That was no problem, but when Frank asked me to join the band, and actually come to rehearsal, the first thing he had me do was play a doo-wop lick. I started playing weird jazz chords over the singing, and he's saying, 'No, no, no! Wait a minute, man. Triads.' [*sings doo wop progression*] And that was where the rubber meets the road. That's the crux of the biscuit, as he used to say. I had to make a decision, because it was a world apart from jazz, and I was like a man out of place. I'd seen a lot of bands, so I was familiar with the rock thing, but I wasn't *in* it. It was the first time that I'd even come close to being in it. I made a decision to stay, and I got thrown into a whole new world.

JEFF SIMMONS I'm in there for about two months, and we do this gig at the Pauley Pavilion, with Zubin Mehta and the L.A. Philharmonic. This is May 1970. Aynsley is on board, and guys like Ernie Watts from the *Tonight Show* band were up there on the finale of 'King Kong.' I was just going, *Man, I shouldn't have smoked any hash before this gig.*

There was quite a bit of rehearsal before the gig. In fact, Don Preston was so *verklempt* that he was throwing up in the shower where Bill Walton probably had washed off just a few minutes earlier. *Don't make a mistake*—that's the motto. *Don't be out of tune.* And I learned the book from Ian by rote, because I didn't read. I'm up there on this plywood stage, practically passing out because I was scared green. The concert ends, and everybody's happy. Frank's in front, accepting accolades, and here comes three guys in tie-dye: John Sebastian, Howard Kaylan, and Mark Volman. Totally tie-dyed out, shirts and pants. And they're going, 'Frank, this is the best thing, we can't believe it.' I'm just a kid from Seattle who doesn't know squat. I'm going, *Whoa, that's the guys—they look different, kind of scruffier and more like hippies—but that's the guys from The Turtles and Lovin' Spoonful. This is Hollywood: anything can happen.*

GAIL ZAPPA Frank was not fond of writing lyrics. He hated the idea of writing them, but you can't just do straight music all the time. People are going to complain. You have to have some levity, and that's best done with lyrics, and that's an opportunity to make political statements and make fun of people who take themselves too seriously.

If you're going to have lyrics, the most important thing is to get the idea across. Sometimes, a singer you've hired may not understand, may not *get* a song in a certain way, and then it doesn't work. It's very difficult to find people that can really sell the song the way you intended it, and with Mark and Howard, Frank had a break there, because he could write anything and they could handle the material and had the right attitude. He could totally write for that. These guys were like clowns—they were funny and were always having a good time—but the difference was that they were extremely musical and extremely talented, and they had an interest in pushing the envelope.

They were perfectly suited for Frank, and they didn't know it, because I don't think they ever thought they were going to be able to do what they did. If Frank had put it to them, 'This is what you are going to do,' they would say, 'No, we can't do that.' But you get them in the door and then you start pushing that envelope, like George Duke: when he came into the band, he was never going to touch a synthesizer. There was no way he would ever do that. And that's true for anybody who has a career beyond playing with Frank. It's because their ego was of a suitable size not to get in their way. And they picked up what they'd learnt and took it to another level and another dimension for themselves.

JOHN SEITER When Mark and Howard joined, it was a perfect fit. They're ace performers and always were. No matter who's playing behind them, they were always tight and right on, and they were the perfect call for Frank, absolutely perfect. They took Frank to a place he'd never been before, and it was a great marriage; a great, great, marriage. And then they brought Ponsy in, and that was like The Turtles with Frank Zappa.

GAIL ZAPPA Frank was like the H.G. Wells of rock'n'roll: he could see things far into the future that other people didn't really see, and he could see Mark and Howard's potential just being in the room with them. He really liked their humor and was very interested in expanding the potential for what they could do, so he invited them to come to that show and see what was going on, and then they came over and talked about working together.

IAN UNDERWOOD I don't know that I would put it exactly that way, that he saw their potential. I think they were doing fine with their own potential. Frank looked at everything that came in front of him as an opportunity to use for his thought process, for his compositional structures and whatever. Mark and Howard had a certain kind of stage presence and sense of humor that really was dynamic and really was great onstage, and Frank was very happy to make use of that.

HOWARD KAYLAN I don't know where, I don't know when, but I'm assuming Frank saw The Turtles at some point, because he certainly knew. He knew the day that The Turtles broke up. At the L.A. Philharmonic gig, he gave us that offer. It wasn't 'join the band.' The first thing he said was, 'Listen, I'm having a barbeque Saturday. Why don't you guys come over and bring your horns,' meaning our saxophones, knowing as The Crossfires we had played, in Mark's case alto and in my case tenor sax. Somehow Frank knew this—I don't know how—but we went over to the barbeque with our saxophones to 'audition' for The Mothers Of Invention. With saxophones! Keep in mind, Ian Underwood was already in the band. It's ridiculous. He was one of the greatest reed players I've ever heard. And we were *honk-honk-honk-honk*. That was our expertise. We brought our horns, he gave us a bunch of things to see what our chops were, and after about three and a half minutes, he said, 'Yeah, all right, put those down. I don't think we'll be needing those.' It was the wisest decision he ever made. Ian Underwood was a brilliant sax player and I'm thrilled that we didn't have to perform musically with that band. Vocally, it was tough enough.

JEFF SIMMONS A couple of days later, Frank said, 'I'm thinking of putting The Turtles in the band.' And I went, 'You're so iconoclastic, this is a far-out band thing, that's like a commercial thing. You're not aligning yourself with that. This is not a good idea, Frank.' I tried to tell Frank it was a bad idea, you know. Mr. Jeff Simmons—fucking neophyte. It wasn't that I didn't like them, but it was kind of an AM thing, and a lot of girls bought their records. Thank God he didn't listen to me, because I didn't know what I was talking about. I was just a punk. As I've grown older and realized what the actual body of work was, prior to them even joining the Mothers, I was flabbergasted. It's just great stuff. But the perception back then was that it was a pop group.

AYNSLEY DUNBAR Frank saw me playing with my band in Belgium, and he brought me to America. Once I was here, I did all the gigs, basically. Mark and Howard came in a few months after me. I was against them being in the band at the beginning. When Frank said, 'The Turtles,' I said, 'Who the hell are The Turtles?' He said they sang 'Happy Together,' so I went, 'What are you doing with those guys in the band?' 'Well, you will be surprised.'

GAIL ZAPPA It came from the band internally as much as externally. People thinking that he just did comedy music. And Aynsley, that's just a reflection of Aynsley taking himself way too seriously anyway. And rightfully so—he was very talented—but you've got to open up. Aynsley came from the British blues scene. British blues? Excuse me, which comes from where, again?

AYNSLEY DUNBAR I was surprised. And I was really impressed. I enjoyed them being in the band. They were funny, they were very humane, and I was very English and very cold. If anybody came up to me and gave me a hug, I'd back off. But after being around those guys, I was all of a sudden forced into hugs all the time, so I sort of got used to it, which was . . . it was very interesting. I really enjoyed them. At that point, they really helped me release that terrible tension you get when you're English. Stiff upper lip, that sort of thing.

Once we joined Frank and he started becoming more successful, people stopped liking him because of us. We brought a certain kind of commerciality to it that Frank liked but his diehard fans didn't. I don't know what they were expecting, but there are certain fans from the early years who are vehement about how distasteful we were to the band, how much they disliked us being part of the Mothers.

AYNSLEY DUNBAR Most people were really serious. I played with John Mayall, who was absolutely serious. We had really serious musicians, and sometimes they forget that they are actually playing for people out there. But there was a real sense of entertainment that these guys brought to it. That was the best thing, and they made everybody laugh and kept everybody amused the whole time that we were out there. Working with Frank was a complete challenge. He came up with these parts: he'd have them doing two different vocal patterns against each other, going up and down, and he would conduct them, and they did it. And they did a hell of a job. So, in the end, I was really happy that they were in the band, because they made a big difference to it.

IAN UNDERWOOD I can understand, from Aynsley's background, if he said that. But for me, anything unusual that came along was interesting, because my interests were similar to Frank's. Something new and unexpected works fine for me, so I thought it was great when Mark and Howard joined. It was very different from the earlier band. Clearly, Mark and Howard were very accomplished in the world they were in and great onstage. Really great personalities. I thought it was terrific.

DON PRESTON Other than Aynsley, I can't think of anyone that wanted to be a pop star. We had too much fun lampooning it.

HOWARD KAYLAN We were already sorta clowns on the stage anyway. We were rock'n'roll clowns, and Frank knew this. It's not like he enlisted our talents because we were dull guys. If I'd been Roger McGuinn, I would not have been a Mother Of Invention.

JEFF SIMMONS Next thing I know, I go down on La Brea to this rehearsal place, where I meet Mark and Howard for the first time. They're early, and I'm there before Frank, too. What does Mark do? He grabs these rolling papers. I smoked weed already, and I knew Frank frowned upon stuff like that, but he wasn't real Jack Webb-ish at that point. We fired up this giant stogie—the three of us—and I realized this is the best thing that's ever happened. No one else in this group smokes weed, but these guys smoke *beaucoup* weed, and in that crystalline moment we become the dearest of friends. Mark turned to me within a week and said, 'Simmons, it seems like we went to high school with you.' Because we just got along. We were grooving. From that day forward we were kind of like the Three Musketeers.

The Turtles' decidedly relaxed attitude to rehearsals was a polar opposite of the Zappa gig.

GAIL ZAPPA For Frank, it was always about having a band that was really well-rehearsed and willing to follow you anywhere. And if the circumstances arose—that you had that situation combined with the audience paying attention and really feeling the energy of what's going on in the room—you had the potential to just go completely out there. And so they were prepared, they had additional bits of material that had been worked out, and then you had something to build on. So, if you wanted it take it out there, you could. They already knew where it could go, and then it was just the question of throwing the occasional thing in there, especially in those circumstances, that would catch Frank and make him laugh.

He'd never say, 'Here's your part, fit it in.' It was, 'Here's your part, sing it,' because everything had its place. Howard and I had studied singing in high school, and we had both played clarinet, so we could follow the charts to a certain level—when we sang, there was a semblance of order. We would get a piece of written music, like 'Wanda LaRue,' and even to this day I can sing it. It was music that, once you learned it, it was embedded in your skull, because you had read the notes, rehearsed it countless times, and by the time you are done with this, which was like a very classical piece, it was there forever. But there was also Frank trying to be a rock'n'roll band, and rock'n'roll bands don't sing notes written on a page. So, it was a combination of elements. You'd have one song really rudimentary rock, and the next one might be completely written out. So, for the next few minutes, you completely blow people's minds, because you're singing stuff that's jumping an octave, from the lowest to the highest point and then back down again, and there were always inversions to the natural instinct, which was to hit something that sounded normal. But Frank would write in such a fashion that we would sing it and sound completely dissident to each other, but in real musical terms it absolutely worked.

IAN UNDERWOOD Frank could ask them to do things, like singing certain notes in certain ways. Not just a note at a time, but certain kinds of singing that would be more closely thought of as being related to modern classical singing, as opposed to just straight pop singing. There wasn't anyone in the original band that could pull that off onstage. But Mark and Howard could do that, and so Frank was able to use that, usually in a more humorous way. Not like, *Okay, now we're doing a serious classical piece*, but it was still that kind of singing. Could anybody else previous or after that do that kind of singing? Not really, no.

GEORGE DUKE I preferred to look at the chart. To memorize all that stuff was just horrendous. But I had to, in the end, because Frank didn't allow any music onstage. That was a big change for me.

JEFF SIMMONS Rehearsals were very strenuous. We'd go twelve to thirteen days in a row before going out on the road, and it was very intensive, getting things tight. Mark and Howard were in the hot seat every day, because they're fronting the group. But those guys created for Frank a power that was something he hadn't had yet. I think that's why Frank made the move to Howard and Mark, because he saw what they were capable of.

Touring was where things really gelled.

GEORGE DUKE It was a dichotomy. He liked things that didn't quite go together, and Mark and Howard were absolutely perfect for Frank. A match made in heaven, so to speak. I'd never worked with two guys that were that proficient and that theatrical onstage. They could act out anything Frank could write.

And not only that, they came up with ideas. They fed Frank as much as Frank fed them, and so Frank would write stuff specifically based on stuff they would do offstage. The band became a display of our personalities. He even brought in the whole jazz thing with me. It was all part of it.

IAN UNDERWOOD Aynsley was different from other drummers. A more powerhouse, technical drummer, but also extremely musical. He's really a seriously musical drummer.

AYNSLEY DUNBAR All I'd ever do was improvisation. The Zappa gig was just a continuation, basically, of what I had done all my life. Most of my cues were from Frank, and for others, you just watched what Mark and Howard were doing, like the big drum roll before they threw the stuffed animal through the burning hoop.

JEFF SIMMONS Oh my God, it was the greatest, because you had those two guys, and then you've got Aynsley, who I'd listened to and worshipped on the *Hard Road* album by John Mayall. I was more aware of him than probably The Turtles, because my earlier groups were kind of leaning toward guitar heroes and the British blues more than pop groups. Well, I couldn't sing like Howard or Mark, either. We went with what we could do.

GEORGE DUKE I had just graduated from San Francisco State with my masters, and I was teaching at Merritt Junior College in Oakland. I wound up sending my resignation from New York, on Holiday Inn stationery, while I was out on the road with Frank. They say if you can make it in New York, you can make it anywhere. I got to New York with Zappa, staying in a Holiday Inn, and I said, 'I've made it. I can make a living playing music.'

JEFF SIMMONS Every Holiday Inn room is the same: to the left is the bathroom, walk a little farther past this little foyer and you're in the room. And Mark would immediately grab the first bedspread, throw it up over the entrance foyer, pin it up there somehow, light some incense, lie down on the bed, pick up the phone and go, 'Hello? Give me the police. Hello, Frank?' And then slam the phone down. Just a shtick. And then fire up some weed and we'd all huddle around.

There was a lot of crazy stuff that came out when you had a large touring group. Before, we were used to being on the road with five or six of us, and here we were, with crew and everything else, with something like twenty-one people.

DON PRESTON It was quite different from the original Mothers. The second band was more about presentation and doing a show, and we always had a set list. That was one of the prerequisites that Mark and Howard asked for. It kind of makes things a little more comfortable, whereas in the first band I don't think Frank was concerned with being comfortable.

IAN UNDERWOOD The shows were still unstructured in a way. It wasn't like we had a set song list. We never did that, ever, really. But it got more and more like that with things like 'Billy The Mountain,' which wasn't actually a song. It was a presentation, a little oratorio, or whatever you may want to call it.

GEORGE DUKE At first, it was enormously difficult for me. I'd never been in a band before or since that was that diverse stylistically. I was amazed with the level of dexterity they had. There was a spontaneity that happened between everybody in the band—well, everybody except for me—it was like I was as a spectator. I didn't even know why I was in that band, but Frank must have seen something in me that I didn't even see. He totally broke down those ultra-high jazz walls I had. He told me I needed to loosen up, as simple as that. He kept pushing me into areas that I might not have ever gone into, to allow my personality to come out. He said, 'Believe in yourself. You can be so much more than you are. You're funny offstage—you say funny things—you should do that onstage. You should sing. You should play synthesizers. You play trombone? Wow. Bring it in next rehearsal.'

I'd never sung before. I didn't sing. It just happened. And when he found out that I could sing falsetto, that was it. He was into that doo-wop stuff, and that opened up a whole new thing for him. Doo-wop was not part of my musical vocabulary, but I learned. Frank—everybody in the band—taught me the joy of simpler forms in music. It was like those walls had to be broken down, and they came crumbling down. And when they came down, all of a sudden, even when I did my own solo shows, I began taking the heat from the jazz community. They were saying that I'd sold out or that I'd gone crazy. But

I didn't care at that point. I saw the value of having a good time onstage. And all that came from being with those guys.

JEFF SIMMONS In Europe, the Mothers were on a par with everybody. In the States, they were looked on as an oddity, maybe a little too beatnik or bohemian, but in Europe we were hanging out with these groups who were like, 'Wow, you're in the Mothers? I can't believe it.' It was a player's band, to them. We'd be hanging out with T. Rex and Free, hobnobbing and hanging, having a great time.

GEORGE DUKE Most of the people, especially when we went to Europe, thought I was Billy Preston. There weren't any Black guys in these rock groups except for Billy Preston. They knew about Billy, and so I'd be onstage and hear 'Bee-lee! Bee-lee!' That was kind of crazy. Everywhere I went in Europe, they called me 'Bee-lee.'

JEFF SIMMONS We toured together for the next year, and Frank was now in a position to revamp his music or soup it up with the new guys. He had everything with Howard, from Pavarotti to Del Shannon, as far as his voice, and Mark, Mr. Bomp-ba-bomp-bomp, Spanky & Our Gang and Mamas & Papas backups and choral arranging type of harmonist. So, Frank could do everything from his doo-wop leanings to souping up songs like 'Who Are The Brain Police.' And that's where some of those Mothers purists jump off the ship and say, 'Well, this isn't right. This should be this old way.'

That era when we were playing together with Frank gets denigrated a bit, because of the science rock that followed. In his later bands, there were so many notes that it didn't mean anything. It didn't say anything. The supposedly so great Steve Vai and how many notes can you play and that kind of thing. I'm proud that we were in there when it was still called the Mothers. I think that it was Frank's golden period, and I think that's when Frank was the happiest. He absolutely loved it.

Frank used to say we were the only group of Mothers where each one of us could have been leaders of our own bands. At the point when we joined, the band was Aynsley, George, Ian, Don, Jeff, Howard, and me. It's been said that this band was the band that Frank had the most fun being in. We were like a real group. None of us ever complained about the crazy shit that Frank would ask us to do.

IAN UNDERWOOD To some extent I would say it was Frank's favorite version of the Mothers. There was a really, really, great energy and flow onstage, because of the people who were in the band and what Frank was writing at the time. It was extremely musical and energetic, and a worthwhile feeling to be doing that. We had some shows that were spectacularly good in that way.

RAY MANZAREK Zappa gave them the legitimacy that they were looking for. It was a kind of intellectual street cred from being with Frank and being Flo & Eddie. Interestingly, they changed their names, too. That worked to their advantage. They shed that skin. They shed their persona and took on a new persona as being ultra-hip. Frank Zappa: that's as hip as you can get. His music was so complex and was virtually classical music. And who's singing with him? Flo & Eddie. Who is Flo & Eddie? Mark and Howard from The Turtles. *Holy shit, man! What a change!* It was the best thing that could happen to them.

JIMMY FINK From their rock-radio standpoint, it gave Mark and Howard more credibility. Previous to that, they might have been like a Brill Building band, just making pop tunes, but here they are with Zappa, and John Lennon is playing with them. It changed the whole persona and made you look deeper. The whole Zappa experience and the Flo & Eddie persona gave them a significant amount of credibility: credibility that Jay Black from Jay & The Americans never had. Even though he had contemporary hits around the same time, he stayed in that pop genre, and Flo & Eddie blended themselves more into the happening music of the time, of the 70s and 80s.

MICKY DOLENZ They definitely had a flair for comedy. And I think that's probably why we got along, because The Monkees had very strong comedy roots, with the Marx Brothers and stuff like that. Rock'n'roll doesn't always have to be political and serious. It can also be fun and entertaining. Mark and Howie got that. They also got what The Monkees was all about, because some people in the music business didn't get it at all. And there are some that didn't get The Turtles. And I think that it's no coincidence that Frank Zappa got The

Monkees. He got it and what it was all about. He was amazing; a genius. And so, it's no surprise that Flo & Eddie started working with him.

IAN UNDERWOOD I don't really know if Frank was intentionally trying to broaden the audience. Certainly, Mark and Howard added another level to the band, a kind of communication which you can't do with a bunch of people sitting around playing instruments, no matter how good they are. The vocal aspect was something Frank was happy to use, and it worked really well that way. As far as the sophomoric humor and teenage sexuality, from the day that I joined the band, that was an interest of Frank's. But not isolated from other things, like politics and other sociological aspects. It was the part that interested me the least of what Frank did. I appreciated that he was interested in it, so, fine. But it got boring for me.

DON PRESTON If you really look at the music that he wrote over that twenty-five-year period, it seemed like he kept getting more adolescent. From 'Hungry Freaks Daddy,' which is a huge political statement, up to 'Don't Eat The Yellow Snow,' which to me is just garbage. Or 'Bobby Brown'—God, that's just sickening. I mean, it's funny, but jeez, it's bad taste. That didn't bother Frank. He didn't care about taste or anything.

DANNY HUTTON In large part, their job was to make him laugh. They are very clever, and I'm sure he pounced on a lot of their ideas, and probably moved on with them.

JIM PONS Frank enjoyed their spontaneity. He gave them a lot of latitude, and wrote a lot of things into the show that he saw them doing offstage. The idea was always to entertain Frank, and he really did enjoy some of the things they did. He got a big kick out of that.

ALICE COOPER I'll tell you what, they always made me laugh, and I always felt like Frank's little brother when I first got with The Mothers Of Invention. I was this little version of Frank, even though I wasn't anywhere near as talented in the way that he was talented. I was talented a little bit more in my stage persona.

DON PRESTON Everybody felt that way. The first band felt that way all the time. It was our job to make Frank laugh.

IAN UNDERWOOD The band wasn't just working to please Frank. We were working together, in a sense, to achieve something. Clearly it wasn't a band with a bunch of hits, going out to play our hits. That wasn't it. I experienced it not as Frank the employer, but Frank the musician and composer, and everybody was working toward that end. Frank is the employer, but, more importantly, he's the creator of these new ideas, and everybody's job is to make all that work as best as possible, and throw themselves into it, because obviously you don't want to be in a project that you're feeling stupid about. So, everybody really gives their best. You're making a contribution as only you can do it. And as long as things are working, that's a very lovely situation to be in. So, I see it without the word *employment* coming into it at all. But I understand what Howard and Mark said, that if Frank is laughing, then that means that everything is going well. Not that they yearn for his approval. It's like playing in a chamber ensemble: the dynamics are complicated, and everybody is a contributor and everybody wants things to go well, and everybody's working at a pretty high level. In those terms.

GAIL ZAPPA Every once in a while, you get lucky, and there's people in the band that understand that that's the thing: how do you make Frank laugh? How do you trick him in the middle of something and just get him going? Because he's just so in the moment, and that's the game. That's the challenge. That is a part of your job description, although you're not hired to do that. But it's more than that. It's that recognition, but it's also having the bond to know that it's okay that you do that.

GEORGE DUKE Just like Mark and Howard, once I was aware of what Frank was looking for, I just created stuff naturally. I knew what Frank wanted, and I'd just do it, and he'd start laughing and say, 'Yeah, that's it.'

PAT VOLMAN Everybody thought Frank's music was a little bit crazy, and they made it funny. They actually made it more commercial. Before that, he wasn't my favorite, but they made him my favorite. They made it easier to listen to, with them being silly onstage. And it's what they did in The Crossfires. I mean, they've always been silly.

MICKY DOLENZ Frank called me in about 1970, because he lived down the street. And, of course, I knew him. He'd been on the television show and in the movie *Head*. He called and asked me to be the drummer for the new Mothers Of Invention. I don't remember why or who'd been drumming before or the specifics of it, but he called out of the blue and said, 'Do you want to be the drummer?' And I was like, 'Gulp—wow!' I said, 'To be honest, Frank, I'm not sure that I'm really up to it. I'm not a studio cat.' And he said, 'I know, but that's cool.'

The Monkees were just sort of coming to its tail end, and I called the record company, because I would have had to have either been on loan or gotten off my record deal at RCA. And they said no. They wouldn't let me out of the contract, and they wouldn't even let me be on it with a 'with permission' or one of those things. But, to be honest, I don't know if I could have cut that stuff. Frank wrote some very, very sophisticated stuff, with very unusual time signatures and stuff. But it was very flattering for him to ask me.

In January 1971, the Mothers traveled to London to videotape their feature film debut, *200 Motels*. Not surprisingly, it was by all accounts a bizarre production.

GAIL ZAPPA Frank wrote a fake documentary. Well, it's not exactly fake. It's more like a surreal documentary on that band, and what it's like to be out there on the road, never knowing what day it is or where it is or what's going to happen. It reflects an exaggerated version of some of the stories that happened, kind of incorporating their hopes for the outcome of the evening of the night of the show. The idea of going to a boutique and all that stuff.

The story of *200 Motels* was a true story that continued out of our live show during the *Live At The Fillmore East* album. Yes, the big hit record with a bullet was true. Frank massaged it into a script. Howard and I received a 'special material' credit for material supplied by us.

JEFF SIMMONS It seemed like a lot of the material in the script was a little too close to truth. He had me saying stuff that maybe I felt was . . . I don't know what I felt, but I read it, and it's unbelievable. Like the stuff we would say about him and about traveling, and how, *that's okay for him, but meanwhile, Frank's up in the President's Suite, and we're down here.*

GAIL ZAPPA Frank could predict what people would say pretty much flawlessly, and the lines that they say are based on their characters and their characters are them. So, it's not like you're playing yourself exactly, you're playing your persona, but your persona is what you've created.

GEORGE DUKE Totally crazy. It was a crazy experience, with Theodore Bikel and Ringo and all of that. I was very young, a jazz player, and I was just watching. It was like going to another planet. These people were just nuts. I had never been around anything like that. How can I best put this? Okay, I'm a Black guy, right? Well, these are some crazy white people . . . I mean that in a funny way. It was just, *Whoa!*

PAT VOLMAN That was fun, but it was boring. They were on set for hours and hours and hours, and it could be stressful, because Zappa was incredibly regimented in how he wanted them to do things. I just couldn't sit there, so I took Sarina to the zoo and rode in the double-decker bus and all that stuff while Mark was on set. And it rained every day.

GAIL ZAPPA I don't remember how long we were there, but it was more than a couple of weeks. There was a whole rehearsal, and then they had six days to film. Everybody wanted to have a good time, and nobody really knew what was going on except Frank, and he was wearing so many hats. It was very difficult for him. Tony Palmer, the director, was a nightmare. Tony just hated everything to do with Frank, and he made up all these stories because he didn't think the film made any sense. And then Jeff decided he wanted to play the blues, and he walked off the set. He quit the band.

With all of the stress from the production deadlines—three weeks of rehearsal and five days to tape the movie—Jeff quit, and we needed to get a replacement actor, which made things even more stressful. On top of that, Tony Palmer, the director, hated Frank and the whole movie. Despite all that, Howard and I had a good time making that crazy, boring, stupid movie.

JEFF SIMMONS This is another case of maybe being too big for your britches, but *200 Motels* really wasn't something I wanted to do, now that I got over there. Led Zeppelin was out then, and I was thinking, *Man, we've got to get some broads, we've got to do some music that rocks. I don't want to do 'Centerville: a real nice place to raise your kids up,' and all that far-out atonal crazy junk.* I made the mistake of telling Mark, and he managed to tape me quitting the group. The next day, Frank says, 'I understand some people aren't too happy with their parts,' and Mark turns on the tape recorder. He's like that: impish, funny. He probably didn't want me to go. But I got uppity and thought I was cool and thought I was heavy, even though I had nowhere to go. But I could have been with Ringo and Keith Moon.

Everything we did in that movie happened. In terms of Jeff quitting and the dialogues about, I want to play the blues and be taken seriously. Instead, we're singing these comedy songs, that was a reflection of the guys in the group who took themselves very seriously. And then there were those who said, 'We're doing this for fun,' and that was basically me and Howard and a few of the other guys, so you had both sides taking place. Frank just caught that and wrote about it. He made that our story. He made that, as he used to call it, the folklore of the band, which grew out of the realities of each of the individual ways we thought.

MARK PARENTEAU *200 Motels* was as close as they got during that period to bridging the gap between The Turtles and where they wanted to go. Not only were they musically interesting but they were visually interesting. They were characters in that movie, and they were hilarious. And they got to tour with that whole Frank Zappa persona. But Frank had his own very unique audience, and it wasn't like The Allman Brothers or any of the more easy-to-grasp-onto rock acts. It was more brainiac music, and Frank had developed them so that they were the living embodiment of hipness and fun and coolness, because Frank certainly wasn't. They made Frank laugh, and Mark's so good at that, he's such a clown, and Frank was so straight-faced. But it was interesting, because Frank was an artist's artist, and to see those guys up there was such a winning combination.

HAL WILLNER They were always comfortable, for whatever reason, in their own skins. And he cast that material around them. It's interesting: someone was telling me how classic a film *200 Motels* is considered over in England and

Europe right now. I loved it, but not too many people saw it back then, and I guess it must have hurt them, because I remember they did something from it at a show, and the audience started applauding, and Howard grabbed the mic and said, 'You didn't like it then, don't like it now.'

GAIL ZAPPA They have some techniques in there that everybody has copied, whether they acknowledge it or not. The scene before the race has been copied in so many ways to the same sort of comic effect, and using animation, all these things that he introduced. And of course, this was the first feature that was ever shot in video and transferred to film.

JACK UNDERWOOD Mark had just been in the movie, and I'll never forget walking into a supermarket with him. He had his tie-dyed big T-shirt and his hair was all over the place. He stood out in a crowd. Somebody approached him and said, 'Hey, aren't you the guy who was in *200 Motels?*' He goes, 'Yeah!' Then he goes, 'I hated that movie.' I think that was pretty much a general consensus. I'd seen the movie too and actually agreed with him.

MADELINE CAMPILLO He made one movie: *1,000 Motels* [sic]. Well, I did go to see it. I told my children I would let them come and see it *if* it was all right. And it certainly wasn't. The only song I can remember certainly made it not all right. So, I went home and said, 'I'm sorry, children, I'd love you to see your cousin, but you are not going to this movie. The next movie he makes, you can see.' Then they did *Care Bears* and *Strawberry Shortcake* a few years later, and that's much better. Much better.

JEFF SIMMONS I did leave under suspicious circumstances, but if you look at what happened with that movie, I almost feel exonerated, in that the director threatened to have the tapes erased. He wanted his name pulled off the credits. The orchestra ripped up their rented tuxedos.

JIM PONS Mark called me from London. The bass player quit, and Frank told him to call me. I had known Frank from when I was in The Leaves, and he knew I had been in The Turtles. Maybe they had recommended me, but Frank had Mark call and see if I would be interested. I told him I would give them an answer by the time they got back. I didn't really love that free-form jazz kind of rock'n'roll, I like blues and country music. I thought about it for a long time. I had a nice little country band going, but it wasn't making any money, so I said I would do it. It was not my kind of music, but I venerated Frank as an artist, and I felt a responsibility to interpret his music properly. We all did.

GAIL ZAPPA Jim wanted to play country with the Burrito Brothers, but that job wasn't available. That happens to a lot of people, doesn't it? The one thing they want to do, they can't, but Frank was paying all the bills. Frank paid for all the equipment, everything. So, it's a gig, isn't it? I don't think that anybody was dreaming of working for Frank, and some people also got fired a lot and some people got fired before they were hired.

JIM PONS In The Turtles, we were all like stars in a band, whereas with Frank, he was the one who always got called away for interviews. He was pretty much the star. We were just sidemen. Sometimes Mark and Howard got included, sometimes they didn't, but the rest of us never did. That was quite a difference. We were just the Mothers *du jour*. It was the nature of his band, although The Turtles brought something different for a while.

JEFF SIMMONS When you're that young, you get the misinterpretation that, *I'm here because of me*. And then you realize, no, it's because of these guys up front. This is the work that they had laid down, all the work they did to get to that point. They're professionals, and what I did was probably unprofessional, but it led me to where I am today. In my post-Mothers career, I've played with Lowell Fulson, Pee Wee Crayton, Big Mama Thornton. I play mostly acoustic piano, that slip-hand, postwar blues, jump-piano kind of thing. I learned by trial and error, and I started with George Duke and Ian—they were my first two heroes in that realm, even though I was playing bass at the time.

JIM PONS I got called into the studio to do overdubs for *200 Motels*, and I wound up doing vocals and some speaking parts, and a couple of bass parts. I was the voice of the bad conscience in the cartoon. And the next thing I knew, we were rehearsing for the next tour. No words were really ever spoken. I sang a lot, too. He always had singing parts for me.

THE FILLMORE EAST

DON PRESTON I'd been in *200 Motels*, but I wasn't *in* the band at that point. Later, I was living in New York and working with Gil Evans, and Frank asked me to sit in at the Fillmore. I was there both nights, and after the show, Mark and Howard said they wanted to get me in the band. I was going on tour with Gil right after that, but I joined right after the tour. I had to learn 'Billy The Mountain' and all those other songs, lots of new songs.

I had no idea John Lennon was going to show up. I was amazed when he started doing hand signals. I think Frank said, 'You can do this, this, this, and this, and the band will do this.' But it wasn't so much that he knew how to do them, it was that he did them so well. And, in the end, he actually created a great little piece when he did that. It showed how creative he really was. That he could be put in that position and do something really beautiful with it, that was mind-blowing for me, to see him come into our world and still be the creative self that he was. He seemed totally lucid and focused.

HOWARD KAYLAN I had one of the best times in my life during those few days. I had this little clay pipe that I had purchased in Greenwich Village, and, as we know, Mr. Zappa was not very fond of drugs in his presence. However, Mr. Lennon really was, and there was an afternoon before John and Yoko sang with us at the Fillmore, where we all went to Frank's room and sat around and worked on the songs that we were gonna do. John asked Frank if he had any dope, and Frank of course looked back like, *Hey, you're talking to me. I don't do that shit.* John immediately turned to us and said, 'Well, you can't tell me you guys don't do that shit.' And I said, 'Oh no, I got dope. If you want dope, I got dope.' That was not a problem. So I let him have the first hit on this newly purchased clay pipe. We got high in that room, and we created some really, really stupid things, and they started going over this idiot riff that would later turn into this song called 'Scumbag.'

The audience was led to believe that it was all just happening and improvised, but for us it was twenty minutes of rehearsed music. We knew what we were going to do, and it took about three meetings—probably three or four hours at each meeting, of us accumulating some of John's ideas, some of Frank's ideas, some of Yoko's, really all of us kind of figuring out what would work and what wouldn't work. And Frank pursued it, and cultivated it, because he knew how unique it would be.

It was great to see John again, but I don't think he felt comfortable being Frank's donkey, because Frank was in control. John was uncomfortable being in that position, which was pretty much the position Howard and I were always in. We were the donkey show. That was what our job was. Frank couldn't have anybody on the stage who didn't realize that he was going to be calling the shots. You have to understand, you never did anything on Frank's stage that he didn't want. It was all planned. If he couldn't be in control, he wouldn't have done it.

HOWARD KAYLAN It was incredible. It's all over YouTube, and if you go to see it, I'm the guy who places Yoko in the burlap sack, pulls it over her head, draws the cord, and puts the mic in front of the bag where she stands for the rest of the show screaming her little ass off. I've never been prouder of anything I've ever done.

JIMMY FINK I was there that night, and it was absolutely thrilling. The word *avant-garde* might fit to that particular concert, and certainly Yoko did take it off into a different direction. It was pretty crazy, basically like an extended set of feedback. It certainly wasn't musical and melodic.

LARRY ZINN I saw all four of the Fillmore shows in June of '71, including the one that Lennon released as *Sometime In New York City*. He was cueing the band, and then they put Yoko in a giant canvas condom, and everybody walked off the stage with her screeching. As far as I'm concerned, she has very little talent. I think she was one of the first people to be famous for being famous.

When that album came out, John took credit for writing all the material, and Frank had to sue him. He also removed Howard's and my voices. They dropped all the frequencies around our voices—dropped them out as much as they could. But the original version of that night is on *Playground Psychotics*, and you can also hear the one song they took off: 'A Small Eternity With Yoko Ono.' That was Frank's title, but he took it from Howard's and my discussions. That was our ribald way of looking at the whole mess of her directing us to put her in that bag. We tied her up and then dropped the mic into the bag, and we all stopped playing while she sat there making a complete fool of herself. And the audience wasn't enjoying this. No one could have enjoyed that. Well, John I think enjoyed it. Frank enjoyed it because whatever happened onstage, that was okay with Frank.

DON PRESTON I thought it was very interesting that Yoko would agree to do that.

HOWARD KAYLAN Well, it's not like I don't get it. I get it, I just don't want it. It was better to see her as an artist than to hear her as an artist. It's unbelievable. And that's her art. Her art is just to cackle like a hen over everything and call that music. I have a feeling John was playing along, just like the rest of us. I think he was able to hold a straight face better than Frank or me or Mark.

That particular evening was not the first event in that series of shows. Grace Slick joined us one night and pretended to hump everyone in the band. We also had Joni Mitchell up onstage with us. Joni's was really an exceptional evening. She used the F-word. In fact, she had a song called 'Penelope Wants To Fuck The Sea.' The chorus was that lyric, and it was pretty shocking for the Joni Mitchell fans at the Fillmore to hear. But Frank brought that out in you. He made it okay to be weird. And he was someone people wanted to be onstage with.

JOHN SEITER They asked me to come into the studio and sing my part on 'Happy Together' on Frank's *Fillmore* album, and I was almost on the next one as well. I went to all these rehearsals for the Pauley Pavilion gig. I was just another Turtle for that, and that was okay with Frank, because now he had four of The Turtles. I was playing congas and I was going to play the gig that became *Just Another Band From L.A.*, but at the same time, I was doing a band with Jerry Yester and Judy Henske called Rosebud. We were on Reprise, and they got their first gig—their only gig—that very night. Honest to God. Their only gig was on that night.

So, I couldn't make the Pauley Pavilion show. But that's where 'Eddie, Are You Kidding' came from. I thought it was the funniest ad I had ever heard: 'Eddie, are you kidding?' 'No, I am not kidding. I have tall suits, I have portly. Come down . . . sixty tailors.' That was his thing: sixty tailors waiting for you, and I would do that riff all the time, I was parroting it all the time.

When it came time for composer credits, I fought them tooth and nail. I fought Herbie, I fought Frank. I fought them all. I said, 'Man, I wrote it, it's my thing, and I just want my piece.' And I actually got my royalties, too. I may be one of the only people that did that, and I still see royalties from that song. I was relentless. But I wrote it. I mean, come on, man. They couldn't deny that.

As Mark and Howard had already learned, Zappa had a close-to-zero tolerance for members of the Mothers: no drugs.

GEORGE DUKE Guys in the audience used to throw joints on the stage, and I could see the cats: when Frank turned the other way, they grabbed the joint. It was kind of neat to see how they were going to do it.

JIM PONS We were a lot straighter and a lot more careful. By the end of The Turtles, we were pretty high during our shows, and all of a sudden it was regimented. It was much more difficult and there was a lot more tension. Frank would watch you, and if you played a bad note, he would make you feel pretty bad about it. He would talk to you after the show about why you failed to do what it was that he needed to be done. It was fun but it was tough. We had a lot of things to remember, and then, on top of that, vocals and speaking parts. I remember at the end of the show being exhausted, and feeling, *Thank God it's over. We got through another one.* As each tour progressed, and the songs became more familiar, you played them with a little more ease. Frank was a little more lighthearted and enjoying it, and it got to be fun.

JEFF SIMMONS You worked to try and hide from Frank so you could smoke weed and have a moment where you're not thinking about how important this music is to the world, and how you should do it perfectly, and never be out of tune.

JIM PONS We used to hide when we wanted to get high. He would get upset with us because he was a business man, and that was not appropriate. He wanted the best out of you when you were doing that gig.

Hiding our smoking from Frank was done out of necessity, because he was really against our using drugs. One of the reasons was that band members couldn't perform his music well if they smoked, and up until that time that was true. Then, when Howard and I came into the mix, we challenged the system, in terms of saying, 'Listen, we're doing just fine with your music. It's not because of pot that we're not learning the music, it's because it's hard—it's just hard!'

Once he understood that we could perform just as well smoking pot as we could without it, he slacked off, and in fact he was able to incorporate that as part of the performance. It became us making fun of that as well.

JOHN SEITER People thought Frank was a big head and all that, because he wrote all that stuff about being a head. Well, it was the stuff that the band was talking about. Frank would listen to the band, and then write it all down. All that crazy shit, that's all just what the guys were doing, because the guys were getting high and they were talking about all this shit, and Frank was writing it down. And taking the publishing.

HOWARD KAYLAN The best thing about *our* Mothers Of Invention with Frank was that it was a group. It wasn't a big band, it wasn't a jazz experiment. We drove around in the same vehicle. We shared the same orgies, we shared the same eating experiences, we lived together as a band, Frank included. And toward the last days of that group, Frank was hanging with us and was smoking dope with us. Against everything he had ever said before and certainly since.

JIM PONS I don't remember Frank getting high with the band. He certainly wasn't with me. I never saw Frank smoke a joint in my life.

In October 1971, the Virginia Beach police arrested Mark and Howard for singing lyrics deemed unacceptable by the community. They were held overnight.

GAIL ZAPPA There was an arrest, but it wasn't considered anything serious. They had to stick to at least who they believed was the offending person. They couldn't arrest the entire band. I think the way that that was presented, because not all communities have the same standards, was, if they arrest these people and keep them, they can't go and play the next gig. And if they've got a contract, and they held them unlawfully, that was a risk. So, a compromise was struck.

There had been problems leading up to that show that had to do with language and the police looking for trouble. Frank always brought that with him, just with the route that he took lyrically. At the time, 'Billy The Mountain' was about as bad as you could get, where the lyric is, 'A mountain is something you don't fuck with / You don't want to fuck with / Don't fuck around with.' A lot of F-words got thrown around, but I'm not sure that it warranted a night in jail.

As the concert began to wane down, the police started making their way to the sides of the stage down on the floor level. It reminded me of The Doors, that documentary where Jim is really letting the police have it. It ended up with Herb making a deal where Howard and I were given up to go to jail for the night so that Frank wouldn't have to go. Frank, Gail, and Herb all said, 'We decided you two would go.'

It's funny, but that kind of politics was something we understood. When you work with Frank, you're going to be singing about penises and donkeys, and there's probably going to be an issue. Frank wrote the words, but they came out of our mouths, and that's why we ended up in jail.

Spending the night in jail was silly, but we had to do it. We shared a cell with four or five other guys, and by the time we were ready to leave we were signing autographs for everyone. It was one of those things. Basically, Herb negotiated that we'd plead guilty, and they—Herb and the Mothers—would take care of the bill. And then they wiped us off the books so it wouldn't show up later down the road. It might have even been expunged. And why all of this needed to happen and be cleaned up was because we toured a lot overseas. We were back in Europe a few weeks after that.

In December, a show in Montreux, Switzerland, ended abruptly after 'some stupid with a flare gun' took aim at the ceiling. While everyone got out safely, the building burned to the ground, destroying all of the band's equipment in the process.

The fire forced us to make a choice, which was done by vote. Frank wanted to go home, but the band won out, and we continued on to London for a series of shows at the Rainbow Theatre. That week was the worst.

JIM PONS I don't recall Frank wanting to come home. He *did* allow us to vote, which I thought was pretty rare. The next gig ended with the accident. I was onstage when Frank was attacked.

DON PRESTON The club burned down, and Zappa got thrown into a pit. So that was the end of that.

HOWARD KAYLAN The world-famous encore: 'I Want To Hold Your Hand' in London, the last night with Zappa. It had been directly preceded by the 'Smoke On The Water' gig before that, and then we literally had to beg Frank to continue with the final two weeks of the European tour, because we were paid by the show. So, there's the Rainbow, and there's Frank, lying *Lodger*-like at the bottom of the orchestra pit. I mean, he was ruined, man. His limbs were at all these impossible angles, his head was wrong … it was like looking at that cover. We thought he was dead.

We visited Frank in hospital once, and that was all we got to see of him. They brought us in shifts because they didn't want more than two or three people visiting him at any one given time. So, when Mark and I were let into Frank's room, he looked awful. All of his limbs were in traction, and he was wrapped from head to toe. He was able to open one eye long enough to look at us, to react as if it were the beginning of the show, and say, 'Ah, you guys. Great, here we go, "Peaches En Regalia," one-two-three-four.' Like it was the beginning of our set.

He was joking. He was joking, but it was wonderful to see, because he hadn't lost his sense of humor. I was most scared about that. We were hearing all these rumors from Gail and from Herb that not only was Frank injured but no matter how he recovered, he was not gonna go on the road anymore, he was not gonna write music anymore, he was certainly not gonna be a part of any group anymore.

It was the end of the band, and the unfortunate thing is the band probably ended in the worst shape emotionally that any musician could have been in. There was no rhyme or reason to it. And a lot of us felt guilty about Frank ending up the way he did, because he wanted to go home, and we forced the issue based on the economics of it all. For all the great things that went on within that band, there were a lot of unfortunate, negative things where it ended up.

GAIL ZAPPA They say that now, but at the time everybody was mad because they all thought that Frank was supposed to take some sort of responsibility for them. And he could barely hang on. He was hanging onto his own health as best he could, and he couldn't make any plans for the future because he didn't know whether he would recover.

JIM PONS He was in pretty bad shape, and we thought, *This guy's never going to play again, much less with the same authority and talent.* That's when we realized we've got to do something else. There was no retainer, and they didn't explain anything to us. We flew home and said, 'Now what? Do we want to wait eight months, and see if he's going to be able to play and wants to ever tour again, or do we try and put something together?' It couldn't be The Turtles, but Flo & Eddie started out of that.

HOWARD KAYLAN It was a very awkward time for us because we didn't know where we stood. We didn't know if we had a band. We didn't know if we had a future. None of us in the band did, but particularly in my case and Mark's case, we were relying on Frank for everything—for everything—because we still had not terminated our litigation with White Whale, so we still did not have our real names to work with. We could not sign a record contract as Mark and Howard. We were losing our brains, and no one from Herb's office would contact us—on Frank's orders. So, we didn't really know what was happening.

GAIL ZAPPA The whole band were collectively pissed that Frank didn't reach out to them. Herb was certainly not the one who was under any instruction to tell them otherwise, but you don't know what Herb Cohen was capable of doing. They could have called here, but if they were calling Herb, that's ridiculous. But again, Herb was probably telling us that they were looking for some sort of compensation.

GEORGE DUKE I was not there when the accident happened. I'd already left the band to join Cannonball Adderley, so I was not aware of what was going on between them. I was a little surprised they had stopped working together, and I did hear that he was not returning calls. He was extremely bitter about being in a wheelchair, no doubt about it, because he almost died. And that was very heavy.

DON PRESTON Frank ended the first group, too. But we, like idiots, thought that he could. We didn't have to end the group. We could have said, 'Okay.

You go your own way—we're the Mothers.' But we didn't think of it. We were having a great time, not counting not making very much money.

HARVEY KUBERNIK If you're not on retainer, you should be allowed to do whatever you want. But I'm surprised that Zappa would even think of it that way. That is really amazing, because he could replace anybody. He would hire and fire whenever he wanted. Let's be realistic, Frank almost lost his life when he was pushed off the stage, and that's not counting the fire at Montreux, so Mark was with him during some very traumatic events of his life. And those things bond you, so maybe that led to Zappa feeling there was a sense of flight or betrayal. But then again, he saw Zappa a hundred times subsequently. They were neighbors. Their kids went to the same school.

GAIL ZAPPA Unlike a lot of people who worked with Frank who just went out there and talked about themselves and their version of the center of the universe, they really didn't take advantage of Frank too greatly. But they did say something that was devastating to us, and this is the *only* complaint I have about them, even though I'm sure they thought it was funny. They said he jumped, and it was really painful. I imagine that they probably meant that as a bit of humor. And if you go through a traumatic experience like that, yeah, they're witnesses, but they didn't experience it. And we were upset that they were making fun of him, instead of understanding the predicament that he was in, because it's not just loss of income to them. It was a loss of a whole lot more—of recordings, opportunities, and other things for Frank. It took a year or more out of his life completely, and all sorts of other expenses that he wasn't anticipating having to deal with.

Frank and Gail were mad at us for saying that Frank had jumped. It was meant as a joke, to ease the stress on how bad it really was. They knew us so well that I'm surprised they took anything we said seriously. In hindsight, it might not have been the right thing to say, but who says we knew any better?

DON PRESTON I was as much in the dark as they were. Frank never bothered calling anyone to say anything, so Mark and Howard finally decided to go on a tour without Frank. And they did pretty much the same thing. In fact, we played the Rainbow Theatre exactly one year to the day that Frank got thrown into the pit. That was kind of weird. When we became Flo & Eddie, I was doing all of it, all the time. I played keys, I played Moog, I played piano a lot. I stuck around and went on a couple of tours with them.

Over the years, numerous members of the Mothers have complained of not receiving proper writing credit.

DANNY HUTTON I did a song called 'Funny How Love Can Be,' and I invited Frank to the session. I used the guys who became the Wrecking Crew, and also a consort of musicians from UCLA that played eighteenth-century woodwinds. I arranged the whole thing. If you listen to that song, and you listen to Frank's stuff, it's insane. Frank completely went in that direction. Just check it out, listen to it, and imagine Frank Zappa being at the session. I think he assimilated something from me. That's Frank Zappa.

ANDY CAHAN Frank wasn't fair. He would take actual dialogue. For instance, Jimmy Carl Black would say something and then Frank would turn around and use that as lyrics to a song. And he didn't treat his guys financially the way he should. According to Jimmy Carl Black and Bunk Gardner, Roy Estrada, Elliot Ingber, Denny Walley, and Artie Tripp—all the guys I've spoken to—he wasn't fair with his band. All the original Mothers really resented what Frank did.

E. MICHAEL HARRINGTON That's the way it goes. Frank learned the business early on. It's so unfair. But that's how it works: if you're not the songwriter, you're not gonna get paid. Legally, they're not entitled to anything.

I worked very closely with him on putting together *Playground Psychotics*, which was the last project released of our group during his life, and most of that was material I had recorded on a tape recorder. So that particular album, other than some of the live recordings—including the John and Yoko show—is what Frank had handpicked out of the tapes I had turned over to him. All the spoken word material is credited as composed by Frank alone.

DON PRESTON Frank didn't give anyone any credit for anything. And not only [no] acknowledgment but [no] payment. In the original group, everybody was constantly complaining about the money. We wanted to know where the money went, because they had some really sharp accountants. I don't want to say too much about that because I'll have Gail after me.

IAN UNDERWOOD I can talk about it. Later on, I think there was maybe some amount of money in some settlement or something, but I never had any issues or complaints about Frank taking credit, and if it did happen or it didn't happen was not even a thought in my mind. So, when it did, I said, 'Oh, okay.' But I didn't feel mistreated. You can put a zero on that column. As far as I'm concerned, I was treated fairly.

GAIL ZAPPA It was their stories, but with every band, every group of people—and Mark and Howard certainly have this in their own friendship—there's folklore that accumulates, and you develop a particular language so you don't have to tell stories over and over again to know what somebody is talking about. And then Frank built on that, so it's all fair game in terms of material. The folklore builds, and it's a reflection of those people doing that at that time, under that baton. It doesn't happen anywhere else.

GEORGE DUKE I spent hours and hours coming up with synth patches, because there was no way to save any sound at that time. We did a lot of that together, just Frank, me, and Kerry McNabb, who was the engineer at the time. We spent weeks upon weeks in the studio, and I never got paid for any of that. They would say we were going to get royalties, and I remember thinking, *Hey, I might get rich off of this*, but most of us never really got anything, or got very little.

Eventually, I think I got paid one check. But I chose not to go after that in court. Gail is still putting out stuff that we did, and a lot of it was improvised, and she's put my name on a few things. But see, the deal is, I'm making a decent living. I'm doing fine, and I think I got more out of it than he took. I tend to look at it that way.

AYNSLEY DUNBAR We didn't get any royalties, but it didn't really matter for me. If I was going to write them, I would have written them, but Frank wrote them, so all the best for him.

LEAVING FRANK

AYNSLEY DUNBAR Flo & Eddie didn't record right after Frank's accident. There was a break, and I did the *Waka Jawaka* and *Grand Wazoo* albums, but I didn't do Frank's tour. I did the *Flo & Eddie* sessions when I was still with him, and I think he was upset, because I asked him what he thought about it all. He said basically, if I joined them, then I would be out of the band. So I went, 'Okay, well, I've got to do something different.' I didn't think it was going to turn into anything other than sessions, but I was with them for a while after that. I just went from one band to the other.

IAN UNDERWOOD There was a *Grand Wazoo*-ish band that went to Europe around '72 for a few concerts and then came back and played a couple of shows. That was a bigger band, and that's the last thing that I did. There were several conflicts that were arising at that point in my life, and when I told Frank that I thought it would be best for me to leave the band, he just said, 'Okay, fine. That's good.' It wasn't like, 'You can't leave, I need you to do this and this . . .' He just said, 'Okay.' I think from his point of view, I wasn't really providing anything absolutely useful that he couldn't have happen in a different way. He just moved on to the next people who were available, continuing on with what he was doing.

I was still not interested in being in a rock'n'roll band, or being in that world and playing songs of that kind, so I went straight into being a session player. Actually, I didn't even know what a session was, really, when I started doing that. I was vaguely aware that that world existed, but only in the vaguest terms possible. I discovered this other world where I could work, that worked well for me, and my interest was and continued to be . . . it was broad, but it was more toward classical music.

After I left, I didn't follow what Frank was doing. Occasionally, I would go up to the house and say hi, but at the point that I left the band, for me, it had become more of a 'playing a part' situation. I still liked the band, but I was ready to move on to something else.

DON PRESTON Frank kept calling and asking me to do this and that, so I went back and did a few projects. I didn't get any sense of bitterness toward Mark and Howard, not at all. But the older Frank got, the less communicative he became. By the time we started doing the '74 band, he was the leader, and everybody else was working for him, whereas in the first band, we were all equal partners. I was never in that real professional band. A lot of times those guys would just stand there and play the notes.

GEORGE DUKE When you left the band, I think Frank was just depressed that it happened. There was probably a bit of that, but one thing I did notice is, once you were out of Frank's world, you were out of Frank's world. I won't say you didn't exist, but it's almost like he knew he had limited time. He didn't have time for small talk, and if you weren't in his world, you weren't there.

I did go back. I went back in 1973, when Jean-Luc Ponty came in. I think I left on good terms. I gave him a long notice and told him that I was still a jazz guy and I wanted to pursue that, and I formed a band with Billy Cobham. After that I tried to be personable with him, and it took him a long time to warm up to me. But he eventually came around and said, 'Hey, George, you ought to come up and let's make some music sometime.' I went up once and I never went back. I don't think I saw him again after that. But I'm not bitter in the least. I enjoyed my time. I think I got a lot out of that.

JEFF SIMMONS I came back on rhythm guitar after Mark and Howard had left. I'd just come back to L.A., and I looked Frank up, and he said to come down and see his new band. I went to the rehearsal and said, 'Man, I couldn't play with these guys, the musicianship has gone up light years.' He had me come up and do this supposed comedy bit. After that, he hired me to play rhythm guitar in the band, so I toured again in '74. So even though I wasn't like Tom Fowler or Patrick O' Hearn or some of these noodlers that came after me, I did play on some of his beauteous music. But I see now that Frank only got me back so he could play the last card: no one quits Frank's group. But that's cool. I think it was just destined to be, that he would have wanted to say, 'You don't quit *my* group.' But I was proud to be associated with Mark and Howard. I was proud to be there for stuff that was worked out that precisely and enjoyed by so many people. It wasn't that I disdained the music. I took from it Frank's love of the doo-wop and roots music more than the compositional or clustered chords or pedal tones. I heard 'Apostrophe' with Jack Bruce on it, and I thought it was terrible. That was after my time, but I listen to these things that are supposed to be watermarks, and there just isn't anything I'd listen to.

AYNSLEY DUNBAR I never was fired. I left because it was over with, basically. He did invite me to play with him again, but not to fire me. He wanted me to go on a tour in place of Chad Wackerman. I think it was back in the 80s.

Frank succumbed to cancer in 1993. By then, any issues between them had long been repaired, and Mark had become a regular visitor.

The last few years of Frank's life, knowing he was dying, we spent a lot of time together, getting back to being friends. God brings you back to places, and there was a definite reason for all of that, for us to get back together. A lot of healing went on. There had been bad vibes circulating about us taking Frank's band away after we returned to America, and there was a lot that needed to be patched up. Frank never would've held a grudge, but there were things that needed to be cleaned up, no doubt about it.

GAIL ZAPPA I'm sure he enjoyed Mark's visits, because whatever negative feelings from before were long gone. In general, he wasn't one to hold any kind of grudge, especially when he was ill. He just let everything go, dropped everything. So, there were people that he did want to see, and people he absolutely would not see.

Was there a change in his attitude once he knew he was dying? Not really. Frank was always in good spirits. He fought like hell against the cancer. He tried a lot of organic remedies, which was more his style. But Frank accepted his mortality graciously. At least in the time I spent with him, it seemed he had accepted the reality of the situation. I think the only regret was that he couldn't eat pizza on the last day of his life, because that's what he loved, along with cigarettes and coffee, and I can honestly say he did that up until the very last days of his life.

Did that diet kill him? I don't know. If it did, it was a hell of a way to go. But I miss him. Even today, I miss being able to talk with him. He always made me laugh. He was a unique individual and of all the people they tag the word genius to, he might be the only one who ever came close.

Each decade since his passing has brought more respect. Today, Zappa is seen as one of America's great composers, with a significant body of work unlike any other.

GEORGE DUKE Frank Zappa was one of the most important musical figures of our time. I don't think there was anybody like him before, and I don't believe there will be anybody like him in the future. A totally unique character, and as important musically to the whole dynamic of the musical world as Duke Ellington or Stravinsky. I think he was misunderstood. He got credit for some things that were not true; yeah, he was a zany character, and a lot of people think he was the wildest drug addict in the world, but that was grounds for being fired in the band. There were a lot of things that followed him that were not true, but then there were a lot of things that followed him and they were true [*laughs*]. But I've never met, before or since, an individual that had that kind of mastery of guitar and music, and self-taught, with that kind of humor and sarcasm. But at the same time was so open to just do whatever he wanted to, and was able to do it.

I would never say it was easy. Working with Frank was probably two of the hardest years ever, because you really had a job to do. It wasn't like you were out there to have a good time. He was the only one allowed to have a good time. You had to fit your good time into when you went back to your hotel room, and when he allowed it. When Frank said it was okay to have a good time, it was okay to have a good time. It was written into the script: *Have a good time.*

When you took the job, it was like joining the Merchant Marine and there was only one leader. We did our best to bring a semblance of personality to it, but that personality was Frank studying us and writing our personalities into the music. And that was what made him so singularly Frank Zappa. He was able to take all these people and make it all Frank Zappa, but utilizing each of the individual personalities and talents, and during that two-year period we were there, we were very fortunate to be involved in the particular group. That was a very unique band, and there wasn't one guy who didn't hold his weight.

7

T. REX

While in the UK with Zappa, Mark and Howard were reacquainted with Marc Bolan, a former White Whale labelmate during his time with John's Children. Under the moniker Tyrannosaurus Rex, Bolan released four albums between 1967 and 1970, all meeting with middling success. After plugging in, shortening their name to T. Rex, and—significantly to our story—bringing in Mark and Howard to sing backup, sales skyrocketed. For the next few years, T. Rex were massive in the UK, and they broke worldwide with the single 'Bang A Gong (Get It On).'

TONY VISCONTI T. Rex had opened for The Turtles in North America, and Marc invited them to come over and sing. This would be 1970, and the reason why we got them to sing in London is because they were on tour with Zappa. I saw them at the Royal Albert Hall. The first time they sang for us was on a song called 'Seagull Woman.' They came in and were swaggering about in the studio, cursing like sailors. I guess from being with Zappa, they had this way of speaking that always had a barbed insult in it, and they would just attack. It was very un-English.

I was in the control room with Roy Thomas Baker, who was our engineer for these vocal takes, and they were asking things like, 'Do you guys know what to do up there? You're sure you know what you're doing?' It was a little offensive at first, because I'd just shook their hands and went to work, and then they started in. But at the same time, it was really, really funny. They called Marc a cosmic punk. They meant it as kind of a semi-insult, but he loved it. They were bantering back and forth, trading insults, but it went down well. It was all in good fun.

JEFF 'SKUNK' BAXTER The interesting thing was, Mark didn't make fun of people because he was cruel. I think making fun of someone is the wrong term. He would leverage people for humor, based on mutual respect. There was no reason for him to be rude or cruel to someone who wasn't really good at what they did. The only way it really works is to be part of a group of folks who are excellent at their trade. Then it can be funny because, after all, it's no fun having a joke at someone else's expense. The humor was to reflect the joy of life. Now, there's no doubt, as they say, 'kill my demon, kill my muse,' that Mark's humor was like all of our humor. It was slightly dry, probably leaning toward the gallows mentality, because the work that we did was really hard. And you had to work with some very interesting people, let's put it that way, and also keep your sense of professionalism. So, humor was an outlet for that. But Mark was never cruel to anybody.

TONY VISCONTI Their vocal was the last thing to go on. All the rest of the recording was done. We didn't know if it was going to work out, because it was very different from anything else they had sung before, but it was no problem at all, because they loved the music and they loved the way they could fit in.

Tony and Marc were two of the good guys. Tony was a smart producer who had really good ideas in that he allowed us the room to sing it our way. We wanted to help them be pop stars, and we came up with ideas that we thought would make them radio friendly.

TONY VISCONTI After the initial sessions we did 'Hot Love.' Mark and Howard happened to be in town that day, and they sang sixteen tracks of absolutely gut-busting vocals. They overdubbed repeatedly: I had to bounce the drums down to two channels to make room for the backing vocals. By then, we had started working more as a team. They dropped the insults, or, if they kept on doing it—that little game—we were used to it. It was more relaxed and really nice to work together. Most of the time it was the three of them. Marc would be next to them to teach them the parts or add his voice, but they overpowered him easily. You could barely hear his voice in the mix, but he was there.

DANNY HUTTON I knew Marc Bolan. He and I used to hang together. I remember sitting in the back of his motorcycle, my arms wrapped around his belly, thinking, *I hope he doesn't think I'm [gay]!*

With the album *Electric Warrior*, T. Rex became massive.

TONY VISCONTI 'Hot Love' was a #1 hit. It was #1 for seven weeks, and T. Rex were touring, so we recorded the *Electric Warrior* album as the group was touring. I just followed them around. The beds were laid down in London and New York, and finally we flew to L.A., where Mark and Howard did all the vocal overdubs on our prerecorded tracks. We recorded 'Get It On' there. I remember going over to Howard's house and rehearsing it. Marc was teaching the guys the song, and they were making up their parts by poolside. The rest of the band was clowning around, picking oranges off the trees. We never saw anyone who had oranges in their backyard.

In the studio, Mark and Howard came in at the wrong place, and we loved it. I've had the pleasure of remixing it several times, and the original track goes on for about seven minutes. There's this whole long ending where everybody's going berserk, and Flo & Eddie are just improvising and howling, but it was such a long song that it was easy to get lost. Some of the verses were three lines long, some two, and some were five lines long, and at the end of the two repeat lines—the two-line ones—Mark and Howard came in with '*get it . . .*' and started laughing. That's what the mistake was. You'd have to crank the track up to hear it. But I come from that generation where we love these accidents, and we even build up on it. Also, those records are so vibe-y. We purposefully wanted things to be a little loose. We didn't want to be too slick. One thing great about Marc Bolan, he was very, very true to rock'n'roll ethics. We didn't really shine and polish things too much. We always let a little bit of rawness in there.

DANNY HUTTON All of a sudden, they're on the radio singing 'Bang A Gong' and it's like, *Why didn't he ask me? What the hell!*

TONY VISCONTI Everyone would get pretty out of their skulls, but Marc never did that much drinking or cocaine in the studio. I think he felt obligated—he thought maybe *they* needed to have all this—but we never made albums under those conditions. We hardly used drugs or booze in the studio, ever. When Mark and Howard came in, we thought they were the type of guys who needed it to be turned into a party. That's the truth. I've got vivid memories of those sessions because they were hilarious. I used to run a tape just to catch the banter between takes, and I don't know where they are. I might have made a copy for Mark—I think I did as a favor, because I felt he was treated so badly.

When we started on the second album, he gave us the time we needed. He knew that we were part of the sound. Because of Flo & Eddie, we were busy with our own careers and never toured with him as part of the band, but Marc always listed us on his records as members of the group—we were not background singers.

TONY VISCONTI During the sessions for *The Slider*, they sang on 'Metal Guru,' 'Rock On,' and 'Baby Boomerang.' They sang on those three songs, and we had more backing vocals to go. For instance, they sang on 'Rabbit Fighter.' Then we had to put some backup vocals on 'Telegram Sam,' and I said, 'Shall we wait till Mark and Howard are back in London?' Marc says, 'No. They're not singing for me anymore. It's a real bummer. They asked for money.'

I couldn't believe it. These guys were integral to the sound of T. Rex. But Marc was such a prideful guy that he wouldn't pay them. He thought once they wanted money for doing it, that it was over. This is already . . . they were singing on their third T. Rex album, technically. And he wouldn't pay them. It was a shame, but Marc thought that people should do everything for him for free. He was very reluctant to give either money or credit to musicians that played with us, and Mark and Howard, they were mates. As far as Marc was concerned, they were doing this for the vibe. So, he never paid them. They never made a cent. Not even basic union rates. Nothing. The musicians had a union, but singers didn't matter. So, money never exchanged hands, because we were supposed to do it as friends, that was Marc's condition. You're just doing this for the vibe. Even the members of his band were paid a stipend, like £75 a week. They didn't enjoy royalties. I'm sure they didn't get gold records either.

All of my platinum and gold records were as a member of T. Rex, and he considered his success very much tied to the fact that we were a part of those records. We sang on entire albums, all the way through, and Marc always considered us part of the band. My record says, 'Presented to T. Rex: Mark Volman,' so he wasn't giving us gold records for being background singers.

TONY VISCONTI Mark Volman's gold records must be out of a guilt trip on Marc's part. That's very, very rare. He should count himself lucky that they got anything. *I* don't even have a gold record. I wonder if Marc just made them up, like a booby prize or something.

DANNY HUTTON That sounds just like Marc. He was just a charming asshole. Of course they didn't get paid, and of course the gold records were fake. That is *exactly* Marc. I loved him for that. He was such an artiste, such a star.

TONY VISCONTI I was okay. I had signed Marc and made the very first Tyrannosaurus Rex album, so I was paid by my label. But when his contract ran out, and it came time to do *The Slider*, he started his own label. From that point onward he was paying me, and it was difficult to get any money out of him. Because we all knew each other, and we all started out at the same time, he felt none of us should put on airs. But it was perfectly all right for him; he was making practically all of the money.

His lawyer came to me and said they wanted to pay me a retainer, which was generous, but wouldn't equal royalties in any way. I mean, he was selling fifty thousand singles a day. So, I quit. I refused, and they ended up reluctantly giving me royalties from that point onward. From *The Slider* onward, I did make some money, but not as much as I was getting from my former label.

By that time, Mark and Howard were off the page, because they had dared ask for money. And it never did get worked out. Marc Bolan felt very bad, and maybe that's why he gave them those gold records. From 'Telegram Sam' onward, if it sounds like Flo & Eddie, it's actually Marc and myself, doing our best Flo & Eddie. That's us sounding like them. And it fooled everyone. It even fooled Mark and Howard, but I can tell, because the sound is thinner. Those guys had beautiful body in their voices: they were very professional, solid singers, But we got the upper part right. We learned the nuances from them. And they learned from Marc what he wanted them to sing. The high men singing falsetto: Marc always had that in his mind for the sound of his backing vocals. And what he really wanted, in the end, was girls. So, finally, he got girls. They could sing higher.

Mark said that in his whole career he'd never met someone with a bigger ego than Marc, and I'd agree with that. It was strange, but anyone who came after us really suffered from his ego. But I had the best relationship with him, and also his wife June. I discovered Marc in 1967, and I introduced him to June about six months later. She was a secretary and basically girl Friday for the management of Pink Floyd. I brought Marc to the management company, and at the end of the day, Marc and June were together. She was very, very influential on him. He was egotistical, but June and I knew him right from the beginning, so he took our advice. He took it from me as a producer: I did the string arrangements, mixing, and was integral to the music from the get-go. If I told him his guitar was out of tune, and I did that with people listening, he would yell at me and tell me I was 'fucking deaf' or something like that. But if we were alone, he would say, 'Okay, which string?' He couldn't be seen to be imperfect if there was an audience there. That was the worst thing he ever said to me, ever, in public. I just took it. He walked away in a huff, and I picked up the guitar and tuned it. So, we kind of had that tacit agreement that if he knew something needed fixing, he would just walk out. I would fix it, and as long as I wouldn't say it was fixed . . .

Later, everyone ended up being some kind of a sycophant, but not June and myself. I saw the signs, and I got out really early, so I don't know Marc from this period. The last album I did, he was going out with Gloria and he was estranged from June. That's around the time I left. But the cocaine use was already rampant, and we didn't need Gloria. June could get the best cocaine in London, and we had a deal—I mean, everyone is dead. I'm surprised I'm still alive—but June had a friend called Chelita Secunda. Chelita was Marc's PR person for a while, but she was also London's elite coke dealer. We would just ring her bell, she'd throw it out the window in an envelope, and you'd put some money in the letter box. It was crazy, that decade. And this is way before Gloria came in. Gloria just put the nail in the coffin. Her and her brother just made it worse, that's all. Marc was already overweight, drinking from the minute he got up, doing cocaine all day. He would position himself so that he was near cocaine at all times, and I think that it was just convenient that Gloria's brother was a dealer. And Marc was always in denial—*always* in denial. He made some kind of a renaissance before he died. He did lose some weight, but the night he died, they were partying, and he never quite gave it up. He was just a little too much rock'n'roll.

It was sad that Marc was just starting to feel good again when he died. We wrote 'Another Pop Star's Life' about him, but I'm not sure he really knew. That era had a lot of excesses, but we were looking at Marc. Everything in there was pointing at how he's so big: 'Another pop star's life goes by / Another pop star's wife / Another pop star's life.' If you dissect it, it's pretty much Marc. I mean, it was his wife driving the night he died in the car wreck. We denied it for years, and it was easy because there were so many people that the lyrics fit, and we didn't want to be pointing at any one artist as being significant enough to write a song about. We certainly wouldn't have wanted Marc Bolan to think he was so important that we wrote a song about him. But we did.

TONY VISCONTI He didn't know how to drive. Yeah, that's about Marc all right.

Over the years, Visconti would use Mark and Howard on various projects, but there was one artist they never got to work with.

TONY VISCONTI They think I kept them from singing on a Bowie session? Oh, no [*laughs*]. I beg to differ. First of all, it really wasn't up to me. If Bowie wanted them, he knew they were around. That's *if* he wanted them. But Bowie on principle wouldn't have Flo & Eddie on his records, because it would be too much like T. Rex. It would be too close. Every week in the *Melody Maker* there would be headlines like, 'Who do you like more this week: David Bowie or Marc Bolan?' So it would have been impossible. Bowie wouldn't use any of the photographers that Marc Bolan used, and vice versa. There were two camps then, very, very strongly divided. So, we had our set of players, which Mark and Howard were members of. I would have introduced them to Bowie, but they wouldn't have sung on his records.

I used them on a session in the early 90s with a French singer called Louis Bertignac. He's very famous in France, a national treasure. We recorded in Paris and did a song called 'Oubliez-moi' ('Who Would Forget Me?'), and we got them in. They were in New York, and we had to fly them in, and they delivered the goods. The song was an homage to 'Get It On.' It was the same key, and I remember Mark turning to me, and he goes, 'Tony, you're asking us to hit these high Es. It's not the 70s, you know.' But they did it. They really squeezed their butt cheeks together, and they got the high notes out. At that point he was working on his nutrition degree, and he looked so good. He was slim and fit. I was surprised; I thought he was going to be overweight for life. He was showing all the signs of a serious heart condition, a potential heart condition coming on.

I used him again a few years later with The Cherry Poppin' Daddies on 'Diamond Light Boogie.' That was, again, a very T. Rex-y single, so we flew him up. Howard wasn't available, so I had Mark do both parts. He tracked about three or four times. I was just there for the one single. I think the track was fantastic, and having Mark on it was just icing on the cake.

SPECIFIC TRACKS THEY SANG ON

TONY VISCONTI I was going through the songs on headphones, because there's a big story to tell here. Mark thinks he's on everything but he's not. I remember in an interview he said that he sang backups on 'Jeepster,' but the truth is there are no backing vocals on it, so they didn't sing on that. I know he believes that, and God bless him, it's a long time ago, but all you have to do is listen, and I defy you to find a backing vocal.

When I say 'Telegram Sam' onward, I know the chronology, but no one else would. They didn't, for instance, sing on 'Children Of The Revolution.' That's Marc and myself, sounding like Flo & Eddie. They probably *think* they sang on it, but it's really hard to find credits on the T. Rex albums. *Electric Warrior* was the last well-credited album. After that, Marc just didn't want you to know that there were people making the sound. It's a real shame, but I hope I can set the record straight.

Mark and Howard entered with 'Seagull Woman' from the *T. Rex* album. They sang on all of *Electric Warrior* and some of *The Slider*. Marc B. and Tony V. started to sing on *The Slider*. Mark and Howard never sang on *Tanx* or any albums afterward. The backup singers were either Marc and myself, or female singers. Ironically, none of the T. Rex band members (Steve, Micky, or Bill) ever sang backups, except for the chant at the beginning of 'The Groover' ('*T–R–E–X*').

We didn't sing on everything, but as I recall, we did sing on a few more than Tony mentioned. We did 'New York City,' 'Telegram Sam,' 'Children Of The Revolution,' plus a few others. But who's counting?

See discography for Tony's list of exactly who sang on which T. Rex songs.

8

FLO & EDDIE

THE FIRST BAND

GARY ROWLES I first met Mark and Howard at the Troubadour. I played in a lot of bands, but as far as *national* is concerned, my recording career started with Love in 1969. I was playing with Emitt Rhodes on a little two-week tour. He was a class act musically, and that was a very, very sweet situation, and it was at that gig that Mark and Howard came up and said that they were forming a new band. They wanted me to play on their record, and they had a Warners deal, so it was kind of an easy thing to check out.

HAL WILLNER The first time I saw them perform live was right after they left Zappa. It was that same band, the Phlorescent Leech & Eddie band, and it was one of the great shows. Especially if you knew the record—which, of course, few people did.

JACK UNDERWOOD He was playing the Whisky A Go-Go on the Sunset Strip with Flo & Eddie, and that would have been the first time I'd seen him onstage since The Crossfires. I was blown out. I mean, just the power. They had morphed from The Crossfires to Flo & Eddie, and it was great. They always worked to make everybody happy and excited, and Mark has known how to do that from day one.

HENRY DILTZ It was a real clever, fast-paced, entertaining show. They had so much fun, and the music was great. All those songs were so upbeat and engaging, but it was beyond that. The force of personalities and their natural, easygoing comedy just drew you in. It was very joyful.

RAY MANZAREK We went to Europe with Flo & Eddie. We toured with them right after Morrison died, and right after they left Frank. Talk about posttraumatic stress, God almighty! I don't remember anything other than banter backstage with those guys. It was hysterical, man. A very funny tour. We had a great time. I don't know what cities we played, I couldn't tell you any of that, but we were on German TV.

In 1973, Alice Cooper's *Billion Dollar Babies* tour was breaking box office records everywhere it went. Flo & Eddie were the opening act for nearly all of the dates, as well as many the previous year.

BOB EZRIN They're great entertainers. They're droll, unbelievably musical, and really funny to watch, and at the same time they would do things vocally that mere mortals couldn't do. Obviously, it's tough to open for Alice Cooper, no matter who you are. And that audience is not necessarily going to be oriented toward this kind of fun pop music. But I think that, generally, they got it.

ALICE COOPER I never had so much fun in my life as I did when they opened for us on that tour. *Billion Dollar Babies* was the #1 album, and we had our own jet. Getting on the plane with the guys, first thing, everybody popped a tall can of Budweiser and the poker game started. And it lasted for seven, eight months. Every day, that game was going. We'd land at the airport and all the press was there and we'd end the press conference with the table turning over. That was really, truly the most fun I ever had.

SKIP TAYLOR I had done many, many European tours, and when Alice wanted to go, it was decided I was the guy to go with. And, lo and behold, the opening act was Flo & Eddie. I lived up in Laurel Canyon and we ran into each other at studios and stuff all the way back to the Turtles days, but until then, we hadn't worked together.

It seemed like everybody on the tour were ping-pong players. Mark and Howard put together this big seating chart, listing each guy's name and who would play who, and who would move on, like a tennis tournament. Every night we rented a suite and had them take all the furniture out and put up a ping-pong table that we carried on the plane. I had these little cards printed with *You are invited to this private Alice Cooper after-show party*. And there was a blank line for the hotel and room number. I would go out into the audience each night and find the best-looking women, and say, 'If you're with a guy or you're married, don't bother coming, but if you want to come alone, fine.'

The whole Alice Cooper and Flo & Eddie crew would get back to the hotel, and it would look like a casting call for all these women. And the funny thing was, everybody would just go into this big suite to watch the ping-pong. It wasn't like guys were running off with these women. There were drinks and beer and whatever, but almost everyone would wind up with a woman as well as a good game of ping-pong.

GARY ROWLES At the college and club shows we had a lot of fun. They were more intimate, but when it got to the Alice Cooper thing, it lost the lightness. Everything got heavy. We did the *School's Out* European tour in '72. All these people were out there with their eye makeup on, and they wanted to see Alice put his head on the guillotine, and that's not really Flo & Eddie. My son was born when I was in Zurich. It was the last gig. The tour was extended so I missed his birth, and they dedicated the last show to me, the new dad. Alice put his white top hat on me, and I kept it. I've still got it in my studio today.

The next spring, we went out and did the *Billion Dollar Babies* tour, which was a ninety-eight-day tour of the North America. The crowds were getting more and more in-your-face, and it was less and less about the music. There was a cynicism that was starting to present itself, especially after being on the Cooper tour, where everything was *I don't give a shit* and drink a beer and throw it in the audience, and a lot of that kind of fuck-you attitude. The music seemed like it was going away, and that was when I knew that I was a short-timer, because the last thing I wanted to do was go out and watch Alice hang himself for ninety-eight days.

JIM PONS We were opening for people that used to open for us, and it started to be a little demeaning, tiresome. That's when I started running out of gas. My last tour was in 1973—an awesome European tour followed by ninety-one one-nighters in a hundred and two days, all over the country, opening for Alice Cooper, sometimes thirty thousand people a night. Alice was a great guy, but after that, I wanted to change everything. The fun was going out of it, and I wanted to change my life, my geographical location, my profession, everything. That's why, when I met somebody in New York, and I turned thirty in Fayetteville, North Carolina, I said, 'I don't want to do this anymore.'

It started out as a lark. I started a band just to play fraternity parties while I was in school, and we had a hit record, and I got sucked into the music business. It was wonderful, but when it ceased to be wonderful, I jumped out of it. I had a new life waiting for me. I was happy to sign away any and all of my rights to the Turtles music, the masters that White Whale owned. The day after I arrived in New York, I got hired as a video and film director for the New York Jets. That kept me busy for the next twenty-seven years.

THE SECOND BAND

CRAIG KRAMPF I was with The Robbs, and that's what got me to California in June of 1966. We became the house band for *Where The Action Is*, and on our third or fourth show, The Turtles were guests, and there was a bond instantaneously. It was an exciting time. They had hit records already. We hadn't had a hit, although there was hope for a single that was out.

Around the beginning of '67, The Turtles, Buffalo Springfield, and The Robbs did a short tour through the Midwest. We were the openers and The Turtles headlined. Now we're not just lip-syncing on a television show, but we're out there playing our asses off. The whole memory of that tour brings a smile to my face. It was like taking the Sunset Strip out on the road. It was an absolutely wonderful, zany time. It was the 60s: a lot of weed. There was always weed.

Eventually, The Robbs changed their name to Cherokee, and we started a studio. I was doing other gigs on the side: I was with Little Richard for a while, and I was playing with The Hudson Brothers. Fall of '74, Mark and Howard do the soundtrack for *Dirty Duck* at Cherokee Studios, so we hook up again. The duck has to do a soft-shoe dance, so I got a board, sand, and sugar, and I'm shuffling my feet so the duck can do a dance. It was nothing but good times, chain-smoking joint after joint, doing these wonderfully absurd tunes. And, shortly thereafter, they decided they wanted to form a band again. They knew me going back to '66, and I recommended Phil Reed, who was in The Hudson Brothers with me. Erik was hanging around Cherokee, so we recommended him for the gig too.

ERIK SCOTT I had just moved to L.A., and I hooked up with the guys at Cherokee Studios. They asked if I wanted to go out on road with Flo & Eddie. We rehearsed three times with Craig, Phil, Bruce Robb, and me. That was the ceiling for Mark and Howard. That might have been a direct result of Zappa. It was three days of rehearsal, music, and entertainment cues alike. The lads were not into rehearsing. They liked the show to come together onstage.

CRAIG KRAMPF Phil and I left The Hudson Brothers and off we went with that incarnation of Flo & Eddie. And at this point in my life, after working so hard and coming close but never having a hit, it was the perfect time to laugh at rock'n'roll. It couldn't have happened at a more perfect point in my career. It was an incredible release.

BOB TRUAX My position was as road manager between '74 and '76, and those were the best years. Skip would get everything booked and then hand it over to me for the hotel reservations and all of that—get them out there and give them their money when they needed money, things like that. I had already worked with Alice Cooper, Zappa, and Tim Buckley, but to hook up with those guys, it was the most fun I'd ever had. Everybody got along, and there was nothing uptight about any of them. I was known as Fucking Bob: *Where's Fucking Bob? Is he getting our tickets? Which airline is this? Does he know where we're going?* They gave me that nickname. I loved them.

ERIK SCOTT December 10th was the first gig, in Ebbets Field. We flew into Denver the night before and hung around the hotel drinking. Bonding is what you call it when everybody in the band gets together and gets drunk and smashed and smokes doobies and shit. That was the first night. We did some Colorado gigs, then came back and did the Troubadour over the holidays, and this was true for all the Flo & Eddie shows: they were such industry favorites, everybody loved them. And for me, a new guy, it was like playing the Super Bowl as a rookie. I was like a supporting player in a rock star zoo, because everybody would come. You'd find, for example, on Christmas Eve they had the Peter Asher / Linda Ronstadt / James Taylor / Joni Mitchell contingent come to sing Christmas carols. They came up, and then the next night Keith Moon and Alice Cooper came up.

It was a good graduate school for an introduction to the personalities in the business, because it was almost a decade after the first hits and Mark and Howard had seen everything. They still had this wonderful appreciation for the business, but they had seen the excesses of the ridiculousness from the industry, so they had this unique perspective and the ability to make fun of it in a way that was both loving and hysterical.

CRAIG KRAMPF Bruce Robb was on keyboards for the December shows. Then the whole studio thing started happening more and more for the boys, so we brought Andy in.

ANDY CAHAN I was with Jimmy Carl Black in Geronimo Black, and we used to hang out with The Robbs at Cherokee Studios. Craig got me a job working with Little Richard, and then he got me the job with Flo & Eddie.

BOB TRUAX They couldn't go out as The Turtles, but people knew who they were. It was always full, and there was never a show that the audience didn't leave satisfied. It was kind of X-rated. When we played in Reno, they told us not to come back. But that's all changed now. Now they're playing Disney World.

CRAIG KRAMPF We had our set routines, but it could change. People would call up the name of a song or an artist and Mark would quickly turn around, count 'one, two, three, four,' and off we would go. And it had to be good, otherwise it wouldn't have been funny. In order to laugh at rock'n'roll, what came off the stage better be good. And we were. That band was able to pull stuff like that off.

ERIK SCOTT From a technical standpoint, it wasn't a hard gig. It was more about timing and being able to change gears immediately. They'd make a satirical reference, and *boom*: we'd go into one of the hits of the group they were sending up; the big hook that's going to be recognizable for ten seconds. It was a little like current events. Come to think of it, it was kind of along the lines of Stephen Colbert and Jon Stewart. From a pop standpoint, it dovetails with their radio show.

CRAIG KRAMPF There were so many different cues. The Flying Sanzini Brothers: 'One hand: bang! One hand, two ducks: bang-bang!' And all of a sudden here's a stuffed hippo getting thrown through the ring of fire. There's these little musical interludes and bam, we'd be right back into the feel of what we were doing. One of my favorites was a lampoon of all the boogie songs. '*You want a boogie / We'll give you boogie / We'll give you boogie, you assholes.*' And then a solo section, and you could go wherever you wanted to. Any key, any groove, as long as you met back at the pass after twelve bars. Some nights the cacophony was absolutely brilliant. And then we'd get back into the song, back to the boogie. That was a brilliant little thing.

ERIK SCOTT Before all the tour buses, it was flying to whatever airport was closest to the gig and renting a station wagon. And we'd race. Mark was at the bottom of this. It was who could get their car rented faster, running through the airport, throwing the stuff in the station wagon and driving as fast as we could, one guy reading the map because the whole band was in the race now. Racing to see who can get to the gig first. But the craziness kept us sane on the road. We acted crazy for any reason.

CRAIG KRAMPF In Hawaii, we played to seventy thousand people. The festival was actually inside Diamond Head crater. That's where we hooked up with Fleetwood Mac. Not a heck of a lot was really going on with their career at that point. Mick gave me an acetate of 'Rhiannon,' which hadn't been released yet. In a few cities they would say, 'You guys are bigger than we are here, why don't you headline tonight?' The last day of us being out with them, we sat with Mick and John McVie. They're doing a lot of blow and telling us that when they get back to L.A., they're probably gonna break up the band. We leave the tour, and all of a sudden 'Rhiannon' starts getting played, and the rest is history. But they were that close. Sure, a lot of cocaine—the philosophy powder—was doing the talking, but still, quite an amazing turnaround.

Then we went out with the Starship. So, all of a sudden, there's Mr. Barbata again. He would sit in and do one or two songs occasionally. There was no bad feeling at that point. Johnny seemed so happy. He was in another big rock band, and he was definitely enjoying the moment. That was at the height of their hit, 'Miracles,' and the *Red Octopus* album. One of the Starship's

1 My parents, Bea and Joe Volman, in our back yard in Westchester, California. They had "happy hour" every evening. My dad would make Manhattans, Martinis, and Margaritas. **2** My mom's side of the family, the Campillos. My grandmother, Maria, is on the far right. **3** My father and me when I was nine years old. My brother was eight years older than me, so my dad was an older father. He let me be obnoxious. **4** In my front yard in Westchester at age ten. The two other boys were my neighbors, Bruce Clark and Ralph Dorsey. **5** My little league team. My dad was the coach. My mom worked for the league, scheduling umpires and running concessions. We won the championship that year. I am in the middle row, second from the right. Interestingly, we used to play on what is now the Loyola Marymount University baseball field. It came full circle!

ABOVE The Turtles, 1966. Left to right: me, Jim Tucker, Howard Kaylan, Chuck Portz, Al Nichol, John Barbata.

OPPOSITE 1 Me on tour in 1966. There are a lot of photos where I'm wearing sunglasses and trying to be hip. **2** Denny Jones (the original Phlorescent Leech) and Carlos Bernal (the original Eddie) with Howard. We'd known them since high school, and they were our crew for the Crossfires and early Turtles shows. We named them that, well ... probably because we were high.

3 Stephen Stills, me in my cool 1966 necklace, and Bones Howe. Bones produced the first Turtles album, as well as The Fifth Dimension, The Association, The Mamas & The Papas, and many more. **4&5** Me playing tambourine in 1965 at McCormick Place in Chicago, Illinois. We were starting to get comfortable on big stages by then.

1

2

3

4

5

1

2

3

4

5

6

TOP In the 1980s, we decided to do one of those goofy old-timey Western photos, and we thought it was so funny that we made it our promotional band photo. I should bring that look back. Left to right: Chris Apostle, Tristan Avakian, Howard, me, Joe Stefko, and Donnie Kisselbach.

BOTTOM Howard and I went on tour with Stephen Stills at Stanford University in the 1970s. In this picture: George "Chocolate" Perry on bass, Stephen Stills, Neil Young, me, and Donnie Dacus. Joe Lala was on drums (not pictured).

OPPOSITE 1 Me, my daughter Sarina, and my first wife Pat in 1969. This was one of the best years of our marriage. We were growing a family, living in the Hollywood Hills, and I was getting to tour. **2** Graham Nash, James Burton, and me at a charity show at the Thomas & Mack Center in Las Vegas in the 1980s. **3** The Turtles onstage at the Hollywood Bowl in 1967. I'm wearing a Mickey Mouse pin. I always tried to pick out goofy things to add to my wardrobe. **4** The Turtles performing "Elenore" on *Kraft Music Hall* (NBC) in 1968. You might notice a short tie, which was a callback to the tie I wore on *The Ed Sullivan Show*. I may have been the first person to "brand" a fashion style. Way ahead of my time. **5** Shadoe Stevens, me, Harry Nilsson, and Howard when we were doing *Flo & Eddie By The Fireside* in the 1970s at KROQ in Los Angeles. **6** Me, Stephen Stills, and Allan McDougall (PR for A&M Records) in 1968. Stephen was staying at a place in the English countryside, and I came to hang out with him and Henry Diltz.

1

2

3

4

5

6

ABOVE Gene Simmons and me messing around before we introduced KISS at Anaheim Stadium in 1976. We dressed up like them for the show.

OPPOSITE 1 Me, Carly Simon, Linda Ronstadt, and Joni Mitchell, among other choir members, at a Christmas show in the 1970s. **2** Me having my face painted like a KISS band member at Anaheim Stadium. That's their makeup guy. **3** David Bowie and me on his Thin White Duke tour, 1976. We were invited to meet David by his press person, Barbara DeWitt.

4 Howard and me on the plane for Alice Cooper's *Billion Dollar Babies* tour in 1973. We were the opening act. **5** The whole crew and band for the *Billion Dollar Babies* tour. **6** Howard and I were on WXRK (K-ROCK) in New York as the drivetime DJs. Gene Simmons and Paul Stanley were our guests that day.

1

2

4

3

5

FLO & EDDIE

ABOVE A promo picture of Howard and me, from when we were on Columbia Records as Flo & Eddie.

OPPOSITE 1 Flo & Eddie had a TV show on CBS in the 1970s. This is Gary U.S. Bonds, me, and Howard doing our Sanzini Brothers bit, where we would light a hula hoop on fire and throw stuffed animals through it. **2** Another bit we did for this TV show was learning how to cook lobsters. **3** Me, Pat, Sarina, and Hallie in a photo booth, 1975.

4 The Eagles Charity Tennis Tournament, 1976. This is Keith Moon (who was paired with Micky Dolenz) and me. I was paired with Olivia Newton-John. The Cycle Sluts were a Hollywood rock band who were also in the tournament. **5** Me at a Flo & Eddie concert with my adopted Telecaster, given to me by Frank Zappa. I had a Martin acoustic guitar that Frank really liked, so we traded.

ABOVE Max Weinberg, Ronnie Spector, Bruce Springsteen, Miami Steven Van Zandt, Howard, me, and Roy Bittan from The E-Street Band. Ronnie came to Cleveland and sang four songs with us because she had been working on 'Say Goodbye To Hollywood' with Bruce.

OPPOSITE 1 Me, Howard, and Garrett Morris on *The Flo & Eddie Show* on CBS. Let it be known that we got along really well with Garrett. Great guy. **2** Howard, Kathleen Turner, and me backstage after a Flo & Eddie concert at the Bottom Line in New York. She fell in love with us. What a swinging time.

3 Howard, Eddie Money, and me at a K-ROCK show in Central Park, 1990. Eddie was a great songwriter. He doesn't get enough credit. **4** K-ROCK engineer Tim Reid, music director Robert Benjamin, myself, Alice Cooper, and Howard at the radio station. **5&6** Howard and me with Ozzy Osbourne at the radio station. I still have that Hollywood High School T-shirt!

1

2

3

4

5

6

1

2

3

4

ABOVE We interviewed Curtis Sliwa and Lisa Evers, the founders of the Guardian Angels vigilante group, for our CBS show. They were wild. We did a bit where Lisa was going to teach me some basic self-defense moves, and she ended up breaking my wrist.
RIGHT One of my favorite promo pictures of the 1980s band. Left to right: me, Howard, Dave Nelson, Chris Apostle, Joe Stefko, and Donnie Kisselbach.

OPPOSITE 1 Howard and me at a Miss Teen USA event, which we worked on with George Honchar. The events were free to the city where the pageant happened, and we performed with Gary Puckett and The Grass Roots. **2** This is one of my favorite pictures of myself. So rockstar! Taken at an outdoor concert at Santa Monica College, during the *Moving Targets* era. **3** Howard and I used to open our shows with a parody theme, and this was the heavy metal era. We had those cheap blow-up guitars you win at carnivals, and we would walk on to a bed of smoke-machine mist and pretend we were shredding. **4** I don't remember where or when this picture was taken. Sometime in the 1980s. My pants were very tight.

ABOVE This is one of many lovely pictures of me from the late 1990s. I believe I was in college at the time of this show. That tambourine is still with me. It's VERY duct-taped now, but it works!

OPPOSITE 1 Alice Cooper, Ke$ha, and me, backstage in Nashville in 2014. Emily took this photo because she was a big Ke$ha fan. **2** Emily and me at a 'Dancing With The Nashville Stars' charity event. I practiced a swing dance for months and ended up winning the Online Favorite Award. Not too shabby. **3** I have always loved bike riding, so Emily and I asked our friends Glenn and Ursula Houghton to go with us on a trip through the North Carolina wine country in 2011. They had a support van to climb into if you enjoyed more of the wine than the biking.

4 Emily and I both became lay speakers in the United Methodist Church in the early 2000s. It required weeks of study and ended up giving us the ability to give sermons in our church district. **5** Aww, those were good times. We had just come back from New Orleans, where we ran a half marathon together. **6** This is a great picture. We don't have too many of these together. This is Sarina, Hallie, myself, and Emily in front of the General Jackson Showboat, Nashville, in 2014.

1

2

3

UNITED METHODIST MINISTRIES – LOS ANGELES DISTRICT
2000 FALL LAY MINISTRY SCHOOL
Certificate of Completion
for
Lay Speaker

This is to certify that

Mark Volman

Has met all of the requirements and successfully completed the

BASIC COURSE IN LAY SPEAKING

*Conducted at Culver-Palms United Methodist Church, October 2 - November 6, 2000 and is hereby awarded
this Certificate of Completion by the Los Angeles District Committee on Lay Speaking Ministry
Given under our hand on this 6th day of November 2000.*

4

5

6

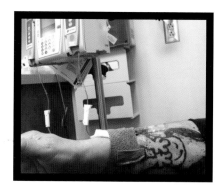

TOP Howard and me, still going strong in concert, 2009.

ABOVE LEFT In 2015, I was diagnosed with cancer and had to come in for chemotherapy treatments. It was around this time that I got that tattoo of Snoopy, originally painted by Tom Everhart. Snoopy covering his eyes was exactly how I was feeling at the time.

ABOVE RIGHT Here are my lovely daughters, Sarina and Hallie, backstage with me in 2001 at the Universal Ampitheatre, which was demolished in 2013. Man, that was one of the best venues to play, too.

biggest times ever. We were treated great. The same with Fleetwood Mac: both incredibly compatible tours. Most of them were.

GARY ROWLES Mark had a Fender Telecaster that he used to throw around onstage, and how it survived that abuse, I will never know, but that guitar should be in the Rock And Roll Hall Of Abuse. It would probably be one of the top three survivors.

ERIK SCOTT He wasn't the lead guitar player, but he played rhythm parts, and he did a fine job of it, and that's him on the records as well. When we were recording and he didn't have to do the theatre, he played all his parts just fine. His parts were important, absolutely.

CRAIG KRAMPF Mark was always the guy in charge. He was the leader, definitely.

ERIK SCOTT As a bandleader, he was always inclusive and generous and gracious. I loved working for those guys. Howard was free to be his intellectual acerbic wit, and then Mark was involved with the band and all that came with it.

CRAIG KRAMPF On one tour, Bruce Springsteen & The E Street Band were a day or two ahead of us on the same circuit. Every club we went into: 'Oh my God—Bruce was here!' People would go on and on. That was the first time I ever heard his name. Later, we played in Montauk, New Jersey. That's Springsteen territory, and several of the E Street Band came to the show that night and came backstage. After the show we went to Max Weinberg's house.

GARRY TALLENT I first met Mark when Craig Krampf was playing drums, so we're talking a long time ago. I went to see them at a local club in Asbury Park, and I couldn't believe it. I'd forgotten how many hits they had. They kept doing one hit after another. I was very impressed. At that point we hadn't had a hit record yet, and they had like a whole string of them.

ERIK SCOTT I got to meet a lot of larger than life rock stars, and you come realize that they're just regular schmoes. It's fuckups like me, who can do something pretty good and got lucky. There's a talent, and maybe that talent is kind of awesome, but the rest of their lives they're not supernatural in any way.

I would accompany Mark to visit some of these pop stars in their hotel rooms during tours. At one point I went with him to Stephen Stills' room during the backgammon craze—this was the thing to do on tour. We're playing backgammon, and I won the first three games. Here I am, just a boob from the Midwest playing with Stephen Stills, my gosh, and I'd won the first three games, and he got pissed and started cheating. And I couldn't . . . what am I going to say? *Excuse me, Mr. Stills, that was a three and a two, not two threes?*

SKIP TAYLOR Mark came to me one day and said, 'Stephen Stills wants us to go on tour with him. I don't know, man, why don't you explore this.' So I talked with him, and Stephen said, 'I want Mark and Howard to open for me—do an opening set—and then they can stay to sing background, but the one thing is, I'd like them to ride on the bus with me.' I said, 'So this is the rent-a-friend tour?' That's exactly how I've always referred to it. They went out to sing background and open for Stephen, and the money was as good as they had ever made, because none of Stephen's band would ride on the bus with him. At the time, he was always coked-out and drunk. So, they were really paid to travel with Stephen. The gig was no big deal, but if they had to be on the bus, they were gonna get paid well.

CRAIG KRAMPF I remember Stills crawling on his hands and knees and not being able to find his room. He was pretty far gone at that time, doing blow and drinking fifths of scotch every night. One time we were backstage, and he called for ice. The roadie brought him a huge bucket of ice and he went face down for about forty-five seconds, which is a long time to be face down in a bucket of ice. That tour he was pretty out there but musically brilliant.

PATRICK SIMMONS I grew up in the 60s, and I loved all the 60s music. The Turtles were at the height of what was happening at the time, so I really listened to their music a lot. Probably more than most bands, actually. I never saw them play live until we started doing shows with them. We did a lot of touring around 1976, '77, and did a lot of shows together, and we hit it off really well. They're just great people, and there's a history there in terms of our respect for them. They'd always sit in and sing with us on a few tunes. And we used to do silly crazy stuff: we would walk on in the middle of their set wearing stupid costumes and do some kind of a skit, and vice versa, they would do something crazy. One night they came out in the middle of our set and set up a table onstage and started having wine and something to eat, like they were in a restaurant. That kind of stuff went on all the time, so that was an added highlight for all of us.

JEFF 'SKUNK' BAXTER It was during Oktoberfest, and we were in Cincinnati, and I just thought, *What the hell, why don't we have Mark and Howard join us onstage.* We had a five-course table set for a meal. We had a waiter, the whole thing. And they just sat onstage having dinner while we did the whole show. I don't know, it just made sense to me at the time.

ERIK SCOTT We did an amazing amount of touring. To go out with the Starship, which had the #1 album in the summer of '75, then the Doobies, who had the #1 album of 1976, and then we'd do Stephen Stills . . . there weren't really any bigger tours at that time. It meant playing sheds and amphitheaters with twenty thousand a night, and we had a very cabaret sort of act. It wasn't particularly designed for the big rock show. It works best in a more intimate setting where you can understand the commentary and their asides, but everybody loved Flo & Eddie and wanted them on their tours.

SKIP TAYLOR The home I lived in was one of the wildest places going. Mark and Howard, Don Henley, Glenn Frey, Stephen Stills, Dave Mason—they all were frequenters at my house, because it was always drugs and women. And that's what they gravitated to. Because I had to get my bands out of jail, or worry about them getting busted, I wound up getting more drugs, so that the guys could get them from me, rather than somebody else on the street. I made sure they were quality drugs, at the cheapest possible price. They were going to get 'em anyway, so the quality was improved, the price was decreased, and the risk was lessened. At least, that's the way I looked at it at the time.

TIM SEXTON Oh, God, I forgot about Skip. He was a dope dealer. There were a lot of guys that were like Skip who had leadership capability but used it in the wrong way. My thing was that I basically confiscated the stuff, and I became the equivalent of the medicine chest. So, I made sure everybody got to sleep at night, even if it meant to take this pill. And I got everybody up in the morning. I never got busted. Truth be told, I was probably terrified of doing the wrong thing, so I was always careful.

BOB TRUAX In the rehearsal studio once, a trunk was delivered and no one paid any attention to it, and an hour later Skip came by and opened it up. There were fifty pounds of cocaine inside. They were blocks, and he stuck his fingernail in there and said, 'Try this.' It was cocaine like you'd never find anywhere else: the highest quality. His cocaine, as far as cocaine goes, you couldn't touch it.

RON NEVISON Skip was deep into that stuff. I remember him freaking out one day when we were at the Record Plant. He had one of these airline bags, and he said he couldn't find $25,000—$25,000 was missing and he was freaking out, running around yelling, 'Somebody ripped me off!' and it ended up that it had one of those false bottoms. That's where the $25,000 was. Another time, he put some coke under the console to dry out with heat lamp. There was like a pound of coke under the console with a heat lamp on top of it.

BOB TRUAX Skip was big-time coke. Our tickets would say Los Angeles to Hawaii to Fiji to Australia, and coming back it was kind of the same thing, Fiji to Hawaii. Skip's ticket said South America to somewhere else in South America to San Francisco. I don't know if I should even be saying this, but I saw the tickets. I don't know if anyone else did. It just seemed funny.

SKIP TAYLOR I had a home invasion robbery at my house one night. They took some drugs and drug paraphernalia and stuff like that, and while they're questioning me, the guy's gun went off—I think accidentally—and went through a stack of albums that were lying on the floor right alongside of where I was laying on the floor. And the top album was *Moving Targets*. When I told Mark and Howard, they were terrified. They thought it was a message. They didn't want to be associated in any way.

PHIL REED

ANDY CAHAN Phil was dealing cocaine, and it was all tied in with Skip. We were on the road and one of the cocaine deals went sour. The guys came into Skip's house and tied them up, and on the living room floor was a stack of albums, and the first album was the *Moving Targets* album. The guy took a gun and shot a hole right through the album cover like a warning: pay up or they would do whatever they had to do to rectify their drug deal.

BOB TRUAX Phil didn't deal [drugs].

CRAIG KRAMPF How honest was Skip? How much do you know? I don't know if Phil and Skip were doing stuff together. At first I thought Skip was a guy that always had incredible cocaine, and then I realized that he was dealing, but I don't think we truly knew until later to what extent. There was a shooting. So that theory also existed: 'Look, Skip, you're not safe.'

ANDY CAHAN After that, we were touring with the Doobie Brothers, and we were at a hotel in Salt Lake City, a Hilton or whatever.

CRAIG KRAMPF The first date of the tour was Salt Lake City. It was October '76, and it was a great show, absolutely tremendous. The Doobies brought us out at the end, and everybody was up onstage, doing 'Black Water.' You could tell that there was going to be camaraderie between the Doobies and our band. There were no star trips, just a bunch of regular guys, and it was going to be awesome.

After the show, several of us went up to Phil's room. He was up on the ninth floor, and we were talking about all sorts of things: that this tour was just going to be an amazing tour, a long one, but how cool? It was going to be a great audience for us, and we could tell already that the bands were going to get along. Phil and his wife, Jeanie, had gotten into CB radios, and they had a big ham radio setup where they could talk to the truckers out on the highways. Phil had brought along a portable CB thing, and I remember him going out on the balcony and trying to get some reception to see if we could hear anybody.

ANDY CAHAN Phil was very much into ham radio and talking like truck drivers, 'Ten-four good buddy' and all that stuff. I was hanging out with him in my room—his room was right next to mine—and we were talking on the radio, and then I said goodnight.

CRAIG KRAMPF And then it was just me and Phil, and I left last, so I guess I was the last one from the band to see him alive. I left his room about 1:20, and it was like, *Okay man—see you tomorrow.* The rest of us were on the fourth and fifth floors, so I went down to my room and went to sleep. And the next thing I remember is the phone ringing. It was still dark outside, and it was Bob, our road manager. I remember the words: 'Craig, you better come down to Mark's room, something's happened to Phil.' Everybody in the band is there, and that's when they told me that they had found Phil. The paperboy delivering the morning papers to the hotel found Phil nine stories down.

BOB TRUAX I got a call saying that Phil had fallen out of the window and it was on the tenth floor but he landed on his feet. It didn't make any sense to any of us.

ANDY CAHAN Somehow he was either pushed or jumped off or whatever from his balcony. I believe it was murder. It wasn't an accident.

BOB TRUAX Mark had left early—he went with the Doobies to the next gig, so we had to call him and tell him that Phil was dead. He had already gone to the next town.

I'm not sure when I left, but I did go on ahead with The Doobie Brothers to the next town.

CRAIG KRAMPF Everyone was in complete shock. And because I went back the longest with Phil, I was the guy that had to go to the hospital and identify the body, and then go to the police station. I knew it wasn't a suicide. The police were asking if he was despondent, and it just didn't compute. He was really trying to investigate the suicide angle, and I'm going, 'I have no idea what happened, but I can give you 100% it wasn't suicide. I find that impossible.' I think the guy finally believed me. I went back up to Mark's room, and we were just baffled, absolutely baffled. And then it was time to make the phone call to Jeannie and tell her that Phil was dead. That was, to say the least, incredibly difficult, giving somebody that news. Pat was going over; maybe she was with Jeannie at that time.

PAT VOLMAN That was a shocker. That was the most tragic thing that happened in a long time, losing somebody that close to you. Phil was such a sweet guy.

I did speak with Phil that night after the show, and I did tell him that we were thinking of having a different band. But it was not about him or anyone specific, just a possible change in the future. After his death, I spent a long time thinking I may have caused the reason Phil killed himself, and I felt guilty.

CRAIG KRAMPF Mark told Phil we might not continue as a full-time band? I never knew that. And we had the three-month Doobies tour ahead of us. It was the first night of the tour.

ANDY CAHAN Mark talked to Phil about ending the band? Are you serious? I didn't know that. That's the first I've heard anything like that. I don't think that was it, though. Mark and Howard loved Phil. I don't know if that happened, maybe Mark did talk to him. See, stuff goes on that I don't know.

CRAIG KRAMPF I went up to Phil's room—and this was bizarre—the hotel was laid out so that it had a long hallway, but then every two rooms had their own tiny three or four foot by four foot little hallway. So, the doors of rooms faced one another. I left Phil's room last, and leaving, I looked at the door that was three feet away, and there was nothing wrong with that door. Now, that room across from Phil's had all sorts of damage, like somebody had taken a screwdriver or a knife, trying to get in, and the door was propped open with an ashtray. That door was not like that when I left at 1:20 in the morning. So that absolutely baffled us. Was it the police trying to get in? Was it something that happened during the night after I left Phil?

BOB TRUAX There were a couple of girls in the room next to his, and the balcony was adjoined. They didn't know if he tried to jump the balcony or exactly how that happened, but his door was locked and bolted. It wasn't like someone came into it.

CRAIG KRAMPF What we were thinking for a while was that something was going on in that room next to Phil's, and either Phil was trying to peer into that room from the balcony—would he step over the rail to try to see what the hell was going on in there? That could have been an accident, then—or, maybe Phil came across something he wasn't supposed to come across.

PAT VOLMAN It was a very strange time after that. There were some negative elements at that point, with the drugs and all. That's the stuff nobody likes to talk about, because I heard awful stories and I just wanted to forget about it. That's when you don't want to know.

PATRICK SIMMONS That was a shock to all of us. We had been having a great time. Almost every night we would play and then we'd come back to the hotel and hang out and have a few drinks. There was a real camaraderie going on there. We had all been together with Phil that night, actually. And the next day we all got up and he was gone.

SKIP TAYLOR I wasn't there. I wasn't on the road with them. I heard about it, and, in all honesty, I really don't have any idea. Nothing ever surfaced, and it had nothing to do with me in any way, shape, or form. There's one theory that it was a suicide, and another that maybe Phil was involved in some drug dealing. But I never had any connection with him other than the band, and didn't know if he was involved in anything further. He certainly wasn't with me. I really don't know about it, never did. That was at the conclusion of our association, at that point. I might have booked that tour, but it was one of the last days, if not the last day, of the tour. As I said, I wasn't on the road with them at that point. I did a lot of dates, and I was out there for some of the time period but . . . you know what? Maybe I *was* there. God, I don't remember. That's terrible to say, but I don't remember.

BOB TRUAX The whole band went down into one room. We changed all our rooms and shared one room all together. There was an apprehension: *Is* *someone after the group?* Every idea was floating around. *Does someone want to do the whole group in?* And so we just settled into one room for the next day, and then we flew back to L.A.

PATRICK SIMMONS They were left in a bind as to what they should do, because they needed to get him back to his family. They also needed to find somebody to come and fill in. They were in the middle of this tour, and they'd made commitments, so they had to find somebody as fast as they could. They were having trouble getting flights and getting things lined up, so we lent them the Doobie Liner, and they all jumped on that.

JEFF 'SKUNK' BAXTER They needed the plane? No problem. You have to reach out to your friends—that's the name of that game.

PATRICK SIMMONS We were so happy that we were able to help, that we had that option, because these days we don't do that. So it was the right place at the right time and it worked out.

CRAIG KRAMPF Flying home, nobody was sure what was going to happen next. Everybody was shellshocked. All we knew is we were going home. We'd just headed out on tour, and here we are, back home two days later. It was just mindboggling. I don't have the right adjectives to describe how it felt. Shit like that doesn't happen to us.

There was a ceremony for Phil out on a boat. We all went on the boat and there was a scattering of his ashes out at sea.

Phil's death sent all of us out of control. After the tour, Howard and I took a year off. To this day, I don't know what happened. Everyone has a different opinion of what went on. It's like each of us sitting in a different corner of the same room, seeing the same thing from a different angle, and I feel that with this part of the story.

HARVEY KUBERNIK It was in the local newspapers. It was even in *Rolling Stone*. We all felt—and remember this is a world pre-internet and TMZ—we all felt it sounded a little weird. It just didn't make sense. You would never associate any sense of tragedy with Flo & Eddie because it was a comedy troupe. You didn't think that there was tragedy, chaos, murder, suicide, or anything around those kinds of people, because they were always laughing and having fun.

BOB TRUAX It turned me off of cocaine. I don't think I ever did it after Phil died. I got so I hated it. I gave it away. I just said, 'I don't want any more of this.'

CRAIG KRAMPF Something happened in that room. But—and the question probably still lingers to this day—what the hell happened? Nobody truly seems to know. Jeannie and her father actually hired a private investigator for a month, and they came up cold.

ERIK SCOTT We came back to Los Angeles and had one day of auditioning with three guitarists. Each guy played three songs with us. The third fella was Billy, and he got the gig.

BILLY STEELE They called me up in November '76. I'd never met Mark or Howard, but Erik and I had played together in a few bands, and I knew Craig from Cherokee. I did the audition, got the gig, and we were on the road in about a week, if that. The first show was Cobo Hall in Detroit, opening for The Doobie Brothers. We stayed out until the end of their tour. Before joining, I'd never seen the band, so I didn't have much of a sense as to how the humor fit in. Mark always said, 'Anything that happens onstage is part of the show.' Crazy stuff would occur spontaneously and we'd just follow along. One time we were sitting in the dressing room, and he said, 'Let's go out there and everybody start out on a different instrument.' So I gave someone the guitar, I went over to the keyboard, and everybody had a different instrument, and we get on there and we start the first song and it's all wrong, because everybody is on the wrong instrument. Mark says, 'This isn't the instrument you played when we started the tour, is it?' And then we changed back to the right instruments. It was stupid stuff like that. Just before we went on, he'd have some idea.

CRAIG KRAMPF Not much after that, in early '77, Mark and Howard decided to go on a hiatus.

ERIK SCOTT Back then, it was an annual thing. You'd make the record and then tour behind it. You'd lap until you'd make the next record, and then tour behind that one, so that fall kind of wound up the touring for the *Moving Targets* record.

BOB TRUAX It just kind of broke up. They weren't going to go out. When I left them, I went to the American College Of Optics and became an optician. It was a big change. I was tired of rock'n'roll. They were gone, and they were my favorite group. There was nowhere to go.

CRAIG KRAMPF Nobody was sure what was going to happen, and I wound up with Nick Gilder. All of a sudden, Nick's album was coming out, and 'Hot Child In the City' was the single. Then, in '78, Mark and Howard wanted to go out and do some gigs, and I was really torn. Here was a band that I considered family. I actually went to a rehearsal, but 'Hot Child' was starting to climb the charts on its way to #1. It was really tough to tell them that I couldn't do it. It was really hard.

ERIK SCOTT By '78 there weren't enough gigs to support a full tour, with the hotels and crew and everything to go out for two or three months, but we still played. It was more one-off dates: festivals, TV shows, or benefits. But we had to get a different drummer, because Craig had moved on. I did every show from Ebbets Field in Denver until the end of '78. And then I went to Europe with Alice Cooper. I ended up producing a couple of albums with Alice, and as a producer, when we had background parts, I hired Mark and Howard to come down.

CRAIG KRAMPF Erik was with Alice before me. They were starting an album, which eventually became *Special Forces*. Erik recommended me, and all of a sudden I'm doing an Alice Cooper record. I actually co-wrote a single from the album with Erik, Billy, and Alice.

BILLY STEELE We always seemed to flow in and out of different groups and projects. Erik and Craig and I worked with Tonio K, and I worked with Craig writing songs with Steve Perry. And I wrote some songs with Erik and

Alice Cooper for a couple of his albums. And with Alice, Flo & Eddie sang background, so we had the whole band plus Mark and Howard on the same album. Crazy. But I was with them a long time. I was always doing other stuff, but they would call me up to do sessions or TV, things like *The Garry Shandling Show*. That was me and Andy, Mark, and Howard. And I played at Mark's wedding as well.

HOWARD KAYLAN After Phil, I didn't think we would ever work again. That it happened meant that we were vulnerable. It didn't mean necessarily that we were looking over our shoulders for a threat, it just put mortality into perspective, so that we were able to go, 'You know what? This is not that important.'

Also, we were still Flo & Eddie then. We had not yet gotten The Turtles name back, so we were still in a physical limbo as far as not only signing record deals but going forward in any way, shape, or form. That's why the 80s, for us, was *Strawberry Shortcake* and the *Carebears* and *Miss Universe*, and all that stuff we did to keep ourselves away from touring.

THE RECORDS

HENRY DILTZ After they left Frank, I took pictures of them for their first album [*Phloresent Leech & Eddie*]. On the back, Mark's garage door is open, and they're sitting with a Zappa poster. I did the front, too. They have cowboy shirts on. I did that.

AYNSLEY DUNBAR With Flo & Eddie, it was simpler, more straight-ahead, not so many time changes, and it was just something I needed to do in between other gigs. They had some good songs—I liked the songs. I like the Flo & Eddie albums.

GARY ROWLES They produced the first album, and there was some great material in there. Mark would write the more heartfelt songs. Kaylan wrote some, but Mark wrote most of the tunes. It took a couple three weeks, and then we did a bunch of college dates, and then all of a sudden Alice Cooper came into the picture.

BOB EZRIN Warner Bros brought me in [for *Flo & Eddie*]. I was having some success with Alice, so I guess they suggested me. I loved working with those guys. I thought it was a fun and wonderful record. It captured who they were, the essence the group, their sense of humor and drama. For its time, and for what it was, it was a great record. And for my level of experience, it was certainly my best work up to that point. There was a bunch of mitigating circumstances that prevented the album from becoming better known, starting with the fact that we didn't have a hit. When you listen back to it now, there's some great songs, but I don't hear anything, even from today's perspective, that would have worked at radio then. So unfortunately, we sort of missed with the block and tackle. We were neither fish nor fowl. I think I brought too much big rock sensibility, and they were very pop-oriented. It was a lot of fun to listen to, and had some really good songs on it. People who knew the band really enjoyed it, and I think on all of those levels it succeeded. On the level of coming up with something that would get to the general public through radio, it didn't succeed. At the end of the day, we didn't really have a hit single.

The other part is that the name was challenging. I think the name hurt them in the long run, even though it was kind of fun. But it was kind of an in-joke, and in-jokes are, by definition, not shared by the rest of the world. Which was typical of a lot of what was going on with us at the time. There was a lot of that stuff, winks and nods and things that we understood, that people outside of the circle didn't really understand. And so, on that level, I think some of what we did was a bit parochial.

I don't recall any drugs at those sessions—mostly because no one had the money.

BOB EZRIN It was a pretty clean session. I don't know if there was a rule—if there was, like, *No drugs allowed*. I don't think any of us had enough money to get into real trouble. Mark's absolutely right about that. I do remember a couple of drunken nights, though, where we got really crazy and laughed our asses off and stayed up until dawn, just being silly. Some of that silliness got on the record, and some of it is lost forever.

GARY ROWLES 'Just Another Town' was a great song. Everybody flipped over that. That was so much fun. I have an old Martin guitar that we used on that record. I tuned it down a whole fourth and then detuned it. That was kind of a signature piece—a winsome, lowdown acoustic kind of sound.

HOWARD KAYLAN Mark and I literally lifted *The Day Manolete Died* for 'Carlos And De Bull.' We shortened it and went into the studio with Bob Ezrin, one of the greatest rock producers of all time—the man who brought you *The Wall*, ladies and gentlemen, let alone all of the Alice Cooper records and everything else—and we brought him this thing that we had written, called 'Carlos And De Bull,' and he cracked up. He couldn't believe it. It was so stupid. But we went into the studio to record it, and neither one of us really could get the accent right. It just sounded like we were riffing, making fun of our Latino friends, and it just wasn't coming off correctly.

While we were going through the machinations of trying to figure out what to do, one of the assistant engineers in the room was listening to our conversation, and he said, 'So, the bull is stubborn today, eh? So, the bull will not give up his ears and his tail.' And we went, 'Who is this guy? He's un-fucking-believable!' I don't even know the guy's name. To this day, I have no idea what the guy's name was. He's not credited on the album. I don't even believe that Bob Ezrin knows who the guy is. He went in, he did this incredible narration in one take, we cut it together, it fit perfectly with the music, and we used it. And God bless him, I wish I knew who he was so I could send him a check for the seventy-two cents he's earned from album sales so far.

BOB EZRIN I think if anyone got as far as 'Carlos And De Bull,' they had already bought the album. I don't know that it hurt anything. It certainly was indulgent, but we thought it was hilarious. And that was actually done in the cold light of day.

The engineer did the voice of Carlos. He was an older chap—for us, much older—because he was in his thirties. He was a really straight guy, as I recall, and we just sort of brought out the goofy in him. He jumped right in there—boy, he participated whole-heartily. And making the sound effects was fun. It was all fun.

They had a great band—an amazing band—some of the best musicians, ever. Some of whom I went on to work with for albums and albums after that, particularly Aynsley. It was the first time that I'd worked with him. Some of that stuff that I did with those guys was a natural extension of some things I had begun with Alice Cooper, but really, doing it with those guys, like really getting into the voices and the sound effects—that more sort of radio theater kind of stuff—that informed a lot of what I did later on, including Pink Floyd.

Mark and Howard became good friends. The thing that I hold most dear about the experience of making that album was the relationship that was formed. They embraced me like family. You often make a family out of the people that you work with, but in this case, it was like working with my cousins, almost. And that made it very warm and cordial, and fun, lots of fun.

JIM PONS Mark and Howard seemed to be out of focus and lacking direction. It seemed like they were looking for Ezrin to provide some. Or maybe it was just me. The sessions we did were not very memorable. I guess my heart wasn't in it anymore.

GARY ROWLES It seemed like they kind of sold out when they went to Bob, because he was this rock guy. The rock thing is all good, don't get me wrong, but I didn't see Mark and Howard as those kinds of guys. They were more personal, not so in-your-face. And the more in-your-face they tried to get, the more they lost the part of the Flo & Eddie thing that made them special. They were being controlled by the record company, who thought, *We'll do this, and they'll sell some records.* Of course, that's what record companies do. That's why you're in the business of making records, to sell them. There's nothing wrong with it. But for me, it was a departure from the things I thought they really wanted to do as their own self.

MARK PARENTEAU Why didn't it sell more? Not for lack of effort on Bob Ezrin's part, because the album he collaborated with them on was stunning. He was a genius producer. Alice had so much success with Bob, but Flo & Eddie? I don't know why it wasn't more popular. Maybe lightening only strikes once and they had all the success with The Turtles, which was stolen from them financially. But they certainly were a working band, and, boy, they never stopped working. They had a work ethic.

SKIP TAYLOR We became friends during the Alice Cooper tour, and because I was a producer as well as a manager, when it came time for them to do a record [*Illegal, Immoral, And Fattening*], they got me involved. I met with Columbia Records. We tried to get Columbia to look at them as a real pop act rather than a comedy act. That was a very difficult transition, and I must admit, I wasn't able to do it. It just didn't happen.

We were trying to do something very, very different, and we were able to do that at the Roxy. The idea was, if you can't go to Hawaii, Mark and Howard will bring Hawaii to you. We had birds in cages and grass mats on the floor, and a Hawaiian band opened for them. To start the night off, we had filmed a whole scene in a dressing room weeks before, which showed piles of cocaine and joints and naked girls running around backstage. That's playing on a screen out front, and you'd see the band leave, but Mark and Howard are still backstage. The band starts playing the *Tonight Show* theme: 'Now! Here's . . . Flo & Eddie!' and they come running out on the screen, and all of a sudden they're onstage.

During the show, a roadie brought a drink out and they said, 'This isn't fair, to drink in front of our audience. Let's buy a drink for everybody.' And a drink, in special 'Flo & Eddie' glasses, was brought to everybody in the audience. At the end of that show, the screen would come on again and you'd see them running outside and all these limos lined up, and they'd run right past the limos and get in these jalopies and drive off, and Porky Pig would come up on screen: 'That's all folks!'

It was a combination of live and pre-shot stuff, and an entertainment night that was just incredible. All done at least a decade before anyone else was trying this sort of thing.

HARVEY KUBERNIK I went to those shows at the Roxy. I was writing for *Melody Maker* and the *Hollywood Press*. I wanted *more* lampooning and parody. I wanted to see the piss taken out of all those people, because I got tired of the media fawning over them. Mark and Howard were the only guys popping the bubble, and it hurt them critically in this town, because it was practically sacrilegious to even say anything that wasn't drooling about Joni Mitchell. And they would mock her, her boyfriends, make fun of her open tunings . . . the audience would just be howling. We thought it was hysterical.

LINDA CAMPILLO I saw them at the Roxy. I had never seen a show like that before because they brought something new, all these skits and stuff. It was very witty and clever, more performance art than just music. The only other group I had seen do that was The Kinks, when they would act out their albums. But this was even funnier. They were making fun of people and being political, and it was way cool.

SKIP TAYLOR On *Moving Targets* we brought in Ron Nevison, who had come over here from England after doing Led Zeppelin, Bad Company, and The Who. I put him together with Dave Mason, and he had a lot of success here later with Jefferson Starship and Heart. He was a big-time producer.

RON NEVISON I think I caught them at a really good time. They wanted to be Flo & Eddie with an edge, to rock a little bit. It just all worked—it jelled. For a lot of artists, being in the studio is a very stressful time, and one of the producer's jobs is to try and get them to relax.

With these guys, I didn't really have to set any tone, because they were setting it themselves. It was all fun. Doing the vocals, I'd have them both out there at the same time, and if you asked a question, it's almost like a tag-team answer: one of them would start off explaining the answer and the other one would finish.

My best recollections are of doing the vocals at the Record Plant in Sausalito. Mark and Howard and Skip and I, the four of us, were staying in the Record Plant house, and there was one night in particular that was priceless, priceless. The house had this old phonograph, and we had a tank of nitrous oxide. We're playing Vanilla Fudge at Warp 10, all distorted and everything [*sings 'You Keep Me Hanging On'*]. We were really high on nitrous oxide, laughing and rolling on the floor, having a great little time.

SKIP TAYLOR I still think it's a masterpiece. It's just a great, great record. We did a remake of 'Elenore' that was very poppy, very hip for those days. I thought that could put them right back, but the label just couldn't get behind it. And the other one was 'Keep It Warm,' which was just an absolute gem of a song, and the single edited version was even stronger, shorter. It was really good.

MARK PARENTEAU They certainly got plenty of airtime on my show. Wasn't 'Keep It Warm' a Top 10 song in America? At FM radio, it was a huge song. It was totally identifiable.

JIMMY FINK I was playing 'Keep It Warm,' there's no question about that. That's just a great, great song. And it brought them back into the fold of people who appreciated album-oriented rock. That was a meaningful song. It was deep and well put together. It was special.

RON NEVISON You needed to have a hit single. And you had two plump guys— you didn't have any kind of a front man. It was okay in the 60s, I just don't think it was okay in the 70s. And it was definitely not okay in the 80s, once MTV came around. No one wanted go 'Sailing' with Christopher Cross. Not on MTV.

SKIP TAYLOR Columbia just didn't get it. They thought of them as a comedy act. They didn't realize that these guys were two of the best at doing what they did. They wouldn't take them seriously and didn't think that America would take them seriously. If they had been promoted in a proper way at that point in their career, there was any number of songs that they could have been hits. But somehow, when you look at two overweight guys—at that time—and long hair and whatever, they just didn't fit the image that Columbia had for a pop star. So, their craft was never really taken seriously. And they were not able to have another big hit. 'Keep It Warm' got a lot of airplay, and we thought it was gonna break through, but the label wouldn't put the money behind it to make it happen.

RON NEVISON By recording as Flo & Eddie, they lost the value of the Turtles name. As far as marketing, a lot of people related to them as being the guys from The Turtles, and Columbia could have done a better job promoting it. More to the point, did Columbia drop the ball? Probably. It didn't happen on the level that we thought it would, and I don't know what to put it down to. I don't know how many fingers you can point. I did my job. *Moving Targets* was a joy, and it sounded great as far as I'm concerned. I had a lot of fun doing that record, maybe as much fun as I ever had working with anybody.

SKIP TAYLOR Things weren't going well at the end. I had a lot of friends at the label, and I just found it very, very frustrating. They just wouldn't take them seriously. I don't know any other way to put it. It just wasn't working.

HARVEY KUBERNIK I know they've been reissued and they're critically acclaimed now, but to me there was a tragic element to the Flo & Eddie records. Those are damn good pop records, but for some reason, when they were musicologists on vinyl, it didn't translate to radio airplay or people with pocketbooks. I could never figure it out. They always picked stellar material. Something like 'Afterglow' should have been a huge hit. It just didn't connect, and I don't know why. Maybe it had to do with budgets and that kind of stuff. When you're older, you realize that budgets and money do inform or impact the wax being made. But they overcompensated and became more of a live act. They always understood touring could make things happen.

BACKUP VOCALS

PAT VOLMAN They kind of buttered [up] everywhere, it seems. Whether you liked it or not, 'We're here!'

HAL WILLNER The sound of the two of them together was crazy and beautiful, like insane angels. I use 'beautiful' in a warped way. It wouldn't be that to everybody. To me, it's amazing, and it has a little bit of a twist in it, because it's not only perfectly in tune, but it's got this juju kind of weird sound there. You could always tell; there was that unique sound. It's incredible the way that both Tony Visconti and Frank Zappa knew to use them in all different ways. Obviously, the balance worked beautifully in Marc Bolan's favor, where it could get played on the radio. Frank Zappa, I guess, was another story.

JEFF 'SKUNK' BAXTER We've been friends for a long time. I first met Mark when I was in a band called Ultimate Spinach, and we did some gigs with The Turtles around the Boston area. We have a lot in common in that the amount of music that we were involved in over the years is quite varied. We both did tons of session work. It's almost like we were part of a tenured group that found ourselves trying to boost a number of different projects forward. The rock'n'roll stardom thing, it's certainly delightful on some level, but for me, the real challenge was being first call in the studio. That was important, and Mark and Howard both—Mark especially—understand that, because those were the guys that you would call if you needed the right thing at the right time. They were pros.

You earn that by your ability: when the red light goes on, everyone around you knows that you're a pro. It's a brotherhood, part of a group of elite folks that everyone can count on to do the job, and a lot of it is done behind the scenes. Many people don't know about Mark and Howard's involvement in Steely Dan, for instance. I was with Steely Dan, which had just started. Mark and Howard sang on a number of the demos and were instrumental in raising the level of quality to the point where people became aware of it and enjoyed it. They certainly helped the band get signed. I don't think that Steely Dan would have gotten a record deal, or the kind of record deal that it did, without their vocals, because they supplied vocals to music which at the time was not well understood by a lot of different parties. Was Howard offered the lead vocal slot? That sounds right, because Howard's an incredible singer. They both are. The fact he declined, and stuck with Mark? That's a very smart move.

PETER NOONE Both Howard and Mark are very underrated as singers. They're two of the best. Most other singers know how good they are. It's an unusual thing. It's not that they're a couple of bloody comedians; they're a couple of really good entertainers. They sing well, they've got different vocal stylings, and so I'm a fan of the whole operation, really. But they play this sort of nonchalant, *We don't care*. Meanwhile, they make fifty million bucks.

TIM SEXTON I was always more taken with them vocally than as performers. The comedy and all that stuff to me was just schtick. They were very, very talented, and when you listen to their catalogue, it holds up. There's a lot of good stuff, no question.

ROLAN BOLAN To be a fan of the songs that Mark worked on, and then eventually meeting Tony Visconti and learning how they did a lot of those techniques to get that T. Rex background vocal sound, it was pretty cool. They had their unique sound, and even to this day, people refer to it as that T. Rex vocal sound.

ALICE COOPER They sang on at least ten of my albums, if I can remember correctly. Any time we wanted background singing, we called for Flo & Eddie. They had such pure voices. Everybody wanted to work with Mark and Howard because they were so much fun. They'd walk in a room, and it was party time. And I don't mean drug party—I mean they were fun. It didn't matter what it was—Mark and Howard were fun to work with anytime it came to doing backgrounds. Truly, two of the most talented guys I've ever worked with.

RON DANTE It has to almost be in your DNA to sing harmonies. As a very young man, I did a lot of that. I was exposed to doo-wop music, that three- or four-part harmony that they do without instruments, and The Everly Brothers, where there's two-part harmonies going all the way through. The key is to submerge your own personality and bring out the personality of the group you're working with. I've sung with Jay & The Americans, Mountain, The McCoys, Steely Dan, Neil Diamond, Neil Sedaka . . . really, I did backgrounds for thirty or forty groups and singers over the years. In fact, every Barry Manilow record I ever produced, I'm singing background. The two of us overdubbed our voices just like The Turtles did and made it sound like a group. You have to adapt, to blend in and make it all sound cool. That's the key, and Mark and Howard were very proficient at it also. That's why we have a lot in common. We did a lot of the same things.

SUSAN COWSILL As Mark and Howard like to say, they've been married to each other since they were fifteen years old. But their vocal prowess, who knows how that happened, because they have a resonant sound that's kind of like the DNA thing. I chalk that up to past lives. Mark and Howard must have been bards—very fucked-up bards—back in the day. And that's how they stumbled onto their genius for harmony.

HOWARD KAYLAN There's something just wonderful about the sound of our voices together. If I go in and overdub myself, I can do it until I turn blue but it's going to be missing an element. It's going to be missing a little sparkle on the top that the two of us get when we sing together. I've got a low timbre to my voice, but only slightly, and Mark has a higher timbre, but only slightly. We stood next to each other in a cappella choir for a reason: I was the last of the second tenors, Mark was the last of the first tenors. We were very, very close in range. Our voices sound very similar. When we sing, we have almost the same tonality. We have the same California accent. The way we pronounce words nasally—California nasally—means that when we sing together, even the pronunciation of words is quite similar, because we grew up within blocks of each other. There are environmental, geographical reasons for the way we sound, including and not limited to, Mr. Wood, who pretty much taught us how to sing, how to open up and how to really project our voices, and I give him a lot of credit for it.

And we're not stupid. We've been singing together for all these years, and, like anything else, you adapt, you change, you figure it out. When you're a performer, you work the room. When you're working with a partner, you work your partner. You figure out how far he is from the microphone, what his propensities are, when he's going to lean in. If he's gonna go flat on a certain note, you know the note that will make him stay on top of it by hitting your note a bit sharp. There are little things that I think it really takes fifty years of partnership to learn; that can't just be taught to anybody, or certainly out of a book, or from a DVD or a classroom. You can spout all you want about the way things should work and what timbres are complementary to each other, and why that works with X harmonically, but it's not the same as living it: living a life with headphones on, if you will.

When we're singing background on records, we have to be chameleon-like to blend in with Hoyt Axton or Roger McGuinn or Andy Taylor, or whoever the hell it is. We're chameleons, not only with each other but with other artists. We've learned how to make records with Todd Rundgren, and it's different than making records with Roy Thomas Baker. You learn how to sing differently for each one of those producers. We know how to do that as a team. If I was going in to a Roy session or a Todd session by myself, I wouldn't have the same clout. I wouldn't be as powerful as knowing that Mark and I can set up one microphone in the middle of the room and show Rundgren exactly what we mean, and he's gonna go, 'That's exactly the part I had in mind. Record it.' It's history—it's bigger than we are. We can try to analyze what makes it work until the cows come home, but I really don't think that it's going to be worked out verbally or consciously. It's just something that is natural and something that has evolved, and I wouldn't have it any other way.

JIM YESTER I've had conversations with Mark about that. It's something they've worked on quite a bit. It's the same approach, the same phrasing, the same ideas about intonation and stuff like that. You can really hear it on something like [*sings, 'You taught me how to do ...'*]. When they do that live, it's different than anything else—it's so cool.

CHRIS HILLMAN In '76, I made an album for Asylum Records [*Slippin' Away*], and I had them come in and sing. It was my first solo album, and, in all honestly, I really hadn't developed as a singer quite yet. I was getting there. Certainly, I had come a long way from The Byrds and The Flying Burrito Brothers. I was just starting to get comfortable being a lead singer, and those guys were really good. They were great duet singers, both in The Turtles and singing for Zappa when they were Flo & Eddie, and all that goofball stuff.

RAY MANZAREK They sang on my second solo album, *The Whole Thing Started With Rock And Roll, Now It's Out Of Control*. It was like old home week. A decade later, Redondo Beach gets together in a Hollywood recording studio, and they were singing. God! They did 'Love It Or Leave It.' I said, 'I want you guys to be like Latinos.' There was a repeating *montuno*, and they were terrific: 'We can do Latino, Ray.' And they ended up doing it in their Latino accents. Everything they did was fun. And they're so adroit—you tell them what you want, let them hear the song, and they were always able to come up with something. They're consummate musicians and singers. They know how to really do backup, so it was a real pleasure. And, on the title song, they were doing stuff that I thought, *How did you come up with that?* It was beyond me. I didn't know what to tell them. I just said, 'I want you guys to sing this,' and they said, 'What do you want us to sing, Ray?' 'Well, I don't know, think of something ... *good*!' And they did.

SKIP TAYLOR Mark and Howard had their radio show going in L.A., and Keith Moon was on when I was handling him. After that, I brought them in to sing on Keith's *Two Sides Of The Moon* project. They sang on almost everything. I don't know if they were credited with all of it, but boy, they sang a lot, and we had a ball. They really made the vocals work, because Keith couldn't sing a note.

HARVEY KUBERNIK They got known as the kings of background vocalists, and it marginalized them. Those guys could sing the phonebook and that would be fine with me, but what happened is, they got relegated into secondary positions when all their background vocal credits kept getting hurled at everybody. I'm not saying that's bad; I'm all for people working. It's just Howard and Mark were kind of voluntarily relegated to being support players on all kinds of records, and they weren't singing lead anymore. Now, maybe that's where the paycheck was, and it's major label credits, it's just all of a sudden they were these background guys. I wanted to hear them sing lead. I want *them* to sing.

HALLIE VOLMAN I think that the big one that stands out is Bruce Springsteen. I was a big fan, and he sang 'Hungry Heart' with them.

GARRY TALLENT 'Hungry Heart' was our first hit single. Bruce just kind of wrote the song in two minutes, and he doesn't take anything that comes too easily very seriously. It was going to be a throwaway, but everybody that heard it went, 'We can have a hit single. All it would take would be making it sound radio-friendly.' That was debated and initially pooh-poohed, but the band had been together for ten years at that point, so, in the end, we figured, let's give it a try, let's see what it would be like to have a Top 10 single. I know how hard it is to have one, and we went without. We had music we were proud of, but you have to make a conscious effort to be on the radio, because you're dealing with the radio programmers. And even then, they might like what you're doing when they listen to it, but it doesn't mean they're going to play it on the radio. So, 'Hungry Heart' was made to be more chipper and happy, and the background vocal was definitely part of that. Mark and Howard added ear candy. And the band wasn't capable of doing that. When we sing, it's not ear candy.

JIM BESSMAN I wrote the first book on the Ramones, and some people were surprised by Flo & Eddie on a Ramones album, but people tend to overlook that the Ramones, besides being simpleton three-chord one-two-three-four, they patterned themselves after the classic rock'n'roll of the 60s, and so it would come as no surprise that they would have been aware of The Turtles. It would seem surprising, but in looking back now, it's not surprising at all.

HAL WILLNER The very first time we worked together was on Gavin Friday's *Each Man Kills The Thing He Loves* record of 1988. All those earlier T. Rex records were big, big, big to Gavin growing up. It would have been his Beatles. On the song 'Man Of Misfortune,' he mentioned T. Rex and its influence, and right off I was going, 'How about Flo & Eddie?' And it was incredible to see it happen. I flew out to Los Angeles to record it, and to someone who had liked Flo & Eddie for at that point over twenty years, it was the session that did not disappoint in any way. I'd sing lines to them, and they would put these cutup things in between, go into vaudeville with all these routines. And then they had their very professional approach. When you explained what you wanted, they just knew how to do it, and the second they start singing, there's that sound.

They came to New York and sang on Gavin's second record, and then many years later we did his fiftieth birthday show at Carnegie Hall [October 4, 2009]. The interesting moment for the night was having Flo & Eddie with just U2, doing one of Gavin's songs. But they sang with everybody that night. It was probably the only show in the world that had Lady Gaga followed by Lou Reed and John Zorn. It was a dream magic night, a perfect show. We had superstars, U2 and Lady Gaga, avant-gardists, jazz players, rock musicians . . . it revived that old Bill Graham Fillmore spirit. And Mark and Howard were the foundation of the whole thing, the secret weapon, one of the first ones we set out to get.

RICHIE FURAY I had him sing on my solo album. It was really neat. I got wind of Mark wanting to sing on it, and so, bingo, I'm going to have him on the record. After he heard it back, he said, 'You're going to turn me into a country artist after all, man.' You're coming down to Nashville; what do you expect?

9

FAMILY LIFE

HALLIE VOLMAN I knew from very early on that what he did was definitely very different from all the other kid's parents, and that it was extraordinary. But at the same time it was very normal, because for as long as I can remember, my dad was in The Turtles. He was away a good part of pretty much every year, but once he was home, he made a huge effort to spend as much time as a family unit as he possibly could, taking us to Disneyland, to the zoo, all those types of things. When he was there, he was there 100 percent. He really made an effort to bring us all back together again, doing things as a family, as a whole.

SARINA VOLMAN I loved growing up in Laurel Canyon. Both Hallie and I went to Wonderland Avenue School. Dad tells me I played with Moon Zappa when I was a child, but I don't remember.

HALLIE VOLMAN I went to Wonderland Avenue Elementary School and then transferred over to Walter Reed Junior High in North Hollywood. There were a lot of other kids whose parents were also musicians or actors, but when you grow up around that, it's just kind of normal and every day. It doesn't impact you the same way as you might think it would from the outside.

SARINA VOLMAN Hallie and I are six and a half years apart, so it's almost like we had different childhoods, different lives. The two of us are like day and night. We're a lot different, which is fine: you don't want to have the same kinds of kids. We were there at the same time, but we weren't close until after we were adults. We shared a room, and I'd come in late at night and wake her up, so it could be tough.

HALLIE VOLMAN Because of our age difference, as we both got older, we kinda didn't want to spend as much time together with each other. It did get tougher as we got older.

PAT VOLMAN Mark used to go down to Wonderland Elementary School and help organize the Halloween Festival. He helped with the setup of the booths and everything. One year he was Flo-nac The Magnificent: he would read everybody's biorhythm charts, and he was the most popular booth. He loved that, and the principal of the school just adored him. See? Everybody loves him!

FELIX CAVALIERE Being on the road meant you missed what was going on at home. We all did. It was horrible. That's just part of the industry. There is nothing we can do about it.

SARINA VOLMAN He wasn't there for my high school graduation. My grandparents and cousins and uncle were there, but not my dad. He wasn't around for a lot of things, because he was always on tour. But he was there for my college graduation.

HALLIE VOLMAN I had no resentment. He had this amazing opportunity to do something with his life that most of us only dream of. And I know that he loves it, and a lot of it he did for the family, and I've never ever held any sort of resentment or anger toward him for taking that career path. By the time I was nine or ten, my sister was out of the house with her friends a lot, so when Dad would come home, he'd spend a lot of time with me. He'd take me to the movies, to the ballet, we'd spend hours in record stores and book stores, where he'd teach me about different musicians and artists, trying to get me to have an open mind and not just listen to Debbie Gibson. I really cherish those years. It was just him and me.

SARINA VOLMAN I'm not musically inclined at all, but we all, the entire family, we all love music. Growing up, music was always on. *Always.* Always on in the car, always on everywhere. Music was always part of our lives. I remember going to record stores. I remember going to bookstores a lot, too.

10

DRUGS

PHIL VOLMAN There weren't any drugs when I went to school. We were drinkers.

MICHAEL THOMAS At the time, nobody was into drugs or anything like that. You were just in a band, like you were into the surf thing or that circle of things. The worst that would happen is the guys would be driving and have a couple of beers. But as time went on, there were drugs, and then Mark and Howard got into each other. And that was really hush hush back then. That didn't happen until the middle to the end of The Turtles. And I don't know that for a fact.

JOHN SNYDER Mark and Howard were always straight up. Maybe they would have a drink or a beer when they were young, but I never saw them do drugs at all. All that came later—it had to. The influence you're under at that level, where anything goes? You can understand that.

AL NICHOL At that point, everybody that we ran into smoked dope. It's really hard to pinpoint. I can't even remember where I first smoked it, but it was in amid some of these people. But the drugs didn't play any significant part. Nobody really went overboard and had a serious problem or anything with that.

HENRY DILTZ I was a grass guy. Still am. In truth, it's been fifty years of smoking grass, and I think it's a wonderful thing. We all smoked, and it was part of what made the 60s flower. We wanted to know more about life. We were interested in Tibetan Buddhism and American Indian spiritualism and yoga masters and all that stuff. So having a little toke turned your mind on and made you start thinking about things. I think people would be surprised to find out that almost every musician smokes grass. I've stood in my photo gallery looking at a huge wall, at sixty or eighty pictures, and every single photograph, with the exception of Donny Osmond and one of the Monkees—Mike Nesmith never smoked, but the other three did, plenty—and I smoked grass with everybody in all those pictures.

CRAIG KRAMPF With Mark and Howard, there was always weed. It was the 60s. It was all fun, and nobody knew any of the consequences, or cared at that age. We loved smoking dope. Everybody did. On the road, you'd meet in one room. Of course, there were towels laid down so the smoke couldn't go out into the halls—oh, you betcha—we could have got sent away for an awfully long time. We had a secret knock. Everybody figured that nobody knocks on a door just once, right? That's the secret knock: *one* knock, and you knew whoever was on the other side was cool. But the secret knock continued well into the 70s, and, who knows, they might still be using it today. Maybe I'm giving shit away here.

DENNY JONES In May of 1969, I was popped at the Philadelphia airport for possession. I had all The Turtles' baggage, and they found drug paraphernalia: Tuinal and this and that. This was two weeks before the White House. I was just the guy that got stuck with it. I couldn't go near the Philadelphia airport for about a year because of it. They arrested me and we had to call the assistant DA out in California. At the time they were managed by Silver, Campbell, and Cosby. Bill Cosby: *the* Bill Cosby. Bill was the silent partner. They managed Deep Purple and The Turtles, and they took care of everything.

PAT VOLMAN I probably shouldn't actually tell these stories, but what the heck. He probably doesn't remember half of them, so we can bust him. Like the rocking chair in the living room with a big cloud of smoke around it. I remember when he had that big Afro-looking hair, he would roll a joint and put it behind his ear and the hair would cover it, and a few minutes later, he would ask, 'Where is it?' I'd have to tell him it was behind his ear—that's how out of it he was at the time. He always had to have an extra, and that was where it would end up: behind, in his hair.

JOEL LARSON Mark and I decided we were tired of buying weed from other people, so I found a guy that was going to sell us a kilo of pot. I had a Vespa at the time, so we both got on it. Mark is a big guy, so just imagine him on the back. We thought we were the big new guys; we were so happy to give this guy our money. We went back up to Laurel Canyon and unwrapped it, and it was soaked in Coca Cola, this really funky weed that we had just invested in. It was so stuck together we couldn't do anything with it. We got what we paid for. It was amateurs at their best.

I used drugs for what I felt in those days were really good purposes. They helped me pass the time and the boredom that set in. The unreal life I was going through was balanced by the numbing that the drugs did to my system. By keeping grounded in a hotel room, totally zonked out during the day, they allowed me to get to the next day on a two-hundred-city tour. In a sense it was self-medicating, because I survived every day to get to the next day.

BOB TRUAX They couldn't go onstage without smoking pot. But it doesn't surprise me that he stopped. I did the same thing. I don't do it. Every now and then I do, and then I wonder, *How can I even drive home?*

HOWARD KAYLAN When Mark jumped off of that train ten or fifteen years ago, he put an interesting spin on his so-called drug years.

DONNIE KISSELBACH That came when he returned to school, and that was on his own terms. I was never a serious pot smoker, so the absence didn't really mean anything to me. Howard, Joe, and Mark, they were the ones. They're super pros who just couldn't do anything without a little alteration. You wake up, you roll a bone, and that's the way you start the day. I'm sure to do the work that he had to do, it was easy for him to put that behind and do the studying.

JOE STEFKO Since he's stopped, he's just became more of an asshole. When you're not high and having a good time, you have more time to think about what bothers you, or how you could piss somebody off. So, he does a lot of that. When he stopped smoking pot, we became the bad guys, because Howard and I continued, and that was a problem, as it would be. I mean, we did it for years and years, and they were doing it way before me. Mark was the guy that, it didn't matter what time in the morning we had to meet to go to the next town, he was always the first one there, and he had a joint in his mouth the size of a cock. Whether it was four in the morning, three in the morning, eight, it didn't matter: it just went on from there, and it was great. But after that it was like he was saying we couldn't smoke in dressing rooms, we couldn't smoke in the cars. So, Howard and I, we were running around trying to find holes in rooms. And I said, 'Wait a minute, I can understand me having to do this, but not you. This is ridiculous.' So I just said, 'Mark, we smoke. We still smoke. That's what we do. That's what we're going to do. You're going to have to deal with it.' And it's okay. This last tour we did, Howard and I were smoking twenty-four hours. I had one onstage, in the dressing rooms, everywhere. But for a long time, if we lit up, he would look at us like, *How could you smoke that shit?* It's like, *What!?* But he cooled down with that.

PAUL WILLIAMS So many of these comments are interesting, because it's just the extremes, all the way from God, I know exactly what everybody's talking about, and then you come along to someone who says, 'Well, so-and-so was an asshole when he quit.' And I thought, *Oh, my God, it's like a band, and the people around the band are exactly like a family.*

CHUCK NEGRON I'd come out to California and was signed to Columbia Records. I'm a college kid: I have short hair, slacks, shined shoes, nice shorts; a real preppy guy. My producer said, 'We've got to get you out, see what's going on.' I went to this party, and the Mothers Of Invention were playing. Everyone was there. Janis Joplin was there, and Danny Hutton, who had a hit with 'Roses And Rainbows,' I met him that night, and I saw what they meant. It was all hippie, but these people were wearing very good clothes, because they were entertainers. They weren't just freaks. I went, 'This is cool. I could do this.' The next thing you know, a beautiful girl is dropping something in my mouth, and I ended getting a little psychedelic trip. They took me down to Sunset, and all the lights were running into one another. It didn't freak me out at all. It was just a wonderful, wonderful trip up and down Sunset Strip with all the beautiful girls and the lights.

That went on all the time. You'd go to a party and see them passing around something. You got involved because it started so nonchalantly. It's not evil, like someone forcing it on you. They pass it, you pass it, many people passed it on to the next person. It was just something that kids were trying. It didn't seem the least bit dangerous. Then, all of a sudden, the scene changed to where people really were addicts or alcoholics.

PAUL WILLIAMS I look back at some of the conversations that were endless all-nighters with other alcoholics, and my God, I wish I'd had a tape recorder running. It was just madness. Did anybody hear anybody? Did anybody appreciate any piece of their life? Was there anything that I thought about, besides impressing somebody? It's been a long ride, boy. But I would not trade those years for anything, because it led me to a place where I could survive. And finally, finally become grateful. Grateful for every breath. I went into treatment. And oh, my God, I was home. I loved it so much that not only did I love being there, but I got involved with the Musician's Assistance Program. Buddy Arnold, who started the Musician's Assistance Program, told me, 'You oughta go to UCLA and get your certification for drug and alcohol counseling—you seem to like these people.' So I did, and I never looked back. I was home.

You have to look at the era, because now it's easy to say, yes, drugs kill. But in 1965, when you're eighteen years old and your record's in the Top 10 and you're just a suburban kid out of a garage with a high-school band, and somebody tells you that if you do drugs, you'll die? I mean, 'Prove it' is the answer there. I didn't know who Charlie Parker was, so you can't say you're going to end up like him and Chet Baker and all those guys. I mean, who the hell were they? There was no list of rock'n'roll casualties yet, and everything that they warned us against just wasn't happening at that point. And, really, we were just unfettered, weren't we? We were just an accident waiting to happen, constantly.

Even a few years later, there was nobody around at that time in my life I was close to that I lost through drugs. So, really, all the warnings weren't working. And I couldn't see the problem in myself—who's objective enough to be able to look in a mirror and say, 'You're going to kill yourself if you continue this'? I was in the prime of my life physically, still having hit records, and everything else just didn't matter. And that's why I say it's kind of hard to blame any of us, even though it was inevitable that it was going to sneak up on us.

It's inspiring when I think of the individuals that were able to withstand the assault, but it's also numbing. The drug scene was very numbing, and, unfortunately, many of the young men I grew up with couldn't handle the amount they took, or lost control and never came back. Eventually, I lost quite a few friends to drugs, and I miss many of them dearly, but without knowing each of their individual stories, it's hard to say drugs are the reason they're not here, or if the drugs just heightened issues in their lives that would eventually kill them anyway.

In many ways, success was probably a bigger drug than any of the pot or LSD or heroin or anything we did. I think the fuel and the fire for us was having hit records, and the problems arose from misunderstanding the needs and the negatives that come along with that. You're never warned about that. It becomes easy to look back now and say, 'If we'd only known.' But those were good times. In pure reality, those were really wonderful experiences, even though I would not recommend them now.

RAY MANZAREK I think people are terrified of LSD. They are terrified they will change their minds. And that is exactly what it will do to you. It will change your mind. And they say, 'I don't want to take it. It's going to make me different.' It *will* make you different. Are you so pleased and so happy with what you are? Do you think you are on the right path? You're on the right road now? I always tell people, 'Look, if you're afraid, don't take it, man.' Only those who are seeking infinity, seeking the heroic, and seeking the answers to, *Why am I on this planet? What's my existence all about? What is God? Am I God, are all things God?* You answer those questions when you take LSD.

DANNY HUTTON You've got to remember that, in '65, there was so much innocence. Acid was still legal. Cary Grant had done about seventy trips of acid. Esther Williams had done about fifty. Eventually you either went away and joined a commune, or if you were still trying to be in the world and functioning, you would plan a weekend. Grab some acid on Friday night and trip out, go somewhere or do whatever, and then Monday be back to what you do.

There was an overt spiritual component to the psychedelic drugs of the 60s that was gone soon after. Those early psychedelic experiences had something about them that were different than today, although maybe for someone doing drugs now there is a path. I can only speak for me. There were a lot of maps, a lot of books that were guiding me through my explorations, like *The Impersonal Life* and *Autobiography Of A Yogi*. Those were very religious books for me. So, everybody was using drugs and fueling their own fires in many different ways. I'm lucky that I grew up in a band that was very family oriented. For all the problems we had, we were drawn to taking our drugs together, and we spent a lot of evenings discussing spiritual matters. We didn't find ourselves running around being dangerous to others or to ourselves. We spent a lot of time putting our heads together and asking questions, and we found a lot of answers in those Eastern philosophies during that era. For us, if you think back to that time, there were a lot of educated people, whether they were beat poets or writers or whatever, coming out of the 50s. A lot of people became guides for us. A lot of the musicians picked up on Indian philosophies, like The Beatles, with the idea that lyrics could open the door toward a higher consciousness. By drenching myself in 'All You Need Is Love': well, love is all you need. And listening to George Harrison say 'Without going out of my room . . . I can know the ways of heaven.' The messages that were coming from my mentors at that time were being passed through in terms that I understood very clearly, because I understood music.

JIM YESTER I remember being up on top of Mount Lee, where the Hollywood sign is, on the top peak overlooking Burbank as the sun is coming up, about six or eight people all on acid, just being a part of nature, and then going back to the house and talking spirituality. These were very positive experiences. Fortunately, for the most part, it didn't go off in worse directions. But you eventually stop. It reaches a point where you've learned enough, and you realize that if you keep going, it starts frying synapses. You can't just keep on doing that stuff. Of course, most of us still smoke a little bit now and then.

DON CUSIC Part of the culture was that drugs were groovy. They took you out of the rat race. The whole 'turn on, tune in, and drop out' thing was a spiritual search, to be above that. Why be in the rat race if you're not a rat? It was seen as part of a higher consciousness. But the other thing is, it was something you checked off in order to be accepted by that audience, or the audience that they were trying to reach. Drugs were a part of it. It wasn't cool to be clean.

ALICE COOPER There were certain guys that didn't know when to turn off their image. I think that's what killed Jim Morrison. He didn't know when not to be Jim Morrison. He had to be Jim all of the time.

CHRIS HILLMAN That's true about Jim. And it was so uncomfortable at times, when you'd be on a package show in those days, and it would be like if you were seeing old friends, let's say a scenario hypothetically: I'd be sitting there talking with Volman and a couple of other people at the show, and then if Morrison came along, everybody would go, 'Oh my God, here he comes,' and everyone would walk away. But he was miserable. It was horrible to see him.

JIM PONS We got high a lot. Most of our drug experimentation was mild by today's standards. Pot. Uppers and downers (pep pills and sleeping pills). Cocaine began creeping into the picture in the early-to-mid 70s, but by then I was on my way out of the music business.

MICKY DOLENZ After The Monkees, I just kicked back and partied for a few years. If I would have continued on that track with Keith Moon and Harry, I would have ended up like them. Maybe I had some sort of governor on me, or just got lucky. Alice was a survivor, but, boy, it took a lot of strength for him. He moved to Phoenix and became addicted to golf. He picked himself up by his own boot straps and realized he had to get out of the environment and change his life.

For me, it was more that there was something inside that knew I had to get out of there or something. I left the country just as cocaine was coming in. Up to then, it was just grass and a few acid trips. Cocaine hadn't quite hit yet, and I had actually stopped doing everything. I had stopped, kind of to dry out, to take a rest from it for a while. There's very few of us left, and those that are, are pretty straight—except for Keith Richards.

TIM SEXTON We used to golf together. We'd go out to the valley and play three or four holes, and then Mark would smoke a reefer. We'd get to the ninth hole and we'd have a sandwich. And Mark would have a beer. And then a little more reefer, and then by the twelfth hole Mark would start to fade, and so he would do a bump of cocaine, and his game would get good for a hole or two, maybe. And then the wheels just came off: 'Oh fuck! What the fuck happened to my game, Tim? I was playing so good—what the fuck happened?' So, being on the golf course with Mark, that would just crack us up.

SHADOE STEVENS Coke was pretty much everywhere. Back in the 70s, doctors would say that it was a social drug, and that it was not addictive. And we all bought into it. None of us knew; it just seemed like fun. All the people dying were from heroin. No one knew they could go into acute cocaine psychosis and end up carrying guns and hiding behind doors and shit. It got really crazy from that ugly nasty drug. Luckily, Mark got out of it, as did I. I've been off of everything since the mid-80s.

TOMMY JAMES People said coke wasn't addictive. Oh, what a lie that was!

LESLIE WEST Not addictive? No shit! I must have missed that fact. That wasn't my drug of choice—it was the other white stuff. But hey, that's why it's all called junk. I'm lucky to be alive. Man, most of my friends are dead, and I'm sure so are most of Mark's. I was very lucky, and not only that, I was finished with it before the AIDS thing came in, thank God. Anybody that says, 'I can stop whenever I want. I can do this whenever I want . . .' Well, most of them can't. Everybody that got out was lucky. I was lucky that I didn't go to prison. A lot of my friends did. You were in the right place at the wrong time or the wrong place at the right time.

SKIP TAYLOR It wasn't addictive until it was addictive—that's it exactly. Everybody thought this was just the good old Hollywood drug. It was social. Everybody's inhibitions went by the wayside, and you had the period of free love and sexual wildness. There was no AIDS. Maybe somebody would get herpes once in a while, but at the time, that was the worst thing that could have happened. It wasn't like you were going to have sex and die. Multiple partners were the rule, as opposed to the exception.

HENRY DILTZ First it was just grass, and that never really goofed anybody up, and then a lot of people got into coke. Now that is bad for you. It's bad for your heart, and it tears you down. I saw that happen to a lot of people. Myself, I never liked coke. I didn't like what it did to me the next day. It's like you're using up your energy in advance, so that the next day you just feel awful. And I was never willing to do that.

PAUL WILLIAMS I did forty-eight *Tonight Show*s. I remember six! If you put up a couch and a camera, I was there. I was loving it and I loved to hear myself talk, but by the time it was over, it was three in the morning, peeking out of the venetian blinds, looking for the Tree Police. So, it makes your world smaller and smaller and smaller.

DANNY HUTTON When cocaine came in, it was seen as this marvelous drug you could take, and the next day you were fine. No addiction, no anything. It was such a pleasant little thing that everybody started getting involved. It was wonderful. Obviously, later, they found out it wasn't what it seemed. But at the time, it was the perfect little drug that made you active. You'd get a lot of work done. But it changed personalities. Overindulgence just made people get really strange. And then you start getting the dealers and people with guns. Then you get violence and all of that awful stuff that happened.

JIM YESTER Coke seemed non-addictive. *Seemed* is the operative word there. But after a while, you could tell, *Oh my God, this shit is dangerous.* In fact, our bass player, Brian Cole, took it a little too far. Actually, it was a combination of coke and heroin called China White. He was shooting, and for a while we thought we had him cleaned up. He would come to rehearsal and show us his arms like, *Look, man, I'm clean.* But he was shooting in his ankles. And he overdosed in 1972.

CYRUS FARYAR Cocaine invited excess. It's easy to take too much of anything, but coke was so cheerful, and evidently harmless, because it was just an enlivening agent. Disguised in that is the fact that too much of it really didn't do, and the price was forgetting what you were doing to start with and losing your way. You'd been distracted by the romantic courtesan who promises you everything and gives you nothing. All drugs will do that, but cocaine was deceptive. Everybody knew that if you did heroin, you would end up like all those terrible, poor jazz guys, so there were dangers and scares, but coke was such a boutique drug. It was very chic, and celebrities could groove on it, but some people cannot restrain from excess, and *boom*—you kill yourself dead.

ALICE COOPER I think there's a crossroads you come to in your life when you either decide to live or die. And a lot of people at twenty-seven just died. I can think of ten that died. And then I'm a little bit surprised at the ones that didn't. I'm surprised at Iggy, I'm surprised at Ozzy—myself—that we're not six feet under. But I think that there again, there's a grace, that maybe there is something better for us.

HOWARD KAYLAN By the time we both pulled the plug on that habit, it had gotten very, very deep. We had begun to experiment with cocaine in the late 60s, early 70s, and we were still doing it on a daily basis well into the 80s. It wasn't unusual. Our entire community was into it. All of our friends, our wives, our musicians, all of L.A. was into it. It was what you did. We were both going through huge quantities of drugs on a daily basis. The amount of money that left our pockets was certainly astronomical. I don't even know how we were paying for this crap, literally, because we were making our money under the table by doing all these children's records and the Miss Universe pageant, and all of these side projects. Our income on paper was very, very small, and yet we had nosebleeds. It didn't really mean much until we started looking at our physical output—what we were really delivering, as far as showbusiness was concerned—and it just seemed like we were treading water. We were getting lazy, and we knew it was the drugs.

The weird part about cocaine is that it's very seductive, and while you feel like you've got energy to burn, you're doing nothing but burning energy. And that was our case, and we came to the realization at the exact same time. We literally looked at each other and said, 'You know what? We're killing ourselves. We're going to die.' 'Yeah, you're right, we're going to die.' And we made it a conscious effort. We each had huge quantities of cocaine on us, and we walked into the bathroom at our place of work and dumped it. We flushed it. I went home that night, and I told my wife, 'It's gone. I'm not doing that anymore, I'm done.'

It was easier, stopping together. It's like quitting anything: if you've got somebody to do it with you, that you can lean on for support, your chances are 100 percent better that you're going to emerge cleaner on the other side. We could do that because, in our hearts of hearts, we knew that we weren't going to lie to each other. We weren't going to go behind each other's backs and do drugs on the fly, because it was literally not only to save our lives but to save our partnership. To save our careers, to save the company, to save whatever Flo & Eddie or The Turtles were. It just wasn't fair, not only to ourselves but to anyone else who had ever believed in us for any reason. We were letting all of those people down by letting coke get us lazy.

HAROLD BRONSON I was working with them during that period. I was aware that they were doing coke, but I don't recall them ever doing it in my presence. The fact they stopped together and helped each other: when do you ever see something like that? Usually, one person wants to stop and the other doesn't, and it causes more problems. That's nice.

JOE STEFKO It was good that it stopped. Coke was a big problem, because they had the money to buy it and people were also just giving it to them. Listen to some of the things on the *Bottom Line*, that two-disc CD I produced. We were all too high and the show was going ninety-five miles an hour. And that was me—I was the drummer. But listen to some of the vocals. His voice is not really there. I had to listen to so many tapes to find one that was okay. Not Howard but Mark. It affected Mark's high notes. It got better, of course, but it used to be just crazy.

JEFF 'SKUNK' BAXTER Sooner or later, you've got to grow up, so it didn't surprise me in the least when he stopped. Although that was certainly part of the culture we all grew up in the 60s, I never really thought that Mark *or* Howard were that deeply entrenched. I think they had the bear; I don't think the bear had them. I just don't think that them being a part of that culture was in their DNA. They could take it or leave it.

SKIP TAYLOR There comes a point where I don't care who you are or how smart you are, addiction and habits become out of control. I certainly crossed that line, and my capacity was probably much, much greater than most of the people around me. I was definitely into cocaine, but what most people didn't know is, I was into freebase. Nobody knew. I did it totally solo. I kept that a secret, and yet I was still thinking I was in control. And, to some degree, I was. I worked my ass off day and night. I could stay up all night and wait for six o'clock in L.A., when it would be nine o'clock in New York, and I could call Clive Davis and really go after him. I was still functioning as a businessman, and to some degree maybe even more so. I always used the drug—mainly cocaine or freebase—as a stimulant, which it is to start with, but in the long run it doesn't. You need more and more to keep you at that level.

I spent a couple of years as a guest of the state of California back in '80, '81. It wakes you up there. One day you realize, *What am I doing with all these non-high-school graduates and I'm the only college graduate here? Yeah, I've got the best job running the transfer office of who goes to what courtroom, and who gets what job in the kitchen, but somehow, this is not how I pictured my life.* Fortunately, my life has been really blessed with some amazing folks in it, and a lot of the things that have happened are probably better left unsaid.

TOMMY JAMES I was not a big cokehead, and not because I'm virtuous. it just wasn't my drug of choice. I'd much rather kick back with a bottle of Bourbon. The two that really caught up with me were booze and valium. When I went to the Betty Ford Centre, it ended up being for booze and valium. I went in '86, and I have never had a relapse, ever. I've been very fortunate. God's been good to me.

For the most part, drugs never became a problem for me, mostly because I didn't have the money. If I had made all the money that I was due, then probably, but I don't know. I really don't know. I was a cocaine user and abuser for a certain amount of time, and I could probably blame my first marriage dissolving on account of drugs. So, there is a good side and a bad side, and the good side does not outweigh the bad side. But it's a human condition. It's the challenges we face in life, just day-to-day. That's not a struggle for The Byrds or Buffalo Springfield or The Turtles. This is not just a musician problem. This is a problem in the priesthood, this is a problem in the churches, and it's a problem in government. It's a problem with lawyers, doctors ... society has not learned from the mistakes we made. We just don't do that. Alcohol and drugs are not a musician's problem, but we were the first that were being covered by the media.

CHRIS HILLMAN It's such a strange thing. Here we were, children of an incredible generation of people who had survived the depression and World War II, and along comes our generation, and we're basically spoiled brats. Not necessarily everybody. It was really depending on your upbringing and everything. I had good parents, or I wouldn't be here. I had great parents, and I firmly believe that those values that you are instilled with from age one to twelve will stick with you through the most precarious times, or the most tempting times. Obviously, Mark had good parents, too. Look what he pulled off. He had those values instilled in him. There was always a stop measure. He would get to that point and then he knew not to go beyond that, over the precipice into the abyss. I'm a firm believer in a religious foundation in a family, a Judeo-Christian foundation in a family's life. However, not having that, I had a firm moral and value-oriented upbringing, as did obviously the people that are walking around and doing things now.

CHUCK NEGRON Good family can help, but you're talking nature and nurture, and it's more nature. It's right on the medical books. If you have this problem, the second you take a drink, it will create an immediate craving for another one, then another one. Then the second phase is, it opens up the door for a mental obsession. Your brain says, 'Hey, that felt good, I'll have some more.' Then you get to a point where you're so physically addicted, you drink until you die. And that's what happens to most. But that is a medical condition. That's alcoholism, and it is a disease. These guys that walked away are no heroes—they just didn't have the disease. It's as simple as that. When everyone was dying, they stopped. They stopped because they weren't alcoholics, and they were blessed. Trust me, the other people who were dying, didn't stop.

MICKY DOLENZ Family background may not be the only factor, but it is certainly a huge factor in the equation. Your upbringing has an enormous amount to do with it, and I certainly give credit to my parents. They were non-Hollywood folks, even though they were both actors and singers. We lived out in the Valley, on a ranch, and my father was Italian off the boat, so he didn't put up with any shit, and he didn't fly with the Hollywood crowd at all. We were brought up in a very sort of down-home, feet-on-the-ground kind of way. I wouldn't say it was restrictive or abusive. It was a disciplined household, but then most of my friends had very disciplined households back then. But other factors can become an influence: your peers, you can just have different chemistry. And some of it was accidental, just the wrong combination of things at the wrong time. All it takes is one little thing going the wrong way. You're at the wrong place at the wrong time. We say that about car accidents.

PHIL VOLMAN Mark's drug use wasn't obvious to me because I wasn't obvious, either. I was involved myself. And it's not like either of us were unhappy. I think it was the times. Eventually, he realized it wasn't a good idea—it got to be expensive—and he stopped. And that was the same as me. It was time to put your life back together. But it wasn't like a dramatic change. It was more practical.

EMILY VOLMAN Mark was defined by smoking dope. But I happened to meet him after that was over. By the time I met him, he'd stopped everything. Once, after I had first moved in, I found something in a pantry cupboard, and I didn't even know what it was, that's how lame I am. He said it was opium, and I remember going, *Whoa!* It was like the Holy Grail. I didn't know what it was, and I didn't know how to feel. There was this confusion: *Am I supposed to be scared of it?* He was like, 'Oh yeah, it's old. I'll just throw it away.' And he threw it away right then and there. So, it wasn't really that important.

PAT VOLMAN It didn't surprise me when he stopped. It was time. He wanted to get healthy, and he was doing all that Nutrisystem stuff. He goes through these phases. He used to smoke cigarettes, too, and he stopped that. Then he stopped smoking pot, then drinking. We all go through our little phases of experimenting and all that stuff. And, when he came home from New York, he wanted to stop everything, too.

JOHNNY BARBATA He's all clean now. He has a glass of wine once in a while, but that's cool. He doesn't smoke dope anymore, and it's understandable. Being a Christian, that's his choice. But who knows why God put all that stuff down here?

SIDE C THE EIGHTIES & NINETIES

11

FLO & EDDIE

THE THIRD BAND

ANDY CAHAN In 1980, promoters in Europe wanted to book The Turtles, but there wasn't enough money to pay for airfare and the full band, so Mark and Howard decided to do The Two-And-A-Half-Man Show. We'd do a vaudeville act and have stuffed animals and a projection screen with stills and movies of their history, starting with The Crossfires going through Flo & Eddie and all that stuff. We did a bit where, instead of Pink Floyd's *The Wall*, it was Floyd & Eddie's *The Fence*. And I was the half man. I had a drum machine and a Yamaha acoustic piano, and we toured around Europe. We did a Swedish television show where U2 opened for us. Bono had dinner with me and Mark, and he actually got my autograph. He got *my* autograph. It was hilarious. We also did the show at the Ice House in Pasadena, and at the Roxy and a couple other places in town. That was a great event.

GREG HAWKES Mark and Howard came to see us the first couple of times the Cars played in L.A.. They liked the band, and we hung out. I saw The Two-And-A-Half-Man Show at the Roxy when I was out working with The Cars. That show was great: just a slide show and then the two of them plus Andy. I found it very funny and clever.

HOWARD KAYLAN The only reason we got back on the road at all was, in 1979, Joe Stefko put the Flo & Eddie band together, and we played those first reunion shows at My Father's Place on Long Island. Otherwise, there was no band. We were not touring. We would not go out on the road again. It was only after we did that one weekend in Long Island that we decided, *You know what? We can do this*. Before that, we were totally out of commission.

JOE STEFKO I was on hiatus from Meat Loaf, and I went to My Father's Place. Eppy—Michael Epstein—ran the club, and he came up to me and said, 'I'm trying to get Flo & Eddie to come and do a show and they won't play. They won't tour since Phil died.' We went to the office and called Mark, and I basically said, 'Meat fell off the stage, we have nothing to do, I'll give you the Meat Loaf band, you give us tapes, no rehearsal, come over here, we'll do two nights at My Father's Place for Eppy. It can't hurt.'

And that's what we did. They'd never heard me play. I guess that is kind of bizarre, but coming off the *Bat Out Of Hell* tour they must have figured, *He's got to be able to play. And if he's getting some of the Bat Out Of Hell band members, how bad could it be?* I rehearsed the band beforehand, but when they arrived, there was no rehearsal. I'm sure we did a soundcheck, but that was it. They brought Andy out. He was like their anchor: they knew they had him and he knew the stuff. We did it once a year, and it grew from two to four shows to a week, and then we did the Bottom Line runs. And it grew . . . we started touring.

That third band was the start of a new chapter in our lives. Great musicians playing with us—who still play with us today.

DONNIE KISSELBACH Joe Stefko contacted me about doing some Christmas shows at the Bottom Line in 1986. I had been with Rick Derringer for about six years, and after Rick's thing wound down, I was in the studio with Alice Cooper in New York, but I was a Flo & Eddie fan. I bought those albums in the mid-70s, and I was excited.

The first night, I just can't wait to fucking tear this show up. We're in the dressing room and there's a deli tray, the obligatory deli tray. Mark picks up a piece of ham and runs it through his hair; he's running his fingers through his hair with a piece of ham while looking in the mirror, and everybody has their own reaction. We're mortified, but we're mostly laughing. He throws the ham down and says, 'Okay, let's go. Let's get out there, and I want everybody to give a hundred percent.' And Howard rolls his eyes and goes, 'Yeah, I'll give a hundred percent, but I'm only going to care forty percent.'

We all went out onto the stage, laughing, happy, ready to rock, and we went out there and killed it. I'll never forget that. The shows ran Wednesday through Saturday, two shows a night for two weeks. Sixteen shows of material that they couldn't do out on the road, because you have to be more family-oriented at these summer festivals. They whipped out all this arcane Zappa stuff that they couldn't do in a forty-minute show, so you'd see the same faces at both shows. It was remarkable.

LARRY ZINN I was the tour manager from '84 to '95. My gig was pretty straightforward. I would do what a road manager does—make sure everything was in place so that the only thing that we had to worry about was showing up and getting money. We were doing everything from playing in a field in Oakville, Washington, to eighty thousand people at Mile High Stadium, and everything in between. We did thirteen years of Bottom Line dates for New Year's, and we did a bunch of Disney World stuff, where we would do three twenty-minute sets and be done before midnight.

TONY VISCONTI I would go when they did the Flo & Eddie show at the Bottom Line. They would sing the T. Rex songs and say, 'You sing the lead, and we'll do the backups'—hilarious, and what a great concept. I saw them recently, and as the audience gets older, the songs aren't as familiar, but the humor is what carries a lot of the show. Mark's humor is sensational. We've remained friends over the years.

JOE STEFKO For a long time, we were just Flo & Eddie, and we were doing small clubs. When they got The Turtles name back, more money started coming in. It just kept getting more and more until we ended up putting those *Happy Together* tours together and we were out for about eight months. We always did the hits. What changed was, the filthy stuff started leaving. All of a sudden they had to watch what they were saying, because we were playing in front of a lot of people, and there were kids. Some of the Disney-type gigs, one slip and it's over. You don't go back. So, the hardcore Zappa/Flo & Eddie stuff was going out the window. It's pretty much the same show, but there's room for stuff to happen. If they get frisky and bizarre, it can go anywhere.

12

ANIMATION

For a portion of the film *200 Motels*, Mark and Howard voiced cartoon characters based on themselves, in the process establishing a relationship with Murakami-Wolf Productions. That relationship would lead to a parallel career in animated features.

CHUCK SWENSON If you lived through the 60s and you remember it, you didn't live through the 60s. So, I don't remember how we met Mark and Howard. Parties—there were parties. Frank Zappa had a rehearsal space down on LaBrea somewhere, and I may have met them there, I don't know. The company I was with was Murakami-Wolf, and then it was Murakami-Wolf-Swenson. We did *200 Motels* with Frank; we did *Puff The Magic Dragon* with Peter Yarrow; we did *The Point* with Harry Nilsson; a number of music-based projects. So, we were no strangers to the music scene. Frank's an L.A. guy, and it sort of came together because his manager's brother was our lawyer. Those guys really got around.

FRED WOLF I did a little film called *The Box*, which won an Oscar. That was an easy one: I did that in about six weeks, sitting at my drawing table inventing my own process, because I couldn't afford to have it inked and painted properly.

CHUCK SWENSON *The Magic Pear Tree* was the first animated film that I did, and it was nominated for an Academy Award in '68. I went to an art school's film department in Los Angeles, ended up in the animation business, and thoroughly enjoyed it. It was a great fun, and it still is. I'm still in L.A. and I'm still doing it.

FRED WOLF Somehow, through osmosis, I met Mark and Howard. Probably through Frank, because we both had the same attorney, Martin 'Mutt' Cohen.

The *200 Motels* production came to us because of Frank knowing me, and that Oscar that I won. That sort of put a different light on Fred Wolf. It didn't seem like a big deal to me because my little company was doing commercials. We were really TV people who won an award for the movie business. The movie people didn't recognize us, but the music guys did, and Frank was looking for a credible animation company. He had a music company but not a production company at that point, so the movie was Bizarre Productions—that was his company—and Murakami-Wolf was us. We had the lab credits and all. I was busy finishing up my own film with Harry Nilsson, so Chuck would have been more involved with the animation aspect.

CHUCK SWENSON It was a great project, great fun to do. Frank pretty much had the script in mind. It was done before they left for London to do principal photography. I already had a script in hand, and I worked directly with Cal Schenkel, Frank's art director. Frank was around, but Cal was the guy I worked with on a day-to-day basis. It wasn't a stretch. Calvin and I stayed and worked throughout the time they were gone, putting the animation part of it together. And then they came back and it all got combined.

FRED WOLF The only time I saw the results was when I went to the opening night with everybody else. I think it's a bunch of nonsense, but that was the time.

CHUCK SWENSON With *200 Motels*, we did the animation, but the movie was known for a lot more than that. You've got to realize where you are in the world. That was done with Frank and his crew, and Frank is legendary. He's mythical in some people's minds, so they're not going to pay much attention to the animation.

FRED WOLF We owned a series of little Hollywood bungalows, and there was always an open bar. The recording studios and TV studios were all in the district, so we were in the heart of everything. We were too old to be hippies, so we played the part. We dressed that way and kind of grooved that way, but all we were after was just having a good time. Mark and Howard started to hang out, using our place as another kind of watering hole/clubhouse thing.

This is around the time Harry was hanging out as well. His film was over with, and he became another fixture.

We would go drinking at Hollywood & Vine, to a place that was really a dive, the Frolic Room. Howard and I would go with Harry Nilsson and Tom Waits—different combinations of the four of us. There was nobody in the place except us four drunks. It had a piano, and Harry would play and sing for hours in the middle of the afternoon. We were right down the street from Zappa's management company. That's how we ended up at that particular bar: we all had office space at Herb Cohen's office.

FRED WOLF The catalyst was usually boozing and carousing, and I came with my own brand of craziness. I had my own agenda—my own equipment, so to speak. I was in the throes of heavy alcoholism, but I could keep up with Harry, and I guess that's one of the reasons we were such strong pals. I was in the middle of The Turtles, and I'd get phone calls from him, and he'd say, 'I got a great idea—The Turtles meet Oblio from *The Point!*' That's not a great idea.

Ringo was another heavy boozer in that crowd. He had a house down the street from us, and in the summertime, while it was still light outside, I would drop by and there would be Ringo, sitting by the fireplace with a drink in his hand, the fireplace fully lit with logs going. And it would be 98 degrees or so outside. He'd say, 'Have a drink—help yourself.' And it was just two alcoholics. We really didn't have a lot to say, so our conversation was just sort of, 'You hear from Harry? Where's Harry?'

Eventually I realized I was an alcoholic. I've been clean and sober since 1983. Mark got sober around that same time. Quite a few of us did. I can't mention all their names because that isn't fair poker. They have to name themselves. But Mark is as open with his sobriety as I am, and how life changed considerably after that. Ringo's sobriety is related to about that time, and so is Alice Cooper.

CHUCK SWENSON I worked with Mark and Howard again on *Dirty Duck*. I'm credited as director, which means I basically made the movie. I designed it, directed it, did the layouts, the backgrounds, the animation, a quarter of the inking and painting, and cut it together roughly myself. And I wrote the story. I have to lay claim to the entire thing, yep.

We did a lot of improv with Mark and Howard on the recording set. Lots of that stuff is just out of their wacky heads. We started with about sixty pages, enough to tell the story, but there was a lot of material that they added to, bringing in their own personalities. We picked that, and then illustrated after the fact. That's the way animation is done: you do the audio track first. It's a real piece of its time, definitely. There's a lot of stuff that's funny and very much of the moment. I don't know that kids today—the moviegoing audience basically being your average eighteen-year-old—I don't know that they'd 'get it,' so to speak. There are so many references that no longer mean much.

FRED WOLF We saw more of them while doing *Dirty Duck*. That was a pure Chuck Swenson thing. We hung out a lot, but I didn't have any working relationship with them until later on. I started doing these little specials like *Strawberry Shortcake*, which needed music, so I called them to do the scores. They had no experience in that area, but they were great.

CHUCK SWENSON They have a very childlike quality to them. They do this wacky hardcore rock'n'roll, but 'Happy Together' is really a silly song. We thought they could be a fit with *Strawberry Shortcake* to try and cut the treacle, and it worked. They did three *Strawberry Shortcakes*. They wrote the songs, but I think they were given lyrics. Romeo Muller was the writer of the *Strawberry Shortcake* things.

The *Strawberry Shortcake* years were really crazy. It was nonstop lunacy, doing those characters' voices.

FRED WOLF For that film, they didn't do too many lyrics, because Romeo did all writing. He was somewhat of a poet, and there were a couple of songs from him as well. On one song, the client, which was really a doll manufacturer, wanted every bleeding toy mentioned. Mark and Howard had to sing 'here comes Strawberry Shortcake' and 'here comes Mickey Mouse' and every toy, going down the line. It became a blur of names.

We all had a very loosey-goosey way of working. They were late all the time, so I tried to be firm and bossy, but it didn't work, because two minutes later we'd be all laughing, or saying, 'Let's go have a drink.'

HENRY DILTZ Mark and Howard did *Strawberry Shortcake*, and that was a big thing. And *Care Bears*. I thought, *That's very clever.* They're really very professional. They knew how to survive through that era.

BILLY STEELE Mark was always looking for new opportunities, and the cartoons are a perfect example. Who would have thought that Mark and Howard from The Turtles would be doing cartoons? Mark would always get into stuff like that and make it work. He always had a business sense. And I learned a lot from him, without a doubt.

CRAIG KRAMPF Every now and then I'd run into Mark and Howard, and one day they were in the studio next door recording. So, in I go, and they're doing the *Care Bears*. I got to witness it. And later, I'm watching the *Care Bears* with my daughter, and little does she realize, here are Mark and Howard, chain-smoking joint after joint, being the *Care Bears*. But that's typical. I've always thought of Mark and Howard as survivors. Regardless of what has happened in their career, whether it's going off to be drivetime talk guys in New York, having a radio show in L.A. on a Sunday night, doing the music for the *Care Bears*... they always had something going on.

CHUCK SWENSON *Care Bears* was done through Disney. Fred had taken on a job at Disney when they started up their TV department, and he brought Mark and Howard in to do that.

SARINA VOLMAN I was already going into high school by the time they started on the cartoons, so I never got into them. That was my sister more. They're cute but... even though I still love *Hello Kitty* today, I never particularly cared for the *Care Bears*.

HALLIE VOLMAN *Strawberry Shortcake* was my favorite. I was young enough that it was really exciting when he did the music. Hearing my dad's voice wasn't confusing at all. I loved it. I might have been a little too young to really put the two together. I had the *Strawberry Shortcake* bed set and the dolls and all the little knickknacks.

When Care Bears was released on DVD, Mark and Howard's voices were replaced.

CHUCK SWENSON That's probably legal stuff. That was probably cheaper, they maybe got it replaced in Canada or some place.

FRED WOLF I tried to give them as much work as I could. They did *Thanksgiving In The Land Of Oz*. I had them in *Peter And The Magic Egg*. That was for the egg coloring company PAAS. In a lot of cases, companies were hiring us to put a story together around their product, and these were glorified commercials—half-hour commercials.

BILLY STEELE *Care Bears*, *Strawberry Shortcake*, and whatever else, maybe even a movie thing, any of that I usually did with Mark. The cartoon stuff was very quick. You'd go in the studio, learn the material, and then record it. But it always worked out. One time, we had Ray Bolger singing on one of the songs, and I wrote him a vocal chart.

ANDY CAHAN Ray Bolger was seventy-four years old at the time, so Mark and Howard and I went over to his house. I sat next to him at his piano, and we rehearsed a song for *Peter And The Magic Egg*. It was really exciting. I'm sitting there and he turns around and looks at me and says, 'Would you like to know what it was like to shoot *The Wizard Of Oz*?' He spoke just like the Scarecrow and I'm going, 'Holy shit!' But just to be able to meet Ray Bolger. I mean, we're talking 1939.

We wrote a song for Ray Bolger called 'It's A Wonderment.' We copied the form of one of his biggest hits, 'Once In Love With Amy.' He told us he hated the song, right to our faces. I don't think he liked us very much, either.

ANDY CAHAN Mark and Howard were never intimidated. They spoke their minds and they took care of business. They never faltered.

FRED WOLF And then we had a full-length feature film, *American Rabbit*. And there, unlike *Strawberry Shortcake*, they had the whole shooting match. They wrote and sang all the songs. But in both cases, they signed off on the publishing, so if they get anything, they've got the composers' fee. In both cases, I, like them, was a work-for-hire. I had no residual commitment. We'd say, 'Here's a sequence: American Rabbit is down, he's lost, trying to run for a position and the public has turned him down. His girlfriend Bunny O'Hare is cheering him on, and we need score music to accompany these scenes.' The vocals they would sing over it would be like, '*Here we go! | We're back in the swing again | Things are going to be okay!*'—these up and peppy kinds of things. They were pretty vacuous in content, but they did the job and were right on the money. They knew exactly how to create that mood. You wouldn't come out singing the song, but you might come out with a happy moment that felt uplifting. And they certainly knew how to put sadness to a thing when it required sadness.

CHUCK SWENSON Voice work was a natural for them, because they weren't doing anything other than being themselves. They're not shy, they can act, and they can improvise, which I encourage, because it adds to the quality when it's not all script driven. A good actor can give you a great performance out of a great script, but when you're dealing with characters—people like Mark and Howard—there's nothing wrong with letting them loose to see what they'll bring to it out of their own wacky heads. That improves the process and the product, because it gives you some reality from their point of view. They always had a script to fall back to, but it opens up the scope of the thing. A little bit like a jazz or a rock'n'roll musician: you've got the chord structure and lyrics, but what they play is up to them. And we could always edit later.

HARRY SHEARER They have strong improv skills both onstage and on the radio show, so I'm sure that if they were allowed to, they took full advantage of it in the studio. It's a very specialized talent. First of all, you need to be able to create unique characters. I tell kids who want to get into the business that you've got to come up with your own voices, because everybody wants to do a tape of, say, *Simpsons* voices, or *South Park* voices. Well, those gigs have been taken. So, partly, it's the ability to imagine a new sound. It's very much like if you are a guitarist, or a songwriter or a producer; it's the same gift. It's imagining a new sound that people haven't heard before. If you can do the world's best Donald Duck, and there's already somebody with the gig, big deal. But if you can do a new voice that nobody has ever heard before, you've got a shot. You've got something to offer.

Voice acting gets a lot of denigration, but the fact is, you're trying to communicate with just one tool what on-camera actors use two or three different tools to express. You've got to get it all out through the vocal cords, so it's a very special talent. It's very, very specialized, and it calls on you to put all your creative energy through that one instrument, to get all that information out.

The actors we did voiceovers with were all superstars of voiceover. Robert Ridgely, Lurene Tuttle, Walker Edmiston, and Russi Taylor. Ridgely might have been the funniest guy ever. He would be working on *Care Bears* voices or *Strawberry Shortcake*, and he would be entertaining Howard and me with four-letter words at every opportunity. Not just four-letter words. The dirtiest things. He would get us laughing so hard that we couldn't stop. That carried over to Dirty Duck, where Ridgely peaked.

CHUCK SWENSON We worked with a lot of sort-of legends, but in every case they were functioning, working actors, and they needed a gig. Animation voice work is a great pleasure for most actors, because they get to overact, and they don't have to dress for it. Nobody needs makeup, there's no shoot. So, they can come in, in their jammies, and they get to go home at the end of the day.

RON NEVISON Mark and Howard remind me of Gene and Paul's KISS, who I did an album with called *Crazy Nights*. They're all smart businessmen. They know how to reinvent themselves, they're good marketing people, and they're all smart Jewish guys. The whole fact that *Moving Targets*—which I think was their best effort as Flo & Eddie—didn't really shake anybody, well, these are guys who reinvent themselves regularly, and they just figured, cartoons . . . that's another thing to do.

CHUCK SWENSON They're not dumb guys. Most of these musicians, they're very bright people, whether they went to school or not. All these people had incredible minds. Harry Nilsson was an incredibly bright guy. Zappa was this very eclectic scholar who had a wide knowledge of many, many things. And the same with Mark and Howard. To some people's minds they made this sort of bubblegum pop music, but they're very bright guys, both of them.

PHIL VOLMAN I was working as an agent at Creative Contemporary Artists in the 80s and I got Mark and Howard some soundtrack work on a movie. There was a pilot for a television show, and a couple of other things as well. I used to do that on my own, outside the company. That's when we started to connect.

MADELINE CAMPILLO I think he's very intelligent, I really do. He's smart enough to change when you need the change, and they needed to change in the 80s. Redefine and move up.

13

RADIO

MARK PARENTEAU Every time on the radio with them was a joy. The first opportunity came around the time of *200 Motels*. Mark was bigger than life, and there he was in my little studio. Those two guys were cool on so many levels, and as soon as we went on the air, they were wonderful—a disc jockey's dream. Your worst fear is to have somebody like Rod Stewart, who decides that day he's going to answer all your questions in French, because his *Ooh La La* album had just come out, and some artists just didn't *get* radio. But those two were media geniuses.

Mark knew where the camera was on *The Ed Sullivan Show* and played to it; he knew the power of being funny. They were loosey-goosey California knuckleheads who had the ability to be so funny on the air, which is great radio. They would argue with each other, Howard being that staid, stoic kind of guy and Volman just being completely wigged out all the time and pushing Howard's buttons, when of course, they were best friends. It was a dynamic that was just winning. The listeners loved it.

Radio was easy. It was going back to when Howard was Howie The K at UCLA, and I was his 'cousin' every day, pretending to be a British singer in a rock band.

MARK PARENTEAU When they were out with Alice Cooper, they really realized the power of radio—that not only could it sell records, it could fill concert halls. If they were particularly hot that afternoon, suddenly two or three more thousand seats would sell. The ability to utilize media was not lost on them. They really got it.

Volman was instantly identifiable. You couldn't walk anywhere. People would not notice Howard so much, because he was just another sort of long-haired 70s musician, but Volman was so identifiable, with those glasses and that hair and those tight bowling shirts. Everywhere you went with him it was instant notoriety, and he always worked it. He could make a room of old ladies laugh at a restaurant in the suburbs of Detroit. He just knew how to be magical.

SHADOE STEVENS I was the first person to put those guys on the radio, in '73. I was at KROQ, and they came to me with this tape of them doing something on public radio. They were so funny and full of life that I totally got the idea of doing a show with them. We came up with the idea of theme weeks: a Mexican night, an Italian night . . . they would build a theme, and we would get a guest in. So maybe Ringo Starr was the guest, maybe Keith Moon or Alice Cooper.

Radio started for us in 1973, when we did *Flo & Eddie By The Fireside* at KROQ. Shadoe was our producer and engineer. It was very loose, even the idea of how long we went. Some nights we'd do two hours, some nights just one. And radio gave us an opportunity to do interviews. We interviewed a lot a lot of celebrities who wanted to do KROQ. Leading into our show was Dr. Demento, who played music from the 40s and crazy comedy songs. You also had *Rodney On The Roq*, which was kind of a pop show. Eventually, Shadoe got a chance to be program director at KMET in Hollywood. When Shadoe moved, he took us with him, and *Flo & Eddie By The Fireside* moved into weekday radio.

MARK PARENTEAU They had gotten so good at doing interviews that they ended up getting their own show on KROQ. I remember going with Shep Gordon and Alice Cooper and doing the show, and it went on for hours. They were my portals; they knew every inch of L.A. Going to the Hollywood Hills, Volman would point out, 'There's Frank Zappa's house' and 'That's the house that Jan & Dean wrote this song in.' They knew every house, every movie star, and every rock star. It was unbelievable, and of course Volman lived it—this was his neighborhood—but to me, it was fantasy culture come true, to be in California with these actual homes where the music of my life had taken place.

SHADOE STEVENS They were very high-energy. They could ad-lib at a hundred miles an hour, be witty, and laugh at themselves and everything else with very little preparation. And then of course they talked on top of each other. And when they had guests, *everybody* was talking on top of each other, and laughing and making jokes.

Shadoe was the director. He kept the whole thing moving. He was really funny, and so important to the success of our radio show. He capped off what was a great team.

SHADOE STEVENS My job was behind the scenes, helping steer the show and keeping it on track and somewhat focused. I would produce, but in return, they would come in every Thursday afternoon and record promos that would give us something to promote. For instance, we would take a track from The Who and they would sing over it, so now we had an original jingle, and it was sung perfectly, and it's hilarious, but, on top of that, they were technically astonishing. They could sing harmonies that just knock you out, and they could do it extemporaneously, at the drop of the hat.

We would never play a song all the way through. The sets would include stacks of 45s, maybe a couple of LP tracks, and we played only thirty or forty seconds of each song. It was all happening live, and as fast as we could go, so there were intoxicants involved. It was a real party atmosphere and totally fun. And that really helped elevate KROQ's position. It gave the station incredible life.

When I quit KROQ and went to KMET, I brought them with me. I produced their show there for quite a while too.

KEN BARNES I was writing for *Phonograph Record* magazine when we started using them on our *Blind Date* column in 1974. That continued for a few years. The format was, I'd play them a record, and they wouldn't be able to look at the label or the cover until they guessed who it was. And not only did they get most of it, but just the names they'd throw around when they were guessing showed such a vast awareness of the pop scene in general. All styles, all genres, all locales, all eras. These guys definitely paid attention to what was around them.

Considering that they knew so many musicians, it was pretty interesting how frank they were in their reviews. They didn't hold back, but they did it with such a fun irreverent spirit that nobody really got offended. The magazine was distributed across the country by FM rock stations, and Flo & Eddie were almost like mascots—the celebrity mascots. They were all over the magazine, and they had the radio show going at the same time. So at that point, if underground credibility was what they wanted and what they hungered for, they got it. But it probably didn't pay the bills.

DANNY HUTTON I did the radio show with them, and then I saw this thing where they were interviewing David Bowie, and holy crap—these guys are good! I really admire the energy of the different things they got into. They just said, *Okay, can't do that? We'll do this. We'll do radio, we'll do cartoons, we'll do whatever we need to do.* I would love to have whoever instigated all that stuff working with me. It's amazing.

K-ROCK

MARK CHERNOFF I was the program director at K-ROCK—that's WXRK here in New York City. We were a classic rock station. We had Howard Stern on in the morning, and my thinking was that we could do a show in the afternoon that was not just classic rock but something more: guys who've been in rock'n'roll, who might be show hosts. Nothing was going to compare to Howard Stern, clearly, but figuring on something that might be of some entertainment value, and everybody bought into it. When somebody said, 'Mark and Howard—The Turtles,' I thought it was a really interesting idea. I knew they had guest hosted shows in other markets, and had worked at one of the stations in L.A. They even had a syndicated radio show for a while, but they didn't have a day-to-day show.

John Sebastian did a monthly show that was syndicated, but I didn't feel there was enough personality, and I figured the two guys would offer more than one guy who is a historical figure. These guys were both historical and hysterical. And they made me laugh. I went to one of those shows that first year at the Bottom Line and it blew me away. I could see why they were invited back every year. I reached out to Mark and asked if they would be interested in guest hosting while they were in town. It was right around Thanksgiving 1989. They hosted a couple of shows and we wound up signing them to a deal for a couple of years.

Eventually we were approached by Mark. We had done one show a week in California, but now we were given an opportunity to move into a regular five-days-a-week show. We kind of fell into that, and we were learning a lot. We applied ourselves to really learn radio. Now we had our own producer, and people working full-time helping the show, and that's how we built our fan base in the New York area.

K-ROCK was famous for hiring Howard Stern. He was the morning disc jockey, and we were shifted into afternoon drive, which was mid-afternoon, 2pm to 6pm. We were doing four-hour shifts with commercials, and it was really fun. New York allowed us to get out of L.A. and really focus on radio. We eventually moved there. When we did that, we weren't going to try and continue doing everything. We signed a very good deal with K-ROCK, and radio kind of took over.

TIM REID They put me as producer with Flo & Eddie about four months after they had arrived. The format was already together when I started; it was all decided by Mark Cheroff. They were a lot of fun to work with. They weren't like your average DJs. Being a classic rock station, not a lot of new stuff happens, so it's really easy to get bored. So, one of the jobs that I had was to keep them entertained.

MARK PARENTEAU They became really popular, because they already had a developed sense of radio, and Mark's ability to get things out of people and have girls says wacky funny things never ceased to amaze me. But it was very, very hard for them to be in New York. They were West Coast guys, and although they did really well with the ratings, it was a strain on both of their lives. It was harder to be away all the time, and radio is very demanding. You have to be there every day, all the time, and be on top of it.

JACKIE MARTLING Radio is unique. You can play to the imagination, and you count on the audience paying attention. People think it's just television without pictures, but it isn't. It's a completely different medium. It's as different as ice skating and bowling.

PEPPY CASTRO They broke into New York radio—who breaks into New York radio? You know what I mean? You don't break into New York; you've got to sit around secondary markets for God knows how long to even be looked at. But—BOOM!—They came in. And it was refreshing because they were totally different from Howard. Howard would shock—he would do anything to shock—but these guys had a playfulness about them. And, coming from inside, they were hands-on in the belly of the beast. They were in the business of music. They worked up through the ranks, whereas Howard was always on the other end of it, on the outside looking in. Mark and Howard lived it, so if they told a story, you could believe it.

We moved to New York and did the show Monday through Friday. Friday late afternoon I would fly home to California, visit with Pat and the kids, and Saturday night we would fly back to New York. We kept that up for two and a half years. We were still touring as The Turtles and Flo & Eddie, picking up shows during the week and on the weekends, but now we had a forty-two-week contract at K-ROCK. We couldn't just not be there, so we started pre-recording some of those shows, and eventually we parlayed that into a job with WFIR in New York City and Virginia.

JIMMY FINK The first couple of years at K-ROCK were very fresh and exciting, especially with the addition of Howard and then Flo & Eddie. Prior to that, we were pretty much a straight-ahead rock station. We played music and the disc jockeys talked, but then everything changed. You could be a little wilder than you normally would have been.

Howard worked the mornings, and I was on directly after him for a year and a half. I was between him and Mark and Howard, and although I was still a disc jockey, my personality came out more. I didn't try to be a Howard Stern or Flo & Eddie, but it certainly was different than being your standard rock'n'roll disc jockey: *this was / that is / read the weather / tell the time.* We did some wild things on the air.

JACKIE MARTLING I was a huge fan, so I was thrilled when they came to K-ROCK. Howard keeps a little bit more to himself, he's a real nice guy, but Mark is all over the place, and me and him were like obnoxious birds of a feather. So, we're pretty good friends right from the word go, but I never really sat in with them or anything, because I was Howard's head writer, and we were all working our asses off. To tell you the truth, for fifteen years I was in a fog. Nobody has any idea what those hours are like. It was brutal. But it was great having them aboard. They're a lot more fun and a lot more energetic than your average disc jockey.

JIMMY FINK My memories are not so much about being on the air but going to clubs and hanging out. An evening with Flo & Eddie was a lot of drinking. You were part of their world, and they were part of your world. They went beyond just being Flo & Eddie. They became friends.

When it came to radio, we never had trouble getting guests. From L.A. to New York, we had our regulars: Harry, Ray, Alice, McGuinn, Iggy, Keith Moon, and others. On special nights we had Marc Bolan, KISS, Richard Lewis ... we even reunited The Move. We had guys from the [New York] Giants. We even had The Runaways. We flew them to Canada to play on TV with us. It was the night the nuns came. They were so loud! The Runaways, not the nuns.

MARK CHERNOFF They knew a lot of celebrities. They were the only people I knew who had a connection to Harry Nilsson, for example. Harry didn't talk to anybody else. He never did interviews, but he was friends with these guys, and they had him on the show a number of times. The fact that they respected Harry and he respected them says a lot, because Harry was as close to a recluse in those later years as anybody. He was the music version of Howard Hughes, in some ways.

JIMMY FINK K-ROCK made forays into personality radio that were not that successful, like the Greaseman, who tried to be like Howard, and he was a flop. David Lee Roth didn't work either. But Flo & Eddie, they were fun and refreshing. They're not native New Yorkers, but you wouldn't know that. They're both Jewish, and they had this kind of New York Jewish personality that went over very well there. They weren't caustic and they weren't putting people down or nasty. They were fun to listen to.

TIM REID There wasn't much difference between their personalities on air and onstage. They're pretty much true to form. Backstage, too. Mark and Howard are Mark and Howard twenty-four hours a day.

MARK CHERNOFF They were never rude on the air. Whatever they did at their live shows was different. They could do a lot more there, because on radio there are FCC rules and regulations about obscenity and indecency. I never had to worry about that with them. They never crossed the line as far as good or bad taste, that was never an issue. These guys were pros.

JIMMY FINK I don't remember anything being crude, and one thing you don't want to be—and this is one of the reasons why the Greaseman failed—you don't want to be crude just for the sake of being crude, or to try to be like Howard. And they didn't do that. With Flo & Eddie, it was something different. They were being themselves.

THE HOWARD STERN DYNAMIC

MARK CHERNOFF When they first started, Howard really didn't embrace the guys. It's not like he hated them, but it was, 'These two old guys were in The Turtles? Big deal.'

JACKIE MARTLING I'm sure there might have been some friction, but I was never privy to exactly what was going on. When somebody new shows up, it's like the new kid on the block. You know: when is it honest jealousy or anger, and when is it just bravado and silliness? Howard was a huge Turtles fan and loved those guys. You can listen to tapes of him saying horrible things about them on the air, but that's got nothing to do with anything. For all I know, *I* said horrible things about them on the air. It's theater!

TIM REID Flo & Eddie had a different dynamic with Howard than a lot of other DJs did, because they already had their own celebrity. He never saw them as any sort of threat. Actually, Howard didn't really think of anybody as a threat. If he thought you were a threat, he wouldn't talk about you at all. Flo was on a few times with him, but I was never a part of that because my time with them was four hours a day, five days a week. That's a lot of time to fill.

MARK CHERNOFF What turned that situation around was, Howard used to do a Super Bowl party, and he invited Mark and Howard to one of those, and Mark made a spectacle of himself. There were certain things with some women that

Mark got himself involved with, and some old stories as well, and all of a sudden now Howard Stern embraced the guys. He loved them. He started using them more regularly on his show.

JACKIE MARTLING I don't know whether we got drunk a billion times or twice, because those days were crazy. Things just went on and on with the Stern show, so between not getting any sleep and not knowing what the fuck is going on, there's a lot of blank areas. But we got to know each other pretty well. We went to the corner bar and tore it up pretty good. And I loved smoking dope, so we hit on that, too.

MARK CHERNOFF We did a lot of charity stuff. World Hunger Year needed to raise money, and we set Mark up for a hunger famine. He stayed in a van for a week outside the station. People came over and made donations through the station on the show. It was really terrific and we got a lot of attention for it. The week in the van, there were some girls that hung out for the overnights. I'd come to work very early in the morning, 5:30, and knock on the door, and there was company in there more than once. It was a little bit wild.

UNIVERSAL CALIFORNIA

RICK CARR I had a company called Remote Possibilities. When stations wanted to broadcast from outside their area, we would put together location, technical aspects—satellite connections back then—and arrange for celebrity interviews. One of my clients was Miller Beer, and in 1990 they had forty-two radio stations from around the country do a three-day live broadcast from Universal Studios. One of the stations was WXRK, and I was hoping it wouldn't be Howard Stern, because Howard likes to take over and control everything, and I didn't want to be put in that position. When I found out they were sending Flo & Eddie, I was almost speechless. I realized, *I've got to make sure this show comes off good, because, my God, Flo & Eddie are going to be there.*

Having never really met them before I'm thinking, *New York DJs, big time rock'n'roll stars: these guys are probably going to be a real pain in the ass to work with*. I had worked with all kinds of major-league jocks from around the country and had dealt with virtually every ego imaginable, and I'm thinking that these guys would probably be the most egotistical of all time. And I was completely wrong. Mark and Howard are just two kids from Westchester—that's who they are.

As they were doing their broadcasts, we would bring different celebrities by, and they would sing with them. It got to the point where certain celebrities were supposed to be pushing their latest movie, but instead everybody is asking to do Flo & Eddie. When Roseanne Barr got there, her handlers were very, very anti-WXRK because of Howard Stern. Howard used to blast her all the time, so I was told from the get-go that they would not do WXRK. And this was New York's biggest station, part of the biggest market that was there, but the handlers were just, 'Don't even talk to us.' I went to Roseanne and asked her, and she goes, 'No, I won't do anything with Howard Stern.' 'Well, this isn't Howard Stern. This is Flo & Eddie. It has nothing to do with Howard.' Roseanne goes, 'The Turtles? You mean the *Happy Together* Turtles?' She was like a little girl. 'My God! The Turtles! That was the first album I ever bought.' And she almost ran over to them. The handler is saying, 'You can't do KXRK!' And Roseanne was like, 'Fuck you! They're The Turtles!' She did a great interview and they got her to sing with them. It wasn't as bad as her national anthem version [at a San Diego Padres game in 1990].

Everybody, when they knew it was Mark and Howard, wanted to be on their show. And they were great to work with. They never insulted anybody. They had fun, but they knew where to draw the line. So, to me as the producer of those shows, I've got forty-two acts I've got to worry about being assholes. Well, now I've got forty-one, because those guys? Completely professional. We went back the following year. The second time, Mark and Howard decided they wanted to do all five days. So, Monday and Tuesday they pretty much arranged their own guests for interviews. They brought Dean Torrence from Jan & Dean, Richard Lewis was there, and they had gone somewhere and taped an interview with Frank Zappa. He was sick then. Mark made the arrangements knowing that I had, once again, forty-one stations to deal with.

ANDY CAHAN They had all these celebrities come to this little tent they had set up. I had a keyboard, so they could sing with the guests. Dean Torrance sang 'Barbara Ann,' Micky Dolenz did 'I'm A Believer.' Bobby Hatfield did 'Unchained Melody,' and Eric Burdon did 'Don't Bring Me Down.'

RICK CARR We loaded Friday with some cool musicians. Spencer Davis was there; Jimmy Messina from Loggins & Messina, Dr. Demento, and Ray Manzarek. We had them all come up. It was one of the first times Manzarek had played 'Light My Fire' live in years. Mark sang, and he hit so close with the inflections and everything that if you closed your eyes, knowing that Manzarek was onstage, it was like … okay, that sounds like Morrison. The people in the audience were rock'n'roll stars, TV producers, all kinds of insiders, and the place just went silent. Mark did such a good job, and then Manzarek, when he started to do the keyboard solo, all of a sudden, he's lowering his head the way he used to play. It was one of those magical rock'n'roll moments, and by the time they finished they probably got a ten-minute standing ovation. It was incredible.

LEAVING NEW YORK

MARK CHERNOFF We did a couple of years, then the guys weren't sure *they* wanted to do it, and I was a little undecided myself. There were all kind of things that worked against continuing on. It became a money situation, and they wanted to be home on the West Coast as well. Ultimately, Mark and Howard pretty much said, 'You know what? We're not sure it's worth the money, because we have to give up all these gigs in order to do this.'

TIM REID I'm not 100 percent sure why they didn't stay on longer. There are hundreds of factors that would figure into it. I don't think their ratings were really slipping. They did great in New York, but it would work anywhere, even today.

MARK CHERNOFF Mark and Howard were at a point where they didn't really want to be confined to the everyday aspect of radio, doing everything 2pm to 6pm. Howard's family was still out on the West Coast. Mark was going through a divorce at the time and his family was on the West Coast, so there were a bunch of circumstances that made it so that it didn't continue. But Howard Stern did embrace them, and on occasion when he's talking about the old days at K-ROCK he brings them up in a really nice way, because at the end he really enjoyed them. I stayed friends with the guys, and I was sad when the radio part of it ended.

Eventually, radio wasn't really happening any more. We were happy to be there, but the last six to eight months we had lots of problems economically, because we did that coast-to-coast travel. We had to make the commitment to live there, and all of the stuff that was going on was beginning to fall apart around us. The show stopped being a cash cow, and they were beginning to get nervous about the station as a whole. We were starting to think of making a record, and decided we needed to come back to L.A. to do that. There was material we were going to assemble from a bunch of different sources: the soundtrack to *Dirty Duck*, songs we had never released, things like that. We had this idea to do *The Battle Of The Bands Part Two*. There were things from a bunch of different albums, material that is actually still kind of hanging around. We never put it out, but it was all mixed. The way we put it together, it was pretty darn finished, as a record goes.

14

FAMILY LIFE

PAT VOLMAN We were in a bowling league for eight or nine years. Mark was the team captain. We've got patches and trophies and everything. We used to go bowling on Sundays at the El Segundo Lanes, near Westchester High, and everybody thought we were brother and sister. How they got that I don't know. Maybe because we didn't act or talk like we were a couple.

SARINA VOLMAN When he was in town, he'd take me everywhere. Mom would say, 'Take her,' because my sister was younger, so he'd drag me around with him. He was part of a softball team called the Vampires. I used to go to the games all the time on the weekends, and I was kind of precocious, because I got to hang out with the adults. I used to hang out with Alice Cooper and Billy Mumy and all the guys on the team. It was cool. And we used to go backstage to all the shows. We had all sorts of privileges because of who he was. When I was twelve or thirteen, Dad MC'd a KISS show in Anaheim, and I had a picture taken with Gene Simmons holding me up. I was always around, and I used to meet all these great people, but I didn't appreciate it. I was like, *Oh yeah, that's just Alice*, or, *That's just . . . Shaun Cassidy*, and I had a huge crush on him. I met a lot of those people, but I didn't really appreciate it because I was so young.

BILLY MUMY I used to drive Sarina home from Wonderland School. She had to walk all the way to the top of Lookout Mountain, so I would give her rides after school because I lived right next to the school. My real relationship with Mark was as a neighbor, but we were on the same softball league for three years, the Hollywood Vampires. It was part of the West Hollywood Softball League. The games were completely scheduled and umpired and all that stuff. The Vampires had Mark and Howard, Alice Cooper, Micky Dolenz, and Meat Loaf.

MICKY DOLENZ I don't even remember who came up with the name. I expect it must have been Alice. We started hanging out on the weekends and playing soft ball, and then it gradually got a little more formal in that we would actually play against industry teams, or we'd play charity things against local teams. We started doing some charity things to get a little attention—mainly it was just for fun, but it got to be pretty good softball. And then we would go hang out in the Rainbow, which could get fairly intense.

TIM SEXTON On Crosby, Stills & Nash tours, we'd play the road crew against the crew at whatever venue it was, and we called the team the Hoovers, for obvious reasons. I decided that we should institutionalize the team at home, so I created the Hollywood Hoovers, which went from 1980 to 1985. The idea was to not only play in the softball leagues, but we would do benefits to help people in need, the L.A. Free Clinic or a food bank or any number of things. I got permission from Hoover vacuums to use their logo, and Nike put up the money for uniforms and shoes. We had Timmy Schmidt as the second baseman, Jackson Browne was a short outfielder, Mark was the third baseman, and there was J.D. Souther, Andrew Gold . . . Henry Diltz was our official photographer. I was the coach. I was the guy who organized the thing. Mark was the guy who was next most intense about it after me, because we were both competitive. Mark is really competitive. He wasn't in the greatest shape physically. He was overweight but he had good legs, and that gave him foundation for sports.

We eventually got into a couple of competitive softball leagues in Southern California where there were guys who were former Major Leaguers who had torn up their knee or one thing or another and could no longer play baseball but were playing in the softball leagues, and they were really, really good players. They're out there warming up, and we've got six guys gathered around a vial at short centerfield. That's our version of a warm up: 'Who's got the $100 bill? [*sniff sniff*] Okay let's go.' Instead of doing batting practice, our guys would be gathered around a vial, because we were the Hoovers, man.

Playing in these more competitive leagues with real players started to become a bummer. We weren't taking it seriously enough, and we'd get our asses kicked. We'd get beat by twenty-five runs. So, Mark and I had this heart-to-heart conversation. We decided that if you wanted to play, you had to come to practice. We would practice one day a week, and everybody got to play. Mark started keeping stats—I mean, he was *on it*. He kept score and we started publishing the stats. We had a little newsletter—our version of a sports page. Every game, Mark would be in the dugout, marching up and down, all fired up. He was a great force for spirit in competition. He wanted to beat Hallie and Sarina at Go Fish, and he wanted the Hoovers to excel.

The funny thing was that the team got really good. These teams that we were getting hammered by, with ex-college and Major and Minor League ball players, all of a sudden we were in the thick of it, and we literally wound up a couple of years in the playoffs against the best softball teams in L.A.

Mark was really competitive. He always played to win. And, by the way, when you look at the music folks who were really successful and whose stuff stood the test of time, they were *all* competitive. They all tracked who did what. If you were a singer/songwriter in L.A. at that time—James, Jackson, the Eagles, Mark and Howard, any of those people—they were tracking what other people were doing, and they knew they had to step up their game. So, the sports stuff was easily understood. Henley and Frey were incredibly competitive guys, and Mark was just like them. And it could be anything. He wanted to win when you played Battleship.

PAT VOLMAN He was very competitive at board games. We went through a phase where we played each other so he could get really good, and then he would invite people over, saying, 'Oh yeah? Go ahead—try me.' Of course, I would beat him, and he'd get really mad at me. We had game nights, and we had this hockey game, and he was, like, pimping me out. He'd say, 'Yeah, you can beat her,' and I would beat everybody, and he would get so mad. We did have some fun times, I must say.

HALLIE VOLMAN I grew up thinking that everyone smoked dope, and that it was an everyday thing. It wasn't until I got older that I realized, *Wow, I think that's illegal.*

SARINA VOLMAN I got to smoke dope with him. That was fun. It didn't really faze me. It was just, *This is normal.* It was always happening, and all my friend's parents smoked, so, it's just . . . normal. And now that I'm an adult, I'm like, *Oh* *my God!* You look back and, *Wow!* We were really unconventional. But I just thought, *These are my parents, this is the way it is. So, it's normal.* And I was very happy with growing up unconventionally. Some of the things I perhaps do or say, my husband is like, *Whoa!* But I say, 'Hey, man, that's the way I grew up.' I can't fight it. That's who I am, that's where I came from. Very unconventional.

HALLIE VOLMAN I was in my teenage years when he announced that he was not going to smoke anymore, and I was a little disappointed, because that's when I had started. I was hoping we could share together.

SARINA VOLMAN I was really sure of myself growing up. And that was instilled by my parents: *Just be who you are.* We weren't stifled at all. And there was no reason to rebel, because they let us do—not whatever we wanted, but it was pretty free. Of course, I had curfew, and if I was going to be late, I'd call. It wasn't a big deal. But there was no need to rebel. From what? They disciplined us—they had to—but it was just me talking back, that kind of thing. Me and my big mouth.

HALLIE VOLMAN I may have gotten one or two talks about trying to stay away from the hard stuff, and to be careful, but never anything too intense. It wasn't hypocritical, it was just, 'Be careful . . .'

SARINA VOLMAN They weren't strict, and I don't think they were too loose, either. I was open about everything. Anything that was going to happen, I talked to them about, so I never had any secrets. I would tell them anything. And I finished high school and I graduated college. I think we had great childhoods, and I don't regret anything about it.

SEPARATION

HOWARD KAYLAN I spent my eighteen months in New York with my family, in an apartment in the city. Mark did not fly his family in. His girls were going to school and his wife was in that house and he didn't want to pay for two rents, all that stuff. So, he became sort of a wild man in New York. And I was still the family guy. Nothing changed for me, particularly.

I looked at New York City as a separation. We were really not getting along, for whatever reason. Just . . . changes. She was nineteen when we got married. I was twenty. I think we were growing up, and changes led our way at that point.

I was separated from my wife, living a single-type life. I partied, drank. I was living like a radio star.

PEPPY CASTRO Mark was subletting my apartment. I had a beautiful apartment in New York as well as a house out in the countryside, and so he sublet the apartment. I didn't witness it hands-on, but let's put this way: my apartment was three floors. It had a steam room and a huge jacuzzi, two fireplaces, a terrace, and everything else. So, if there was ever a place to sow the wild oats while being single in New York, that was it. It was a fabulous bachelor pad, and I'm sure he had many a wonderful night in that place.

TIM REID He was definitely a single guy. He became an instant bachelor, really living a New York single guy's life. Were there girlfriends? Not that I was privy to. I would say it was a revolving door.

SARINA VOLMAN New York changed everything. That same time, as soon as he left for New York, was my first time leaving home. I went to school in San Francisco, and when he left, I left. We left the same time.

HALLIE VOLMAN When I was about thirteen or fourteen he moved to New York, and he was gone a couple of years. We would go up to New York whenever I had time off from school, but you could sense that his being away was starting to have its wear and tear on the family. I was becoming a teenager and probably needing that father figure to be around, and it started to get tough. I don't think we ever even talked about it. A father trying to talk about something like that with a fourteen-year-old daughter is difficult in general, but it was tougher not having him in the house. I didn't know how to reach out to him, and his not being there kind of put a strain on the relationship as well. But that's no longer an issue. The years have taken care of that.

SARINA VOLMAN I went to see him a couple of times in New York. I guess he had had a wild time. He was smoking, and he never smoked.

PAT VOLMAN Everything kind of stopped, and the rules were changing, and when he was gone for two years—don't come home and change my world all of a sudden.

SARINA VOLMAN I wasn't living at home when he came back, but I did move back to L.A. at that time. I lived in Hollywood for a while, and then I moved to Studio City. So, I'd go up to the house and have dinner, and I could tell things weren't right.

HALLIE VOLMAN When he came back home, it was kind of like, *You've been away for all this time. Who do you think you are, coming home and trying to tell me what to do, or what time I need to be home?* He was trying to be the father and trying to be the husband, and maybe a little bit of respect had been lost in the time that he was gone.

SARINA VOLMAN Oh no, you can't do that with my mom or my sister. No, uh-uh. That's a little tough. And there was no compromise on either side. My mom's like, 'My way or the highway,' and my sister was like, 'You can't come and tell me what to do after you've been gone.' I was out of there, so I was thinking, *Thank goodness I don't have to deal with this.*

PAT VOLMAN I was still bowling, and he didn't want me to bowl anymore. 'Stay home!' 'I don't want to stay home. Don't my take bowling away from me! That's my fun thing I do.' It was time for me to stop, anyway. When a fingernail pops off and ends up in somebody's drink a couple of lanes away, it is time for me to just hang up my shoes. Put the ball away, put my shoes away.

SARINA VOLMAN At the time, as far as mom and dad splitting, I had no idea. I don't think they did either. It's just . . . yeah.

HALLIE VOLMAN Any time your parents are having problems, it's tough. But I was old enough to realize that that kind of thing happens. Relationships fall apart. You try and work it out, but sometimes it's just not gonna work. You never want it to happen, but sometimes it does. And I was old enough to understand that it had nothing to do with me, so I didn't feel guilty or that it was my fault.

PHIL VOLMAN The radio show in New York kind of crimped the marriage. He had been with Pat since they were sixteen years old. He told me that if she had taken the kids and gone to New York, everything would have been fine. But she stayed in California, because she didn't want to take the kids out of school. And because he wasn't here, she had to make her own life. The kids were growing up, and she started doing her own kind of trip with the bowling and the drinking. And the drinking became a problem. When he came back, he wanted to be the leader of the house again, and she wanted to continue. He understood that she had never had her own time, and this was it. And she continued to drink, and it was a major problem for him, and he said, 'Well, I'd better leave.'

HOWARD KAYLAN Mark returned home to California, and at the dinner table he made the suggestion to his youngest daughter about cleaning up her room or some crap like that. And she came back with some very predictable but mundane response, like, 'Who are you to tell me to clean up my room? You haven't been here for two years. You don't tell me what to do.' That sort of thing. Then it started unraveling for him. And he realized that he'd been away too long. He wasn't in charge of that family anymore, nor could he sort of control his wife, who had gone into a sort of alcoholic tailspin. I can say that because my wife at the time joined her. And both of those ladies—in fact, they weren't the only two ladies, there were two others—were part of this fearsome foursome that would get together on a daily basis around one of our pools and just start drinking white wine, and it would change to vodka in the evening, and they would come home all just . . . it was horrible. And it went on for a very, very long time.

PAT VOLMAN That was a really bad time. Everything changed after New York, that's all I'm going to say. Two years of being gone, and then coming home? He changed a little bit, and then he wanted me to go back to the way it was. Anyway, those regulations were being mislaid, and it wasn't going to work. You can't be away from somebody for two years and expect them to be the same when you come home. It was hard.

RICHIE FURAY That was devastating, and a shocker to a lot of people.

LINDA CAMPILLO I was surprised when I heard, because they had been together for so long. We all knew that they had some tough times. It was pretty well known that Mark had not always been faithful, and they'd had their ups and downs, but Pat had always been there. So, it was kind of a shock when we found out they were getting a divorce.

HALLIE VOLMAN The split really didn't change our relationship too much, because he'd gone from being away from long periods of time to not being there at all. It was normal again, because pretty much all through my life, he wasn't there a lot of the time.

PAT VOLMAN Sarina was very upset about the divorce, even more than Hallie. She thought we were the poster couple for marriage, and it really hurt her when we got divorced. I talk to her every day, and I didn't know she felt like that until recently.

SARINA VOLMAN I was like, 'What are you guys doing? You guys love each other. You've been together for thirty years. What are you doing?' It took me a long time to accept it, because they were such a great couple. And if you see them together now, they still get along. I had them both walk me down the aisle at my wedding. It was fabulous to have them both there. There's no animosity or anything like that. They were at junior high school together; they met at the age of fourteen or something, so they have a long, long history. She knows all the stories.

PAT VOLMAN I still love the man. I'm not married to him, but I still love him, and I'll always love him. He's my best friend. I've known him longer than I've known my parents, if you think about it that way. I've known him since '62. The secret to our managing to stay friends through all this is probably silliness. And because I like him. Even if I wasn't married to him, I would like him. You like him. Everyone likes him. See? Okay, there you go.

JOHN SNYDER Even his ex-wife is still friendly, and his daughters haven't thrown him under the bus. I think that typifies what kind of guy Mark really is. You can't hate him.

SARINA VOLMAN I was hanging out a lot with Dad after he and Mom separated. He was having a really hard time, so I was there for support. We'd ride our bikes a lot, just have lunch, because my sister was going through her sixteen- and seventeen-year-old stuff, Mom was going through her thing, and we were all doing our own things. But I was hanging out a lot with Dad. He was getting into his body and the health food and everything. He was trying to better himself, is what it was.

JULIE

JULIE SCHAD I owned a health food store called Sprouting Wings. It had a deli in it, and it was not too far from the gym where Mark worked out. His trainer sent him in for the tuna and I made him a sandwich. He had started losing weight, but he was still getting there. His wife was already seeing someone else, but he was still living at that house with her. I had the sense that they had grown apart, and it was easier to stay together because he spent so much time on the road. At that point, he hadn't filed for divorce. It was a hard step for him to make, but it was a prerequisite of us having a serious relationship.

I liked the fact that Julie was independent and successful. It took the pressure off of me, because I came from a life of taking care of everyone.

JULIE SCHAD Once we became a couple, he moved into my apartment, and we were together for five years. We loved being together. When he was in town, we were together all the time. He used to have his breakfast, lunch, and dinner at my restaurant. Because he was there all the time, he would jump in and help out. He'd get behind the cash register, and he started working at the store. A lot of people recognized him, and he was okay with that. He was very much the same as he is now. He had lots of responsibility, and he took his responsibilities seriously. He was able to compartmentalize very well, and get everything done in his life. He was very good with people. And we were active. I'm three years younger than Mark, and we golfed, we rollerbladed, we rode bikes.

SARINA VOLMAN He rode his bike from San Francisco back to L.A. He did that right after the divorce, and he said he needed to do it to clear his mind.

JULIE SCHAD The bike trip was clearly something he needed to do alone. I couldn't—wouldn't—have taken time away from my business anyway, but it had a deep significance for him. That was clear to me at that time.

Julie bought me a massage, and I haven't had once since because of that bike trip! Two-thirds into the massage, I jumped up, wrapped the sheet around me, ran into Julie—who was having her own massage—and I told her, 'I know what I have to do! I have to take a bike trip.' I don't know why I needed to do that. I flew to San Francisco, put my bike back together, and rode down Highway 1 by the ocean. It was really windy, and it took me eight days. I took a sleeping bag and slept in little campgrounds. Two nights I stayed in hotels: one night in Carmel and one night somewhere else. I almost quit a few times. I figured I'd rent a car and tell everybody I rode it, but I couldn't do it. That's the thing I got from that bike trip: I knew I could make it. And by 'it,' I mean anything. Anything I want to do, I can do it. I still feel that way.

JULIE SCHAD I'm getting emotional over this, but I felt like Mark was a gift to his audience. I didn't know he was a performer when I met him, and when I got to see him perform, it was wonderful. He was onstage singing, and with one wave of his arm, he gestured to the audience to stand, and everybody stands, and that energy that you only get at a performance—where it's contagious and larger than life—that thrills the people, and I'm sure it energizes the performer.

I was so happy for the audience, that they had him, and that he does that for so many people—that he lifts their spirits. That's an incredible gift to be able to give people. I told him how great it was afterward, how lucky those people were, and he told me that it was really nice to hear, and that Pat had never said anything like that.

She didn't know who I was. And when she found out, she didn't like me because I was in The Turtles, I think she liked me because I worked hard and I cared about her. Actually, I don't know why she liked me, but I think eventually she wanted to get married and have kids.

JULIE SCHAD He was getting healthy, and I wanted the certification for my business, so we took a correspondence course in nutrition together, and we became certified nutritionists. I think it was the first step for him in realizing that he had a future—that maybe there was something more for him. After that, we started school together at L.A. Valley College, taking General Ed.

SARINA VOLMAN It's like an AA—one of those degrees that you get from junior college, a vocational degree. It didn't surprise me at all, because, once he makes up his mind, things happen.

JULIE SCHAD I didn't pursue it. I went back to work. I'm a hard worker and an entrepreneur and I'm successful, but I am not good at school. But he thrived. He was on a track, and once he got started there was no stopping him. I think he lucked out. He had some teachers that were fans of his, which couldn't hurt. They were thrilled to have him as a student. Plus, he likes people. And as an adult, with an adult perspective, school was good for him, because he had the maturity to approach it that he didn't have when he was younger.

By that point we had moved into a house. We rented a house, and he bought a grand piano, but I don't remember him playing it a lot. We also got some dogs together. One of his classmates at Valley College, their dog had puppies, and we went to check them out and came home with two.

Before we were together, I was asked out a lot. Men would hang around, and I was not interested in them, and I realized I needed a ring, just to send a message. So, Mark bought me a beautiful ring—not an engagement ring, but it was wonderful, and men stopped asking me out. It wasn't too much later, within a year, he gave me an engagement ring. We were happy, and we had fun, but I think I knew from the start—and I might have fooled myself at times—that I could never marry Mark, because I never believed that he could be faithful or monogamous, and that was very important to me. His history with Pat was that he was not monogamous. We would discuss it. I wouldn't call it a problem. I'd call it a choice. It just wasn't my choice to be married to someone that was not monogamous. He was able to compartmentalize— that's one of the things I'm referring to. And maybe that's why it's so easy to be friends, one of the reasons that makes him still part of my life, because what I have with him, I'll always have with him. It was usually that easy. We didn't judge each other by the way it should be. We would explain if somebody had a question, but we respected each other as individuals. It was a pretty mature relationship. I could have married him if I wanted to, but I never pursued it. We never picked a date. But if I had, I'm sure he would have gone along with it.

Our breakup is hard to describe. There wasn't any animosity and there was no fighting, and there wasn't anybody else for me on my end, but I had a strong sense that it was going to be over about six months before he moved out. At about that same time, I heard a phone message. I was in the office when his answering machine went off, and Emily called. She said that he wasn't where he said he would be to meet her, and that she had waited for quite a while. I didn't know her, but I could tell that there was something going on. For some reason it was just clear to me that it had run its course. I asked him to move out, and he quickly found a house and bought it.

I didn't tell Emily the truth about Julie and me. I told her that it was pretty much over and I was living in the office now. So, I relinquish any guilt on her for that breakup.

JULIE SCHAD We stay in touch, and he is just completely dear to me. I love him, he's a dear friend.

15

THE BUSINESS

HARRY SHEARER I spend a lot of my time in New Orleans, because the ratio of love of the thing to the amount of time you spend dealing with the assholes is pretty much reversed from what it is in L.A. But you have to be adult enough to realize the thing you love is not the assholes who run it. The religious cliché is 'love the sinner, hate the sin.' The show business version would be 'love the show, hate the business.'

HARVEY KUBERNIK One of the best qualities Mark and Howard had—and it shows in their music—they were unabashed fans of rock'n'roll, so that even when it was time to do *Turtle Soup*: 'Let's go find Ray Davies to produce us.' They're fans first, and unfortunately their fandom got in the way of their business acumen sometimes. They were so caught up making the best music, finding the best songs, doing so much touring—and having a good time, by the way—that the business became secondary. This has been a vocation for the last forty years, but the first ten years I don't think they looked at it as business.

BILLY CIOFFE When you get down to the nitty-gritty, he didn't make a lot of mistakes. Not near as many mistakes as a lot of the other boneheads. Hey, he owns his masters. Any time you hear 'Happy Together,' Mark Volman is making money.

TOMMY JAMES I cannot believe that the record industry for this long has been able to hold to the rule that the artist pays for the record and the record label still owns the masters. There's no other business in the history of the world that's ever been able to operate like that. It's like buying a house, and when you pay off the mortgage, the bank still owns the house. It's outrageous.

I feel terrible watching the business fall apart, but it was bound to happen simply from the fact that the industry, from a technical standpoint, had to change. Virtually all the decisions after about 1975 were self-destructive in the industry. I can't think of one that didn't turn out to be bad in the end.

CORKY LAING The record companies did nothing but steal. I know: I worked for one. I knew the whole thing was a farce and that it was not going to last. I was in the tail end of the golden years, up until '96, '97, and you could feel everything falling between the cracks. But the industry was blind and didn't see it coming. The focus was in the wrong area.

Any culture, any era, it always starts with the creative juices, and it has nothing to do with that anymore. It's all marketing and bling. The very best of the creative era came about because of a naiveté. There was no ulterior motive and there were no rules. The Byrds were changing everybody's life, but it wasn't like they knew what they were doing. All of a sudden, industry people didn't know what was happening, but they were trusting in the musicians because they admitted they didn't know. Labels like Warner Bros, the guys that worked there had no idea, they just knew what they liked. It was real simple. Nowadays, the deceleration of everything is unbelievable. I don't know that I would even touch a drum set right now if I was starting out. There's nothing. I don't even know where the money is.

CHRIS HILLMAN It was around '67, '68, when the companies realized there's money to be made here, because it was really a little cottage industry, and it was run by music people. All these guys, from Ahmet Ertegun and Jerry Wexler at Atlantic to Mo Ostin at Warners—all these guys were music-oriented guys. And you know the old story: if you were lucky enough to be signed on a label deal back then, they'd keep you around for four or five albums. So, it's changed. It really isn't that type of business anymore, the way Mark Volman or Richie Furay or I remember. It's not that same business. And we are all lucky we're playing. It's a blessing. We get to go out and still play, and if it ends tomorrow for me—I speak for myself only—I had a great, great, life. It's not over. I'm not done yet, I still find it . . . I almost have that passion back that I had at eighteen.

PAUL WILLIAMS It's all changed. We went through a terrible period following Napster and the like, with the audiences moving from owning music to streaming. At first, we saw the value of our copyrights plummet. But it's gotten better. As far as true value, we're not there yet, but we're getting closer. [At ASCAP] we have an amazing CEO, a dedicated board, and we've found ways to improve again and again. A large part of what I do is spend time on the Hill on both sides of the aisle and make sure that the legislators know who we are and what we do. I bring other music creators with me and put a face on the songs, so guys like Mark and Howard, walking in to a senator's office, a congressman or congresswoman's office, that puts a face on a song that they've loved for years. It's an amazing asset. I would say the one thing that I am absolutely sure of is that these days, one of the things you need to add on really quickly if you're going to try and make a living, if you're a musician, you need that advocacy.

HIPPIE FEST & THE HAPPY TOGETHER TOURS

LARRY ZINN Howard still had a ponytail and hair, and Mark was not completely grey, so we weren't an oldies act yet. There was this circuit where all those guys that are now considered oldies, in the late 80s we were considered classic rock.

JOE STEFKO There were a lot of people on Hippie Fest, especially the first one we did. Mountain, The Zombies, us, and somebody else. It was about forty or fifty people on that tour.

JACKIE MARTLING I hosted a couple of Hippie Fests. That's a great show, but they didn't really need me with Mark and Howard on the stage. Country Joe hosted before they came along, and he was like watching paint dry. I co-hosted a couple with Wavy Gravy, but the ones they were on, it was kind of redundant, having me there.

TIM SEXTON They refashioned themselves as the toastmasters; they're kind of the toastmasters of that evening of music.

LESLIE WEST The first time Mountain did Hippie Fest, they had Wavy Gravy as the MC, and I said to the promoter, 'Jesus, Howard and Mark would be great, man, before they even do a song, let them introduce people,' and they were really good at it. They're funny and entertaining, whether they sing or not. And then they have hits to go along with that.

SKIP TAYLOR Hippie Fest was one of the originators of this touring concept. Country Joe was doing the hosting for a couple of years, and when they wanted to get rid of Joe, I said there are only two guys for the job, because in one act, you get the Turtle songs and you get the two best MCs. It was all in one package. And that's the way they got the job. And I do take full credit for that, whether Mark knows that's how it happened or not.

CORKY LAING Hippie Fest turned out to be quite a cash cow for them, because they can host it as well as play it. They made that whole thing feel like camp. Howard said, 'This is just a rock'n'roll vacation. This is not a career move.' And that's what it was, and it was enjoyed for that reason.

HOWARD SILVERMAN I first started working with Mark in 1984. He was looking after The Turtles. At the time, we represented a bunch of 60s bands and it was hard to book them all and keep it straight. Necessity is the mother of invention, so we decided to package it. We put the tour together as the producer, and a couple of agents over at William Morris said, 'Let's call it the Happy Together tour.'

What makes Mark and Howard different is they have a deep catalogue that's spanned the years, and that includes all the crazy stuff they did with Zappa. They've got solid gold hits under their belts as The Turtles, but it doesn't really represent what it's all about, because it's more than the songs. These guys have a true body of work. That's what causes such fervent fans in the music business, and these guys have it. They're always coming up with ideas; they don't just sit back and let people lead them around. When the phone rings, you never know what they're gonna say, in terms of creativity and stuff.

SPANKY MCFARLANE I was on that first tour with them, and it was really fun: The Turtles, the Association, Gary Puckett, and Spanky & Our Gang. All those groups had strong vocal harmonies, they really did, although somebody might have to lower a key here and there.

RUSS GIGUERE We did the first Happy Together tour—it was 225 concerts! We worked like sons of bitches. In fact, a few guys quit the band because we were working too much. So, we replaced them and stayed out on the road.

NICK FORTUNA The first time we reunited with The Turtles was in 1985, with us and Gary Lewis and The Grassroots. That was a great tour. It went for seven months and was the highest-grossing tour of the year.

CARL GIAMMARESE That's where we really got to know those guys. We had done some shows together in the 60s, but not that many. The tour lasted about seven months, and we played about two hundred cities together, so you get to know somebody pretty good. And it was grueling, because the producer of the tour, David Fishof, was cutting corners, and we were all on our own traveling in motor homes or whatever to get around the country. We rarely were flying to any of the dates, and some of the jumps were really long. I couldn't imagine doing it today. Back then, I was still in my thirties, so it was a lot easier than it would be now.

RUSS GIGUERE Touring today, I love it. In my twenties and thirties, I took all of this stuff for granted. Believe me, I don't take it for granted anymore. I'm so grateful that I'm able to work and still be doing shows. I've never had plans for retirement. If I'm lucky, I'll have a heart attack and die onstage, and everyone will know I'm gone and where I went. That'd be cool—that'd be better than lying in bed with a bucket of piss, dying slowly. Beats that by a long shot.

RON DANTE I opened for The Turtles years ago and we hit it off, and over the years my name had been mentioned when they were thinking about who's going to be on the tour the next year. Finally, they said they wanted me. I started on the tour in 2017, billed as 'Ron Dante of The Archies.' We spent three months together, and I got to know Howard and Mark really well. We realized we have a similar history. My first hit was around the time they had their first hit. I was in a novelty group called The Detergents, and we had a record called 'Leader Of The Laundromat.' We were on TV shows like *Shindig!* and *Hullabaloo*, and we were doing Dick Clark tours. We toured all the states.

Despite that, our paths hadn't crossed that often, because they were L.A.-based and I was New York-based.

I was what they call a demo singer. I did demos for everybody at Aldon Music, including Neil Sedaka, Tony Orlando, Carole King, Barry Mann, and Cynthia Weil. I was the guy they'd call in to sound like Gary Lewis or Bobby Vee or The Everly Brothers. That was my beginnings, but I was a staff writer as well. I didn't have a big hit, but I did get some singles released. It just wasn't in the cards for me to be a solo artist for some reason—of hits, at least. I have no kicks, though. I got my shot many, many, times. And then, in 1969, I had two records in the Top 10 as a singer, even though they were under different group names. I was very happy, because you wait all your life to have a #1 record as a singer, and the Archies hit #1.

CYRUS FARYAR A hit song can reward you and then it can take your reward away, because society won't tolerate you changing. But don't misunderstand it. You're a young couple sitting in the car, a song you've never heard comes on the radio, and as you fall in to one another's arms, this song is imprinted in your mind for the rest of your lives. 'Happy Together.'

Do you remember that great group? Where are those guys? That can't be them, they're all old now. But I get it. A beautiful song becomes a memory, and what do you do about that? What you're supposed to do is you let the source of those memories continue to flourish, so that new memories will come along, but that's . . . in another universe. There's imagery there. You, the musicians, are there because of what you are remembered for. It's an emotional charge. You're bringing them briefly back to their past, which was probably a very happy moment, and they deserve to re-experience their happy moment in a parked car with Sally. And you can't say, 'Here's a brand new song you've never heard before. Grab your girlfriend and let's see if we can recreate the effect it had on you back in the car.'

FELIX CAVALIERE I've known Mark for many, many, years. Because we lived in separate parts of the country, our social life has been via work. Many of our concerts were done together, and we met mostly backstage. When I did work with them, they were just crazy onstage—totally nuts. But when it came to sitting down backstage and talking business, it was a whole other thing. They are very astute businessmen. And Mark being a professor now, that speaks volumes. Because the status quo in the music industry—and The Rascals unfortunately were living examples of that—the intelligence quotient is not really that high. And these guys are an exception to that rule. These guys got their catalogue back, God bless them. They're not dummies.

JIM YESTER The first couple of weeks of the tour, I had the opportunity to sit and talk with Mark, and I was blown away. He was not who I thought he was. I'm absolutely amazed at his grasp of the whole music scene and his perception of how to put this thing together. To be part of and to see how the tour is structured, how incredibly brilliant that is and how it works. We basically sold out everywhere we went. And then on top of that, being a professor at a university—I mean, unbelievable. I have incredible respect for him. All these years, he puts himself up there as the clown, and yet he's the brains. He's the guy who knows the whole thing. It's so mind-blowing to find that out.

CHRIS HILLMAN I have two wonderful children, what more could I ask for? I wouldn't trade my life for any amount of acclaim and gold albums or whatever. Grammys, this or that, it doesn't matter to me. And I'll always think, *Okay, I had a great life*. I may be just a mere footnote in the history of it all, but I don't care. I don't really care. Because when I got into music—and I'll speak probably for all the people we've talked about—we all got into it because we had a passion. We loved it, but we never thought we'd make a living at it. We weren't inundated with the materialistic side of it all, that the kids are getting now. It's a different world, it was just pure passion—*Gosh, I wish I could do that*—and I never thought of how much can I make, or how much do I get if I do this or that.

GREG HAWKES Often, we'll be on some of the oldies bills, where you get a twenty-five-minute set, so you do the hits, but if it's just them on the bill, we'll do a Frank Zappa medley and more of the Flo & Eddie material and go over more of their history. The audience loves it. We even do 'Gas Money,' which wasn't a hit but it's so appropriate, especially when we're at four dollars a gallon. Playing with them is great. It's not completely structured; they're very loose and easy. And as Howard always says, let's not over-rehearse. We'll be learning a song and we'll run through it once, and it will be, 'Okay, we don't wanna be over-rehearsed.' That keeps it fresh.

CRAIG KRAMPF Of course, Mark and Howard were the stars, but the feeling among all six of us—you can't force something like that. When that incarnation of the band went out at end of '74, it just gelled, and it felt extra special to me because here I am married with a child, and it's cool, because there's Mark and a child or two. And then Phil got married. And Andy was married. So off we go, a perfect time to be out there. I'm making money, there's a lot of touring, and the wives would get together and go bowling, take the kids to a park, go swimming.

ERIK SCOTT We'd go to Mark's house for dinner and then play backgammon for hours. Mark got into it big time. He organized a league, the Flo & Eddie Backgammon League, and we had our own names—the Chieftains, the Warlocks, whoever—and a sanctioned tournament at the end of the year, with playoffs and a champion that got a T-shirt that Mark made.

PAT VOLMAN It was always close, and it was always family. Any new person that came into the band at all, it was just like family. A lot of wives and girlfriends went in and out during those years. Mark said, 'Don't you become good friends with them, because you never know . . .' And I went, 'Oh, be quiet.' But it's true! When the women left, it was hard. I mean, they were my friends.

DONNIE KISSELBACH This band has been through so many marriages and divorces and births and deaths, and it makes it family-like in the best and the worst that that conjures up. There's a tightness and a loyalty factor that's just unbeatable. Even though I was one of many, many players that they had been through, that was irrelevant. You can't say or do anything wrong; you're not going to get fired. And that was clear from the beginning.

My very first night, Howard told me, 'Nobody gets fired from The Turtles. We've had this guy and that guy'—he names them—'it doesn't matter what problems you have, it doesn't matter, and even if you die, if you think you're going to get out of this by dying, you're going to die a Turtle. It's going to be a dead Turtle.' But that was his way of making a point. He was saying, *You're here with us, we're all one, now let's go make music.*

I remember going to Woolworths on my bike, because I loved 'It Ain't Me Babe' when I was eleven. I looked up at the shelf and all I knew is, The Turtles—I heard it on the radio. I see this album cover up there and go, 'Oh, my God, they don't look *anything* like The Beatles.' They're not thin, they're not well dressed, they're not pretty like Paul McCartney. What the heck is this about? They look surly.

When I think about looking at that album and seeing them on TV, seeing them on *Ed Sullivan*, and then seeing them live in high school—it was in me from back then, so getting to play with them and being part of it, even as a sideman, has been wonderful. When I fast forward to now, I feel like I'm the luckiest guy alive. There's no one better to work with than the two of them.

ANDY CAHAN I'm the longest lasting band member at this point. There was a strange little episode that happened back in 1983. We had two keyboard players, and finances got to where they could only afford one, and they gave me first option to audition. It was like re-auditioning for the band a decade after I first got the gig. They gave me a shot, but at the time I was getting a divorce and my piano chops were down and I failed the audition. Everything was just lousy. My wife took my kids and moved out of state the same week The Turtles fired me. That was a tough week. I became a truck driver and worked all these straight jobs just to pay the rent. But I built my life back together. I was doing really well when Mark called six years later and said, 'Would you mind playing with us again?' And so I got re-hired.

I had a six-year sabbatical. It was never anything personal. Oh, they loved me, and during the really tough times when I was down and out, they would hire me for three or four hundred bucks just to go with them to Vegas and wear a suit and tie and pretend I'm a road manager. I didn't have to do anything—all I had to do is sit there and eat food and smile and shake hands.

PAT VOLMAN They did that a lot to Andy. To bug him. You know, 'This week, let's do it.' 'No, let's wait a week.' Every time Mark would say, 'Yeah, he's back,' I went, 'When did he come back?'

HOWARD KAYLAN He got better because of that absence. It's not like we were slapping him on the hand and stuff. It's just, 'Andy, please. Please learn this stuff.' Eventually, he did. But we had to hire two other guys in the interim. He could have held onto that gig, had he learned that stuff in a timely manner. I don't think we're cruel bosses. I think people like to work with us. The fact we've held on to the same drummer for thirty-odd years, that sort of thing is testimony.

LARRY ZINN I always say that when I win lotto, the first thing I would do is go back out on the road with The Turtles, because as grouchy as I was, I was happy doing that. All these year later, it didn't leave a bad taste, not at all. I remember the good things. I mean, I also remember the bad things. I remember the 110-degree weather in Tampa with the shitty sound system and wanting to kill somebody. But I'd still do it again.

RICK CARR When The Turtles do a longer set, they can include Zappa and Flo & Eddie material and people really enjoy the versatility. I really think there would be some legs in them doing *An Evening With Flo & Eddie*, where they could actually sit there and go through their history, maybe with some backing video. People would find it completely amazing.

HAL WILLNER Flo & Eddie are in their own category. Some people talk about outsider music. Yes, they're outsiders. Occasionally, they get invited inside. But they're in that outsider thing, which is great and difficult. None of us that understood them understood how, when they were at the height of their solo careers, Flo & Eddie didn't become a lot more successful. It was surprising to us. For whatever reason, that combination of the vaudeville humor, music and beauty just doesn't go down with everybody. But when people see it, they get it. And then you're looking at the bigger picture and finding it frustrating, like, *Wow, this could have an impact.* But they'll have their own chapters, and the work will be discovered. Because as it all keeps coming out, it's the one Zappa band no one seems to be able to duplicate. The T. Rex records? There's nothing like them. The Turtles records? They're great pop records. And they're consummate performers and comics and actors. True song and dance men. I'm proud—very proud—they're in my resume, and I'm in theirs.

HAROLD BRONSON Rhino first started putting out albums in 1978, with The Turtles. Originally, we put out a picture disc: *The Turtles 1968*. It wasn't the first reissue but the first major one. And when we made the deal for their catalogue it was the biggest advance we'd ever given. We dealt with Mark and Howard directly, because they owned the catalogue. We leased the records.

The original deal was maybe three years, and we just kept renewing. We were fans, so for us it was a matter of what would we like to see? We would like to see a generous helping of songs, good photos, informative liner notes, and really good sound. It was a matter of putting that personal passion into it, and a consequence was that people appreciated it, and we had good sales because of that. You could contrast it to other artists or bands that might have been big at the time. For instance, Herman's Hermits and Dave Clark Five were even bigger, but their catalogues were treated poorly. None of the original albums were out, there was no promotion, nothing. Because there wasn't visibility, their stature receded, while The Turtles, because of what Rhino was doing, their stature rose.

The most enjoyment I had at Rhino was when I would get together with Mark and Howard and work on projects together. And it lasted all the way through. I left Rhino around the end of 2001, so it was not only a very successful relationship, but it lasted that full duration. That was twenty-three years.

JIM BESSMAN It upsets me to no end that they don't have the recognition of a Rock and Roll Hall Of Fame, which they so deserve—they *so* deserve. I used to be part of the nominating committee, and I always used to push The Turtles. I might not have been the only one who would have supported it, but I was the only one who would ever bring them up. There are a lot of sad omissions, and this is one of them. It's unfortunate. They're as great a group as there ever was in terms of the quantity and quality of the hits that they released, number one. Just on that count alone, they are as worthy as anyone else in the Hall Of Fame. You can take it further if you don't put a lot of weight on hit singles by saying that they also were an album band. They experimented with album concepts. And then just narrowing it down to Flo & Eddie—to Mark and Howard—who continued and of course have sung with everyone from Bruce Springsteen to the Ramones, and it goes on.

It goes on and on, and it continues to this day. The longevity is extraordinary. The two of them got together in 1962 and they haven't broken up yet. That's over fifty years, and they've kept it going at a top level in terms of presentation, sounding great, playing great, and performing great.

SKIP TAYLOR The Grammys are a joke, and so is the Rock and Roll Hall of Fame. Both of those are just so political. I was on the NARAS Board of Directors for about fifteen years, and it was embarrassing to be a part of it. I swear to God, it's ridiculous. And the Rock & Roll Hall of Fame has no bearing on what's really happening, none at all. The people who get ignored, still, it's a crime. And the people that they'll put in now make no sense. But the board of directors—the ones that have a vote—it's the who's who of the political end of the music industry, which is close to falling apart anyway.

MICKY DOLENZ I call them the *hipoisie*, and they think they're very clever. Those are the people that would never let The Monkees or The Turtles in the Rock and Roll Hall of Fame. But the Hall of Fame is not an official representation of the music industry. It's a private club, like a golf club, and they have the right to let in whomever they want. It's their prerogative, and there were certainly a lot of them around at that time in the music industry. There was such a political and social thing going on that for anybody to come out with something that didn't have some dire social, political, revolutionary message, or eight-minute guitar solos . . . that if you came out with something like 'Happy Together,' the hipoisie would go, 'What the fuck does that mean?' But the proof is in the pudding, and at the end of the day, the recurring success of The Monkees and the recurring success of The Turtles and Flo & Eddie and those songs and that music, it stands up, and it stands up years later much better than what was considered hip back then. That's not saying that the other type of music wasn't good and it wasn't important, because it was important. It was good, but it didn't mean you had to exclude everything else.

DEAN TORRENCE We didn't hobnob with the right people. It was kind of the East Coast thing, too; the East Coast never really wanted to admit that the West Coast artists were as strong as they were. So, any chance they got to try and not recognize the West Coast guys, they took that opportunity to do so.

CHRIS HILLMAN Mark had some sort of radio thing going in New York. We got inducted into the Rock & Roll Hall Of Fame, so we're at the Waldorf and a live radio broadcast is going out the night of the induction ceremony. Now, mind you, in 1991 it was not televised on MTV, none of that was going on. It was a very private affair, a very special occasion at the time. I've lost a bit of my adulation of that organization, but anyway, they had a radio show, so I run into them again, I talk to him on the radio and everything. That was fun.

KEN BARNES It's interesting that The Lovin' Spoonful is in the Hall Of Fame and The Turtles aren't. I can't say the Spoonful's music is any hipper. It may have been more innovative in some ways, but I always tended to like The Turtles a little better. And The Turtles wrote as well, so it's just . . . you're starting to think there's a debt to be paid here, that The Turtles are getting the short end of the stick.

GREG HAWKES They're one of the more underappreciated acts in music history. If it were up to me, they would be in the Hall Of Fame, but they had that goofy persona, so music critics took them less seriously than, say, Procol Harum.

SHADOE STEVENS The real proof of their quality is the longevity. Think of the number of bands who were around at that time. Almost all of them are gone. The Turtles just keep on. It's iconic music that seems to transcend time. They reflect the happy side of the psychedelic era.

16

BACK TO SCHOOL

Howard graduated as valedictorian and was accepted to UCLA. He was jumped ahead, and I was the only member of the band still at school. Howard, Al, and the others graduated in the summer of '64. I graduated in Spartan class, February of '65.

HOWARD KAYLAN Neither one of us were social elite in high school. Mark at least had the Westbury Surf Club. I didn't even have that. What I had going for me was academics. So, while Mark was barely able to skate out of school with a high D average, I had an A average, and I had a UCLA scholarship, and I was able to bump myself up six months at the last minute and graduate with the class of '64 instead of '65. So, I was out and about and already at UCLA when Mark graduated high school and then started to attend junior college.

ANN BECKER [Mark graduated with a 1.9 GPA] because he was the class clown! Not because he didn't have the ability. He certainly did, even as a child. He had a curious mind, always asking questions. I remember one time, Mark was about six or seven years old, and he was with us when we were driving, and he was going on this long dissertation about dinosaurs, and he was pronouncing all the names correctly. I never will forget that. My husband and I just looked at each other and shook our heads. He's always been a very intelligent person.

MADELINE CAMPILLO I honestly think—and I was a schoolteacher too, a school librarian—I think he was too bright. He was so bright that he was bored in school. I had a son that had that same problem. Mark got bored and got into mischief. The schools weren't equipped for that back then, and they're not equipped for them now. If you teach math and the kid is way ahead and the questions other kids around him are asking seem stupid to him, he'll start poking the girl next to him or passing notes. He didn't concentrate because he was too bright, if that makes sense. He couldn't do what he's done since, particularly in later life. He couldn't possibly have achieved what he's done if he wasn't bright. I think he just misplaced his energies.

MARY BREDEN It just proves that there are different kinds of smarts, and that grade point average—although it's very important and we want students to excel—there are different ways to approach your successes. Mark was ready to come back and be a student at forty. And now he's running a music department in Nashville. That's just amazing.

SUSAN VOLMAN When he went back to school, particularly when he started going to graduate school, he started calling my dad. By then, both of Mark's parents had died, and I think he may have called more for some family history questions, but there was that period of time where Mark would call asking academic advice. And my dad was very proud of that. My father was quite proud of him for going back to school and getting his degrees and everything.

Returning to school had a few elements to it. The band was beginning to slow down, and we weren't really sure what was going to happen. At that point I wanted to be a little bit more . . . I don't want to say 'in control,' but school was a test for me. It was my first significant project without Howard's involvement. It was something I would do on my own— something that didn't count on anyone else to be there. As well as that, after I graduated high school, we were immediately thrown into the music business, and I never had a chance to see what I could do academically. So there was that. And there was a third level, which was the business. The Turtles created this craziness with all of the lawsuits, and that was where I started realizing that I was good at managing the group, and eventually I began looking after us. And so, I felt like it was my responsibility at that point to really put the time in with the band stuff.

JACK UNDERWOOD The Turtles didn't really come out as great as they could have because of those lawsuits, and I think that gave him impetus to go out and start learning about the business of music on his own. First through the school of hard knocks, and he then refined that by going to school.

PHIL VOLMAN He had to do something, because you get to a point, age-wise, where doing what he was doing all the time wasn't too healthy. So, I knew he was going to be doing something. This Jesuit priest at Loyola got him interested in starting a music business class, and based on that—that he was going to do that—he went back to school.

DEAN TORRENCE I wasn't expecting it, but when I heard, it seemed perfectly natural, and good for him. He's just one of those kind of guys that would want to move forward and not get stuck in the past, always thinking about getting back on the charts. Those are the guys that make me nervous. You've got to be pleased with what you did and know that that was your time. We had our time in the sun, and it was a good one and hopefully you did the best you could and came out of it with some bucks, and move on. I'm not saying that you can't ever be involved with the music business, because you can be a teacher. You could teach music, you could produce music.

CHRIS HILLMAN Mark must have had some great epiphany, to all of a sudden go, 'Hold it, what am I doing here?' and go back to school. It took a lot of guts to relearn how to learn, relearn how to retain information, to go back into a structured situation. That took a lot of guts. What an accomplishment, to do that and be successful.

TIM REID He's always been confident enough to grab any bull by the horns. Remember, this is the guy who didn't play an instrument but joined an instrumental band. One day he said, 'Okay, I need this many credits to be a teacher? Let's go get this many credits.'

MARK CHERNOFF They owned their music, which is extremely smart. I mean, how many guys own their catalogue? And he was a good business man. In negotiating, there was an agent—I don't remember who it was—but Mark was able to negotiate for the both of them as well. Howard would speak up when he had to, but Mark was really the spokesman for the two of them. And he was very much involved in the business decisions of The Turtles. When they were touring, he would deal directly with the concert promoters and make the deals for the group. He was a brilliant guy, so I was not surprised when he went back to school.

RAY MANZAREK Isn't that amazing? It did surprise me. I think it surprised everybody. Sure as hell did. But it just goes to show, these are not *dummkopfs*; these are not cracked-out, pot-headed, alcoholic rock'n'rollers. Both of them were very brainy guys. Mark was always intelligent. The 1.9 grade average? There's the motivation—perfect motivation. It's just what he needed to motivate him. It's not that he wasn't smart, he was just going to get it certified. Like his *Ed Sullivan* imprimatur, he was going to get his university stamp and seal of approval. It's like, 'And here is your diploma' to the Scarecrow in *The Wizard Of Oz*. He got his diploma. I'd say that's a pretty full life, especially for the class clown.

CHUCK SWENSON It's surprising because it's a big life change. Not that he *could* do it—that wasn't the surprising part—but that he *did* do it. That he actually stepped up to the plate and went back to school. I'm sure a lot of people just shake their heads. But if you hang around for any length of time and talk to him, it's clear he's not a dumb guy.

PHIL VOLMAN Six years, right through. It made perfect sense to me. Because they still were doing concerts making their nut, making $200,000–300,000 in just the summertime. That took care of the bills for the year, and the rest of the time he'd have this other teaching income that started slowly. He taught at Loyola and then he taught the same thing at Cal State in L.A., so he had both.

Why did I keep going? I don't know how much I would have stayed with it if I wasn't doing well. And it showed me what I wanted to eventually move into, which was even more studies. I started at L.A. Valley College, then shifted over to Loyola Marymount, and eventually moved past that to Belmont.

COMMUNITY COLLEGE AND LOYOLA MARYMOUNT

GEORGE ATTARIAN There are lots of alternatives at community college. L.A. Valley College has everyone from kids who haven't even finished high school to ninety-year-olds. Students can just take courses for enrichment, or they can take courses that lead to a profession. The very oldest come for enrichment classes. As far as specific degrees, they aren't goal-oriented like that. But to have someone who at that time was in his late forties pursue a broad and thorough education from that point on, is really unique. The guy had a goal, and he went right after it. Not very many do that.

He joined our chamber singers group, which was the best small ensemble we had at that time. The classical stuff was new to him, but he learned it and mixed in well with the younger guys. When we took our tours, he was instrumental in making sure the arrangements were made. He took over on a lot of the stuff, and when he went to Loyola Marymount, he went right into the choir there and became an assistant. Was I surprised that he went on to Loyola Marymount to get his bachelor's degree and master's degree and all the rest? Oh no. My gosh, I knew the guy was driven to do it.

I was very much supported by several professors who were fans of the band but were even more inclined to help me understand the system, helping me to apply myself through L.A. Valley College and then onto Loyola Marymount. I did about two and a half years of full-on Loyola Marymount, graduating with honors, and I just held on.

MARY BREDEN The first time I met Mark, I was adjudicating and clinicing at a community college choral festival and he was in the L.A. Valley College choir. After the session he came up and said how much he had enjoyed it and inquired about Loyola. He was looking to finish his degree, and he was . . . older. He was not your normal college-age student. He had grown up about five minutes away from Loyola at Westchester High, and it was sort of coming back to his roots.

The next fall he joined the concert choir. Given his experience in a totally different genre, it was a whole new experience for him, but I could tell there was a voice there that I could work into the choir. It was a different style of singing, different type of repertoire: working for a certain blend and tone quality, finesse of phrase shaping, and singing in different languages. And all this classical music that in many ways was brand new to him. But he went into it full energy and fit right in. It didn't seem like an older person had joined the ranks. Because he was a student, he just went about his business. He didn't make a big deal about what he had done all of his life, but it was such a fascinating set of circumstances that I found it fun to let people know who he was. These kids weren't even born when The Turtles were popular, but they all knew 'Happy

Together' and they'd kid around with him, and he'd help keep some of the kids in line, too. He loved being around the students, and vice versa. When we were on tour he watched out for a lot of the kids. They were doing home stays, and he would say, 'I don't like the look of those people that they are going home with. I think we should put them up in the hotel.' That sort of thing. He stayed with some people on one of the tours up in Northern California, and they were just beside themselves getting to meet him. We happened to have housed him with these people, and it turned out they were Turtles fans.

We had a lot of laughs. He always wanted to call the concert 'shows,' and I'd say, 'Mark, it's not a show,' but what I value so much is just what a wonderful human being he is. He's kind of kooky and off the wall, like a little boy who never grew up, and yet he is. I always appreciated that about him. I went to one of their concerts when they were performing here in the area. He got me tickets. It was turning the tables, because I'm a classical musician, and that's basically the kind of concert that I would not go to or perform at. Seeing this really in-your-face type of energetic show was fantastic, an eye-opener to something I wasn't aware of. I could see skills he had that I might not have appreciated before. I got to see a 'show.' It was fun.

STEVE DUNCAN I graduated from Loyola, too. I got my master's before Mark did, even though we're pretty close to the same age. I was a career naval officer, and I was going to run the film program for the navy in the Pentagon. I needed a master's degree, so I went to Loyola. The first screenwriting class, I realized, *Whoa! This is what I want to do*, and so I decided I was going to get out of the navy and pursue a career as a screenwriter. It was real clear what I had to do to get where I wanted to go, and going to grad school when you're older, especially when you have a family and a mortgage payment and all that stuff, is what helped to focus me. And Mark was the same way, so we were kindred spirits. I tell my students, you never know what life experiences are going to hand you. My whole career as a writer started off with me creating a show called *Tour Of Duty* for CBS Television. That came from my experience in the military. If I hadn't been in the military, I would have been some drugged-out artist somewhere, painting or doing sculptures or something crazy like that.

When I met Mark, I wasn't full-time faculty. I was part-time and still chasing the business real hard, so it was nice to have a student in class that totally understood that show business is show *business*. That was good. I'm African American, and I grew up in the South in the 50s, so The Turtles were not a real bright spot in my music repertoire. I remember them, but it wasn't that big of a deal to me, so we hit it off.

He was in screenwriting because the music department didn't have a Master of Fine Arts program, which is what you need if you want to be a serious professor. He ended up writing a feature script told from the point of view of a roadie who had some father issues, and it was an interesting and mature story. If he wrote a scene about somebody using drugs, if felt real. It wasn't so much an assignment as something he was trying to sell and turn into a movie. And why write it otherwise? It was one of the bright spots in the class, because most of the students are writing as assignments. Yeah, he was writing as an assignment, but he was also thinking about what he was going to do with it, and in fact was trying to set the damn thing up. There were a couple of conference calls we had with people who were interested, and a lot of it had to do with who he is and the fact that he's writing a script. He'd get a lot of buzz in this town just from that. He didn't pursue screenwriting, but he could have been successful if he put his mind to it, because he was a talented writer. He instantly understood story and character from his songwriting experience. It's just grappling with the artform. This is a much bigger canvas to work on.

ROLAN BOLAN There was this rumor that some older guy with a lot of hair was on campus, saying he was looking for Rolan. I was thinking, *I'm a fairly decent guy, I haven't done anything wrong to anyone, but an older gentleman trying to find me?* Finally, he walks up and goes, 'Are you Rolan?' I say, 'Yeah, and who are you?' 'Mark Volman. Does that ring a bell?' And then I realized, holy shit, I remember seeing his name on my dad's records. We were in all the same classes, so we got to spend a lot of time together. He brought me into his home. I'd go over there and have dinners, and from there it was like we were partners in crime. He was the man around campus. I thought I was busy, but Mark was on this fraternity for academics and helping the choir and just making the most of his experience. I've been in class with other mature students—people going back to college at midlife—but he was different. It wasn't like *Back To School* Rodney Dangerfield. He embraced his classmates like we are all the same age.

I eventually realized how deep of a tie he had with my father. He filled in some blanks for me about my own family. It was almost as if my dad was up in the sky, saying, 'If there's two people I need to meet, it's these two.' It was like a physical connection, because up to that point, besides some of my immediate family, the music was all I had. Years later, I ended up performing in the musical *Hair*, and that's an interesting story, because that's when my mom met my dad, and that's when Mark was around; that was all '69 at the Aquarius Theatre on Sunset Boulevard. Meat Loaf and Jobriath and Nell Carter and Ben Vereen were all in the cast. Mark and Howard were both asked to be in that show, so that's another circle. Jobriath introduced my mom to my dad, and then, eventually, here I am.

Mark knew what he was doing in the studio, and he had the best engineers in the world working on his own records, but in a weird way, he was the student this time as well. I helped assist the engineer on some of the projects he was working on, and where he'd really shine was his personal approach in making the musicians feel comfortable and really bringing up the songs. So, even though he was a student himself, he was a mentor. He definitely helped a lot of up-and-coming artists to find themselves. At one point, I was helping get The Black Eyed Peas off the ground, and we brought them into the Loyola studio to cut them with a live band. They already had a band at the time, but I introduced them to some other players, and then with Mark in the studio we were able to bring that rock element to the hip-hop vibe, at least on the production end of it.

RICHIE FURAY He earned three degrees? Wow, that's ambitious, man. That's ambitious.

PAT VOLMAN Back in high school, Howard was a smarty pants, but Mark never applied himself. And I knew he had it in him. He was just being a silly little boy, making everybody laugh, instead of paying attention to the teacher. I just told him, 'You can't keep getting D-minuses the rest of your life.' I was proud. I was there the day he got all of those awards, with his parents. It was quite impressive; I came to tears at one point. To think that he had achieved that. Hey, this guy could do anything that he wants to, let's put it that way. But I always knew he was smart. Except that he wore that zebra shirt. That was not smart.

EMILY VOLMAN He was the valedictorian speaker, and he was very, very nervous. He can sing to the masses, but to get up there and have to read this speech, he was super-nervous and a little shaky. But he did great, and the crowd started singing 'Happy Together.'

ANN BECKER When he graduated from Loyola as a valedictorian, I didn't believe it. I figured my sister must have misunderstood. I said, 'Well, that's a complete 360-degree turn.' I went to his graduation, and he brought tears to my eyes, because his speech was so great. I just thought, *That's such a good example, that it's never too late.* I can't tell you how many times I've told people in their forties who say, 'I should go back to school but really I'm too old.' 'Don't you believe it! My nephew, blah, blah, blah.' You know, that shows his intelligence.

MARY BREDEN It was one of the best speeches we've heard at a graduation. Very entertaining, but it had a good message and the kids loved him. And he was comfortable in front of a crowd, obviously.

TEACHING AT L.A. COMMUNITY COLLEGE

GEORGE ATTARIAN Was I responsible for Mark coming to Valley College to teach? [*laughs*] Yeah, I did that. I knew he had a lot of success in the business, and we were starting a class in music as a profession, so I had him teach. It was just a night class, but boy, it did very well. I was chair of the department, so I had to visit all the classes, and I was impressed. He related well to the younger kids. They knew his group, and that makes a lot of difference, but also, he knew a lot. That's one of the things students want to know: *How much knowledge does the guy have? How practical is it for me? How can I use it, and is this really meaningful?*

EMILY VOLMAN When I met him, he hadn't decided he wanted to be a teacher yet. He was also thinking about becoming a lawyer. He was throwing around ideas of what he could do with a degree. His first bachelor's was in communication, with an emphasis on recording arts. It was a regular sort of liberal arts degree, but with an emphasis on recording and engineering and that kind of stuff—practical skills. But even before graduation, he started to talk to the teachers at school, and they thought he might be a great asset to them: perhaps he could teach there once he secured his bachelor's? The only problem was, to teach at the college level you have to at least be going toward your master's. So, he started in on his master's right after graduation, and he ended up graduating with a screenwriting degree.

His first year teaching, I actually took the class just as an observer. He was still trying to figure out what he was doing. There were absolutely no music business courses in all of Southern California; no college was teaching music business. They may have had lecturers in a time or two, but there were no official classes on the music business. There were on the other coast, and especially in Nashville. That was one of Mark's early resources. He found this book by Larry Wacholtz, a teacher at Belmont, not knowing that he would be sharing an office with the guy six years later.

LARRY WACHOLTZ He called out of the blue and said he had found my book. It was an educational thing called *Star Tracks: Principles For Success In The Music & Entertainment Business*. He discovered I was teaching this stuff and asked me, 'How the hell did you do all this?' And I've got to tell you something about Mark. It's no big thing to me to talk to somebody who is famous. I've done a lot of that. But for somebody who wanted to teach? That was really cool. I wondered if he could actually teach it, but once he told me how he was using my book, I realized, *You know what? He may have it.*

MICKY DOLENZ He invited me to a community college class that he was giving in Santa Monica, something to do with how to survive in the music business. Just have a chat with the students, a Q&A, basically. I'm so proud of him. It's just so admirable, but that does not surprise me, because he's such a smart guy. From day one, when I met Mark, it was clear that this was a very, very bright guy.

HENRY DILTZ He asked me to come down and do a slide show. I just thought it was brilliant, because here's a guy who's come up through the music business and now he's teaching a class on it. Who better? It's not book learning, its experience, and he was a fantastic teacher. When I went to show my slides, I got to sit through a class, and he had all that energy. It was very, very interesting, kind of like seeing him onstage.

GEORGE DUKE I went out to one of his classes and gave a little seminar. I hadn't seen him in years. It was like, *Wow, this is a different cat—he has really changed his life*. I was really proud of him. Mark is one of the most dynamic stage performers I've ever worked with. He could sing, act, and was very theatrical and spontaneous onstage, so I imagine that, as a teacher, he must bring a lot of that to the class. It's not just a guy giving a lecture. He brings with him a lot of character that can work in an intellectual setting. That makes things interesting, and keeps people interested in what they're learning, which is a big thing.

EMILY VOLMAN That first year he relied very heavily on guest speakers. He had musicians, managers, lawyers, and publishing guys. He had everything, and there were very few weeks when he got up and lectured, mainly because he had these resources. I mean, why not hear from the source? Anybody taking that class loved it because they were meeting amazing people with amazing stories.

After the first year, he realized he had to start creating a class without relying on guests, and that's when he put the syllabus together. He's good at assembling things in that way, so he had a really good class. It was very popular, but he was still an adjunct, which means you come and teach your class and leave. And because he still had connections at L.A. Valley College, where he first went to school before he went to Loyola Marymount, they asked if he would be interested in teaching over there. So, within two years, he was teaching two courses at each place. He would switch off days at one college and then the other. But the kids loved him. At Loyola he was voted numerous times by various sororities and fraternities as favorite teacher. All the while, he was getting his master's. So he was touring, getting his master's, and teaching at that same time.

He loved teaching. He got to stand up and tell stories, and everybody sat there wide-eyed. Not much to argue, that way. There are a lot of similarities for him being in The Turtles, and it's funny, he doesn't really care about touring anymore, but that's because he gets to stand up in front of a group of people every day. So he's onstage all the time. And they all have to pay attention to him. What better audience? And he loves that so much. He is always going to be a performer, and teaching is right up there with that.

DANNY HUTTON Mark is so bubbly and loose, and yet there's a part of him that compartmentalized into putting part of everyday toward, *No, I've got to stop. I must spend X amount of hours preparing, because tomorrow I have to do this.* There's a responsible side that you just wouldn't expect, because of his ability to be an entertainer. It's amazing, and very, very unusual. He's one of those guys where the doctors are going to tell him, 'Mark, when you die, we're going to have to dissect your brain, because you, dude, are very unusual.'

JEFF 'SKUNK' BAXTER I'd always thought that he should become a teacher. Mark and I would stay up late sometimes and just talk, and he had a very engaging and very lucid and cogent way of explaining things. And I always thought, *Hmm, this is the kind of person you'd like to be around when you're having conversations,* because he's not dull, but it also doesn't go really far off the reservation, either. I thought he would be perfect.

CHRIS HILLMAN I had run into him over the years, and then, gosh, all of a sudden my daughter ends up in his class.

CATHERINE HILLMAN CLARK I was a student at Loyola Marymount from 2001 to 2005. My junior year I needed another class to fill my schedule, and my roommates were all signed up for *History Of Rock And Roll.* It sounded interesting, so I thought I'd join the waitlist and see if the professor would add me. Luckily, he did, and I ended up taking not only that class but also his *Intro To The Music Business.* It was a really interesting connection Mark was able to make, because growing up, my dad would sing those songs, and my brother and I would sing along with him, not really placing any context with the lyrics or if there was a meaning behind it. Mark started talking about the 60s and what was going on in the country, and how important 'Turn, Turn, Turn' was, and getting that whole context, and thinking about those lyrics in a different sense than just, *Oh, this is something my dad sings.* He really bridged that gap for me.

You can be in so many classes in college where you have professors who have written books, and they can be very pretentious. They think that they know everything, and they come off very, very condescending, but Mark wasn't like that at all. The *History Of Rock And Roll* class took us through the blues and early African American music, all the way up into the 80s. There was music and styles that I didn't even know in those other decades, and especially the 60s, and learning about what was going on at the time and the historical connections made. Business class was incredible; I still have my textbook from that class, actually.

My parents are both in the music business, but it's not really what we talk about around the house, and when I was taking that class, I'd talk to my mom, and say, 'I learned about contracts today,' or 'I learned about band partnership agreements.' And she'd go, 'Well, this is gonna be useful for you, because when you eventually take over the publishing that your dad has, you'll know what to do.' So that was a really practical class for me because I never really thought about the business side, just that my dad sings, he performs. But there's this whole other side to it. He said, 'When you're young and you're starting out, people don't tell you all this stuff you need to know, all of the business side to it, so learn from my mistakes.'

Mark was looking through the roster of who was in the class and came upon my last name. He goes, 'Any relation to Chris Hillman?' I said, 'Yeah, that's my dad.' And he said, 'Oh, great—I know your dad. I sang on one of his albums.' So, we had that little connection from the first day of class. When I said, 'My professor's name is Mark Volman,' Dad said, 'I know him.'

CHRIS HILLMAN And it was so funny the way it happened. The last minute she signs up to take his class. She didn't know who he was, and of course her being a late student, he does the roll call: 'Catherine Hillman. Hillman. Chris Hillman?' And she said, 'Yes.' 'Do you know Chris Hillman?' 'He's my father.' And the funny line was—and here's our generation—he goes, 'Well, do you know your father?' 'Yeah, I know him real well. I've been with him for all my life. He brought me home from the hospital.' She said he was so much fun. He would show them all the dances of the 60s, literally show them. He had no inhibitions about any of that, he just loved it all.

MARY BREDEN He taught it in a totally different way than somebody from an academic background, in that he had firsthand experience with all these people that he would bring in as guest speakers. Having grown up in the industry, he really offered a different sort of a class. It was very popular.

CATHERINE HILLMAN CLARK He would really make those classes fun. It wouldn't be a three-hour lecture where you're taking notes all the time. It would be, 'Hey, I'm gonna talk to you about this. Let me share a story with you. Let's listen to some music.' And it was like you were hanging out with friends. It's great, because he does what he loves, and he's able to pass that on to other people. Everybody loved being in his classes, and they really had a greater appreciation for it, because he was teaching with such a passion. That's kind of infectious, so everybody got that passion from him.

CHRIS HILLMAN She ended up doing a paper on Richie Furay, who of course was as close to Mark as I am, or maybe even closer to Mark as a friend.

CATHERINE HILLMAN CLARK Richie did the rock star thing in Buffalo Springfield, and then with Poco and all that, and then he became a minister. He had a story similar to Mark, where he started out in the rock world and then ended up changing careers and doing something else. So I talked to Richie, and he was incredible. Just hearing his story and how he got to where he is now.

CHRIS HILLMAN And she loved it so much she took the next class he offered, which was more emphasis on business.

CATHERINE HILLMAN CLARK He was only teaching two classes at the time, and I liked the first class so much that I made sure I got into that second one. He just came across so genuine, an everyday down-to-earth guy. When you're in his class, you forget that this is a rock star. This is somebody who's achieved so much fame, and so much recognition, and yet he was able to relate with everybody so easily. He was by far my favorite professor at Loyola because he was so easy to talk to, and so genuine with what he taught us. He never did that whole 'I'm a rock star' thing. You never would get that from him.

CHRIS HILLMAN She wanted to go to law school after she got her bachelor's at LMU, and that wasn't the right thing, it didn't work out, so she ends up teaching high school, and wants to keep teaching, and go to a college level. I'm sure he had a big part in that. He inspired her in more ways than he'll ever know. There was something there. Something touched a nerve, because she didn't know what she wanted to do.

CATHERINE HILLMAN CLARK He said he had realized there was more to life than what he was doing, and that he decided to go back to school, and then decided to teach. And I had no desire to teach. It never even crossed my mind. I just thought I'd graduate, get my degree, and look into something else, maybe go into a different career field or something. But Mark went straight through—bachelor's, master's—and that really inspired me. Hearing his story and seeing him be able to do that, especially so late in life, inspired me to go on and get my master's. I graduated with my bachelor's in English, and then went on to graduate school at Cal Poly San Luis Obispo, where I got my master's in English. He really inspired me to be able to go and attempt my hand at teaching. Seeing how he was able to relate that subject to all of us made me think of how I would love to be able to do that with English, with students of my own. And when I got into my graduate program, my passion for English really peaked, and his passion as a teacher really influenced me. I thought, *If he has so much passion about what he is doing—and I have all this passion for English—I'm gonna try teaching.* And so I've been teaching for three years now. I'm going into my third year of teaching high-school English. He's one of those teachers you never forget.

CORKY LAING Unequivocally, this is probably the most unusual, exceptional situation, because Mark helped me reinvent myself from a rock'n'roll drummer to a professor lecturing at one of the top universities in Canada. If it wasn't for Mark, none of this could have happened.

A few years ago, I did a guest lecture at McGill University. At the time I was doing international marketing, among other things, for Polygram, so I went and spoke, and I really enjoyed it. Then, when I did Hippie Fest, Mark said he had to leave early to go back to Belmont and teach, and we started talking. Instead of getting an eight-ball and going back to the room and getting drunk, he would tell me about the syllabus and how his course is outlined, and he just sucked me into this whole academic world. It wasn't sitting around bullshitting. We really focused. I remember going out of his room at two o'clock in the morning going, 'I gotta do this—I gotta write that out.' And I applied. I applied two, three years in a row. I kept at it, and Mark was constantly helping me along the way, guiding me. Prior to that, I didn't know him from a hole in the wall.

He must have thought there was something there, because, sure enough, the call came from the University of Western Ontario: 'Corky, would you like to come up and teach this course?' It blew me away. This is big time for me. Radio City, Carnegie Hall, playing in front of a hundred thousand people? Forget it—no problem. That was wonderful, beautiful. Woodstock, the whole deal, but lecturing at a college? That, to me, is the real shit.

After I got hired, I flew down to see Mark, because I'd never taught. I invested in going to Nashville and sitting in on his courses, seeing what he's doing and emulating it. He's very funny, but he's also very sincere. And he brings it home. When he wants the students to know something, he knows how to nail it. It was very, very impressive. After his lectures I happened to see a couple of kids from his class and asked a few questions, like why they were taking the course, what they thought of it and things like that, and it all came back to Mark. It all came back to: they love the content, they love the consistency, the sincerity, because Mark is presenting that. And you can't plan that. It's either there or not. I went over his résumé, and he has a vast, vast repertoire of experience in all phases of entertainment, television, comedy, music . . . the guy has been through so much shit, and yet he loves this. He plays with his students, and he has that wonderful disposition. It's wonderful.

All this humor and the rock'n'roll is one thing, but this is genuine: he's my mentor. He is my mentor for university. I don't know what he did with everybody else, but for this little drummer boy from Canada, he changed my life, because now, in my sixties, I'm going into the academic world and really working it, and just the nature of this whole thing, it's so *not* rock'n'roll, yet because it's not predictable, it is. The ultimate rock'n'roll move is to do something that nobody would expect. And that's what he did to me, and I'm still in shock.

BILLY CIOFFE I had a band out of L.A. that did a lot of work backing up people. Del Shannon, Ben E. King—you name them, we played with them, and it seemed like every time I was playing a gig, The Turtles were on the bill. So we wound up hanging out, and then Mark called us and we played a few shows as The Turtles. I did some stage direction, and he hired me, so I was doing that as well, not to mention playing golf and hanging out together. Around that time, he started talking about going to school, and it made incredible sense to me. I could relate because I didn't go to college either. When I was in high school, my group had a record deal. We were opening for The Byrds, The Rascals, and The Spoonful, so who the fuck cares about school? I wanted to be a rock'n'roll star, so I wasn't going to go to college.

I kicked around Hollywood for years. I loved every minute of it, but after thirty-five years of being on the road, I wanted a change, too. It doesn't mean I'm not a rocker and that I don't love it, but I considered myself a writer as much as a musician. I was contributing editor to *Guitar World*, I wrote for *Creem*, and I was musical instrument editor for a bunch of magazines. I always wanted to take a crack at doing some serious literature, so I decided I would get a degree, and in 2002 I moved to Scottsdale and went back to school. When I told Mark, he flipped. He thought it was great. I said, 'It's because of you. I was inspired by the fact that you had gone back to school.'

I graduated with a degree in English literature. I wasn't the oldest, but I'm about two years younger than Mark, so that tells you something. We invited him to my graduation party. This is his busy season, it's not like I expected him to come, but out of courtesy I invited him because he's my buddy, and he wrote this really beautiful email. And then, the night of my graduation, he called to tell me how proud he was. It made me feel terrific. I felt like a seventeen-year-old: *Hey, guess what? The guy from The Turtles just called!*

JULIE SCHAD He's a great teacher, in part because there is a confidence about him. He's always had that. I think that's part of what I found attractive about him: his confidence, his easygoing way. He's not out to take advantage of anyone. It's all positive motives.

DON CUSIC The key to Mark is that he has always been that friendly connector. He gets along with everybody. He's the man with no enemies, and that's the key here in the academic world. Everybody knows him, everybody gets along with him. I'm not saying he doesn't have depth—in fact, there's a depth that you don't find in most musicians—but at the same time, what you see is what you get. He is one of those open, friendly, one-of-the-guys people. He's got charisma, but he's not stuck on himself. Not an egomaniac.

EMILY VOLMAN If you meet him and you don't know what he does—say you're someone that knows me and he introduces himself to you—he will tell you he is a teacher. The first thing he tells you is not that he was in The Turtles or even that he is a musician.

DON CUSIC You've got to be part-entertainer, and Mark fills the bill there. He's a ham. He can entertain as well as educate. He was voted top teacher more than once, and students like him because he has a perspective. So many academics come through the academic world and don't really relate to a 'C' student, or can't relate to someone who doesn't put all their energies onto getting a grade. And Mark's not caught up in that.

SIDE D THE TWENTY-FIRST CENTURY

17

EMILY

EMILY VOLMAN I met Mark when he was forty-seven, and I would have been twenty—I was born in May 1974. We met in '94, but we didn't really start dating officially till the beginning of 1997. We moved in together maybe six or seven months later, and we were married April 1st, 2000. That was intentional. Everybody thought we were huge fools, so it seemed totally apropos.

At Loyola I majored in music, and you were required to be in the concert singers, as well as the choral choir. There were about a hundred members in the choir, and not just students. There were alumni, and people in the community could join as well. I was a soprano, and I made a couple of friends in that section, and we would just kind of cut up in the back. I would be cutting up in this choir class, and apparently Mark was doing the same. He would entertain the troops back there in the tenor section with his road stories. I didn't know it at the time, but the tenors used to sit across the room and pick out girls they thought were cute.

I had heard rumors that a guy from The Turtles was in the choir, but that didn't really mean much to me. I knew who The Turtles were. My dad was really into 60s music, so I knew many of their hits because of him. Dad was a big Beatles fan, and I became a huge Beatles fan, so when I heard that a guy from The Turtles was in the choir, I thought, *Well, he's not Paul McCartney, so who cares? That's nice for him, but he's not in The Beatles.*

That first year in choir, we went on a tour up and down the California coast, and it was on that trip that I met Mark. I'm usually very cynical and sarcastic, and that tends to be my sense of humor, but my first real encounter with him was nothing like that. I feel silly even saying it, but it was very magical. The first night, he talked to me, and I kind of blew him off. It wasn't, 'Look out for Mark.' That will come, but not yet. And yeah, Mark *is* charming. He's been around the ladies for a long time, so I am sure he knew exactly what to do to put the moves on. It wasn't creepy, but it was definitely not my bag. Older guys just weren't on my radar. But then somehow at one of the stops we had a day off and we got to walk around this small town. He asked if he could buy me lunch. I accepted, and we talked, then we walked around together, and he was—and still is—very charming and very easy to talk to. That day he won me over. And, for whatever reason, it wasn't like anybody I had ever been with had given me that sort of feeling. I was smitten—after that I was very smitten.

After the tour it was time to say goodbye. That was the first time we kissed, and it hit me a little bit like, *Whoa, this guy is so much older*. It seemed weird because now you're back to reality. Even though the entire tour was no more than a week, you still have that desert-island mentality, where you connect with people, and then you go back to reality and it's not the same. It was mixed emotions of *I really like this guy* and *He's older than my dad*. It was awkward yet exciting at the same time, but reality sets in. My friends want to know who that old guy I'm hanging out with is. They don't understand, and I begin to lose interest, because the fantasy is over. I dated other people, but Mark and I remained friends, and eventually we started dating, and it just grew from there. It turned into a relationship. That's when it got bad with everybody else at school.

HARVEY KUBERNIK He was doing a nutrition/herbalist thing. I thought that was kind of cool, and then all of a sudden he goes to LMU. Plus, he met a girl on campus? Like, how rock'n'roll is that?

EMILY VOLMAN Mark was in the communications department, so it wasn't that big an issue for him, but it became a big deal in the music department. My voice teacher called me out on it and said that we can't have this older man going around pursuing these girls their parents have trusted us to take care of. She had a prior marriage with someone much older that hadn't worked out, so maybe I was getting her baggage. I love her still to this day, and she has come to grips with it all, so it was more that she was worried about me, which I can appreciate. That's really what it boiled down to. Eventually I moved in with Mark. I had a job and I could have lived on my own, but it just seemed silly because I was there all the time, and half my stuff was already there.

At this point we had already been friends for about two and a half years, so my mom had met him a few times, and she loved him. From the very beginning, Mom understood it, because I'm such an old lady at times. I'm saying, 'Don't run!' I'm that mother. He's running and I'm screaming at him to stop running. So in that way we completely balanced each other. My dad, on the other hand—well, until we were getting married, I hadn't even told him that we were more than friends. It's silly, because we lived together for three years, and he knew. My dad is not a dope. I'm sure he knew, but his side of the family is very southern, and they don't talk about anything. So we didn't need to discuss it. And he accepted it when we said we were getting married.

Before, there were moments when I was embarrassed to be seen with Mark. Not because I was embarrassed *of* him, but I got so many comments from younger people, mainly younger guys, like, 'Is that your dad?' So I was always conscious of people staring. Mark sensed that, because several times early on in our relationship he would say, 'You don't want to be with me, I'm an old man. You need to be with people your own age.' He would constantly push that on me, but of course I am a total contrarian as well, and I would say, 'Don't tell me what to do.' Even today, I have a hard time holding his hand in public. That sounds horrible, and I hate even saying it out loud, but a lot of that has to do with how I was raised. I come from one of those families that worry about, *What will the neighbors think?* That's a big deal.

Mark asked. I was twenty-four or twenty-three, so I wasn't thinking about marriage. I wanted to see the world and do everything I could possibly do, so marriage didn't enter into my mind. But I said yes because we were already living together. We were already kind of married. It was like, *Okay, sure.* And then we went through marriage counseling at the church, and those were really good sessions. Those sessions have been amazing for the rest of our marriage, because it brought up a lot of stuff we were not thinking about. The obvious being age. Counseling addressed how that is going to affect having kids, what about when he's seventy and you won't have done this or that or whatever. Obviously, this has waned over time, because we're an old married couple now. When Mark and I are together alone, I don't even think about it. We are, if you can use the word, soulmates. We just click. We get each other completely and I don't even think like that.

MARY BREDEN Him marrying one of our students, that was interesting. When he first met her, he was still a student. It was a little bit, *Hmmm, what's this all about?* But she had graduated by the time they got married. It's lasted, and he's helped her find her niche too, so . . .

STEVE DUNCAN He got married to one of his classmates. That caused a few raised eyebrows, because she was younger than him, but nobody made a big deal out of it. In the last decade, Loyola has actually written policies about professors and instructors and students. So, he definitely couldn't do that now. But there were no real policies, plus he was a student. So, as long as there was no trouble, everybody's happy. My wife and I hung out with them after he got married to Emily. I was like, *Hey, I don't usually hang out with my students, but we can hang out with Mark.*

JULIE SCHAD I was at Mark and Emily's wedding. I had one of my kids there. I was the foster mom for a while.

HALLIE VOLMAN It was a shock. Emily and I are very close in age—we're about three weeks apart. So, I'm older, and it was a shock. But for the most part, I could see that he was happy with her, so if he's happy then I'm all for it.

SARINA VOLMAN I declined to be in the wedding. I wasn't thrilled with the whole idea, and it was weird having a stepmother younger than me. A letter was sent out to everybody that was going to be in the wedding party, telling what was expected of them, and I took a big offence to it. We already knew he was getting married, it was just this attitude of, *If you're going to be involved in the wedding, these are the rules and regulations that you have to abide by.* I thought it was a little inappropriate. I just thought, *Wait a minute, you're my dad. What the hell is this?* It just didn't feel right. It really put a bad taste on it, so I declined to be in the wedding.

EMILY VOLMAN Pat was invited to our wedding but ended up declining. It was a little too much for her, and we understood. And there was a little bit of a weird thing with Sarina. I asked both Hallie and Sarina to be bridesmaids, and I don't think Sarina was that excited that her dad was remarrying, let alone me.

PAT VOLMAN Emily is a pussycat. I just love her. She's very good for him, and she takes care for him. I think that's why he married a younger girl, so when he gets old and has to put those Depends on, he'll have somebody to buckle them up for him. Because I would be right next to him—I wouldn't be able to help him.

EMILY VOLMAN Pat and I never ever had a moment of awkwardness. I can honestly say that I liked Pat a lot right from the start. I've never felt uncomfortable around her at all, and I don't think she felt uncomfortable around me. I probably had more awkwardness around Sarina. Hallie is so easygoing that I don't think there's much that would faze her. Well, I know it bothered her when her folks split up, but she's definitely the Mark personality type. Whatever comes, she'll go with. So, we always got along.

SARINA VOLMAN I was not thrilled with it for many, many, years. But it got better. I eventually realized I was wrong and being childish. I finally grew up, and I apologized. Emily is a fantastic woman, and she's good for Dad. She makes him happy. She grounds him, and she's a great lady. I've come to realize that. It just took me a long time because—and I don't want to hurt Emily—I always had that hope against hope that mom and dad would get back together. And once he got married again, that hope had been banished. But she's a fine lady. She's a fine, fine lady. And it's a great marriage. It is, definitely. But I also thought my mom and dad's marriage was good, so . . . it is what it is, and we all move on, and she's fine and they're happy, and that's what matters. As long as my dad is happy, right?

LINDA CAMPILLO When I first met Emily, she was really, really shy. At family things she would barely say a word, and I just thought, *Oh, my gosh.* But one time they babysat my daughter, and then she started becoming more talkative and was really funny. I could see what they had in common. She liked all the same movies that I liked, we listened to the same kind of music. She was really sweet and very mature for her age.

JACK UNDERWOOD Emily is great, she really is. At first, I was surprised by the age difference. Then again, when you think of somebody that's in the music industry, marrying a young girl is not that unusual. So, Mark fell into this one. Having met her, she's very outgoing and a great girl, but she obviously has a bit of what I guess you would call an old soul. I think she's been great for Mark.

JOHN SNYDER She's lovely, and they have a great relationship—you can tell. She seems to be a lot more mature for her age, if I can say it that way. My wife and I both liked her a lot. We just thought she was very mellow and a perfect fit for Mark.

18

FAITH

Grandma Campillo would take young, preschool Mark on long bus rides to a Catholic church on Alvera Street. It was a secret they both kept from his parents. At least, that's how Mark remembers it.

ANN BECKER Grandma would take care of Mark when he was little, while his mother worked. The church we went to was in our parish area, but the church she took him to, that's a mission church on Alvera Street, in the city of Los Angeles, and that was quite a distance from where we lived, probably about twenty-five miles. Joe and Bea would let their children make up their own minds—that was their philosophy—but she was very religious, and that might be why she took him there. But I don't think she would ever not tell them, because she had a very good relationship with my brother-in-law.

MADELINE CAMPILLO We had no idea they took the long bus rides, but it doesn't surprise me that they didn't tell. Bless her heart, it says a lot that she got him there. I think she just wanted him to have some faith, too. Children need to be steered toward something. I've been Catholic, and I've been Protestant, and I really think they are pretty much alike. Same God, same basic teachings. I became Catholic so my children would have a religion. Bea and Joe chose not to. They weren't giving Mark any, and that's why Grandma spirited him off to church. I never knew before, but I'm so pleased.

My brother and I never felt that pressure. We were very fortunate that our parents allowed us to make those choices. I'm sure there was an understanding, but the age I was, I didn't witness any negative part of that. Rather than let it turn into Bea and Joe having dueling religions, they just let us alone. You're not going to be able to change Joe, anyway. At that time, Dad was like, *I don't care what's going on as long as it doesn't affect anything.* And that was the way that a lot of people thought at that time. Even the trip with Jack Underwood and his dad when we were kids: the experience of being in the chapel in Notre Dame in Indiana (the Basilica Of The Sacred Heart in Notre Dame, on the campus of the University Of Notre Dame). That was one of the places we visited, and it was interesting because a big part of growing up was having my grandmother take us downtown to the Catholic church. That was a really good side of the family. My grandmother was very spiritual, and my other grandparents were not, but considering they were Jewish, and it was just after the war . . . but I don't remember there being any problems between my mom and my dad about being Catholic and being Jewish.

LINDA CAMPILLO Our grandmother was very religious, but Mark's memory is weekdays taking the bus? I don't know what memory that would be, because she didn't really take the bus. Maybe when he was very young, but by the time he was eight, I started living with her. I was three. I went to church with her, because I lived with her, and he never went to church with us.

FELIX CAVALIERE I think that the key word there is *search*. You're on a quest to find truth, and our generation was really on that quest, consciously. And I'm not sure that there is any other quest that means anything, seriously, except for that. Once you find it, whatever it is that you're looking for, you've really completed your life's purpose. And the rest of the things that you do while you're alive on planet Earth are affected by those beliefs, and by those truths.

PAUL WILLIAMS I have no God of my understanding. My Higher Power is too massive for my mind to comprehend. My god is the Big Amigo, and there's a newfound level of trust and belief. I don't understand, though. I don't understand electricity either, but I use it.

JIM PONS All of us were influenced by the culture of the day, and that included psychedelic drugs and Eastern religions. I was definitely looking for something new that I could believe in, and Christianity represented the faith of my youth—something I had left behind in my search for higher spiritual consciousness. I introduced Mark to a book called *The Impersonal Life*, and that's when I realized he was a seeker like myself, but we were pretty much all over the place when it came to any kind of spiritual discipline. We would smoke pot and practice transcendental meditation while listening to Ravi Shankar. We even bought Indian clothes and musical instruments. Whatever we saw The Beatles doing, that's what we decided to try. But God was definitely calling us. I guess He let Mark and me take the long road around the mountain before bringing us back to where we started.

AL NICHOL Mark and I have been following the same spiritual point forever. During the Vietnam War and the hippie revolution, he was really eager to explore a lot of spiritual areas that were opening up at that point. And he did a lot of exploration. He wasn't satisfied to lock in and be part of any religion. He was constantly searching for the underlying meaning, the driving force of positive existence. And I've been doing that all along too, only maybe in different ways. So, I can relate to that. It didn't surprise me at all that he would finally find a level that he could lock in on a more secure, frequently visited area.

CHRIS HILLMAN That was the era of 'God is dead' and all these other stupid clichéd things that came along. I don't look back at it as quite as wonderful a time as everybody else. I do think the decade was really exciting and innovative on a musical level in the early days, from right when The Beatles came out, up until 1969. That's when it started to get edgy. That's when Altamont happened—we played at Altamont—and all these things sort of took a real sharp turn to a darker place. That's when a lot of the people I knew started to pass away. It was such an indulgent time in the 70s. That was the *make it or break it* time for a lot of us, where we knew there was something more to be done with our lives than to waste away into nothingness. And some people just didn't quite make it. It's all down to making choices.

TOMMY JAMES Everybody in our band became a Christian in the late 60s, and I think our music—songs like 'Sweet Cherry Wine' and 'Crystal Blue Persuasion'—reflected light. There was nothing politically incorrect about stating how you felt about things. It was considered kind of cool and very artistic. There was no downside to it. *Jesus Christ Superstar* was huge, 'My Sweet Lord' by George Harrison . . . basically it was kind of chic. Of course, everybody thought 'Crystal Blue' was about drugs. If they didn't understand the words, it meant you were taking drugs. *Everything* meant you were taking drugs back then. And most of it was true. But it doesn't surprise me that Mark returned to the church. It may have surprised *him* more than me. I don't think we ever discussed religion. It was just that he was always very big-hearted when it came to people. Very outgoing and very, very friendly. It doesn't surprise me at all.

ALICE COOPER Mark had to get through all that. And maybe a lot of us did. Because we were still rebelling against what was conventional. In other words, we were going, *Well, maybe this whole Buddhist thing, and maybe this transcendental thing, and maybe this Hindu, and maybe this* . . . And you know what? They didn't lead anywhere. They didn't go anywhere. There was no promise to it. There was no future to it, really.

STEVE DUNCAN One of the things that surprised me about Mark was that he was so spiritual. But then I realized it made sense. How do you survive the business he was in without having some kind of spiritual center about you? And so, I hardly raised my eyebrow. My wife is a born-again Christian and they hit it off like, *Bam!* I'm an agnostic most times and some days an atheist depending on my mood, but he doesn't feel a need to convince anyone. My wife's the same way, otherwise we wouldn't have gotten married. I think we all kind a gelled and got along really well because of that.

GARY ROWLES Does it surprise me? Based on what I saw back in the Flo & Eddie days, especially on the Alice Cooper tours, because that was some insane stuff, it does surprise me in a way, but not really, because I knew he had a tender spot in him. That was one of the things that drew me to them, was his personality. It certainly wasn't Kaylan. I mean, I like Kaylan fine, it's just that every now and then he'd get real salty, and that was the way it was. He was one of the guys who was in charge—one of the bosses. But Mark was the one with the true vision, the one who had more of the overview. And, like Mark, I ended up returning to the church, too. In 1981, I was basically dragged to the throne kicking and screaming. But ever since then, it's been the grandest life I could've ever imagined.

LOYOLA

PHIL VOLMAN He came out of Loyola pretty turned on with the Jesuits, and pursued it from there.

EMILY VOLMAN At the tail end of his marriage, Mark probably didn't do a lot of religious practicing, but at Loyola, we had to take religious classes. It was part of our degree. And there were masses, not because you necessarily *had* to go, but if it was attached to something else, like our choir concerts. The liturgical music is all Catholic, so a lot of times we had to sit through a mass. He hung out a lot with the Jesuit priests, too. Especially Father Trame.

Father Trame was one of the priests who worked in the university. He lived right on campus and was a very interesting, outspoken, really fun guy. He was twenty-five years older than me, and because of my age, the priests felt comfortable having me around. I'd go over to where they all lived, and they would have wine tastings. It was funny because you saw this kind of backstage world at the university. Most of them taught on campus . . . at least, the ones still young enough to do that. He got tickets—for the opera, theater, or whatever it was—to the Music Center in downtown Los Angeles, and then invited me. I said, 'Sure,' and he says, 'Well, you'll have to drive.' That was the first sign that I should have known we were headed for something a little off the wall. We got our car together, I picked them up, and on the way we got cut off in the middle of traffic. I can't really relay the whole story, but there was language coming out of Richard that would have shaken the foundations of any church. He was yelling at these guys that had cut us off, 'You son of a bitch!' and just ranting at them for almost killing us on the freeway. And that always made me laugh, because he was such a real guy. He felt I was in a good place to pursue becoming a professor. It was all twisting into place, as long as I was willing to put the time in.

EMILY VOLMAN They had a lot of great times together. Father Trame was a little man, hunched over, pushing his little audio-video cart. He just thought the world of Mark, and vice versa. I'm sure they had great philosophical discussions. So, in that way Mark got a lot just from being at that school. Definitely, his time at Loyola started him on his own journey into faith again, because you couldn't get away from it. It was a Jesuit school, and a lot of people actually practiced it. So, he was exploring again on his own.

We talked a lot about religion. My mother was Catholic, my father was Russian immigrant Jewish, and his parents had come from Hungary. I was beginning to understand how lucky we were that we didn't have any tension around that. We discussed how that was something he could accept as plausible, that we really were fortunate, just in life after World War II and everything that my parents and their parents had experienced. Mostly because everybody else thought it was such a weird combination.

MARY BREDEN Mark thought very highly of Father Trame, and vice versa. Richard was a history professor by training, but he just loved chorale music and had long been a helper with the choruses. Mark worked with him, helping him with the recordings, and when he died quite suddenly, in 1998, Mark stepped forward and helped record our concerts for the rest of the time that he was at the university. He was so helpful. When Father died, he had all sorts of recording equipment and books and recordings that he left to the music department, and Mark helped me go over to the Jesuit residence and put everything in storage. I needed to do it right now or we were going to lose the stuff, and Mark was there when I needed him. And he helped us put out a CD with LaserLight. The university has long been known for its excellent choirs, at least among people who are aware of choral music, but we hadn't done anything commercially like that. That was a good opportunity. It raised our profile, to some extent.

I was singing in the LMU choir. They were a very professional group of singers. Paul Salamunovich, a renowned conductor, had been involved in basically starting the choir, and they became quite famous. Father Trame loved music and was hanging out already, and Mary Breden asked if I would be interested in working with him to put together the music. I went to Laserlight—a CD company that did jazz, some old rock, and other stuff—to discuss recording the choir. We did the choir record, and then we started to work on a few other things. We ended up making a Christmas album and a couple of other recordings.

STEVE DUNCAN The Jesuits are an interesting bunch of guys. When I first got hired, I said to the president, 'You know, Bob, I don't believe in God,' and he looked up to heaven and said, 'Well, Steve, that's why we're in business.' I thought, *Okay, this will be cool.* Their idea is that you educate the whole person, and your spiritual life is a part of that. Math is a part of that. Art is a part of it. At the heart of the institution is this Jesuit philosophy of social consciousness, of service, but you're free to pursue whatever religious interest you have. In that environment it's difficult to understand the schism between being out there in the worst business of the world, dancing with the devil, yet having some spirituality about yourself, having ethics and morals even though you cross the line all the time, because that's just the way the business is.

The Jesuits don't always quite get that. Sometimes they see things very black-and-white and get a little stuck in that, especially the old school guys. It was that tail wagging the dog from the academia side: 'If you're a good artist, you go out and be successful,' and Mark was like me. We're going, 'No, that's not quite how it works. This is a *business*, so all this shit we're doing here is nice and you can call it art if you want, but really, it's about how much money people are going to make off of it. And until you can prove that you can make some money, nobody is going to take you seriously as an artist.' So he had a real-world view that few of the students understood.

JACK UNDERWOOD He said he was getting involved with the church, which I thought was great. We never really talked religion over the years at all, so I suppose Emily kept him on the right path.

EMILY VOLMAN I don't think you can necessarily credit me for his exploration of faith, because he was doing that on his own at the Jesuit school. Now, afterward, I am definitely the one that influenced the switch to becoming Methodist.

PAT VOLMAN I was a little bit surprised when he started going to church, because he was hippie-dippy, peace and love. We never really talked or put that in our kids' heads about heaven and God and all that stuff, so I was surprised. When his parents died, back-to-back, I think that kind of hit him a little bit.

EMILY VOLMAN Pat's dead on. Mark's parents passing away played a huge part in his moving toward faith. And Jack, God bless him, he knows my churchy background, but I definitely didn't influence Mark to become religious. His parents did, in their passing. That's really what got him interested in faith again.

At the time, a lot came down to Richie Furay. Richie is a pastor, and I remember Mark calling him when his parents were passing away, and he had these really wonderful, deep things to say about the whole situation. Mark found great comfort in talking with him. Richie has been very influential in Mark's life and exploration toward Christianity specifically. He really loves Richie and looks up to him in a lot of ways.

RICHIE FURAY Whatever role I played in it, if I played any, it was just that he would see my life, the things I'd gone through, maybe the things I've said about my walk and how the Lord affected my life. And maybe those things affected him. I don't think I had any direct interaction with Mark as far as helping him make a decision. I don't think that was it. I think it was something along the line: somebody planted a seed, somebody watered it. Maybe I watered it with some of the things that I did at the same time. But when I found out about it? Man, it was just like, this is really too cool. And then we talked about it, and after talking to Mark there was no doubt in my mind. Yup, he's had a conversion in his life.

Before that, I would see Mark when he'd come to town, and one time they played down here, and to tell you the truth, I left. It was like, *You know what? I'm just uncomfortable here with my friend and what he is saying*. This was obviously before he accepted the Lord, and they were still pretty wild and crazy guys. I had heard this concert, probably in the late 80s or early 90s, and I'm thinking, *Mark's just having a good time playing music, and he's just going to be having a good time like that until his life is over. It's just going to be like that. It's not going to change*. Of all my old friends who came to faith, he was probably the biggest surprise. But I shouldn't say that, really. The Lord can do anything.

EMILY VOLMAN Mark's parents dying was hard. I don't think he thought that would ever happen, and it really made him question things. He was trying to figure out what it all meant, and I suggested we check out a Methodist church in Westchester. He knew nothing of any denomination other than Catholic, so he was wary, but he went, and the pastor was really good. He was a young guy, charismatic and thoughtful, and Mark loved the sermon. They really connected, and we started going there, and we ended up being very, very involved with that church.

SARINA VOLMAN Apparently Dad had religion when he was younger, but I didn't know that. I had no idea until years later. My sister and I grew up with Santa Claus and the Easter Bunny. Both of my parents may have believed, but they didn't press it on us. Just believe in what you want to believe in—it's everybody's path.

It did surprise me when he became a Christian. And the way he gets, he goes full force. So, when he first got into it, he was full force, oh yeah. He talked about it a lot. And at first I wasn't interested, and then, as I was starting on my own path a little bit, I found it interesting.

CHRIS HILLMAN Of The Byrds, McGuinn is a very devout Evangelical Christian, and I'm an Orthodox Christian. And it's not because we're all getting older, it's really, truly, a calling, and it hit most of us in our forties or late thirties.

RICHIE FURAY I was thirtysomething when I came to faith, and Mark was fortysomething when it happened for him. So, how awesome is that, man? It's like the Lord is always reaching out to us. And what happened? What happened to flip that switch on at that particular time? I don't know, but praise the Lord, whatever it was. I think about that: *Why me, Lord?* Awesome.

HARVEY KUBERNIK I didn't know that Mark and Howard were Jewish. I didn't know that Howard defanged his Jewish name from Kaplan to Kaylan. I didn't think about those things. All I knew is they looked like guys you go to Hebrew school with. But you have to understand that Mark *always* thought outside the box. He was not going to become somebody who'd be a cantor at a synagogue, okay? Both those guys, you think with their name and their shtick they might be, what's the term . . . *demonstratively* Jewish or something. But it doesn't really go with them. They never catered to any Jewish youth groups or the Jewish angles of the record business or doing B'nai B'rith events. You can work all that stuff, but they weren't going to show up and do a fundraiser for a Holocaust museum. I'm not being negative, they're just not in that world. And it doesn't surprise me at all that Mark got involved with church groups, whether it be for harmony or just the organized religion aspects.

TIM SEXTON Underneath all of that stuff, Mark's a very solid citizen, family kind of middle-class guy. And he is not in truth all that complicated. So the return to church doesn't surprise me. I'm really glad to hear that.

LINDA CAMPILLO Mark has really changed over the years. He was very liberal and very much a 60s kind of guy for a long time beyond the 60s, but now he's become much more conservative, and that surprises me. That he found religion and became spiritual was not that shocking, because he did have a spiritual background. But the fact he's politically conservative ... I don't know if I believe this or not, but he pretends that he voted for Ronald Reagan. And I'm like, 'Mark, you've got to be kidding me.' It could be just to get a reaction.

BILLY CIOFFE He started going to church, but he's not the kind of guy that proselytizes at all—at all. He keeps that business to himself. I mean, I knew it. I knew he was singing in choirs, going to church every Sunday and all that stuff, but I don't think anything of it one way or another. Everybody needs a system.

FRED WOLF I heard he had found religion. I didn't know what the hell that meant. By the time it gets processed through my mind, I thought he had become a born-again guy and was very close to Christ and all that stuff. So, I called. I said, 'I thought you were a minister or something,' and I found out that none of it is true. And God bless him. He took his life and went further with it, way beyond The Turtles. Professor Volman, huh? Amazing.

JIM YESTER I was totally blown away by the whole spirituality thing and the whole Christianity thing. I had not a clue, because he doesn't wear that on his sleeve at all. I had no idea, and I was with him for a month and a half. But I didn't see anything at odds with that, absolutely not.

EMILY VOLMAN There was nothing for the youth, so I tried to start a youth group, and one of the parents put the kibosh on that because Mark and I were living together. Everybody else at that church was pretty West Coast liberal, but this one lady didn't want me to head up a youth group because I wasn't married. We were living in sin. This became a big church crisis, and we had a meeting with the pastor and all the other parents, and what was so ironic about it all was that *I* was the one attacked. Mark was there, but unlike back in college where he was seen as the predator, this time *I* was the one wearing the big scarlet letter. It was bizarre, because I was only twenty-three or twenty-four. I didn't get it, and I felt such shame. We weren't talking marriage at that time, and it wasn't like we were going to get married so I could run a youth group. All my friends at church were older, and they said, 'Don't worry about it, we love you just the way you are. We're fine with you being with our kids.' So that worked out okay.

We both became lay leaders. We took the schooling they have so that we could preach on Sundays. There was a lot of continuing education. I did a lot of women's studies, where Mark focused on Old Testament studies. He was into the scholarly bible stuff, and I was more into the social aspects of church. We really liked that church. We got married there in 2000, and stayed until we moved to Nashville in August 2004.

19

NASHVILLE

Outside of the New York City radio days, Mark had spent his entire life based on the West Coast, so it was a shock to all when he and Emily moved to Nashville.

DANNY HUTTON The thing that surprises me the most is where he's living—in Nashville. I didn't expect an L.A. guy to end up there.

EMILY VOLMAN He was teaching at the two colleges and he wanted to retire. I was doing improv and comedy stuff in Los Angeles, but in our minds—to both of us—it seemed like a good idea to get a house, get a porch with a swing, and retire. Here I was, I'd just turned thirty, but what's funny about me is I'm just an old soul kind of person, so at the age of thirty I was ready to retire.

Originally, we were going to move to Nashville to be closer to my family. My dad lived in Chattanooga, my grandfather was in Georgia, my aunt and uncle were in South Carolina, so they are all very southern/southeastern. And because I was with my mom much of my childhood, I really missed growing up with my dad's side of the family. Dad suggested Franklin, his reasoning being it's in the richest county in Tennessee, and a lot of musicians live there. And, sure enough, it fits us to a *T*. There are a lot of Californians that moved to Franklin. That's why we like it here, because it is like Southern California but not—it doesn't have the traffic and the people are much nicer. We moved here for that, but at the same time, Mark had gotten so much from Larry Wacholtz via his book that he decided to call him to say he lived here now, and maybe they could meet in person. And it just so happened, Larry asked Mark if he could substitute for his class. Well, the ball started rolling at that point, the buzz: 'One of The Turtles is the substitute?' Now it starts with, 'He's got his master's? Would he like to teach a class here?' And from there his relationship with Belmont grew. And here we are now, where he's the chair of the whole department.

LARRY WACHOLTZ He kept in contact. I'd send him books, send him suggestions and all that stuff. Well, finally, he called and said he was moving to Tennessee. And as soon as I met him, I knew that he was a teacher. I knew because he has that ability to be more than an artist and more than a star. He's real. He is what he is, and he doesn't put anything on. He will talk to anybody. He's totally there when he talks to you, but he has the ability to explain things honestly and with a sincerity that most artists can't do.

To find a person who is a big star—and he is really one of the bigger stars on the planet—and is able to teach it, is an absolute godsend. We have had many, many people who are big stars, huge stars, but when they talk, they have enough that they can talk for an hour or two. Well, that's it. They're great for one or two classes and then default to the old stories. The kids love it because they're hearing story after story after story, but they're not really learning how the business works. It's more anecdotal, whereas Mark is giving them the information they really need. And that is such an incredible gift. Students ask the most technical business-oriented or creative questions, and, every time, Mark can handle them.

E. MICHAEL HARRINGTON Belmont is way too conservative. There was a job opening, and I was on the committee and Mark's one of the applicants, and I'm thinking, *He wants to be here?* I said, 'Drop everything—don't even look at anyone else—this guy puts everyone to shame.' And there was all this hemming and hawing, and they went against it. The next time there was a job opening, I wasn't on that committee, and again they didn't hire him. They had different reasons. They wanted to go with their Baptist buddies, and so and so won't rock the boat, he goes to church with the president of the college . . .

How many of the other teachers have played with Zappa and John Lennon? Half of them don't even know who Zappa is, or they'll think he is satanic or something. I was mad as hell at the school, and Mark must have been, too, but he's just an easygoing guy, because he applied again, and they finally hired him. That program he's running, Entertainment Industry, that's just fabulous. He's the one to do it. Belmont doesn't deserve someone that good.

LARRY WACHOLTZ It's very hard to get administrators to realize what a treasure, what a unique and tremendously effective recording artist, teacher, person,

Mark is. They're so incredibly rare. Now I will say this: the president of the university didn't think that. The president *loves* Mark Volman. Anytime Mark's there and the president is there, they're having a good time, and the president doesn't do that with many people. He knows that Mark is a gift. The president *gets* him . . . it was the committee, and some of the other faculty, that may not. I'm not talking about music business or any of that, because we're all so glad he's here. It's so rare to have anybody with his talent come in and be able to teach. He is truly a gift.

ALICE COOPER Mark's one of the smartest guys in the world. Mark and Howard were maybe the two smartest guys I knew in rock'n'roll, next to Frank [Zappa]. When you talk about intelligence, here was this little pop group The Turtles, but come on, these guys could be professors. And Howard looked like one. But that doesn't surprise me one bit. I would be surprised if Mark and Howard had a problem with academics. It seems to me that if they put all the energy they had into academics, they could be doctors of whatever they wanted to be.

BOB EZRIN Surprised? Totally. First of all, I lost complete touch with him. I had heard he'd got to Nashville, so that was surprising to start, because I always saw him as quintessentially Californian. He and Howie were such L.A. dudes that I could not imagine Mark being in Nashville. So that took me by surprise.

And then to hear that he had actually become an academic? Not so much surprising as interesting, because it's something that I've considered, too. I love teaching. I just love it, so I get that he loves to do that, and I get that the kids relate to him. He's a big kid—just a big overgrown kid. And he always will be. I'm not quite as big, but I'm an overgrown kid, too. So, I get that. I have to say, I'm proud of him—and, on a certain level, envious. Because I think he's just got the greatest life.

JACK UNDERWOOD Not a whole lot of people do that, but it didn't surprise me, because Mark is somebody that's always testing boundaries. I was impressed when he'd pulled that off. When you hear about famous people that played rock'n'roll, rarely do you hear of anybody that's changed their life like this. In fact, you don't. They're generally recovering from some kind of a drug or something.

SPANKY McFARLANE Well, Mark loves to talk. He loves to explain his musical trip, and I thought that was perfect for him. Let him do it to the people that really want to hear about it, who will take it to heart and can learn something from him.

PAT VOLMAN He likes to be in front of people, still. Even if he quit touring, he would still want to be in front of everybody. I would guess that's part of why he ended up being a professor.

FELIX CAVALIERE He's educating young people coming into the music world with his experience, so that they don't have any illusions about what they're getting into, whereas in those days we didn't have that. We had to learn by our trials and tribulations.

DANNY HUTTON Mark and I both got screwed, on different levels, the same way. In fact, any musician—we've all gone through versions of the same thing. And now he's teaching about it. He's used the problems he had and communicated that to people. He's said, 'You're here to find out about music, but here is what you didn't know.' I don't know of anyone else who's pulled off what he's done. *And* it's not like he retired and did that. He's doing both! Holy crap, how the hell do you do that? Talk about energy. But he was always a driven kind of guy. He's just one of those light bulbs that when you walk in a room: boom!

DONNIE KISSELBACH He has an experience and intelligence that you can't get out of a book. So, what did do he do? He came up with, *I'll write the book.* He essentially has written a book on the music business. Yeah, you can sing your scales, you can practice your instrument, you can be hot shit in your hometown, but guess what? When you go out in the real world and you're competing in the marketplace to be somebody and to get attention and to get recognition, here's what you're really going to be up against. That's how smart he is.

PATRICK SIMMONS I thought that was an amazing thing for anyone, let alone a guy who was a rock musician. I went to college when I was younger, and I loved the learning process, and it's one of those things where at the back of your mind you always think, *Maybe when I have time, when I'm not doing this* *anymore, I'd like to go back and re-learn some things I never paid attention to then, that I'm interested in now.* But Mark is one of the few people that has actually done that. And that's an incredible accomplishment. It gives everybody else hope that maybe we can do something like that someday.

JACKIE MARTLING I respect his talent and his brain so much that I would be lying if I said I was totally shocked. I was thrilled for him, but it wasn't like, *Jeez, I can't believe he could do that.* Of course he could do that. He's a guy who could do absolute whatever the fuck he wants, you know what I mean? He's that talented.

B&B

URSULA HOUGHTON My husband and I ran a bed-and-breakfast, and that's how we met Mark and Emily.

GLENN HOUGHTON They were looking for a piece of property in Tennessee and stayed with us a few times. I'm about nine years older than Mark, and I didn't know he was an entertainer. We grew up in the same era, but I was busy doing other things. I'm more of a fan of the big-band era. I played baritone horn in the Military Band—the 101st Airborne Division Band—for three years. But we became good friends.

URSULA HOUGHTON We clicked right away. Glenn is twenty-five years older than I am and Emily is twenty-seven years younger than Mark, so we had a lot in common.

GLENN HOUGHTON Even though there's a difference in age between Mark and Emily, they complement each other quite well. I've never felt that it was a big issue, anyway. It's how you handle it yourself. As you get older you can't just put yourself in the box and forget to do anything. I can dance and I can run, and I do everything I've always done, maybe not as fast, but I can still do it quite well.

URSULA HOUGHTON They have a few differences, like any couple does for that matter, but it doesn't seem like the age plays a role at all. It's like with me and my husband, I never think of him as being that much older. He's just my husband and friend. And Emily and Mark are the same way. The friendship just evolved from there. Mark had never owned a big piece of property, so he had to know about lawn mowers and all that stuff. He always came to Glenn for help about things like that.

GLENN HOUGHTON They're like anyone else, and I treat them like any other friend, and they're receptive to that. We just call a spade a spade, sir. And that works. They actually ran the bed-and-breakfast for us. That was on Emily's bucket list. And they did a good job.

URSULA HOUGHTON They did that for us a couple of times. One time I had to go out of town because Glenn had emergency surgery in Minnesota. I had guests scheduled and I was desperate. I didn't want to cancel our guests out, and they said, 'You go and take care of your husband, and we'll take care of the business for you. Don't worry about a thing.' They enjoyed hosting. And Emily was so funny, because she doesn't like to cook—Mark is the cook in the family—but they managed quite well, and of course, with Mark being such a good storyteller, he really had a good audience with our guests. So, if you need a friend, they are right there, and we can say the same thing about us for them.

We've taken a few trips together. Glenn kept saying he wanted to take me to New York, because I had never been there. He kept threatening and threatening, and then one year, for Christmas, Mark and Emily surprised us with a trip to New York. They made all the arrangements. The four of us went and had a grand time. It was pure fun.

GLENN HOUGHTON I've been trying to get Mark and Emily to accompany us to Italy, but so far I haven't been able to do that. Mark gets a little tired of being on the road, and I can see his point of view also. He grew up on the road.

URSULA HOUGHTON Mark doesn't like to travel too much unless it's for a show. Emily is more of a go-getter in that regard, and she would like to travel more. But she goes on trips. She went to Paris with Mark's daughter a few years ago, and she took her little sister to Paris as well. So, she gets to travel with other people. Mark's got shows and school, so he is pretty busy, and he's just happy when he has time to hang around at home and be with the dogs.

EMILY VOLMAN When we moved to Nashville, we quickly got to know my cousin. He's a senior pastor, so we started going to his church, which is a Presbyterian church. We were going to Methodist before, so we made the jump. And it was a cool church. There are a lot of musicians at this church working in the music industry, and it's small—not more than three hundred people—so it was everything we liked. After we were going there for a little bit, they hired an associate pastor who became more focused on the youth and the children's programs. He gathered a whole bunch of youth advisors, as they called them.

ALAN BANCROFT I'm the associate pastor at [Harpeth Presbyterian Church] for the youth and family ministry. Our church is relatively small, but about fifty kids are in our youth group. Mark and Emily served for three years as youth advisors with the ninth through twelfth graders, so ages fourteen to eighteen. When I first asked, he had concerns: 'Man, I've got kind of a wild past. You think I need to be in there?' And I told him, 'Absolutely! The kids need to know there are lots of different people out there, that faith is not just for one kind of person.' And so he offered a perspective that, really, none of the rest of us could, because not only was he the oldest advisor but he had lived a totally different life. And to be able to say, 'I tried this, I tried that, and as I've come around, this faith story of God and Jesus has had more meaning for me in my life.' That was really great. He'd tell them, 'Don't forget what you've got here. I had this foundation and I abandoned it. And I think my life might have been a little different had I held onto some of that.' He's very frank. He was willing to say, 'Value this. You've got a church community here that cares about you, and adults in this church that care about you.' Of course, we've got a few broken homes and maybe some weird situations, but by and large these kids have adults in their lives that really look out for them, and Mark wanted them to be aware: 'Hey, you've got a lot going for you. Don't mess it up.'

One Sunday he was worried, and he asked if he had shared too much. I said, 'Absolutely not.' Because Mark's Mark. And, from my perspective, that's the most valuable thing. I don't look for theologians or people with all the answers. I look for authentic people that can be role models for young people, and Mark is just awesome with that. And he brings this personality. He has gravity. People are drawn to him, and in a good way. He brings a good vibe. Everybody walks away from a conversation with Mark feeling uplifted.

DANNY HUTTON There's an audience, so what the hell else is he going to do? Is he going to sit there? I can see him on the Sunday. He's full of energy, and he loves being in front of people since he was a kid. It's that five-year-old, little Marky Volman, here to preach to you, man!

ALAN BANCROFT We all eat dinner together on Sunday nights, all the senior highs and middle schoolers, so they all know him, and it's a mutually beneficial, inspiring relationship. The youth group goes on at least one mission trip a year, and, with Mark and Emily, they picked a doozie. We took about thirty youth on a bus out to a little church near Taos, New Mexico. We did bible-school stuff for local kids in the morning, and construction projects, yard work, household visits, that kind of thing in the afternoon. And some of our older ones were conducting a middle-school camp for kids in the area. Mark and Emily were my point people on that. I figured with both of them having the music and the drama experience, they'd be better out there. It ended up being a nine-day trip, and it was great.

EMILY VOLMAN For the most part, Mark really doesn't care what anybody thinks. And that's why kids love him. We would go on these mission trips, and Mark goes and does something without even asking. He just does his own thing. And all the kids just giggle because they can't believe someone is like that.

ALAN BANCROFT We've probably got about a dozen music-industry folks—session players and producers and publishing types—who all know each other, but most people just know him as a guy at church. And he's happy to be known as that: just a guy at church. The kids all knew who he was, because they thought it was cool, right? *Wow, a pop star.* But I've never seen him introduce himself as 'Mark Volman of The Turtles.' He's just Mark. We sing various worship songs and stuff in our youth group, and he'll bring his

NASHVILLE **313**

guitar and help out, but he's not usually in the choir. He may have done one of our special cantatas one time, because Emily was doing the reading for it, and Mark got roped in at the last minute, but for the most part, when he's there, he's just a guy in the pews.

CHRIS HILLMAN I never knew Mark even had those leanings. I sort of felt it—I had an inkling—but I never knew he was a committed Christian. But it doesn't change anything one way or the other. I always saw him as a good person, and it's only natural that he would be.

ALICE COOPER I was the prodigal son. My dad was a pastor, my granddad was a pastor, my wife Cheryl's dad is a pastor. I grew up in the Christian faith. Alice Cooper pulled me away from it, and I became the symbol for everything that was opposite of that, except that there was nothing ever satanic about what I did. I really had that knowledge of good and evil and Christ and God and Devil, and I knew what side I was on. I would never do anything anti-Christian, or I would never give Satan any due. But I certainly was perceived as that. Basically, nobody knew how to look at us, and they just didn't know how to categorize us, so this whole vaudeville thing became satanic.

I got to the point where I had my alcohol problem and was throwing up blood, and I went into the hospital. People say, 'Thirty years without a drink, wow—that's really a cured alcoholic.' And I say, 'No, I'm a healed alcoholic.' And it really is true, because I never had a craving. I never had a mishap, I never slipped. It never occurred to me to have a drink, to the point where the doctor said, 'That's impossible. You were the classic alcoholic.' But I can sit down and watch everybody drink, and it doesn't even occur to me to have a drink. So, to me, that was God taking it away, and just lifting it out of my life. And it was a healing, rather than a cure. So, when Mark was telling me how he became a Christian, I totally got it. It wasn't surprising to me. That can happen to anybody.

JOHNNY BARBATA I'm born-again and so is Mark. Jim Tucker and Jim Pons are, too. I guess I was the first one. I was surprised to hear the other guys became Christians. I didn't expect that from Mark, because he's part Jewish. So, family-wise, that must be a little bit different.

JIM TUCKER I went back to church thirty years ago. I was the first. I'm not going at the moment, because I'm living in sin with my other half, but I've been there for thirty or thirty-five years at least. Howard is Jewish, and I don't think he ever will. But the rest of us have all done that, and people say, 'Why don't you guys get back together?' Especially now that most of us have become religious. And Mark doesn't care. He's just selfish. He's left everybody else—the guys that put him there—out in the cold. After finding the Lord and going to church, usually you're supposed to take a step back, but he just keeps on moving. Usually, when you get into the bible, and you get into God's word and everything? Yeah, we all thought that he might figure out that it's not all *you*. We were the ones that got you there. But it doesn't matter. It's all about him.

JIM PONS I was surprised to hear about Jim Tucker, and actually amazed about Barbata. He was the least likely person I could've imagined to come to Christ. God definitely works in strange and wondrous ways.

AL NICHOL Am I a Christian? Sure, I'll be one. I've gotten deeply involved with a lot of different churches, and years back, through all this chaos that my life has gone through, I became—and still am for that matter—an alcoholic. And I got involved with Alcoholics Anonymous, which is a very spiritually guided group, if people want to find it that way. I've gone to synagogue services and lots of Christian services, and I've performed with Christian groups, and I've also gone into the Catholic diocese, so I've been involved. Nothing really specific, although being involved has helped me get to where I am now. You know, I'm still alive.

HOWARD KAYLAN I'm sure you can tell from my conversations I am not a converted man. I don't feel myself to be a religious person, and I'm not a born-again anything. I've never lost my faith in the God that I always loved, so I figure I'm in pretty good shape. In your own head, you've just got to be secure, to know that, if the trumpet blows, you're going to be all right leaving this planet and not having any issues to settle. Not having guilt about things you could have done better or people you could have treated differently. All of us have done some really crappy shit, and I don't ever expect to atone for those things. I don't think anybody can, so you take the good with the bad.

PHILIP AUSTIN He's handling his Christian life of late with intelligence and grace, from what I see. You don't have to burn your past to embrace your present.

JACK UNDERWOOD I think it's been good for him. We went to his church the last time we were in Tennessee to visit him. He introduced us to the congregation, and I could tell he was really loved by all the parishioners and that a lot of the kids looked at him like *Uncle Mark*. A lot of people seek religion, and get a little overzealous with it as far as you either do it their way, or you're a sinner and you're going to Hell. I didn't get that from Mark, but I did get a little between-the-lines thing. I believe in God myself, but I'm not gonna shove it down everybody else's throat and judge somebody else about it. But then that tempered to where he realized where I'm at and I realized where he's at and we accepted each other for that, which is wonderful.

EMILY VOLMAN Mark's a spiritual person. Now, what religion of the week? That's kind of negative, I guess, and it's not that he changes his worldview. Since I have known him, he has not been in any other religion besides Christianity. I think it's a phase thing. If he was into biking, he would be too hardcore on you at that moment. It's like when he lost all the weight. He did it initially via Nutrisystem. Anybody that would say, 'Oh, you've lost weight,' he would start selling them Nutrisystem, even though it has no financial incentive. They thought he was getting a kickback, but he just had to share it and tell you how he did it. He's that kind of person. If he's into it, he thinks everybody should know about it. And that was especially true when he was really interested in religion. It makes him sound fickle, but it's true: he's not beating anybody over the head these days with religion because he's not that into it. Not that he's lost faith, but he's not engrossed in it, he's not reading religious books.

A few years after they settled in Nashville, there were major changes on a number of fronts, beginning with Mark and Emily's relationship.

EMILY VOLMAN The one thing I don't want to do is make Mark sound bad, because I love him very much, and I wouldn't want a negative light passed on him at all. I always said I was looking forward to growing old with him, and I still feel like I'm doing that. I'm at his house all the time, and we laughingly say we co-parent a dog, so we have to see each other a lot anyway. I consider him family forever, so to be there and to take care of him has never gone off the table for me. I met him when I was, gosh, twenty, and when we got together he was very active. He was gone almost every weekend and busy with school during the week. That left me open to whatever I wanted to pursue, and then we'd just do stuff together, and it felt very partner-like.

When we moved to Nashville, his schedule changed. He would go out for the summer and then be home for the rest of the year. Even though he was teaching, as soon as he started to be home, he wanted me there as well. But I was kind of hitting my stride in my thirties. I had opened up a comedy place, and then I got a production deal for writing, so I was going to Los Angeles a lot. Mark didn't like that, and it was impacting our marriage. It was frustrating, because it was all starting to take off, and this was exactly what I wanted to do. I was excited but Mark was not. He wanted me to be home a lot more.

We went to counseling, and the biggest issue that became apparent was our age difference. Finally, it reared its ugly head, because our pastor who had done our premarital counseling had told us, 'This is going to come up. It's just a matter of when.' And we said, 'Okay, that's fine. Whenever it does, we'll deal with it.' And it really came up that age was a big difference now. It wasn't back when I was in my mid-twenties and he was in his early fifties, but now he was sixty-plus and I was thirtysomething.

When I hit forty, I ended up taking a Master of Arts in professional counseling on a program with a mental health specialty. I learned a lot about myself, too. That's part of the program, because obviously if you're telling other people to get into therapy, they want you to have done your own work around that, so you better have worked that out already. By then, I was the age Mark was when he did all his changing. He started school at that age. I said, 'Don't you see the parallels?' and he was like, 'Nah, that's different.' So I started to be resentful of the relationship. I mean, in a lot of ways not, but in certain ways definitely. It was really hard, and marriage counseling wasn't working. As far as making clear where the issues were, in that way it was working, although I'm not sure Mark even saw that. Maybe it was working for me, and maybe it was working for our therapist, but not for Mark. We would leave the sessions with him going, 'I don't understand the problem.' And that's true—he just didn't see it.

In August 2015, Mark was diagnosed with cancer, both throat and partial tongue. He went through forty-one chemotherapy sessions and forty-six radiation treatments. There was also esophagus surgery to help him swallow. The first surgery was unsuccessful and had to be repeated in 2016. Through it all, he never missed a show.

The various treatments took a while. It was about two years that I was going through stuff, and it was a pretty miserable time.

EMILY VOLMAN We started talking about separating early in 2015, and I moved out in May of that year. And then, in August, he was diagnosed with cancer. On the way home from the doctor, Mark said, 'Can we *not* get divorced right now?' And I said, 'Of course. Let's not do this right now.' And so, even though we were living separately, we postponed the divorce. We talked to the attorneys, and said, 'Just postpone this until . . . I don't know when. No date specified.'

And then we flew Pat in, because I now had a house in a different place and I was going to school up there, so it was impossible for me to be around. I couldn't do it all. So, once Mark started chemo and radiation, we asked Pat, 'Can you please come and live with Mark and be his caretaker?' He really needed to have someone around 24/7, and not because he was physically incapacitated. Mark grew up a rock star from the age of seventeen. His entire adult life has been a catered-to lifestyle. He's used to just yelling and someone jumping, so for him to be going through such a stressful experience alone wasn't going to work at all. He needed someone there. And so, reluctantly, Pat agreed. Not because of Mark and not because of the job. She hadn't flown for decades and was really afraid of flying. Sarina and Hallie got onboard and were like, 'Mom, just go. Take care of Dad. You need to do this.' So, she agreed, and she moved in upstairs and stayed about three months. I was still there a lot, just not overnight.

So, now we've got two ex-wives looking after him. Pat and I both knew him really well, and we're trying to make this go as smoothly as possible and not let him be anxious. Because when he gets anxious, that's when he physically goes downhill, very quickly. And so we made that happen. We're all extremely grateful for Pat doing this, to put her life on hold and come out here.

20

HOWARD

SUSAN COWSILL Mark told us about the cancer, and then he came back out after recovering. That was the year that Howard fell, and Howard was completely beside himself, because he wanted to be there for his pal. He wanted to carry the weight that summer: 'I am here for my guy.' And then less than a week in, Howard's bag got caught on the handle on the way down the steps of the bus. He slipped, his Achilles went out, and it became the summer of Howard in the wheelchair. He was just heartbroken, and he would not leave. We asked the doctor how long it could stay in the state it was in before surgery, and they said two weeks, so my brother Paul and I hopped on being Howard's medics. We were icing Howard morning, afternoon, and evening to keep his ankle in an optimal state, because he was not going to leave this tour, period. So, he went and got his surgery and came back. And it was rough. He was heartbroken, because all he wanted to do was step up for Mark.

It happened in upstate New York, in Tarrytown. The buses can be dangerous, and there are a lot of ways that things can go wrong: a computer or iPad or anything you might be carrying. You could find a million reasons why just about anybody could have fallen, but Howard was always having problems with his legs, and the buses have really high steps. When he fell, he knew he had injured himself, but he finished the show and we got him a brace, which he had to wear until he met with a doctor, and they told him he was going to have to have surgery, so then it was a matter of whether or not he would be able to do the shows, all that kind of stuff. He did complete the tour, but by the time we got him to the doctor, they said he wasn't going to be able to go on much longer.

I sat down with everybody and asked if they would feel comfortable with me doing it on my own, because there wasn't really any other choice. We could sit back and say we're going to wait for Howard, but that wasn't possible, because he wasn't coming back—at least not anytime soon. I had done other dates without Howard in the past when he couldn't be there for various reasons, so I was never really worried about me. I wanted to make sure that the crowd would enjoy it, and that was really the key.

RON DANTE Traveling back and forth to the hotels, the gigs, singing every night, sometimes four and five nights in a row, I got the feeling that Howard might not want to do the tour again. All through the summer he kept mentioning that his back hurt and his energy was lagging, so I figured he might not come back, but then I got the call. In January of '18, Mark asked if I would be interested. I was surprised, but I knew that I could. I have basically the same range as Howard, and some of my songs sound like Turtles songs. 'Tracy' from my Cufflinks days is really a homage to The Turtles, because I did all kinds of background parts the way they would have done it. So, I went from the opener of the show to the closer.

SUSAN COWSILL Mr. Dante is adorable, and we love Ron, but as lovely as he is, that wouldn't make the show work. He could be as nice as he wants, but if he can't sing, that's not going to cover it. Fortunately, Ron is a consummate professional vocalist. He can sing anything. But when we first heard about it, I'm not going to lie, we all went, 'Wait a minute . . . you're having Ron being Howard?' But that's because you're thinking of Howard's personality. It's like he's Reggie, the big bully in *Archie* comics, and Archie is going to replace Reggie as lead singer? Howard is tough. And you're bringing out the frickin' Good Humor ice-cream boy to play the part of our villain? It's hysterical! You're thinking the audience is going to freak out when they're not being told to shut up and sit down—and, not only that, they're probably going to be offered a seat by the nicest boy on the planet. So, the irony ain't lost. But it was only for that ironic moment.

With Ron, everything about it pointed in that direction. He was perfect. It's hard to describe, but there's a feeling of continuity that was just there. We're pretty close in the timbre of our voices, and I never really thought a second about it. Howard was fine. We agreed if we can't do it, we won't. We'll stop. But Ron came in, and it just didn't have any problems.

EMILY VOLMAN If Howard can't be there, Ron is perfect. Show-wise, it was great, and people really liked it. It gave Mark room to feel he was contributing more to the show. And that's not to take anything away from when Howard was there—I mean, that's The Turtles, no doubt—but Ron let Mark be the leader for the first time ever in that dynamic, in the show dynamic. I think it was a little frightening for Mark. He was anxious about being able to handle that position. But as soon as he realized he could do that—that he was capable and actually maybe even good at it—he got into a groove and started building confidence, and by the end of the tour he was talking about doing a one-man show. So that gave him some confidence that I'm not sure he ever had.

SUSAN COWSILL The first couple of nights, we had to push Mark onto the stage. He's trotting out there like Snoopy on his tiptoes: *Go! Go now! You can't wait any longer!* They'd finish the song and not know how to do the shtick. Mark would go, 'So anyway . . .' and Dante's just sitting there. It was hysterical, because you can see them working through that. They didn't want to be fake. The whole idea was to sing Turtles music but not try and *be* Howard, not try to make their dynamic happen with somebody else. It was so cute, because they were tripping over each other trying to figure out what they were doing. Well, who doesn't want to see that? That's fun. And boy, by the end of the summer, it was Martin & Lewis. They were sauntering and dashing and had it under their belts. It just became cute and cuter.

RON DANTE Mark's goofing off, patting my head, caressing my cheek, and it's all off the top of his head. He's making it up as he goes along. I never know what he's going to do, and it's a joy to be in that. He's kibitzing with the audience, and they just roar with laughter.

SUSAN COWSILL And when they open their mouths? Perfect! Beautiful! And Mark absolutely shining on vocally. He's being challenged to sing more and head it up. He can't just sing back and have a good time. He had to be *on*, and that was different for him, and he totally rose to that occasion. A total pro, *and* he had me in tears the first night. He's singing 'You Showed Me,' and he was amazing. He made me cry.

EMILY VOLMAN The difference between Ron and Howard is that Ron has a huge amount of respect for Mark, and, with Howard, I don't think he'd ever say that unless he said it in a joking way. That's just their dynamic. Here's the thing: you know when you go back home to visit your parents and they treat you like the little kid you've always been? Like, certain dynamics just don't let people grow up? It's ingrained. You become that person again when you see them. You always are and you even feel like it again. And maybe you're a little resentful. They've made a million movies about that. People go home for the holidays and they're treated like a little kid and they don't like it, et cetera, et cetera. Those two have been friends since they were kids, and it's really hard to get beyond that, to move into adulthood and change. And the way Mark came into the band was not as a leader. And so, does he ever get to be the leader? I think that's what they're trying to figure out. It's a change, and they're trying to figure it out in their seventies. And it does seem to be working. I was surprised. I've spoken to Howard, but it's typically been business-y stuff. I spoke to his wife Michelle, and he actually has liked staying at home. And of course, for his health, he needs to do that, too. I mean, he was really in a lot of pain.

RON DANTE Howard was very generous about my coming in. Every once in a while, I'll hear from him asking how's it going, and when I started, he sent an email, saying, 'Can a fella thank you enough for doing this for me?' He appreciated the fact that I honor the songs, their legacy. I don't deviate. And that's the most important thing I can bring, to do them as close to possible to the original records. And no fudging—no lowering the key so that I can sing it. I'm doing the same keys and the same arrangements.

Howard was very supportive of my first tour with the group, when he was still singing lead, and he was very supportive of me doing subsequent tours. He's got a big heart. He's very smart and he's very sensitive, and I learned a lot that first tour from him.

SUSAN COWSILL I text with Howard once or twice a week, and he's like a fifteen-year-old girl on text—he *loves* to text. I can't predict the future, but Howard is on board with Ron, and I could see him saying, 'Look, I'm good. Y'all are good. Are we good?' I hope he comes back, not because I don't love Dante, and of course he could stay with us, but because I miss him, and because there is a certain tangible reality that occurs when those two hit the stage. But it is absolutely not missed. Nobody—no audience member—is getting short shrift on this tour, that's for sure. Unless you were hoping to have Howard tell you to shut the fuck up and sit down. If you're that type, then you're missing something.

FELIX CAVALIERE I'm not sure that The Turtles were ever a band. What I remember of The Turtles is what we see now, which is a duo; a singing duo.

CHUCK NEGRON Mark and Howard acknowledged and embraced the fact that they needed one another, and they liked one another. That doesn't last long with most relationships in showbusiness, because inevitably one guy wants more or thinks he should be getting more. When Howard had a hit, Mark could have gone cuckoo. But they came together and realized, *Hang on, you're going to have the lead, and I'm going to do the high parts,* and they accepted who was best at what, and they were friends. But take a band like Three Dog Night. These guys almost hated anyone else's success but their own. Even within the group.

HARRY SHEARER The first time I met Michael McKean, we just talked about the records that we each had growing up and realized with delighted shock that we were probably the only two people in our—forget zip codes, in our entire states who had the same strange records growing up. And you don't run into that all that often. So, when you find that not only do you have those things in common, but that you work well together, you sort of spark each other on both the comedy and the music level, you tend to want to hang onto those relationships. Because life doesn't deal that many of them. The shorthand, the references, and also—I don't know about Mark and Howard, but in my situation, none of us, the guys that I work with, has enough functioning memory to remember everything that we've been through. So, the other guys are like part of the institutional memory. It's like, *Oh yeah, that's where we were that night.* And that becomes more important as time goes on. *What was that? What was that gig? Who was that person? What was that company?*

FELIX CAVALIERE I did not have the good fortune of having a partner that stuck with me. My partner went a little south on me, and that makes a huge difference. Our team didn't function together like their team did, and we can only blame ourselves. We would have had our catalogue. We would have had our lives together if that had happened, but it didn't. So, I really respect Mark and Howard for that. That's another accolade: the people who were able to do that, that speaks for itself. That's very, very, cool. They're very fortunate.

JEFF SIMMONS It's hard to separate the two of them, because they were like a modern day Martin & Lewis. Obviously Mark can sing a little better than Jerry Lewis, but he's just as funny.

LESLIE WEST They're like Frick and Frack.

GARY ROWLES Mark was the clown, of course, because he was big and round and had that wonderful hair and that shining face. When he smiled, wow, the whole room lit up. Kaylan was kind of dark, morose; everything with him was a little bit sarcastic. He's a curmudgeon. And the two of them together were great, because they were like Mutt and Jeff.

BOB TRUAX They were perfect together. I never saw any arguing. Howard was always the one that would get upset, but Mark seemed to control it. Whether Howard agreed or disagreed, Mark seemed to say what was going on. He was like the rock: I don't think I ever saw him upset. Howard had his comments, but it always worked out after Mark talked with him. He was wonderful as far as all that goes.

HARVEY KUBERNIK Most partnerships break up or have volatile endings. This partnership is at half a century and going strong. Something is different here. They're both students of the game, and rock'n'roll lifers. But they're not like each other; they are different people. Mark is quite different than Howard, and maybe that's what's good about it.

IAN UNDERWOOD They are *completely* different people. Clearly, they're very different personalities, and at the same time, that's the great thing about how they are onstage. Because it's not just two peas in a pod, it's these two different personalities that can both work together and really create something very unusual.

KEN BARNES In my interactions with them as a team, when we were doing the *Blind Date* reviews, it certainly wasn't one dominating over the other. It was impossible to attribute them separately. I don't have a real idea of who spoke more. They were both right there with the humor, and they played off each other as you'd expect with guys who've been together for more than ten years.

ERIK SCOTT When it came to something new, Mark would come in and announce, for example, that the band's going to go to Australia, and he's all excited like a little kid bouncing around: 'We're going to have so much fun!' and Howard already knows he hates it. That was the dynamic, constantly. Off days as well as on, they played off of each other. I guess they're always onstage that little bit.

PAT VOLMAN It's like they were married to each other. It was for better or worse. You take the good and the bad, and work through it. I mean, could you imagine being married to somebody for fifty years? Well, it does happen. They need each other. But Howard has had five wives! Oh, he's been busy. Busy, busy.

He used to be such a handful, personality-wise, but I've seen him change. He used to be really, really, really—and this is not very nice of me to say—moody. Everything, up/down, up/down. When you'd walk into the room, you could tell if he was in a bad mood or not. But he's changed a lot. He grew up. It took him a long time, but he grew up.

JOHN SEITER In some ways, Howard held Mark back. We all felt that. That until he had his own professorship and his own life and his own world that had nothing to do with being second banana, he was always Ed McMahon, and that's the way it was.

JIM TUCKER I don't think Mark and Howard like each other anymore. They still work together because that's all they've got. Howard has never had a job besides that. Well, Mark's got teaching. But he and Howard don't even get along. He'll send Howard the plane tickets, tell him where to be and when to be. Howard shows up, they do their deal. *Phwwt*, gone.

After all these years, we're still able to talk without fighting. I think it's because we just listen to each other. Neither of us wants to stop. We both know that we have a good thing going on. We just talk about whatever is happening, make a decision, and then do it.

DONNIE KISSELBACH It's amazing. Their personalities are as different as their look, and it's just perfect. It's fraught with all the fragilities of a marriage, and it's imperfect, but at the same time, they're the perfect yin and yang, the perfect opposite poles. They feed off each other, and it makes it very interesting. They both know that they're lucky to have each other, to have had this career. When you have a team like that, there's got to be many points over the decades where you just go, 'Fuck it, I don't need that guy. I'm going to go do this alone.' And that never works. People don't want the one guy. You're not the whole reason. You're just a part of the reason.

BILLY CIOFFE If you were going to have the model of a rock'n'roll business association, that's the one, right there. And the reason why is that they don't live each other's lives. They are two very different people, but at the same time they are intensely loyal to each other. They don't make decisions without consulting each other, and there's another thing about Mark: he's way more stable. Howard's been married a bunch of times. Mark was married for twenty-eight years or something like that. He's much more conservative in his own way, personality-wise. He's very erudite and thinks about things other than rock'n'roll records.

CORKY LAING I don't know how Howard and Mark get along in private, but I've walked in backstage and they always seemed to be like brothers. It's very civilized, very polite, and there's absolutely no awkwardness. And the fact they've stayed together, that's incredible. I remember when Leslie and Felix had their problems in Mountain. I'm saying, 'Can't we just treat this like a business?' But Felix had to announce that the band was breaking up. And the thing with Felix and Eddie in The Rascals was so awkward, it's silly. You'd think after twenty or thirty years you'd get over it. It's an ego thing. Look at the Grateful Dead: they broke up fifteen times over the years, but they didn't tell anyone, and they kept the business together. They kept it going. But I was out in California with Journey and Cheap Trick, and they all had their soap operas, too. The things that come in first are the ladies—the partners, the spouses. They push. They push hard because they want the best for their people. If you point a finger, probably eighty percent of the problems come from the families. That and drugs. It's Spinal Tap. Even The Beatles went through it. It's too bad, but it's a reality.

HAROLD BRONSON When I spent time with them, I was always impressed with how well they worked together, and it was a good model for myself and my partner Richard with Rhino. We're not the same as those guys, and our relationship was different, obviously, but the fact that they had this partnership, how they worked and did business and created with each other. They were good role models, that you can have a successful relationship of a long duration in a business like this. How they related to each other and did their business through the years, that was a good thing for me to see.

KEN BARNES Sticking together and keeping the rights to The Turtles name has proved a wise decision for many summers. Would you want to go see *The Flo Show*? Or *The Eddie Band*?

PAT VOLMAN Oh, I don't know. I'd probably go and see Mark.

HOWARD KAYLAN Of the bands currently on the road from our generation, not a lot of people even have one member. We're very lucky that we've been able to be very smart about our friendship/business relationship. And I think that's what's kept us afloat. I remember my jaw hitting the ground when I learned that Emerson, Lake & Palmer were coming to their shows in three separate limos, because they just couldn't stand each other. How hard could it be, guys? A million dollars a night! All you have to do is put up with each other long enough to get to the show, to do the show, to leave the show, and lock your door. You can't be friends with each other long enough to do that?

And then you think even farther back than that, to Don and Phil Everly. What? What do you mean you don't like each other anymore? What do you mean, you don't want to do any more shows? That's just stupid. You can't be in the same car with him? He's your brother, for God's sake. How about Ray and Dave Davies? What do you mean you don't want to be The Kinks? It's absolutely fucking insane. And the fact that Simon & Garfunkel won't work together nine times out of ten, because they don't think they *need* each other, or Paul's attitude, or Art's attitude, or whatever it is. To me, it's incredibly stupid. If you hate the guy, if you love the guy, it doesn't matter. I would ride in the same car as Al Nichol. What do I care? I'm just going from point A to point B. I don't have to love the guy. I've been married five times. I know what futile love feels like.

INSECURITY

JULIE SCHAD Mark was always confident, but he did tell me he never considered himself 'smart,' and that Howard was the smart one. I think he surprised himself, but it didn't surprise me. I saw him run the business end of The Turtles. I never saw Howard run the business end of The Turtles. I saw how he planned, and he's a great businessman. He was talented, ambitious.

EMILY VOLMAN I only know it from Mark's side, but my theory is this. Mark joined the band as an afterthought in high school, and from the very beginning he was not treated as an equal. In the sense of musicianship or any kind of talent, he—knowing from his stories—was just a goofball who wanted to hang out and do fun things. And Howard is really good at being condescending. He's always smarter than everyone else. He definitely can make you feel like shit, and over the years he's done a really good job at putting Mark in that place. What I see at home, what I see at his school, what I see of Mark at every other place is different, but the minute he's around Howard, he turns into this kind of bumbling idiot, and the butt of all the jokes. He takes that on, and that's not him. And partially because of that, Mark has pursued his own interests, to be a success on his own terms.

I don't think he feels like being in The Turtles was something he succeeded at—which he did, obviously. He felt he was just lucky to be in the band, so he constantly has to prove himself. Nobody else feels that. Everyone that meets him is amazed at all he's done and accomplished, including being a teacher. But for some reason, he doesn't take ownership in any of that. And that's where their dynamic comes from. Howard *is* a smart guy. He didn't go to college, but he is self-educated, and he knows a lot of things, and—honestly—so does

Mark. He's amazing. And yet, it's that dynamic where Howard is just better than Mark. And no matter what, Mark can't keep up, so I'm sure the class clown versus valedictorian dynamic was part of his inspiration for wanting to go the academic route. Mark is the only one with an issue, because Howard is more secure. He probably worked harder, and Mark *was* a slacker in high school. But Mark has made up for that tenfold. The dynamic now is that Mark works his ass off and Howard is still smoking pot. Smoking pot and watching TV seems to take a lot of time for him, so they've actually reversed in a lot of ways, and, if you were to be very truthful, that probably makes Mark feel good.

TIM SEXTON Howie had intellectual horsepower, and he played that. That was his differentiator, and it worked on Mark. But Howard's a good spirit, too. He was not a user. And I don't mean user of drugs but user of people. Howard wasn't that kind of guy.

SARINA VOLMAN Dad always felt a bit in awe of Howard. Even though he didn't say anything, I could tell there was a bit of an insecurity complex. But he's a very smart man. It's learning through life and the business. It's him taking what happened with The Turtles, and then starting Flo & Eddie, just everything. He's a very smart man, and he still runs the show. He's still the one who handles everything, and he's always done that.

PHILIP AUSTIN Mark is a talker, and I talk for a living. We've always got on with each other, and we do to this day. And Howard is a soulful person whom I've always liked a lot. One of the best things about them is that they get along. I find in my own work that my good relations with my partners at this stage in our lives are increasingly dear to me, if for no other reason than it's so rare in the entertainment business. Burnt bridges are generally a way of life among all of us, and it's fun to see that there are some other idiots like us in it.

PETER NOONE It's not being married when you're in a band. You don't have to be married to the people. They all make this terrible mistake of hanging out with each other. I don't hang around with the Hermits. They're not my type of people, but they're my type of musicians. You put a band together based on how good they are musically, not how good you get along, and I think that's how Mark and Howard survived it. They probably did hang out at the beginning, but over the years, they've grown. One lives in one town and one lives in another. They're not having dinner together five nights a week. That's how we do it.

HARRY SHEARER I don't want to make too draconian a comparison, but you hear of kids who've been through battle together, and how that is a bonding experience that lasts for the rest of their lives. Well, the music business and showbusiness is an unending battle. And to have the same scars, and the same war stories, and be survivors of that, and come out on the other side and still be standing and have most of your limbs, is a very strong experience.

PAT VOLMAN Mark runs everything. On show days, he gets there early and makes sure things are together, and Howard goes to the hotel. He's been doing that for years. He sets up the flights, the hotels, the per diems, and all that stuff. That happened partly out of necessity, because of all the bad managers, but he likes to do it. He's like a camp leader: he's got to be in charge, and it makes him feel better if he knows he did it. And he manages to do it without making enemies. How do you like that?

EMILY VOLMAN Ultimately, in any kind of relationship, someone's got to give, and I think Mark has always been the one who gives in. In general, Mark is not a confrontational type kind of person. He will be if it's a promoter or something over money—over money, he will happily confront you and take you down—but in reality, he really doesn't want to fight. He doesn't want to fight with me, he doesn't want to fight with Howard, he doesn't want to fight with his ex-wife if something like that comes up. He just doesn't want to deal. He's really great at just not dealing. And that's what's kept them together. It's so much easier. If Howard doesn't like something, Mark just says, 'Okay, you don't have to do it.' Howard has the final say, but at the same time, Mark has control of everything else, all the daily stuff: the micromanaging. And Howard has faith in him that he can do that. And that's what blows my mind, because here Mark has this big hang-up with what Howard thinks of him, yet Howard has given him everything. He's placed it all in Mark's hands. So . . . it's not to be understood.

21

VAUDEVILLE

The comedic dynamic Mark and Howard employed throughout their career—the straight man and the stooge—has roots stretching back long before rock'n'roll. More than a century ago, comedy duos were favorites in music halls and on vaudeville stages across the globe. As technology advanced, they moved to radio, film, night clubs, and television. Almost forgotten, the once popular shtick is rarely seen today.

JIM BESSMAN No one knows popular culture—be it music or television or film—like Mark and Howard. Those guys, they're both geniuses. They are two of the most intelligent people that I've ever been around. It's dizzying when you're around them. It's just so brilliant, so quick, and so fast.

HOWARD KAYLAN Even before we hit, The Smothers Brothers had sort of taken everything that we were thinking about doing with our band, and almost turned it into the identical sort of act, but in the folk genre. But getting to hang out with those guys later on, there were an awful lot of similarities between us and The Smothers Brothers. And they took a lot of credit in 1967 for 'discovering' us. Which I love—*I love*—because they were incredibly hot at the time, and on their show's first season, we did two appearances. The first time we went on, they said, 'Here they are, we just discovered these guys.' The song was already something like #39 on the charts. Two weeks later, it was #1, and they asked us back.

PETER NOONE It was good to run into an American band who kind of got the plot—that it was actually showbusiness. Some people just want other musicians to like them. Well, that's no good. That won't get you anything. That's like being a journalist for all the other journalists, and nobody reads you. But he made a great choice—to have the audience like them. That was my choice as well. I think Mark made a great choice.

ALICE COOPER That was the connection: not taking ourselves so seriously, but when you got onstage, certainly taking the show seriously. When I go onstage as Alice Cooper, to this day, my show is still vaudeville. Now, Flo & Eddie, they would fit right in. They would be the guys who do comedy; the two comedy shtick guys. I didn't want to do a press conference without them. They were so much fun to play off of. Because we had the same exact sense of humor, I could go in there, feed him a line, he would throw it back. I knew exactly what they were going to say. In other words, we were pretty much the Three Stooges when it came to our shtick. And a lot of times we'd get done with the press conference and go, 'I would say six people got 10 percent of that.' Some of it was pretty random. A lot of it was references to *Leave It To Beaver* and all these 50s shows that we lived on, 60s shows that all of us liked. We'd sit there and go, 'Who was the secretary on *77 Sunset Strip*?' 'Jacqueline Beer.' 'What was her name?' 'Frenchy.' It was great stuff.

HAL WILLNER I got to witness all this as a kid. I got to see the last period of a lot of these people, but they were *in it*. They were on *The Hollywood Palace* with Jimmy Durante introducing them: 'We got elephants, now we got The Turtles.' They were right in the midst of that. And it's like the Holocaust survivors: we'd better treat them with respect and be around them now. It's a dying breed, people that were in the middle of that transition of showbusiness to rock'n'roll. The young generation has the same sort of reference points, coming up on *The Simpsons* or whatever, but they don't seem to incorporate it into their work. They don't use it. You don't see *South Park* in Green Day's music. And you did see whoever—Louis Prima—in the Flo & Eddie show. Or Alice Cooper. Or even David Bowie. The Beatles are a big example of that. People tend to forget how showbiz-oriented they were, but their producer produced *The Goon Show* before them.

RAY MANZAREK There you go: Martin & Lewis, Louis Prima. It's a fast-paced patter—they always had patter, and that's who they are. They were twisted. They're Soupy Sales.

HARRY SHEARER If you were a two-man team, Martin & Lewis was one of your models. That was one of the major touchstones of any two-man act at that point in time. We all grew up either in reaction to, or in aspirations, to be them. It certainly wasn't Sandler & Young.

JACKIE MARTLING If there's two guys acting like idiots, it doesn't work. It's like the under-sung Bud Abbott—look how boring he was. Bud Abbott was Bud Abbott so Lou Costello would look like Lou Costello. Lou looks easy, but without Bud, Lou's not funny. It's when you get a magical combination, and those guys have that chemistry. They're like Sonny & Cher: Cher would be so bored, and Sonny would be having the time of his life, and it's just . . . if it works it works, you don't question it.

TIM REID I would say more Abbott & Costello. Flo is the bumbling cute fool, and Howard is the guy who's got to keep him in line. And it was the same thing from the very beginning of their career, how The Turtles were doing this all-instrumental band, and Flo kept showing up trying to join, but he didn't play an instrument.

HARVEY KUBERNIK Onstage, Mark's role is the facilitator. He's everything from master of ceremonies to class clown. In a weird way—a weird good way— Mark is the bandleader only because he has such a visual component. He's such a funny part of the show. When you look at the buffoonery around The Turtles, Howard is singing his guts out. It's a real strain for him to enunciate those words so perfectly. Mark didn't have that responsibility. Mark had his own responsibility to keep the band going, play the tambourine, do something funny, distraction, put some horns behind Howard on camera . . . that was funny, wacky energy. That was the Spike Jones component, and it lightened the seriousness of Howard singing these songs.

LARRY ZINN Mark was in charge. He was the bandleader, he would make up the set list, and he was also the clown of the band. Howard was the lead singer. Mark sang well enough, but he was the comic relief. Howard was always a straight man. It's an Allen & Rossi, a Martin & Lewis . . . you think about the great comedy teams, and that was Mark and Howard.

DANNY HUTTON They have that dynamic of all the great comedy teams. Mark is so gregarious, and Howard works off of that. He's intelligent. He knows how to bat the ball or catch it when it's thrown at him. It would never work if Howard tried to get the laughs. It would blow it if we had two funny men out there.

HOWARD KAYLAN Our shows are totally vaudeville. But to make it work, it's like *good cop, bad cop.* If Mark is the guy over on stage right who is twirling tambourines, who is bouncing around, who is being the buffoon doing the introductions, who's got the *I don't even know why I'm here* kind of attitude, then I've got to be the one who stands there, non-reactive. If I react to him, it ruins everything. I'm Dean Martin. It's Martin & Lewis. It has to come back to that. If it's not a clown and a straight man, two people onstage don't work.

PHILIP AUSTIN I always thought of them as being in the Zappa world at heart. Smart people doing material that the world thought of as dumb. In their case, pop, goodtime music. In Zappa's, that kind of doo-wop fifties soul stuff. They're in the tradition of tongue-in-cheek satirists. They're not so much making fun of the songs they sing as they are the business they're in.

KEN BARNES Vaudeville is probably what gave them that early ability to look at both the rock scene and the 60s scene in general with a bit of a jaundiced or at least comedic eye. That's where you get things like 'Elenore' and *Battle Of The Bands,* and that's why they were a natural fit with Zappa, although I've always found Zappa's approach a little more corrosive. But you can still see how they would fit easily. Did Turtles fans understand the humor? Probably not. They probably came to hear the hits. By the 70s, audiences understood more. If you made the commitment to see Flo & Eddie, certainly in L.A., everybody knew what their intent was.

DON PRESTON I hope they forgive me, but I always found them totally funny and hilarious all the time, *except* when they were trying to be funny. That was usually on a radio show or some other place where they were under a lot of pressure to be funny, and they somehow got the notion that they had to try to *be* funny. And of course, any time you try to be funny, you are not funny. And it wasn't actually that they weren't funny, it just they got a little bit broader than what I cared for.

CORKY LAING They have a total handle on what it means to entertain. When you saw them on TV, they were real characters. For instance, 'Happy Together'—there was a character that went with the song. You have Mark clowning around and it was beyond the song, and you can't make that up, that was serendipitous. Anybody could have recorded the song and it would have been a hit, but it became a classic because of them.

MARK PARENTEAU Mark's ability to be a clown is really what first caught my eye when I saw them on TV. So many bands were intimidated by the TV camera, but Volman embraced it. For him it was just another prop, another thing to make goony eyes at. So that sense of vaudeville was there from the beginning.

RICK CARR Mark comes off so personable onstage. I saw them in Milwaukee, and if you live in Wisconsin, there are a lot of towns that have Indian names, like Oconomowoc, and Mark was doing the opening to the show backstage with the microphone. He says, 'Live from a two-week engagement at the Holiday Inn in O-con-o-mo-woc . . .' and he couldn't pronounce the word. At that point he was laughing, and the audience was having a riot with him trying to say these Wisconsin names. So, he knows how to work an audience and make them love him before they even see him.

When the show's the thing, the line between entertainer and real-life can blur.

EMILY VOLMAN Howard's more dramatic, but Mark can be a complete liar. Mark is as good at storytelling as Howard could ever be. It's about the show. It always comes down to the show first and foremost. I have been in situations where Mark will tell the story later and I don't even remember what he is talking about. It didn't even happen. But it was a better story. It was a much better story, and people really get into that. We don't really talk about it, but that's a little bane in our marriage. Because it's fine for other people, but when you are married to someone who is a great storyteller, that's not something you want out of your relationship. If you are able to just make it up as you go, we're going to have some problems.

BEGINNINGS
PART TWO

SUSAN VOLMAN My grandfather left the Ukraine, as so many of the European Jews did, around 1905 or 1907, to avoid being drafted. He snuck away and went across the Black Sea and ended up in Hungary, where he met my grandmother. They came to United States on a freighter, or a cattle boat, and their port of entry was in Galveston. That's where my Aunt Sherri was born. They stopped in L.A. because they both had relatives there. They were actually on their way to San Francisco, but they stopped to visit relatives and ended up staying there. Grandfather was a tailor; he was a jacket maker and had his own shop. During the Depression he didn't have as much work, as many people didn't. When they started gearing up for the war, he went back to work, something about needing uniforms. By the time I knew them, in the 50s, he wasn't working. He would have been pretty old by then.

MADELINE CAMPILLO Grandma entered the United States before 1917, so therefore she was considered a citizen. Maria Saenz was her maiden name, and she was from Chihuahua, Mexico. She was a college graduate from the university in Chihuahua, which—in those days, anyway—was unusual for a girl.

Fernando Campillo was American born but his family roots are from the Sonora area of Mexico, on the west coast. They kind of lived on either side of the border in those days, and that's how he met Maria down in Chihuahua. He was the treasurer for the Mexican army under Carranza, which was the same side that Pancho Villa was on. Apparently, Pancho liked him, so when they got married in Chihuahua, Pancho stopped in at the wedding. According to her, he just about ruined the whole reception. The minute he arrived, the music stopped, and all the guests pulled back against the wall so they wouldn't be noticed. I guess he could have a terrific temper, and the whole thing came to a halt—everything stopped. He said, 'My good friend should never get married without my coming to wish him well.' It was like suspended animation. He only stayed for a half-hour, and when he left, the party started again.

LINDA CAMPILLO Our grandfather was a very colorful figure. He worked on a gambling ship called the *Rex*, off the five-mile limit in the late 1930s, before gambling was legal. That was a big thing in Southern California. He was a croupier. Before that he was involved in starting the Agua Caliente gambling resort down in Tijuana. It was this whole gambling area across the border in Mexico. That was the precursor to Las Vegas, and then, when Las Vegas came up, he knew all the guys that were involved in establishing that. So, the stories I've heard, from more than one aunt, they all remembered their father bringing people over to their house, and then Grandma would see later, in the paper, that they were gangsters. They were all involved in the gambling industry. But he wasn't a major player. There were times where they would have lots of money and times where they would be dead broke, but it was never like they lived a very luxurious lifestyle. In fact, he was a barber by trade. I never knew him because he passed away before I was born, but he was the love of her life. She never said anything discouraging about him. But she was like that: she didn't like gossip or bad-mouthing people. She was very sweet about everything, and she was a very intelligent woman. Even though our grandfather was a strong traditional male of a Latino household, Grandma actually got a lot of things accomplished by making him think it was his idea. According to my aunts, he ruled the roost, but they could see her strength, too, and they must have gotten that from her. All the women in our family are very strong-willed. We have a very matriarchal family.

ANN BECKER Mark's mother was my sister. There were seven of us—four girls and three boys—and his mother was the oldest girl. I was the youngest, so we were probably about fourteen years apart. I was born and raised in Los Angeles and lived there until I married. We were all pretty much in the L.A. area. Mark's father's family was Orthodox Jew, and we had always been Catholics. They married in the 30s, when you just didn't do that sort of thing. I was probably ten or eleven years old at the time, and I remember a priest coming to our house, because my sister wanted to marry a Jew. I'm sure he was going through the same thing with his family. Once they decided to marry, well, then they were married, and of course the family would never come between husband and wife. We knew one another's philosophies, and there was never any conflict in that regard.

We always got together. We would go to my brother-in-law's home on the high holidays, and then they would come to our house and celebrate Christmas. He would even go to church with us sometimes. When you look back at it now, it really was a wonderful situation, because both families had been so—I hate to say this—but almost dogmatic in their religious beliefs. And then there was a little bit more understanding.

LINDA CAMPILLO Joe led an interesting life. He hitchhiked across the United States during the Depression, ending up in New York and living with an older woman for a while. Not an 'older woman,' but older than him. She might have been five years older. My aunt would say, he was a gigolo when we were younger. He would have these really colorful stories about when he was hitchhiking, and the rides that he got, the people that he met.

MADELINE CAMPILLO I was married to Bea's brother, Robert Campillo. There were three brothers, and Bob was the middle one. He lived in Westchester with his mother and two unmarried sisters before I married him. Anyone that wasn't married stayed together with Grandma. They were in the same general neighborhood as Bea and Joe and the boys. As a mother-in-law, she never interfered at all. She was absolutely fantastic. After Bob and I got married, we moved to Manhattan Beach, which is not terribly far from Westchester, and his mother and the two girls bought a house there as well, about four blocks away. That whole group was pretty close. Both sisters eventually married, and then we all chipped in and helped Grandma out so she could stay in the house, and one of her youngest son's daughters came to live with her.

LINDA CAMPILLO My father Hector was the youngest of the Campillos—the youngest son—but my parents separated and kind of abandoned me when I was younger, so I was raised by our grandmother since I was three years old. Grandma babysat my other cousins, and everyone was always in and out, so even though I was an only child, I grew up in the middle of a large family. And

I saw Mark all of the time. I'm five years younger than him, and he always told me that I'm his favorite, and the cousin he knows the best.

SUSAN VOLMAN My father Dave, Mark's father Joe, and Sherri were siblings. They were all raised in L.A. My father is the youngest. Joe was his older brother, but not a lot older. Their mother was Orthodox. They kept kosher in the house and he went to Hebrew school and so forth, but his father really didn't believe it. He was taking them out for ham sandwiches and that sort of stuff, so it wasn't like something he broke from. Like a lot of families, the mother was religious, and everyone went along with it.

PHIL VOLMAN Mom and Dad were both working, and I'm nine years older than Mark, so Grandma would take him out. This is pre-school, and when he was really young, kindergarten, maybe first grade. She took care of him in the daytime, and then one of them would go by and pick him up at the end of the day. Mom would stay home for a while, and then get bored, and she'd go back to work. And then she'd come back home. So it was kind of off and on with her.

LINDA CAMPILLO We had a very close-knit family. It's kind of like *My Big Fat Greek Wedding*. They loved to get together and drink and party and dance. We would go over to Mark's house on the weekend, either Saturday or Sunday, and then over to another aunt and uncle's for dinner the other day. Mark was always the cut-up, always doing crazy things. And his dad was like that, too. Joe was our favorite uncle. We adored Uncle Joe because he was so funny and a really good storyteller. Even in his later years, he could tell stories that would have all of us crying with laughter. When we were at the Volman house, the kids hung out in this little family room where the TV was. The adults were in the living room, having their cocktails and visiting, and we were all in the family room. Uncle Joe would come in and tell us knock-knock jokes, always the same ones over and over again. Or he would come in and start reciting *The Owl And The Pussy-Cat*, because he knew that by heart and he was real dramatic when he told it.

Uncle Joe had a huge record collection. He loved to play music, and when we'd be over there, everybody would start dancing in the living room. In fact, that's how they met: Bea and Uncle Joe actually met dancing, because during the war years everybody would go to the Palladium in downtown L.A. Aunt Maggie and Uncle Elton met there, and Uncle Frank and Aunt Ida as well.

ANN BECKER We would have friends over for dinner or whatever, play records and dance, and just have a wonderful evening. Mark was probably eight years old, and he would always be dancing right in the middle of everybody, all the adults and everything. He didn't have any inhibitions in that respect. He was just doing it for the fun of it.

He would tell vivid stories, and he was a terrible tease, too. One time my husband and I had to go someplace, and his mother was taking care of our son John, who is about twelve years younger than Mark. They were sharing the bedroom, and Mark scared him so badly, telling him stories about these monsters on Hollywood Boulevard. Later, we were driving there—we didn't know this—and he's almost crying: 'I don't wanna go there! Mark said all these monsters live on Hollywood Boulevard!' So he could be a tease, but generally, he's always been a caring person, as a child and as a teenager, too. He was very sensitive, always concerned for people, never wanting to hurt their feelings. He saw it in other members of family; there was this closeness. That's the way it was in our family.

MADELINE CAMPILLO The family were our friends. We all lived in the same area, and everyone got along, except for the times they fought. But even when they fought, it was a nice friendly fight. People just got together. That's unique nowadays, but we didn't think they were terribly special at the time. My children still talk about the get-togethers. Mark's parents' house had what they called the racetrack, and the kids would be running this trail. No matter what room you were in, you would have a little bit of conversation until they came running through. But they were just playing, and that was accepted. They didn't want us around really any more than we wanted them to break into our talking. It was a very permissive household in that way. Not for breaking the rules—it was just, the kids were kids.

ANN BECKER Because of my husband's work, I was the first one that left the city, and then the family started gradually moving away. My two brothers stayed in the Los Angeles area, but one sister moved to San Diego and my two other sisters moved up here to Washington state, and then Mark's mother and father moved here to Bellevue.

All my siblings are now deceased. I'm the only one left. Looking back on my life, I was so fortunate to have such a great family. We all got along. We had our faults, no question about that. But we always got together and did things together. We had wonderful parties, both at our house and at his parents' house. We were very fortunate.

LINDA CAMPILLO When Bea and Joe moved up to Washington, I would visit them there, and the nights were filled with music. It was wonderful, getting him to play different things. He introduced me to Edith Piaf. And Bea was right there with him: 'Oh, listen to this next!'

PAT VOLMAN His parents were like my family. I loved them.

SARINA VOLMAN I loved my grandma and grandfather. We used to go over to their place all the time. Every Sunday. Everyone would be there: my cousins Ray and Mitchell, my uncle Phil, and the Campillo family were absolutely fantastic. My grandparents always had the parties. I have a picture of my father with a lampshade on his head. Grandma was an absolutely wonderful woman. All she gave off was love and happiness and joy, and she was just a fantastic woman. I absolutely loved her. My grandfather was fantastic too. He just didn't give off as much warmth as my grandmother. I guess that's true with grandparents, but they were wonderful people.

EMILY VOLMAN I met Mark's parents at graduation and saw them after that. I wasn't around his mom as much because she passed away soon after, in the summer of '97.

PHIL VOLMAN She hadn't been well for a long time. She had high blood pressure and had been taking medicine for it. I had been there that weekend, and could see Dad was concerned. That was Sunday. Monday, the next day, they called me. And then I got in touch with Mark. He was in Atlanta when she died, touring. I managed to track him down, and he got back here.

EMILY VOLMAN After that we started visiting Joe in Escondido a little bit more, because now he was alone. He started to go downhill really quick, because he had cancer. Mark's mom had known, but apparently the doctors said there wasn't much they could do, and she decided not to tell him. I think she thought she would deal with it when it came, but then she died, taking it to her grave.

PHIL VOLMAN Our father died soon after, six months to the day. They had been married sixty-three years, and when she died, he didn't really want to continue to live.

EMILY VOLMAN When she passed away, Joe was devastated. He never ever expected to outlive her, and he wanted to die, too. Then the doctors told him he had inoperable cancer, and that he had three months to live, and suddenly he turned around 180 degrees, saying not only did he not want to die but he was going to beat it. But, to the day of the doctors telling him, it was three months. It happened very quickly. We would go down there and see him as it progressed.

Joe cracked me up. He had asked for a picture of me to set by his bedside. He was pretty cognitive at the time, and I would wonder why he wanted a picture of me. But we gave it to him, and he would always say, 'Hi, Mark, where's Emily? Let me talk to her.' So, like father like son, he was just one with the ladies. In fact, a few years ago I was talking to Joe's niece's husband, and I said something about Joe being a ladies' man, because of my own memories of him always wanting to chat it up with me, and this guy started saying, 'Oh yeah, Joe had this secretary he was banging.' My mouth dropped to the floor, and I thought, *Oh dear, this is bad. Oh my gosh, I don't want to have to tell Mark.* And he kept talking about this secretary that Joe was having an affair with. I debated telling Mark, but I did eventually, and he didn't seem to care. He was like, 'Oh, interesting.' I guess it runs in the family. It made sense I guess, because, like I say: like father, like son. I think Phil has had his moments, too. They are the ladies' men, the Volman men.

PHIL VOLMAN She was eighty-three when she passed away, and Dad was eighty-six. So they lived good lives.

SARINA VOLMAN When they passed, that devastated my father.

PHIL VOLMAN Because of the difference in our ages, Mark and I weren't that close growing up. It wasn't until our mother got sick that we became close. We became really close, and we've maintained that. I was the best man at his wedding, and I felt honored that he asked me to do that. Besides being brothers, we are probably best friends. Except for my ex-wife, I'd consider him my best friend.

LINDA CAMPILLO We're all kind of spread out now, but we still have family get-togethers up in Washington. I have quite a few cousins up there: Auntie Annie lives there and so does Uncle Elton, who was Aunt Maggie's husband. We all get together for Christmas and Thanksgiving up there.

SUMMATIONS

JULIE SCHAD I think part of what makes somebody successful at reinventing themselves—especially in his case—is, he just kept moving forward. He never knew what the future would be, but he was open to the future and what it held. He came from a place where it's not so much about where you end up, it's about what you do with where you are, and the decisions and where they take you. And that's how he has lived his life. It's quite inspiring. He tells me he's finished; he's gone as high as he wants to go. But I don't think he's finished. I think the track he's on, there's more to it, and he is still on it.

JEFF 'SKUNK' BAXTER I wouldn't have a problem with just being known as a musician, and neither would Mark. He's an incredible talent. But, like him, there were other areas I was interested in, and a couple of opportunities presented themselves. I'd done some writing on missile defense, and taking advantage of certain kinds of radars to do certain things. A couple of the right people saw it, and the next thing I knew, I was working at the Pentagon. What had happened is that I had discovered something that was in its very preliminary stages, in terms of just being thought about, and so I kind of nailed it, and then I ended up working at Lawrence Livermore as well, a Laser Advisory Board on things having to do with missile defense. But I can't talk much about it.

HAROLD BRONSON It's such an inspirational story, this guy in his forties who was the class clown, goes to college and excels, and then teaches at a university level. It's a really great story, meaning you're never too old to do something like that. And I don't think we see enough messages like that.

Over the course of his cancer treatments, Mark transitioned from his position as full-time professor and chair of Entertainment Industry Studies (the department he had created at Belmont), eventually retiring in 2019.

RICHIE FURAY Mark is so real. There is no pretension there. What you see is what you get. He's a fun-loving guy yet obviously a serious man as well, and a very talented guy. I consider him a friend, even though he is not someone that I see on a daily basis. Sometimes I see him maybe once a year, but I know that if I need to call, talk over any situation or whatever, he is a friend that I can depend upon.

CHRIS HILLMAN Look what he's accomplished. My God, going back to school in his forties? Unbelievable. To do that—and they still were doing The Turtles— what an amazing guy. I hold him on a very, very high pedestal. Some of the knot-heads I've worked with? My God, they couldn't hold a candle to Mark or what he's done. So, I'm proud to know him, I really respect him. I really don't think that man has any enemies. He's a sweet man, and he's just great. He's a great guy.

CYRUS FARYAR Anytime you ran into Mark, it was a happy occasion. There's something about him, he's just immensely likeable. Their rise—Mark and Howard—was not meteoric, it was evolutionary and substantial, and they got more popular, but nothing weird happened to change them from being groovy guys. There's always been a sense of depth. As goofy as Mark has been, he's very down to earth. People were always glad to see him because he was cheerful and never took from you to enhance himself. He was always a contributor: to the party, to the conversation. He was somebody you could talk to at four in the morning when you got home from the club, and he'd be right in tune.

Some people, when you're in their company, they heavily take away from you to aggrandize themselves. And some people, when they enter a room, they bring something more than themselves. They bring lightheartedness, they bring enthusiasm, they bring an interest in *you*. They are as interested in you as they are in themselves. It's a truly simple and a remarkable equation. And it is much to be desired.

DEAN TORRENCE He's no mystery. He is who is, and he's one of my favorite guys. I don't have that many friends in the industry, but he's one of them, just because he's a good guy, very talented and very bright.

JACK UNDERWOOD I feel very fortunate that he's been in my life. Everybody should have at least one true friend like Mark. We've known each other for well over fifty years, and I wouldn't change any of moments that I had with him. They are all great memories.

PAT VOLMAN He's such a nice guy. He's only been married once before, for a *long* time, and he hasn't really pissed anybody off. It's not like there's five wives down the line, saying, 'I can't stand him.' There's nothing like that. There's no sadness. Nobody is waiting in line to slug him. We still talk. When he calls, it scares the crap out of me—excuse my French—because he's always calling to tell me, 'Did you hear who died?' When I see his number on my phone, I go, 'Okay, who died now?' And then we talk about the dogs. When he has surgery, I call him, when I have surgery, he calls me, and sometimes he comes here at Christmas and then we all get together. It's so cordial. And I love Emily. I still like him. He's a good guy. There's nothing bad. I can't say anything, even though we went our separate ways.

After growing up and spending most of their lives in Southern California, the Volman clan are now based in Tennessee. Mark, Sarina, Hallie, and both of Mark's ex-wives are again, together, happy forever.

OUTRO
BY JOHN CODY

As Mark mentions in his introduction, our model for this endeavor was *George, Being George*. The big difference between the Plimpton book and ours, of course, being that Mark is still very much alive, so he could offer comments where needed.

For every quote that's included, there were far, far more left out. Many interviews were multi-part and frequently extended into hours. Everyone has strong feelings when it comes to Mark. All told, I conducted well over two hundred interviews. Contradictory statements appear throughout, as should be expected with this many individuals recalling events, many occurring more than a half-century before. It's not a bug, it's a feature. Witnesses offering conflicting accounts? Chock it up to the Rashomon effect.

This is a man who has run the gamut from being jailed for public obscenity to leading church youth groups. If there was an issue, it was the almost complete lack of negative comments. There are a few, along with the occasional beef—and some rare bad blood—but for the most part, Mark simply has no enemies. If George Plimpton was referred to the as the best-loved man in New York, it's quite possible Mark Volman is the best-loved man in rock'n'roll.

There are so many roads taken: music, animation, radio, a return to academia in later life, a faith journey, life-threatening disease . . . it's a *Movie Of The Week* multiplied many times over.

The fact this book took well over a decade from inception to final draft means there are more than a few who have passed away since we spoke. Phil Austin, Ann Becker, Jim Bessman, George Duke, Ray Manzarek, Erik Scott, Jim Tucker, Leslie West, Hal Willner, and Gail Zappa are all missed.

Thanks to John Einarson for spotting issues that needed addressing early on, and Fiona McQuarrie for help making everything that much more focused. And most of all, Mark, without whom . . .

DISCOGRAPHY

THE CROSSFIRES

'Dr. Jekyll & Mr. Hyde' / 'Fiberglass Jungle' (Capco 1963)

'That's Be The Day' / 'One Potato Two Potato' (Lucky Token 1964)

Out Of Control (Rhino 1981)

THE TURTLES

Singles

'It Ain't Me, Babe' / 'Almost There' (White Whale 1965)

'Let Me Be' / 'Your Maw Said You Cried' (White Whale 1965)

'You Baby' / 'Wanderin' Kind' (White Whale 1966)

'Grim Reaper Of Love' / 'Come Back' (White Whale 1966)

'Outside Chance' / 'We'll Meet Again' (White Whale 1966)

'Makin' My Mind Up' / 'Outside Chance' (White Whale 1966)

'Can I Get To Know You Better' / 'Like The Seasons' (White Whale 1966)

'Happy Together' / 'Like The Seasons' (White Whale 1967)

'She'd Rather Be With Me' / 'The Walking Song' (White Whale 1967)

'Guide For The Married Man' / 'Think I'll Run Away' (White Whale 1967)

'You Know What I Mean' / 'Rugs Of Woods And Flowers' (White Whale 1967)

'She's My Girl' / 'Chicken Little Was Right' (White Whale 1967)

'Sound Asleep' / 'Umbassa And The Dragon' (White Whale 1968)

'The Story Of Rock And Roll' / 'Can't You Hear The Cows' (White Whale 1968)

'Elenore' / 'Surfer Dan' (White Whale 1968)

'You Showed Me' / 'Buzz Saw' (White Whale 1968)

'House On The Hill' / 'Come Over' (White Whale 1969)

'You Don't Have To Walk In The Rain' (White Whale 1969)

'Love In The City' / 'Bachelor Mother' (White Whale 1969)

'Lady-O' / 'Somewhere Friday Night' (White Whale 11969)

'Teardrops' / 'Gas Money' (as The Dedications, White Whale 1970)

'Who Would Ever Think That I Would Marry Margaret' / 'We Ain't Gonna Party No More' (White Whale 1970)

'Is It Any Wonder' / 'Wanderin' Kind' (White Whale 1970)

'Eve Of Destruction' / 'Wanderin' Kind' (White Whale 1970)

'Me About You' / 'Think I'll Run Away' (White Whale 1970)

Albums

It Ain't Me Babe (White Whale 1965)

You Baby (White Whale 1966)

Happy Together (White Whale 1967)

Golden Hits (White Whale 1967)

Present The Battle Of The Bands (White Whale 1968)

Wooden Head (White Whale 1969)

Turtle Soup (White Whale 1969)

More Golden Hits (White Whale 1970)

Happy Together Again (Sire 1974)

1968 (Rhino EP 1978)

Shell Shock (Rhino 1987)

Chalon Road (Rhino 1987)

The Turtles Featuring Flo & Eddie Captured Live (Rhino 1992)

Solid Zinc (Rhino 2002)

The Albums Collection (Demon 2017)

MARK VOLMAN & HOWARD KAYLAN

'Goodbye Surprise' / 'Nikki Hoi' (Reprise 1972)

FLO & EDDIE

Singles

'Afterglow' / 'Carlos And De Bull' (Reprise 1973)

'You're A Lady' / 'If We Only Had The Time' (Reprise 1973)

'Let Me Make Love To You' / 'Come To My Rescue Webelos' (Columbia 1974)

'Rebecca' / 'Illegal, Immoral And Fattening' (Columbia 1975)

'Elenore' / 'The Love You Gave Away' (Columbia 1976)

'Keep It Warm' / 'Hot' (Columbia 1976)

Albums
The Phlorescent Leech & Eddie (Reprise 1972)
Flo & Eddie (Reprise 1973)
Illegal, Immoral And Fattening (Columbia 1975)
Moving Targets (Columbia 1976)
Rock Steady With Flo & Eddie (Epiphany 1981)
The History of Flo & Eddie And The Turtles (Rhino 3LP 1983)
The American Rabbit: Original Soundtrack (Rhino 1986)
The Best Of Flo & Eddie (Rhino 1986)
New York 'Times' 1979–1994 Live At The Bottom Line (Manifesto 2009)

For Kids Stuff Records
The World Of Strawberry Shortcake (Kid Stuff 1980)
Strawberry Shortcake In Big Apple City (Kid Stuff 1981)
Strawberry Shortcake's Pet Parade (Kid Stuff 1982)
Let's Dance With Strawberry Shortcake (Kid Stuff 1983)
Introducing The Care Bears (Kid Stuff 1983)
The Care Bears Care For You (Kid Stuff 1983)
The Care Bears Adventures In Care-A-Lot (Kid Stuff 1983)
The Care Bears Christmas (Kid Stuff 1983)

With Frank Zappa
Chunga's Revenge (Bizarre/Reprise 1970)
Fillmore East—June 1971 (Bizarre/Reprise 1971)
200 Motels (United Artists 1971)
Just Another Band From L.A. (Bizarre/Reprise 1972)
You Can't Do That On Stage Anymore Volume 1 (Rykodisc 1988)
You Can't Do That On Stage Anymore Volume 3 (Rykodisc 1989)
You Can't Do That On Stage Anymore Volume 6 (Rykodisc 1992)
Playground Psychotics (Barking Pumpkin 1992)
Carnegie Hall (Vauternative 2011)
Road Tapes, Venue 3: Tyrone Guthrie Theatre 1970 (Vauternative 2016)
The Mothers 1970 (Zappa/Ume 2020)
200 Motels: 50th Anniversary Edition (Ume 2021)
The Mothers 1971: Super Deluxe Edition (Ume 2022)

Rhino's 'Beat The Boots' Series
Freaks & Motherf*#@%! (Fillmore, November 1970)
Tengo Na Minchia Tanta (Fillmore, 1970)
Disconnected Synapses (Palais Gaumont, Paris, France, 1970)
Swiss Cheese/Fire! (The Casino, Montreux, France, December 1971)
At The Circus (Uddel, Belgium, 1970)

T. REX VOCALS (ACCORDING TO TONY VISCONTI)
Mark and Howard (sometimes including Marc Bolan)
'Seagull Woman'
'Hot Love'
'Mambo Sun'
'Cosmic Dancer'
'Monolith'
'Get It On (Bang A Gong)'
'Planet Queen'
'Metal Guru'
'Rock On'
'Baby Boomerang'
'Rabbit Fighter'
'Main Man'
'Chariot Choogle'
'Sunken Rags'
'Woodland Rock'

Marc and Tony (sounding like Mark and Howard)
'Children Of The Revolution'
'Mystic Lady'
'The Slider'
'Spaceball Richochet'
'Telegram Sam'
'Baby Strange'
'Thunderwing'
'The Groover'
'Jitterbug Love'
'Born To Boogie'
'Free Angel'
'Rapids'
'Shock Rock'
'Mad Donna'

Various Female Vocalists
'Solid Gold Easy Action'
'20th Century Boy'
'Truck On' (Tyke)
'Teenage Dream'
'Sitting Here' (Marc and Gloria only)
'Explosive Mouth'
'Satisfaction Pony'
'Left Hand Luke'

BACKUP VOCALS

John Lennon *Sometime In New York City* (Apple 1972)

Navasota *Rootin'* (ABC 1972)

Roger McGuinn *Peace On You* (Columbia 1974)

Hoyt Axton *Life Machine* (A&M 1974)

Ray Manzarek *The Whole Thing Started With Rock & Roll Now It's Out Of Control* (Mercury 1974)

Keith Moon *Two Sides Of The Moon* (ABC 1975)

Michael Quatro *In Collaboration With The Gods* (United Artists 1975)

David Cassidy *The Higher They Climb* (RCA 1975)

Stephen Stills *Illegal Stills* (Columbia 1976)

David Cassidy *Home Is Where The Heart Is* (RCA 1976)

Chris Hillman *Slippin' Away* (Asylum 1976)

Tim Moore *White Shadows* (Asylum 1977)

Roger Voudouris *Roger Voudouris aka The Finger Painter* (Warner Bros 1978)

Alice Cooper *From The Inside* (Warner Bros 1978)

DMZ *DMZ* (Sire 1978)

Good Rats *From Rats To Riches* (Passport 1978)

Sorry *Oh!! Kathy* (Kiswell 1978)

Terry Mace *Confessions Of A Sinner* (Mercury 1979)

Alice Cooper *Flush The Fashion* (Warner Bros 1980)

Blondie *Autoamerica* (Chrysalis 1980)

Bruce Springsteen *The River* (Columbia 1980)

Livingston Taylor *Man's Best Friend* (Epic 1980)

Tonio K *Amerika* (Arista 1980)

Van Wilks *Bombay Tears* (Mercury 1980)

Albert Hammond *Your World And My World* (Columbia 1981)

The Knack *Round Trip* (Capitol 1981)

Al Stewart *Live/Indian Summer* (Arista 1981)

Ava Cherry *Streetcar Named Desire* (Capitol 1982)

Alice Cooper *Zipper Catches Skin* (Warner Bros 1982)

Espionage *Espionage* (A&M 1982)

Sammy Hagar *Fast Times At Ridgemont High* OST (Elektra 1982)

Psychedelic Furs *Forever Now* (Columbia 1982)

Paul Kantner *Planet Earth Rock And Roll Orchestra* (RCA 1983)

Burton Cummings *Heart* (Epic 1984)

Bruce Springsteen & The E Street Band: *Live 1975–86* (Columbia 1986)

Andy Taylor *Thunder* (MCA 1987)

Darlene Love *Paint Another Picture* (Columbia 1988)

Gavin Friday *Each Man Kills The Thing He Loves* (Island 1989)

Jefferson Airplane *Jefferson Airplane* (Epic 1989)

Southside Johnny & The Asbury Jukes: *Better Days* (Impact 1991)

Gavin Friday *Adam 'n' Eve* (Island 1992)

The Ramones *Mondo Bizarro* (Radioactive 1992)

Louis Bertignac *Elle Et Louis* (Columbia France 1993)

Steely Dan *Citizen Steely Dan* (MCA 1993)

Duran Duran *Thank You* (Parlophone 1995)

Johnny Popstar Luv Explosion *Lizz The Supermarket Drag Queen* (CD Baby 1999)

Cherry Poppin' Daddies *Soul Caddy* (Mojo 2000, Mark Volman only)

Adam Bomb *New York Times* (Get Animal 2001)

Richie Furay *The Heartbeat Of Love* (RF 2006)

Alice Cooper *Welcome To My Nightmare II* (UMe 2011)

ANIMATED FEATURES

200 Motels (1971)

Dirty Duck (1974)

Texas Detour (1978)

Loose Shoes (1980)

Thanksgiving And The Land Of Oz (1980)

Strawberry Shortcake (1980–82)

Care Bears (1982)

Peter & The Magic Egg (1983)

The Adventures Of The American Rabbit (1986)

ALSO AVAILABLE FROM JAWBONE PRESS

Lunch With The Wild Frontiers: A History Of Britpop And Excess In 13½ Chapters **Phill Savidge**

Wilcopedia: A Comprehensive Guide To The Music Of America's Best Band **Daniel Cook Johnson**

Take It Off: KISS Truly Unmasked **Greg Prato**

Lydia Lunch: The War Is Never Over: A Companion To The Film By Beth B. **Nick Soulsby**

I Am Morbid: Ten Lessons Learned From Extreme Metal, Outlaw Country, And The Power Of Self-Determination **David Vincent with Joel McIver**

Zeppelin Over Dayton: Guided By Voices Album By Album **Jeff Gomez**

What Makes The Monkey Dance: The Life And Music Of Chuck Prophet And Green On Red **Stevie Simkin**

So Much For The 30 Year Plan: Therapy? The Authorised Biography **Simon Young**

She Bop: The Definitive History Of Women In Popular Music **Lucy O'Brien**

Relax Baby Be Cool: The Artistry And Audacity Of Serge Gainsbourg **Jeremy Allen**

Seeing Sideways: A Memoir Of Music And Motherhood **Kristin Hersh**

Two Steps Forward, One Step Back: My Life In The Music Business **Miles A. Copeland III**

It Ain't Retro: Daptone Records & The 21st-Century Soul Revolution **Jessica Lipsky**

Renegade Snares: The Resistance & Resilience Of Drum & Bass **Ben Murphy and Carl Loben**

Southern Man: Music And Mayhem In The American South **Alan Walden with S.E. Feinberg**

Frank & Co: Conversations With Frank Zappa 1977–1993 **Co de Kloet**

All I Ever Wanted: A Rock 'n' Roll Memoir **Kathy Valentine**

Here They Come With Their Make-Up On: Suede, Coming Up … And More Adventures Beyond The Wild Frontiers **Jane Savidge**

My Bloody Roots: From Sepultua To Soulfly And Beyond: The Autobiography **Max Cavalera with Joel McIver**

This Band Has No Past: How Cheap Trick Became Cheap Trick **Brian J. Kramp**

Gary Moore: The Official Biography **Harry Shapiro**

Holy Ghost: The Life & Death Of Free Jazz Pioneer Albert Ayler **Richard Koloda**

Conform To Deform: The Weird & Wonderful World Of Some Bizzare **Wesley Doyle**

Johnny Thunders: In Cold Blood—The Official Biography **Nina Antonia**